Victorian women's magazines

MANCHESTER
UNIVERSITY PRESS

for Essy, Leila, Helen and Kate

VICTORIAN WOMEN'S MAGAZINES

an anthology

edited by
Margaret Beetham and Kay Boardman

Manchester University Press

Manchester and New York

distributed exclusively in the USA by Palgrave

Published by Manchester University Press
Oxford Road, Manchester M13 9NR, UK
and Room 400, 175 Fifth Avenue, New York,
NY 10010, USA
http://www.manchesteruniversitypress.co.uk

Distributed exclusively in the USA by
Palgrave, 175 Fifth Avenue,
New York, NY 10010, USA

Distributed exclusively in Canada by
UBC Press, University of British Columbia,
2029 West Mall, Vancouver, BC,
Canada V6T 1Z2

British Library Cataloguing-in-Publication Data
A catalogue record for this book is available
from the British Library

Library of Congress Cataloging-in-Publication
Data applied for

ISBN   0 7190 5878 3   hardback
        0 7190 5879 1   paperback

First published 2001

07 06 05 04 03 02 01   10 9 8 7 6 5 4 3 2 1

Designed in Scala and Scala Sans
by Max Nettleton FCSD

Typeset in Hong Kong by Graphicraft Limited
Printed in Great Britain
by Bookcraft (Bath) Ltd, Midsomer Norton

Contents

Acknowledgements

The research and writing of this book has been enabled by staff in the various libraries and collections on which we have drawn including the British Library and Manchester Central Reference Library. In particular we wish to thank the staff of our own university libraries at The Manchester Metropolitan University and the University of Central Lancashire in particular Hilary Higgins and staff at the Interlibrary Loans unit. Special thanks, too, to the Keeper and Assistant Keeper at the gallery of English Costume, in Manchester, the staff at the National Library of Scotland, and Colindale Library in London. Without the love and support of our families and friends and the generosity of colleagues this book would never have been completed and we want to thank them all.

We are grateful to the following for permission to use material: to the Trustees of the National Library of Scotland for figures 4 and 32, to Manchester City Art Galleries for figures 1, 6, 29 and 33 and to the British Library for figures 9, 19, 24 and 26. Every effort has been made to obtain permission to reproduce the figures illustrated in this book. If any proper acknowledgement has not been made, copyright-holders are invited to contact the publisher.

Introduction

At the start of the twenty-first century the magazine – along with that other periodical, the newspaper – is the most pervasive form of print in our global media culture. Periodicals are by their nature ephemeral, each number marked clearly with its sell-by date. However, this stress on the moment obscures the long history of the form. In Britain, which is the focus of this anthology, the first magazines appeared in the eighteenth century but it was in the nineteenth century that they moved into that place at the heart of popular reading which they have occupied ever since. Central to that move was the specific targeting of women as magazine readers and this book is about the magazines which effected that process.

We have deliberately chosen the concept 'targeting' from contemporary marketing, where potential consumers are identified and wooed by producers. Magazines in the nineteenth century, as today, were in the market. They were, and are, primarily commodities. The print industry was an important part of the burgeoning commercial activity of industrialising Britain and magazines, like other commodities, had to attract purchasers and to keep attracting them. But, in addition and equally importantly, it was in nineteenth-century print media that the ground was laid for twentieth-century marketing techniques. From the first, producers of periodicals also used them as a way of advertising other commodities. To begin with these were mainly other magazines or books but as the potential value of magazines for advertising began to be realised so different kinds of goods became advertised in their pages. By 1900 magazines were not only established as central commodities in the market in print but also were an important medium for selling other commodities.

Print media, however, have been important not only in the market economy but also in the circulation of meanings. Magazines for women not only addressed women as consumers but also as readers, as in search of entertainment or in need of instruction in various social roles. From the start magazines which defined their readership as 'women' also took on, more or less overtly, the task of defining what it meant to be 'a woman', or what it meant to be a particular kind of woman; a mother, a London lady with time and money, a working woman, a 'New Woman', or some other specifically female identity.

In this anthology we work with both aspects of the magazine, its role as a commodity in the market and its role as a text. By text we mean that it engages its readers in the process of negotiating their own identities as (women) readers and also negotiating the meaning of what the magazine offered, whether that was advice, or pleasure, or information on a range of social relations and institutions in which readers were caught up at that particular historical moment.

Nineteenth-century women's magazines are a wonderful resource for scholars and ordinary readers who are interested either in the history of popular reading or the ways in which various definitions of femininity have been disseminated, contested, accepted and enjoyed. However, access to such texts is difficult. Because they were ephemeral and often regarded as unimportant, copies were thrown away rather than kept or put in libraries. In Britain even those put in libraries have not always survived. For example, important parts of the collection of nineteenth century periodicals stored in what is now the British Library were destroyed in the bombing of London during the Second World War. Today only scholars with ready access to important collections are likely to be able to see original examples of many of these texts. Where they have survived, these magazines were usually bound into volume format, a process which meant removing the covers and advertisements. In addition, the beautiful fashion plates or other illustrative material, the needlework and sewing patterns, the sheet music and many of the special attractions or inducements to buy which the original magazines included have disappeared, removed by their first purchaser or by subsequent collectors. This means that even copies we have in libraries are often incomplete. Ironically these problems of absence go along with some equally daunting problems of excess and unmanageability. The sheer bulk of material involved in reading even one magazine over the space of several years can dishearten the most assiduous reader. Added to this are the difficulties of dealing with a huge variety of genres. Magazines are miscellanies and they characteristically include a mixture of different kinds of writing and often different kinds of visual illustration, each of which has its own history, and its own relationship to the technology of print and the development of popular reading. However, in considering magazines for women we are dealing with not just one title or even one kind of magazine but a huge variety of different kinds of magazine, which share many characteristics but differ widely in tone, type and target reader. How to make sense of the field as a whole as well as the individual example is therefore another problem which has contributed to the difficulty of making use of these resources.

We hope that this anthology will begin to open up the riches of Victorian women's magazines to readers who either do not have physical access to the works we discuss or find it difficult to make sense of the material which they have. It offers representations of a range of different kinds of magazines and includes examples of the kind of material, like covers and advertisements, which are often hard to find even in library copies. We hope, therefore, that in the first place it gives you as a reader some sense of what these magazines were like. Secondly, the anthology also offers various ways of making sense of a vast and relatively uncharted field of enquiry, a field whose extent we have indicated in the list of titles at the end as well as in the variety of material actually represented in the various sections.

The scope of this book

Chronologically, the focus of this book is the period when Victoria was on the British throne (1837–1901). All periodisation is problematic, since histories are not tidy or compartmentalised. We are not arguing that the history of the women's magazine fits neatly into the 'Victorian' period. It does not. There was, for example, a radical shift in the 1880s and 1890s which affected the number, the types and the format of women's magazines across the price range. We know that the term 'Victorian' has been and is still contested as a meaningful label, and this book is part of that debate. We argue that 'Victorian' usefully defines the period of our project, covering as it does so much of the nineteenth century in which lie the roots of the modern women's magazine and also the roots of the feminist movement which has consistently both critiqued the women's magazine and used it for its own ends. During Victoria's reign the significance of having a woman at the centre of public politics was much debated, not least in magazines addressed to women. Our retention of the word Victorian for a book which deals with women's interests is also an oblique reference to that set of debates and an acknowledgement of our foremothers of both the previous centuries, on whose work this collection draws.

Geographically our focus is on magazines produced in Britain. Mainly this means London, since the publishing industry became increasingly centred on London but we have included some magazines published elsewhere in England and Scotland, though not Ireland. Britain, particularly London, was in the Victorian period the metropolis of a world-wide Empire and many of the magazines we represent here were sent abroad to be read throughout the world where English was spoken. However, we have not included magazines produced in the rest of the Empire.

The third element which dictated the contents and shape of this anthology is that our interest is mainly but not exclusively in the commercial press. We are dealing with magazines as commodities rather than those which were either house journals or the publications of special interest groups. This excludes a range of important magazines, including those produced by suffrage societies on which feminist scholars have done much important work. However, inclusion of all these magazines would threaten to make this project unmanageably large and unfocused and it is in part because comparatively little work exists on commercial magazines that this book concentrates on them. As with so much else in this large and untidy field of enquiry, the boundaries are not as clear cut here as they would seem. Religious journals were crucial in the dissemination of cheap print and had an impact on the commercial magazines which we have tried to reflect. Ostensibly commercial journals were sometimes maintained even when they made a loss because they served some other purpose of the publisher. Where the lines are blurred we have tried to indicate this and in particular we have included in the Bibliography journals which we have not included in the body of the book. Broadly, however, this is a book on commercial journals.

Despite this particular emphasis, what follows is not a history of the *production* of magazines. Its focus is rather on defining magazines through their consumption, or readership. We define 'women's magazines' as those which were aimed specifically at women as readers. We have not included the broad range of 'family' or 'household magazines' which could include everything from literary magazines like Dickens's *Household Words* to general publications like *Good Words*. The magazines included here were aimed at women rather than at households. Of course, this does not mean that women were their only readers. There is considerable evidence, including from letters pages, that men have consistently read and enjoyed magazines which defined their readership as 'women' and we give examples in what follows. Because married women had few legal rights over property for most of Victoria's reign, it was often men's names which appeared on subscription lists or who may actually have bought reading matter for their wives. The difficulties of defining actual purchasers or actual historical readerships are notorious and are not our concern here. We focus rather on target readers, those whom the text addresses and whom the producers sought to attract.

Characteristics of the woman's magazine

Throughout the Victorian period, magazines for women were involved in a general process of disseminating print to wider and wider circles of readers. This meant not only producing cheaper version of older kinds of magazine but also the invention of completely new types, like the ladies' papers, the broadsheet format, the girls' magazine or the cheap domestic magazine which became very important in the 1890s. However, throughout the period and across this diversity of types, certain basic characteristics of the magazine as a form persisted. These had evolved in the period between 1770 and the 1830s and still persist today.

These characteristics were firstly, of course, seriality, that particular relationship to time which is the distinguishing mark of all periodical genres and which gives them their generic name. Magazines came out either weekly, monthly or sometimes, quarterly. (Though there were annual publications aimed at women we have not included them here.) From this apparently obvious point flows much that is particular to the magazine as a print form.

The second crucial characteristic of a magazine is, as already suggested, that it is a miscellany. It is characterised by heterogeneity. A journal which consists of only one kind of writing is not a true magazine. Therefore, we have not included in this collection examples of the serial fiction which remained a staple part of women's reading for much of the period. Working-class women were often characterised as being particularly addicted to reading cheap part-issue fiction or the complete novels which were sold at a half-penny or a penny. Though it is difficult to assess the precise extent of this kind of reading, excluding it means that working-class women's reading is probably under-represented in this collection. However, this anthology is not about women's reading but about a particular kind of publication for women, namely the miscellany.

As well as variety of genres, variety of authorial voice was another element of the magazine. For much of the period represented here most journalism was anonymous and this is true of women's magazines, though even from the 1830s some well known writers were given by-lines. By the 1890s, this practice was much more common throughout the press but even then most magazine writing was not attributed to named authors or was written under pseudonyms. Nevertheless, variety of voice remained a part of that heterogeneity which distinguished the magazine from some other serial forms.

The seriality of the magazine, the fact that as a commodity it had to ensure that purchasers kept returning every week or month, deeply affected its characteristics as a text. Central to these has always been the particular relationship which readers have with this kind of publication. Magazines have always aimed to create a loyal readership who feel a particular attachment to 'their' magazine. The early women's magazines relied almost entirely on contributions from readers to keep up the flow of copy but by the 1830s most commercial magazines were more professionally produced. However, they still relied on readers to write in with comments on the last number, requests for advice, or sometimes with poems or articles for inclusion. In return the magazines developed commercial, rhetorical, and structural strategies to involve the reader. Commercially magazines sought to involve the reader with competitions, special offers and inducements to buy. Rhetorically, they constructed a role for the reader which suggested a particular relationship with the magazine. In the 1840s and 1850s these magazines often offered to be the reader's guide and mentor; by the 1890s they more often constructed themselves rhetorically as the reader's 'friend'. Structurally every magazine developed a particular lay-out and mix of genres which readers could recognise. The serial form meant that magazines could simultaneously offer their readers a constant diet of novelty while at the same time every number was reassuringly familiar. This familiarity was re-inforced by constant references to what was coming up in future numbers and by references to past numbers. Crucial to this structural engagement of the reader was the use of serialised fiction which hooked the reader into the magazine for months or weeks. Although each magazine thus claimed to be unique and sought to engage its readers in a relationship special to itself, the same strategies recur across very different types.

This similarity across difference is also characteristic of the range of ingredients which made up the woman's magazine as a recognisable form. Not only was the magazine well established as a mixed form by the beginning of the Victorian period, but also many of the characteristic elements of that kind of magazine which addressed women had more or less been put in place. These included: fiction, usually serialised; poetry; the biography or exemplary life, sometimes illustrated; responses to readers' letters, particularly requests for advice, and specifically advice on fashion, usually with a beautiful plate where the most advanced techniques of illustration would be deployed. The most basic element of most magazines was the general article, the discursive prose writing which could be political, religious, scientific, gossipy or take any other form according to the tenor and type of magazine. As suggested above, from the first magazines included some advertising but before the 1880s this was mostly confined to the end-papers, that is the pages immediately inside the back and front cover. It was only in the 1880s and 1890s that advertisements began to take up a far larger proportion of the magazine's space and to be spread throughout the magazine, mixed with editorial material. This went along with changes in technology which enabled the much greater use of illustration not only in the advertising but also in the copy. Throughout the period more magazines for women included some illustration. In the fashion and drawing-room journals this was a single plate or other engraving and well into the Victorian period the fashion plates were often engravings of high quality. In the mid-Victorian period more extensive illustration depended on the wood-cut but with the development of the half-tone plate in the 1890s, magazines at the end of the period, from the ladies' papers through to the cheap domestic magazines were lavishly illustrated with pictures on most pages. All these genres remained the staples of women's magazine contents pages. Towards the end of the century some new forms were added, notably the interview, which was often illustrated. These typical genres of the miscellany we deal with in detail in Part II below.

Each of the sub-sections in both Parts I and II is arranged chronologically to enable you as reader to begin to grasp the complex and inter-related histories involved in the development of this kind of print. In general the story is one of widening readership and increasing access to the market in print. Running through this development is another which we have not focused on here. That is the development of technologies of print, paper-making and illustration. There is another story to be told here which you may be able to piece together from what follows but which is not the focus of our book.

How to use this book

Like the magazines which we discuss, this book can be read in a number of different ways. You can flip through it looking at what particularly interests you, or you can take one section and look at it closely. You can read it from the back forward or from the middle outward or you can track the various connections across from one section to another.

However you read, please remember that what you have here is a representation and a selection. Any selection, especially from such a vast field, is liable to distort; any representation will be liable to misrepresent. The difficulties we have faced in constructing this anthology have been both intellectual and material and the two cannot be separated. This is because the magazine is both a material object with certain physical qualities and a text whose meaning is tied up with those characteristics. Form and content cannot easily be separated.

Our primary problem, then, was how to show the magazine's material or formal qualities (appearance, size, quality of paper, typographical and visual features) and how they related to its content. Each number of a magazine constructs its meaning through the particular juxtaposition of articles, illustrations and other items. Different kinds of type-face, size and quality of paper, quality of illustration all enter into what the magazine is and means. One way of solving the problem of how to represent this would have been to include only one or two magazines but include complete numbers in facsimile. This would have given you a better sense of how a particular magazine worked but it would have misrepresented the immense variety of different kinds of magazine and the way they relate to each other in time.

We have therefore chosen to draw from a wide range of journals and use a mixture of modes of representation. The substantial number and range of facsimiles will give you a sense of how this material looked on the page and of the wonderful diversity of styles and types which Victorian publishers used. However, most of this book is in modern format and standardised size. We have tried to reproduce some elements of the type and lay-out found in these journals, but we cannot do so consistently. For example, the difference between single and double column text is not always visually represented. There were various conventions in the use of type which are no longer current. But we have tried to be as faithful as we can in signalling the visual and spatial qualities of the texts. We have reproduced spelling mistakes and other errors which occasionally occur in the originals. We have also reproduced as closely as we can the variety of different kinds of titles and authorial attributions. Most journal articles were anonymous but the use of initials, pseudonyms, or other oblique forms of identification were common and are reproduced here. Where we have had to cut, we still give you substantial extracts. What you have here is a likeness which you may think of as a mixture of photograph and sketch.

The other major difficulty we faced in planning the book was to find a structure which would represent the diversity of different kinds of magazines for which no agreed typology has yet been devised by scholars. We also wanted to enable you as a reader to gain a sense of the historical development of the various kinds of magazine and of individual titles through the years (or sometimes decades) of their publication. For magazines exist not only in space but in time and this book seeks to situate each example both in a chronology and in relation to other contemporary publications.

We have therefore organised this book by cutting along two dimensions of what is a multi-dimensional field. In Part I, you will find a taxonomy of the different kinds of magazines for women. Any kind of classification raises issues of blurred boundaries. However, some attempt at a classification is needed and we have found this one works well. The taxonomy works on two principles; it seeks to classify both by formal features (the ladies' papers, for example, were distinguished by their large size and use of columns) and by aspects of position and content (the feminist and religious journals were formally similar but ideologically different). This demonstrates the need to make sense of different types of magazine in terms of formal qualities but also acknowledges that in some instances ideological position is as important as style and formal presentation. These two methods of classification show the complex relationship of form and content at work in the production and consumption of magazines. We hope this will prompt further consideration of the relationships between the various categories and the implications of this mapping process.

We have identified and described eight groups of periodicals in Part I; the fashion magazines, drawing-room journals, general illustrated, and religious magazines, ladies' papers, feminist journals, magazines for young women and girls, and the cheap domestic type. These groupings, which we believe best illustrate the range of periodical reading aimed at women in the period, do not aim to be absolutely comprehensive. However, they do signal both the range and development of this kind of reading and offer a route through a bewildering range of available titles.

Part II is organised to show how the different elements of the magazine work and how they evolved in the period of our study. Here we identify the different kinds of texts which were combined in the magazine, a form which characteristically mixed visual and textual material as well as putting side by side genres which would not elsewhere be found together. The categories we employ here are: the masthead and cover, discursive prose (both articles and short pieces), prose fiction, the fashion plate and fashion feature, poetry, advice columns and readers' letters, political journalism, reviews, advertisements, competitions and inducements to buy, illustrated biography and the personal interview. Again this list is not absolutely comprehensive (paper patterns, sheet music and recipes are not represented) and a slightly different set of categories could be generated. We believe, however, that this taxonomy not only gives attention to the most important of the genre's constituent elements but also provides a useful way of reading the magazine as a complex form.

The Bibliography at the end is the fullest that currently exists of titles addressed to women and includes some categories we have not represented in Part I, such as trades union and suffrage journals. We hope you will be able to use it both on its own and in reference to the specific examples and the introductions to the various sections.

These are only some of the ways you can begin to build a complex model of the Victorian women's magazine. We hope you will find other ways of using this book and that, like the magazine it describes, you will find what follows provides both amusement and instruction.

PART I

in which we represent the different kinds of women's
magazines which existed in the Victorian period

1

The fashion magazine

These magazines were characterised by a primary interest in fashion and fashion promotion. Most women's magazines covered fashion in varying degrees of detail, but this group dedicated the majority of their pages to such coverage. The first generation were usually monthly, expensive (ranging between a shilling and a shilling and sixpence), presented in a high quality format and included a number of exquisitely coloured fashion plates. As a luxury commodity this type of publication presented the contents in a decorative and well spaced format. Typical contents included fashion coverage, short fiction, short features, fashion plates, entertainment guides and advertisements. Long running titles include *Le Follet*, *The Ladies' Gazette of Fashion* and *The London and Paris Ladies' Magazine*. The first and longest running example of the cheaper fashion magazine is *Myra's Journal of Dress and Fashion* which began in 1875 priced at 3*d* and was edited by Martha Browne. *Myra's Journal*'s successful presentation of fashion in a cheap and practical format was part of the general democratisation of the press. Dispensing with the expensive fashion plate as the primary promoter of new styles, it included detailed illustrations in the main body of the text and provided patterns in a supplement available at the cost of an extra 3*d*. Its long run is also testimony to the fact that the fashion magazine could survive in a market already saturated with other magazines which also covered fashion and dressmaking.

1.1

During its near sixty year run *The World of Fashion* (1824–79) was subject to a number of mergers and was known by a number of titles including *The Ladies' Monthly Magazine* and *The London and Paris Ladies' Magazine*. In this extract, a new editor, announces her aims and objectives.

'To the Readers of the World of Fashion', *The World of Fashion*, vol. 17, 1840, p. 1.

THAT arch-inciter to curiosity, investigation, invention and literary expedients of every nameable description, called NOVELTY, has surely by this time done its worst; and the conductor of such a periodical as this, who undertakes to supply readers with *neauvoutés*, makes the contract with the comfortable assurance that there really *is* "nothing new under the sun."

Every path of civilized life has been scrutinized with the most penetrating eye, in order to discover something fresh in character, or peculiar in feature – the most elevated minds have descended to the lowliest abodes, and the purest hearts have been led to investigate the darkest deeds, to bring forth whatever is curious, or extract whatever may be useful; hence the task of catering for the public taste, becomes one of much difficulty.

The time has gone by, when a fair damsel could sigh over the loves of Strephon and Chloe – or luxuriate on rebuses and epitaphs. In the present day, the female mind requires food of a more wholesome nature than the "trifles" and "whiped creams" (*sic*.) which pleased the palates of our maiden aunts, and great Grandmammas, half a century ago.

The somewhat circumscribed limits of a periodical like *The World of Fashion*, and its character, as offered by a female editor, to female readers, render all pretension to learned disquisition, or philosophic investigation needless; apart from which objects are continually floating around us, like motes in the sunbeam, that appear of far less importance, but yet are of sufficient interest to be caught up by the pen of fiction, or heightened by the graceful wand of fancy. Misfortune that could not be forseen; imprudence that would not be warned; love, – in all its effects of good or evil; the stubborness of pride; the pliability of tenderness; the meltings of paternal affection; the constancy of conjugal attachment, whether displayed by history, biography, or imaginative pictures, furnish never-ending materials for amusement, interest, and instruction. True delineations of feelings and circumstances in their effects on different persons and distinct situations, afford the best medium of conveying the fruits of experience to the young and the uninformed – while to those in more advanced life do they not continually afford recollections which can hardly fail to be useful and pleasurable?

One of the most agreeable tasks which devolve on the conductor of such a periodical as this, is the opportunity it affords of lending a helping hand to latent talent. Magazines are the cradles in which the infancy of genius is rocked, and are, as Southey expresses it, "Of great service to those who are learning to write; they are the fishing-boats, which the Buccaniers of Literature do not condescend to sink, burn, and destroy." The diffidently-forwarded Tale or Poem, accompanied by the timid regret made hardly intelligible by a preponderance of "hopes and fears," which are employed to express it, claim a deep interest in the mind of an editor. Without arrogating any great merit on this score, the present conductor of the *World of Fashion*, has, for many years, had daily opportunities of enjoying such a pleasure, and it is with no little satisfaction that she can now scan the list of authors, whom the public "delights to honor," and find amongst them names which first passed the formidable ordeal of "print" under her auspices.

The grand object of the work, viz. its being especially intended for the perusal of females, will never be lost sight of, and such rigid watchfulness exercised over the tone of its contents, as to adapt it peculiarly for the junior branches of the family circle.

Fashions. – A correspondent, resident in Paris, will continue to furnish monthly reports of the prevailing and most tasteful costumes, illustrated with accurately drawn figures, engraved in the first style of the art.

Her Majesty's Courts. – The gay scenes of Her Majesty's Courts, Drawing Rooms, Balls and Evening Parties will be correctly reported.

The Fashionable Chit Chat of the Month will be also given.

The Genealogy of the Nobility will be continued with many amusing anecdotes.

Fiction. – Original Tales and Romances by esteemed and fashionable writers, will appear in every number.

Literature and the Fine Arts. – All publications of sufficient interest will be slightly but candidly reviewed – especial preference being given to works calculated to improve or interest the female mind.

The Poetry will be original, and contributed by popular pens.

Music and the Drama, will be made a feature in *The World of Fashion*. Notices of the principal theatres, will be found in every number; and an analysis of new musical publications will also be given. With such views the present Editor advances into the field, and sends forth this her first number as a herald to proclaim to her own sex, who are willing to enter the lists and enroll themselves, under her banner a free and fair course, while those of the other have full permission to break a lance in her cause. To drop metaphor, contributions of merit will be received and impartially dealt by, and the hand of encouragement will be held out to the young aspirant for future laurels.

1.2

The fashion plate was a crucial part of the fashion magazine and the more expensive titles included up to six of them in each issue. These plates provided a visual spectacle which was striking in a press which was largely unillustrated in the early part of the Victorian period.

See FIGURE 1.

FIGURE 1 Fashion plate (originally in colour) from *The World of Fashion*, vol. 40, 1864

This short article (originally presented on a bordered page) from *Le Follet* (1846–1900), a magazine also published in French, is typical of the short topical articles found in fashion magazines.

'A Word to Young Maids on Old Maids', by Ella, *Le Follet*, vol. 19, 1865, pp. 77–78.

"We know not the inward canker that eats out all their joy and delight." – BISHOP HALL.

WHY are those two little words "old maid" seldom uttered without the leaven of a certain amount of contempt or ridicule, and but too often used as synonymes for bad temper, prudery, or ill nature – in short, for all the faults that go to make up the acids of life without one counteracting sweet?

Oh! younger and more blooming sisters, has it never crossed your mind that, while revelling in all the charms of that golden age – YOUTH, your conduct has often engendered those very faults you condemn? If a sister (once past the first bloom of womanhood) dare to enjoy a dance, a lively conversation with her partner, or to take up any cause with enthusiasm, there are a dozen pairs of bright eyes immediately filled with astonishment, and a dozen pretty mouths pursed ready to express their wonder at her "doing such a thing at *her* age! It seems as if really she thought herself young!"

Fearing, on the other hand, to call forth undue censure, action and feeling are frequently so restrained that she falls into the opposite extreme; her manner becomes cold, and, to some extent, forbidding, and confirming the old proverb of "try to please all, and you satisfy none," she is set down by her fair (may we not add, and *unfair?*) judges as a positive prude, while, on reflection, they would be surprised to perceive how far *they* had conduced to render cheerless a life already shut out from the one place, above all others, most fitted to call forth those shining qualities of woman, devoted love and self-sacrifice – her own home!

As to ill temper, the outward effect only is judged; whereas if the *cause* could be laid bare, many a poor and slighted "old maid" would become a heroine!

I will not say that there are not any, but there are certainly very few women who have not loved during *some* time of their lives; but their love was unreturned – or the loved one died – or poverty, with its cold barrier, came between, to send the warm love – crushed, chilled, but not dead – back to its source, there to lie concealed for ever! It is too sacred to be laid bare to idle curiosity: too deep and hopeless even for sympathy.

We know that illness of the body too often affects the temper and disposition to the discomfort of those around. No wonder, then, if the *mind* enduring a continual and unshared pain, should show, in word and action, the cruel struggle; yet it is denied the same indulgence.

Did you ever have an "old maid" for a *confidante?* You smile at the idea; and yet, why not? Has she not the same thoughts and feelings? – and, trust me, she *has* had the same hopes. Circumstances – who shall say of how deep an interest? – have not brought them into action; let yours be the influence to draw forth her dormant qualities. Share with her your *griefs*, that the softening tears so long frozen over her *own* trials may once more flow, even though for another. Share with her your *joys*, that, with the smile of sympathy, her past may rise, subdued by the twilight hue of time, like a soft shadow to your glowing present.

There is no stated time when a woman's heart is old. We love the same flowers at sixty as at sixteen; the same emotion to which a sweet song long ago gave rise, inundates our hearts, though there are grandchildren at our knees.

I do not demand that you should look up to an "old maid" as a superior being, though there are many names in their ranks worthy of a world's reverence. I simply ask for your womanly love and sisterly feeling, and bid you remember that, with all the attention and affection you may lavish upon them – tenderly as you may judge their failings – there is a void you can never fill – a want you can not supply – and that, amongst the varied places filled by every other home member, the *"old maid" has none.*

Happy sisters, mothers, wives – have I pleaded in vain?

1.4

The editor of *Myra's Journal of Dress and Fashion* (1875–1912), Martha Browne, was a journalist of much experience, most of it gained whilst working with Samuel Beeton on *The Englishwoman's Domestic Magazine* (1852–79) and *The Young Englishwoman* (1864–77). In her journal, Myra produced a successful combination of lively and informative advice on fashion and health and beauty with stunning illustrated material.

See FIGURE 2.

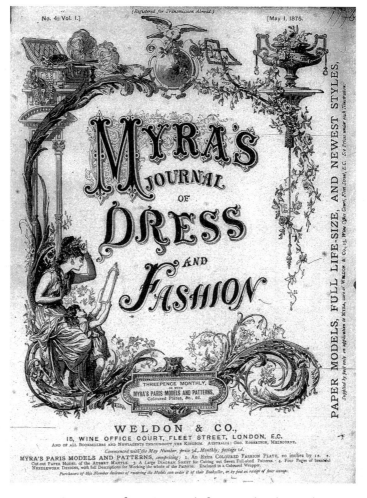

FIGURE 2 Cover page of *Myra's Journal of Dress and Fashion*, vol. 1, 1875

'Spinnings in Town' was a regular feature in *Myra's Journal of Dress and Fashion* (1875–1912) and it combined the chatty tone of the editor with product information presented in the form of the 'advertorial' in which goods were recommended that were being advertised elsewhere in the paper, a technique popular also with general illustrated magazines and ladies' papers.

'Spinnings in Town', by Silkworm, *Myra's Journal of Dress and Fashion*, vol. 1, 1876, pp. 261–66. See also FIGURE 3.

FIGURE 3 'Spinnings in Town', p. 261

Lesbia! are ladies' hearts more cold
Than when your prototype of old
    Wept over one dead sparrow?
Has fashion iced that snowy breast,
Where Cytherea's doves might rest,
Till sighs of Songland, sore distrest,
    Its feelings may not harrow?

O sex, whose softness lords of rhyme
From soft Catullus to our time
    Invoke in songs and sonnets,
Can you look on with smiling face
While La Mode's myrmidons apace
Exterminate our harmless race
    To trim your hats and bonnets?

Think when you trim your hats and "things"
With linnet's breasts and finches' wings,
    How many songs you stifle;
Swallows that charmed with daring flight,
And nightingales which gladdened night,
In myriads die to deck aright
    The moment's modish trifle.

Conceive how feathered bosoms throb
When roughs' rude hands, intent to rob,
    In our loved haunts invade us!
Yet not with them dear ladies, lie
The wrong, the shame, the cruelty, –
For did we plead, they might reply,
    "T'was gentle Lesbia bade us". – *Punch*

IT is too bad! It is positively wicked! That we women submit to be made by imperious fashion the destroyers of the harmless feathered tribe. I am a lover of birds, and waste many a precious moment in watching the fat blackbirds and plump thrushes hop on the lawn in front of my "den". I have a host of pensioners – robins, chaffinches, wrens, tomtits, and sparrows – who daily wait the signal of the opening window to flit around: nay, my robins boldly venture in, and, undisturbed by pen-scratching, inspect the room with interest. All the wire baskets which hung gay with flowers in each side of the verandah which shelters my home are taken down at this season; but a wren has built in one, and still seeks her nest nightly, though her family have long flown; and so the basket will hang in its place all through the winter, and Madame Wren will find her little home unaltered; and I am sure that I am not more tender-hearted than the hundred thousand ladies who will wear this winter, without a sigh, the wings of the dear little songsters I love so well. It is the "want of thought" which works as much evil as "want of heart." It can be imagined, then, that the new chapeaux find no favour in my eyes, and that the chapeau Mercure, with its crests of thrush's wings is an abomination in my eyes. This hat, designed for the skating rink, is sold for 21*s* – by Madame Delamode; it is of felt with velvet edge, and the wings can be replaced by velvet bows, which look quite as stylish. I beg, dear ladies, that you will each one exercise your influence to discourage the crusade against the birds, and not say "everyone wears birds' wings: one more bonnet can make no difference."

I have another little word to say, another appeal to make, before beginning an account of the novelties of the month.

At Christmas time it has been my habit for many years, after mentioning the pretty novelties prepared for Christmas, and enumerating the gifts which are likely to please the dear ones at Christmas, to ask my readers to consider those to whom Christmas brings no alleviation of their physical suffering, and but little share in the almost universal rejoicing of the season.

I have asked, and not in vain, for small sums for various charities, and for some of the hospitals which stand noble monuments of national charity. The Childrens' Hospital, the Royal Free Hospital, and the Hospital for Foreigners of all Nations I have severally pointed out as deserving objects of your charity, and my few words have always met with a cheerful and general response. Now that I have such an immense number of ladies to appeal to, a few pence on the part of each would give a handsome subscription to the Hospital for the Diseases of the Throat, Golden Square. This hospital, partially self-supporting, has, during the past year, received 174 in-patients and treated 3,120 out-patients. The diseases for which the hospital has been established are so well known and too much dreaded for it to be necessary for me to enlarge upon the good work done by this noble institution which has for its object the prevention as well as the cure of throat disease, unhappily so prevalent in England, and especially among children. Throat disease is often fatal, and always most alarming. All mothers must know this by experience; they also know the relief it is to see "the doctor" at the bedside of their darling. Give then, dear ladies, to other mothers this relief and this boon by extending the executive power of the Hospital, and by enabling the poor mother to see her child restored to her by timely assistance and timely medical aid. The hospital is entirely free to the *necessitous* poor. This class includes not only those who are actually in receipt of parish relief, but also those who can barely support themselves by their earnings during health and who, in time of sickness, cannot obtain the necessaries of life. Other poor persons, not belonging to this class, are required to give a small monthly payment, graduated according to their means, or to procure a governor's letter. The hospital is thus made in part self-supporting, and the pauperising influence which gratuitous medical relief exercises on the working-classes is checked.

. . .

"Many a time and oft" have I been reproached with a tendency to visit the West End only, and with neglect of the many excellent City houses. I pleaded guilty to the charge (which I find is much the best plan with MYRA), but was told to "reform" for the sake of the numerous ladies who find great convenience in shopping in the City. Among the names submitted to me, I selected the house of Messrs. Goode, Gainsford and Co., because I have heard so high a character of it; and because "the Boro" is so intensely "City;" and I was well rewarded, as all explorers should be, by the pretty sights and useful information. I begin with the first articles shown me, although I am dying to get to the children's department, which is really too fascinating, at least to me.

. . .

. . . Dainty little silk and satin bonnets – real bonnets – for infants and little girls. Gipsy hats of felt, or of quilted satin, trimmed with feathers. Hoods, rivalling the far-famed red Riding Hood in her own colour, and in all the pretty tints suitable for children and infants, at most moderate prices. Costumes for children from two years of age – not mere repetitions of mama's toilet, but the veritable *sacque* of "Miss Pen" in Joshua Reynolds' works, in silk, 45s., and in merino, 25s. These dear little dresses can be worn by both boys and girls, but are designed for the little ladies. Some of the sacques have hoods, others are finished by Valois collars. They are all nicely quilted, and are warm yet light, an advantage all mothers will appreciate. A charming costume for a child is made of merino trimmed with pleatings of poplin, arranged in very original style. A velveteen dress, trimmed with braid and buttons is sold complete at 25s., suitable for a little boy of five or six years. I feel sure that mothers will enjoy as much as I did an inspection of the lovely layettes and trousseaux, and the outfits for school. They will see some pretty dressing-gowns for their own wear, from one to three guineas, in cashmere, Watteau and princess shapes, and the sacque model also.

And now, dear ladies, I must, with best wishes, leave you—

> "'Tis the voice of the 'Bouncer'—I heard him complain;"
> "Oh, naughtiest of Maters! What, writing again!"

That appeal is irresistible; and I was very good last month, and helped MYRA immensely!

1.6

Although fashion magazines were popular and successful there was an anti-fashion position taken up by the rational dress reformers. The following extract from *The Rational Dress Society's Gazette* (1888–89) states the aims of the magazine.

'Editorial Note', *The Rational Dress Society's Gazette*, vol. 1, 1888, pp. 1–2.

MANY attempts have been made in the present century to protest against the tyranny of fashion, but they have had little effect, chiefly, I think, because the protests have always been made against the frivolity of fashion, that is, against its changeableness on the one hand, and its foppery on the other.

Now against neither of these things directly do we war, although we regret as much as anyone, the constant and meaningless changes of fashion. Still we remember the old saying, "L'ennui naquit un jour de l'uniformité," and remembering this, we stay our hand, and turn our eyes in another direction.

For we have a larger ground on which to take our stand, namely, science, and we have a greater war to wage, namely the war of health.

Not till our women have learned how far more important than anything else in the world is the cultivation of health – more important not to the individual only, but to the race at large – will they have fully seized the meaning of that great problem of women's rights.

The knowledge of the value of health is being gradually given to us by means of wider education; the health itself by a freer life and by a proper use of athletic and gymnastic exercises. Our girls are no longer chained to a backboard, nor kept in-doors while their brothers run about and play.

But the whole value of this liberty is gone if we do not give our girls a properly hygienic dress while they are growing. And not only should we clothe our girls hygienically, but we should ourselves adopt the same costume, for a girl when she is growing up rebels against wearing anything different to what she sees daily around her, and on the first moment of freedom reverts to the dress that her elders wear.

The aim therefore of the Rational Dress Society is to suggest a dress that shall give at the same time a minimum of weight, an even distribution of warmth, and perfect freedom of movement, and we hope, through the pages of this little Magazine, to express to our readers the dangers and inconveniences attendant upon our present system of dress, and to point out such suggestions for its reform, as may prove of practical use.

For this purpose we cordially invite the cooperation of all who are interested in this important question, which is so closely connected with the physical well-being of women, and consequently with the higher development of the race as an organic whole.

1.7

The society review became very popular in the late Victorian fashion magazine and its emphasis on society life and the 'upper ten thousand', that is the elite group that made up London and County society, formed an important element of the magazine's ethos of wealth and sophistication (something that was also very important to the ladies' papers).

'Society is Now One Polished Horde', *The World of Dress*, vol. 2, 1899, p. 133.
See also FIGURE 4.

"SOCIETY IS NOW ONE POLISHED HORDE, FORMED OF TWO MIGHTY TRIBES, THE BORES AND BORED."

ALL the gaieties lately seem to be confined to the country, and house parties, shooting parties, hunt balls and county balls, have followed one another in rapid succession.

Mrs. Charles Wilson's Ball, at Warter Priory, was perhaps the best of the private dances, and the cotillon, led by Mr. Herron and Miss Enid Wilson, a most cheery one. All sorts of presents and favours were distributed, but none were more appreciated than the bouquets of pink roses with long ends of blue satin ribbon.

"SOCIETY IS NOW ONE POLISHED HORDE, FORMED OF TWO MIGHTY TRIBES, THE BORES AND BORED."

ALL the gaieties lately seem to be confined to the country, and house parties, shooting parties, hunt balls and county balls, have followed one another in rapid succession.

Mrs. Charles Wilson's Ball, at Warter Priory, was perhaps the best of the private dances, and the cotillon, led by Mr. Herron and Miss Enid Wilson, a most cheery one. All sorts of presents and favours were distributed, but none were more appreciated than the bouquets of pink roses with long ends of blue satin ribbon.

The four smartest balls in the country have been those of the Market Harborough, the Melton, the Meynill Hunt, and the Lincoln Ball. At the last all the ladies wore purple and yellow, and the decorations of the room were arranged to match.

Lord and Lady Raincliffe had a very large party at Blankney, including nearly all the smart and beautiful women of the day. Princess Henry of Pless, Lady Warwick, Lady Westmoreland, and Lady Norreys were amongst those of the party, and the Duke of Roxburghe, Lord Chesterfield, Lord Cairns, and Mr. Laycock were amongst the men present. Lady Raincliffe owns just now a charming mauve and yellow chiffon gown—a triumph of Machinka's, and most becoming. She gave a delightful ball a couple of weeks ago, not very large, but very brilliant.

The Melton Ball was another great success. The Duke and Duchess of Marlborough had friends for it at Sysonby Lodge, including Mr. Cecil and Lady Lillian Grenfell, whilst the Duke of Roxburghe, who is one of the "dancing young men" of the day, was present with his sister, Lady Victoria Innes-Ker ; they were staying with Captain and Lady Sarah Wilson, as were Lady Gosford and her daughter, Lady Aldra Acheson, Lady Colebrooke, and Lord Crichton. Bettine Lady Wilton and Mr. Pryor, who have been doing a lot of quiet entertaining at Egerton Lodge, brought Prince and Princess Victor Duleep Singh. Princess Victor is the niece of Lady Wilton, and wore some gorgeous emeralds. Mr. and Lady Elizabeth Taylor also came with this party.

At the Harborough Ball, Lady De Trafford was certainly the handsomest woman present, and looked wonderfully well in white. Mrs. Brinckman's blue gown trimmed with black chenille was effective, and Miss Muriel Wilson and Miss Naylor were also greatly admired. The great drawback to this festivity was, alas ! the want of men.

If one wants to see who really is in town a visit to the various smart restaurants will generally inform you. Prince's is crowded every night. Lady Craven —whose father and mother, Mr. and Mrs. Bradley Martin, have just taken a house in Chesterfield Gardens—created quite a small sensation the other night at this restaurant by appearing in a most gorgeous old rose velvet cloak trimmed with lovely sables.

The Duchess of Sutherland, ever attractive, Princess Henry of Pless, who is looking more beautiful than ever this season, Lord Herbert Vane-Tempest, and Lord and Lady Rossmore, were dining at the Avondale one night ; and another evening there mustered here a large dinner party of sixteen, including Lady George Gordon-Lennox, Lady Parker, who wore a dress almost composed of black paillettes, Mrs. William Cavendish and her husband, Sir Squire Bancroft, Mr. and Mrs. Cyril Maude, the latter in white satin with some beautiful old lace, and Miss Gertrude

Kingston, in black velvet and a handsome diamond ornament in her hair.

At Claridge's one sees no end of smart people lunching, dining, and supping. Lady Charles Beresford has been staying there for a time. Church parade has been a failure—weather insisting.

The Sirdar's Ball, at the Hotel Cecil, on the 7th inst., was a most tremendous function, and the big ball room crowded to excess. The boys from the Gordon League lined the marble staircase, with bunches of ivy in their Glengarry caps and little buttonholes of Egyptian lilies and mimosa. The Gottlieb Band was a joy, but the ball opened very tamely indeed, and the company at first suggested a suburban dance in full swing ; strange couples were to be seen reversing, and the provincial style of most of the dresses was amazing. Things improved about 11 o'clock, when the Duchess of Devonshire, and the Duchess of Marlborough, and Lord Chesterfield, and Lord Herbert Vane-Tempest's guests entered the room. The dresses were even then not as smart as they might have been. The Duchess of Devonshire wore a very ordinary watered silk with trails of violets, but her tiara of diamonds and necklace of pearls were magnificent.

LADY RAINCLIFFE IN HER MAUVE AND YELLOW CHIFFON GOWN.

FIGURE 4 'Society is Now One Polished Horde'

19

The four smartest balls in the country have been those of the Market Harborough, the Melton, the Meynill Hunt, and the Lincoln Ball. At the last all the ladies wore purple and yellow, and the decorations of the room were arranged to match.

Lord and Lady Raincliffe had a very large party at Blankney, including nearly all the smart and beautiful women of the day. Princess Henry of Pless, Lady Warwick, Lady Westmoreland, and Lady Norreys were amongst those of the party, and the Duke of Roxburghe, Lord Chesterfield, Lord Cairns, and Mr. Laycock were amongst the men present. Lady Raincliffe owns just now a charming mauve and yellow chiffon gown – a triumph of Machinka's, and most becoming. She gave a delightful ball a couple of weeks ago, not very large, but very brilliant.

The Melton Ball was another great success. The Duke and Duchess of Marlborough had friends for it at Sysonby Lodge, including Mr. Cecil and Lady Lillian Grenfell, whilst the Duke of Roxburghe, who is one of the "dancing young men" of the day, was present with his sister, Lady Victoria Innes-Ker; they were staying with Captain and Lady Sarah Wilson, as were Lady Gosford and her daughter, Lady Aldra Acheson, Lady Colebrooke, and Lord Crichton. Bettine Lady Wilton and Mr. Pryor, who have been doing a lot of quiet entertaining at Egerton Lodge, brought Prince and Princess Victor Duleep Singh. Princess Victor is the niece of Lady Wilton, and wore some gorgeous emeralds. Mr. and Lady Elizabeth Taylor also came with this party.

At the Harborough Ball, Lady De Trafford was certainly the handsomest woman present, and looked wonderfully well in white. Mrs. Brinckman's blue gown trimmed with black chenille was effective, and Miss Muriel Wilson and Miss Naylor were also greatly admired. The great drawback to this festivity was, alas! the want of men.

If one wants to see who really is in town a visit to the various smart restaurants will generally inform you. Prince's is crowded every night. Lady Craven – whose father and mother, Mr. and Mrs. Bradley Martin, have just taken a house in Chesterfield Gardens – created quite a small sensation the other night at this restaurant by appearing in a most gorgeous old rose velvet cloak trimmed with lovely sables.

The Duchess of Sutherland, ever attractive, Princess Henry of Pless, who is looking more beautiful than ever this season, Lord Herbert Vane-Tempest, and Lord and Lady Rossmore, were dining at the Avondale one night; and another evening there mustered here a large dinner party of sixteen, including Lady George Gordon-Lennox, Lady Parker, who wore a dress almost composed of black paillettes, Mrs. William Cavendish and her husband, Sir Squire Bancroft, Mr. and Mrs. Cyril Maude, the latter in white satin with some beautiful old lace, and Miss Gertrude Kingston, in black velvet and a handsome diamond ornament in her hair.

At Claridge's one sees no end of smart people lunching, dining, and supping. Lady Charles Beresford has been staying there for a time. Church parade has been a failure – weather insisting.

The Sirdar's Ball, at the Hotel Cecil, on the 7th inst., was a most tremendous function, and the big ball room crowded to excess. The boys from the Gordon League lined the marble staircase, with bunches of ivy in their Glengarry caps and little buttonholes of Egyptian lilies and mimosa. The Gottlieb Band was a joy, but the ball opened very tamely indeed, and the company at first suggested a suburban dance in full swing; strange couples were to be seen reversing, and the provincial style of most of the dresses was amazing. Things improved about 11 o'clock, when the Duchess of Devonshire, and the Duchess of Marlborough, and Lord Chesterfield, and Lord Herbert Vane-Tempest's guests entered the room. The dresses were even then not as smart as they might have been. The Duchess of Devonshire wore a very ordinary watered silk with trails of violets, but her tiara of diamonds and necklace of pearls were magnificent.

2
The drawing-room journal

This was the earliest kind of miscellany for women, and one which from the first not only addressed a specifically female readership but also encouraged women as writers and producers. These magazines were expensive monthlies, usually costing at least a shilling, and addressed an upper-class readership who were concerned with the accomplishments appropriate to their gender and status. They assumed a good knowledge of French, a capacity to read music and an interest in (or readiness to read) serious educational articles on historical or social topics. They also typically included fiction, reviews, poetry and a fashion plate and sometimes an illustrated biography. They were well produced and the older examples were printed like a book, rather than in columns. Though they lacked the profuse illustration of the later magazines, these journals often included one or two high-quality engravings in each number as well as the fashion plate. Serious in tone and broadly liberal in their politics, the drawing-room journals exemplified a tradition which pre-dated Victoria's accession, as did some of the titles which continued well into her reign, for example *The Ladies' Cabinet* and *The Lady's Magazine and Museum* (which went through various mergers and title changes). One of these, *The Ladies' Cabinet*, lasted until 1870. In the 1860s there were at least two attempts to revitalise the drawing-room journal as a broadly liberal form with a tradition of giving women leading roles as writers and producers. These were *The Victoria Magazine* and the Edinburgh based *The Rose, the Shamrock and the Thistle*, both of which were edited, produced and printed by women. However by the mid-1880s, these more old-fashioned journals had been superseded completely by the general illustrated magazines.

2.1

This contents page from *The Court and Lady's Magazine and Museum* (1832–48) shows the typical range of material offered by the early drawing-room journals.

Contents page of the 'United Series' of *The Court and Lady's Magazine and Museum*, vol. 12, 1843.

CONTENTS OF LE FOLLET, COURRIER DES SALONS.

PLATES, IN THE PRESENT NUMBER.

July and August—Walking Dresses, 1095. 1096. Toilette de Théâtre. Toilettes de ville, 1100. 1101.
September and October—Toilettes d'Interieur. Toilettes de Ville, 1114. 1116.
November—Toilettes de Ville, 1120. 1122.
December—Walking Dresses. Toilettes d'Interieur, 1128. 1129.
Modes for July and August, September and October, November, and December.
Memoirs of Charles Premier—Agnes Sorel—Oliver Cromwell.

List of the Portraits in the present number.

Henry Stuart, Earl Darnley, No. 122 of this series, by Lucas de Heere.
His Majesty King Charles I., No. 123 of this series.
Their Majesties the King and Queen of Prussia.
Agnes Sorel.

Memoirs in the present volume.

Henry Stuart, Earl Darnley.
Their Majesties the King and Queen of Prussia.
Agnes Sorel.

Descriptions of the Portraits of—

Henry Stuart, Earl Darnley.
Agnes Sorel.
Their Majesties the King and Queen of Prussia.

2.2

Mrs Ellis's Morning Call (1850–52) was a monthly with many of the characteristics of the drawing-room journal as this frontispiece shows, but it related also to the expensively produced table books and annuals.

See FIGURE 5.

2.3

The Victoria Magazine (1863–80) edited by Emily Faithfull, a figure close to the mid-Victorian women's movement, combined the traditions of the drawing-room journal and the shilling monthly aimed at a more general readership. This abridged article utilises aspects of the biography, a popular form in the drawing-room journal, to make a public exhortation to the Queen (to whom the journal is dedicated) to come out of mourning for Prince Albert.

'Elizabeth and Victoria. From a Woman's Point of View', *The Victoria Magazine*, vol. 3, 1864, pp. 97–103.

"Uneasy lies the head that wears a crown."

WE women have a voice in the nation—let the men say what they will. Nor, I think, will any good man say aught unkind of it, or of us, so long as we take care to keep this voice what it should be—what God and nature meant it to be—low and sweet in their ears as the voice of Eve in Adam's: yet clear, firm, and never to be silenced or ignored, like the voice of conscience in their hearts. For the condition of a nation where it ceased to speak and to be listened to—this soft, feminine utterance, appealing less to reason and expediency than to instinct and feeling—would be analogous to that of a strong, bold, active man, with every physical and mental power in full perfection, only—without a conscience.

It can do no harm to speak a little, in this said woman's voice, upon a subject which has been very much discussed of late, in newspapers, social circles, and, since it touches on family and

MRS ELLIS'S

Morning Call

A
TABLE BOOK

of Literature and Art

"'Tis always Morning somewhere in the World."

Morning Hours.

JOHN TALLIS & COMPANY, LONDON & NEW YORK

FIGURE 5 Front page of *Mrs. Ellis's Morning Call*, vol. 1, 1850

fireside things, at almost every family fireside throughout the kingdom. We shall come to it by and by; but previously let me refer to two other subjects which drew my meditations towards this one, and are, in fact, illustrations of it. The first was a book—the second a picture.

The book was Froude's history of the reign of Queen Elizabeth. What a wonderful history it is! Not written after the ancient pattern, viz., laying down the law: stating certain received facts, concerning which no evidence is either given or expected to be required. . . . His part is to place before you, as perfectly and truthfully as he can, the people and the events of the period, which you then judge for yourself. If he assists your judgment by any personal bias of his own, it is concealed so artistically that you never discover it. And you become so deeply interested in these historical personages—these long dead men and women, once so living and warm—that you scarcely think of the historian at all; which is the highest compliment you can pay him.

Most lifelike among all these portraits—now reproduced almost in flesh and blood, after being mere historical shadows for three centuries—is the young Queen. Not as yet the Queen Elizabeth of our school-days, who cut off the heads of Mary Stuart, her cousin, and Essex, her supposed lover—(wicked lie!)—whose terrible deathbed scene fixed itself on our youthful imagination, as she lay raving on her palace floor, with her gray hair torn, and her three hundred dresses, stiff with jewels, all disregarded. Not this Elizabeth, but Elizabeth, still not much over twenty, the learned, accomplished, handsome princess—with qualities sufficient to exact personally the homage necessarily given to her station: acute, determined, liking to rule and quite capable of doing it: given to "indirect, crooked ways" and diplomatic deceits—rather, perhaps, from the excessive cleverness of her scheming brain than from any absolute untrueness of heart. For she had a heart—this poor Elizabeth—a heart as passionate, proud, capricious, artful, and yet sincere, as ever tormented a woman.

To students of human nature, there is hardly a more pathetic passage in history than the facts we have now learned, with tolerably certain accuracy, concerning England's favourite "virgin Queen"—Shakspere's

"Fair vestal, throned in the West,"

at whom throughout her long and glorious reign Cupid shot unheeded—

"And the imperial votaress passed on
In maiden meditation, fancy-free."

So the poet puts it; but history records, almost with pity, that restless, solitary, unloved life— that miserable death. And the root of all, as we now know, was what is at the root of most women's characters and lives—love; her persistent, imprudent, and yet most pitiable attachment to Robert Dudley, Earl of Leicester. A passion which, however unworthy (that it was guilty, is impossible to believe), was yet deep and sincere enough to contrast strongly with the falseness, vanity, and ambition which made up the other half of her character; and which, in after days, combined with outward circumstances, brought her, from her youthhood of promise and bright-ness, to be that wretched, old, forlorn, and dying Queen, upon whom the sternest judge cannot look without a certain compassion.

True, she had earned her fate, the inevitable fate of a woman who fixes her affections upon an unworthy man; she is dragged down to his level; or else, undeceived at last, she lives to unlove him and to despise him—happy for her if she does not at the same time, and by the same pitiable process, learn to despise and to deny love itself.

But, nevertheless, as she passes from the scene, as her brilliant reign closes, and the curtain falls upon that busy, troublous, splendid, empty life of hers, wherein this combination of a man's brain and a woman's heart brought upon her the faults, weaknesses, and sufferings of both, and the happiness of neither—our strongest sensation towards her is absolute pity.

25

Glorious as the Elizabethan era was, we cannot but draw a parallel between it and what we are now thankfully and proudly beginning to call "the Victorian Age." Alike they are in many points, especially in one—that in both the centre and nucleus is a regnant queen. Two queens, belonging to two as different types of womanhood as could well be found: yet both stamping their own individuality, not only on their personal court, but on the country at large, and indeed on the whole era through which they move. What strongly contrasted figures they will make in future history! Elizabeth, with her masculine intellect, her iron will, masculine also, yet often womanish in its fitfulness; her stately court, all etiquette and outside show; and the utter blank of her domestic life, a hollow crater wherein burnt fiercely the ashes of one consuming passion, which first conscience and then ambition forbade should ever become holy, peaceful, wedded love; —Victoria, gifted with moderate not commanding talent, who if not born a Queen might have been much like an ordinary gentlewoman; refined, accomplished, wise, and good: in everything essentially womanly, and carrying through life a woman's best amulet, the power of loving nobly, deeply, and faithfully. Loving and fortunate in her love, as such women, in some relation or other, are almost sure to be—happy daughter, wife, mother—aye, and happy widow, to whom even the memory of her dead is a crown of honour; the honour of a love wisely and worthily placed, and fulfilled on both sides, steadfastly and purely, as the marriage vow promised—"until death us do part." And this brings me to the picture I spoke of, which contrasted so vividly with the picture I had formed in my mind's eye of Queen Elizabeth—Froude's Elizabeth.

It is a very small thing, only a woman's head: one of the studies for an unfinished painting, which, however, has been so publicly and widely mentioned that there can be no breach either of confidence or decorum in my referring to it here—the memorial picture in honour of the late Prince Consort, commissioned by Her Majesty the Queen from J. Noel Paton, R.S.A. A mere sketch in crayons, and with nothing either tragic, dramatic, or even picturesque about it: simply the portrait of a woman, no longer young, and who even in her youth could never have been very beautiful. One of those faces, the most trying to artists and most unsatisfactory to friends, in which the principal charm lies in expression, and that expression so fleeting and variable that it is almost impossible to catch. But here, by a rare chance, this is done: and the imperfect outside forms are idealised by a certain spiritual grace, which in these sort of faces is continually seen; the momentary outward shining of the inward light, which friends recognise, strangers never.

. . .

In spite of this excessive simplicity, there is an inexpressible benignity and sweetness about the face. A something better than beauty; a quiet motherliness, a composed sorrow—sorrow not succumbed to, but struggled with, as only a woman can struggle. Yes, that is the heart of the portrait, its exceeding womanliness. The sort of portrait which, whether met with over a family hearth, or on an Academy wall, you would involuntary stop before, and say: "I am *sure* that is a good woman, one whom I should like to know and make a friend of." But you cannot, dear reader, for she happens to be Victoria, by the Grace of God, Queen of Great Britain and Ireland. Placed by her high estate above all friendships, at least all equal friendships, and all equal bonds of every sort, except one, which it has pleased Heaven now to remove from her for ever.

. . .

And yet there have been many hard things said of her, this Queen of ours, in speech or print, and especially by men; words which, if spoken of any other woman, a widow too, her "next friend" would have been justified in fiercely resenting. But she, in her splendid isolation, has no next friend. She has to take the unprecedented step of writing a letter—for in point of fact it is that—through the *Times* newspaper to her people. A letter with all her heart in it, her honest, candid, womanly heart.

There are people who doubt the wisdom of this—people who regard royalty as a mere State machine, to which forms are indispensable. They could hardly imagine a queen without a crown on her head and a sceptre in her hand, making due public appearances, and fulfilling to the last iota all ceremonial observances. They require, in this as in all else, not merely the thing itself, but the outward demonstration of it, almost at any personal cost. And in a sense, they are right. Such persons are to be highly esteemed, for they are always very conscientious. They keep society safe and smooth, and contribute greatly to maintain that fair conservatism without which it would soon crumble away into anarchy, disorder, and misrule. And they are very loyal too. It is in sad and sore earnestness that they believe the Queen, in giving up State ceremonials, is perilling the life of the nation.

But they forget one thing—that the life of a nation is not its ceremonial but its moral life, to which such a letter as this, out-spoken, honest, and free, from the Sovereign to the people, contributes more than the holding of a hundred drawing-rooms. And why? Because it is a true thing, a real thing. Because it sets forth, the more strongly because unconsciously, the truth, that human nature is deeper than outside show, and that womanhood is higher than queendom. Even though never a queen did the like before, it is a grand thing in this our Queen—loved and honoured as such for twenty-seven years—to have the courage to stand forward, quite by herself, and in her own identity, without intervention of ministers, or counsellors, or parliament, and say to the country, "I am only a woman, I have lost my husband, my one love of all my life; my heart is broken, but I will try to do my duty. Ask of me no shows or shams, and I will try to fulfil all that is real and necessary. 'The Queen will do what she can.'"

Surely, when we consider what courts are, what queens are, and what they have been in our own past history and that of foreign countries, there is in the intense trueness of this letter, with its solemn open recognition of two things, only too much ignored—the reality of love, the reality of grief—an influence which cannot fail to have the strongest moral weight over our own and other nations. It is the woman's voice, deeper than all diplomacy, higher than all earthly shows, speaking, neither loudly nor dictatorially, but with that honest sweet humility which most persuades mankind—and, thank God, always will, to the end of time.

But still a word may be said on the other side, and it should be said, not harshly or cruelly—as many have spoken and written of late—but still with very great earnestness.

There is something in our strong, reserved Saxon nature which recoils exceedingly from much outward demonstration of grief—indeed of every kind of emotion. We do not beat our breasts or tear our hair. We follow our best beloved to the grave in composed silence. We neither hang *immortelles* on their tombs, nor wreath their memorial busts with flowers. Not that we condemn these things, there is nothing wrong in them, but still it is not our way. After any great affliction we rarely speak much about it, but as soon as possible we go back to our ordinary habits, and let the smooth surface of daily existence close over the cruel wound. We bury our dead in our hearts; there they soon arise and live, and live for ever. And we believe it is best so.

It would make us only the more tender over her, our widowed Queen, if she would try as much as possible to remember this. Men would esteem her all the more for making her sorrow a silent sorrow. Incurable we know it is, but it is bearable, and it has many blessed alleviations. We women, so many of whom are also widows, or childless, or solitary and forlorn, we should feel all the more keenly for her if we saw her try to suppress, in every suitable way, all outward tokens of suffering. We suffer too, and are obliged to bear it; we cannot mourn externally, at least not for long; some of us, after the very briefest season of that dead stillness and passiveness which nature allows to a great sorrow, have to rise up again and resume our daily burthen, fulfilling unremittingly, and at any personal sacrifice, all the duties of the station, low or high, to which Providence has called us.

We are compelled to do this: and we should love her all the better, and revere her all the more, if, so far as she can, our Mistress, God bless her! would do the same. Not in one thing, or two things—but in everything. He would have done it—that noble, virtuous husband, of whom it was his highest praise that all his virtues were so silent; and who, for this very reason, has been taken into the deepest core of the strong, silent British heart. For his sake we ask this, and for the upholding after his death, as during his life, of that truth which *we* know to be true—that as men are what women make them, so women are what men make them; that everyone of us grows more or less after the pattern of the man we love—for his sake, therefore, who was so perfect a man, we would appeal to our Queen, as honestly as she appeals to us, that she should do her best to overcome her grief, and to rejoice in the many comforts that are left her. We would cry to her as with one voice—the echo of her own—"Be strong! You do but love as we love, suffer as we suffer. We understand it all, but still we ask you to bear it. Live through it, as many of us have done, expending wholly for others the life which is no longer sweet to ourselves; until there comes a time, as comes in every righteous life, when it pleases God to send the peace which is securer than joy, the blessedness which is better than happiness." In words which—to so truly religious a woman as, for the nation's ensample and hope, she is—must be far more precious than any words of ours, "Be strong, and He shall comfort thine heart. Put thou thy trust in the Lord."

2.4

The Ladies' Cabinet (1832–70) was, as were drawing-room journals generally, sympathetic to the development of opportunities for women, particularly educational ones. This article provides a historical backdrop to what had become a very topical debate.

'The Higher Education of Women', *The Ladies' Cabinet*, vol. 34, 1869, pp. 221–22.

THOUGH the University education and examination of women is an experiment new to England, it is by no means, as some of our contemporaries have too readily taken for granted, a perfectly novel institution. It has already found favour to some extent among our transatlantic cousins, and those who are familiar with the history of Italy ought to know that at Bologna, at Milan, and at other Italian Universities, women were not only educated, but in some cases the professorial chairs were occupied by learned and distinguished creatures of the better sex. In 1732, La Dottoressa Laura Bassi became Professor of Natural Philosophy in the University of Bologna, in which she had passed the brilliant days of her undergraduateship, and when she died, honoured of all as she deserved, her Doctor's gown and her silver laurel wreath were carried in funereal pomp to her grave. One of the most successful teachers of the Greek language known at any time in Italy was Clotilde Tambroni, a lady Professor at Milan University. We are by no means inclined, with some writers, to attribute the comparatively high education of Italian women to that reverence for the gentler sex which comes naturally, we are told, from "the cultus of the Blessed Virgin," with its tendency to elevate woman in the scale of society. We, on the other hand, solve this problem, simply by pointing out the fact that the Italian language is to the old Latin very much what the Italian woman is to the old Latin matron, as we find in each the essential elements still extant.

Now, of all women of antiquity none displayed a more marked predilection for arts and literature than did the Roman. The position of a Roman matron was the very reverse of a Greek wife. The Roman presided over her whole household *educated her children*, and, as the materfamilias, she shared the honour and respect due to her husband. Italian women have degenerated less from the old Roman type than have Italian men, notwithstanding that their minds have been thwarted and twisted by the pernicious influences of Popery. Another solution may be found in the fact, that Italian women are more remarkable for their *public* than their *private* virtues and capacities; and a country that was once ruled by a Pope Joan is by no means a country unlikely to encourage a staff of female professors in its public Universities.

Cordially do we rejoice at the prospect now spread before the educated womanhood of this country. It is to our reproach, as a nation, that the higher education of women amongst us has declined since Queen Elizabeth harangued a University in Latin, and Lady Jane Grey wrote Greek. It is something for the Universities to put forth worthy aims and objects to those who would otherwise be aimless and objectless in their studies. It is something to encourage studies which have a marked and incontestable tendency, not only to supplement the wants and to strengthen the weaknesses of the female mind, but to add grace to its grace and beauty to its beauty. It is something to bring the heads of our girls to apply themselves to what is more valuable and enduring than chignons, and to subtract something of the time and attention now dissipated upon the *modiste*, for the purpose of investing the mind with a garment of glory and beauty which changes with no changing fashion and grows in beauty as it grows in years. It is something for our big girls to practically learn by patient study and settled plans, and a rigid economy of time, those moral and social virtues of patience, self-denial, self-restraint, regularity, and order, which go very far to make up the good woman, the exemplary wife, and the true and tender mother, as well as those intellectual excellencies, such as judgment, taste, prudence, and quickness of apprehension, which, when sanctified by religion, strengthen the weakness of women, and entrench her behind a wall of adamant. Such, we conceive, are some of the social advantages which may be derived by the fairer portion of society from these University examinations. Of the literary advantages we say nothing, as these speak for themselves.

We are especially pleased to notice that Cambridge has not forgotten its duty as a Christian University in holding forth the study of the Christian religion to its aspiring candidates. Without a knowledge of God, in truth, all other knowledge is but folly. The light that leads to Heaven is verily worth more than all other lights, and sad evermore is the life voyage of him or her

"On whom there shone
All stars of heaven except the guilding one."

Knowledge and wisdom are not far apart from each other. Society has no such ally in the cause of civilization and Christianity as that of a woman, true to the innate tenderness and the purity of her sex, going forth with a richly cultivated intellect, with a disciplined mind, and a heart sanctified by the indwelling spirit of her God, to teach by the silent eloquence of a noiseless, charitable, gracious, and gentle life, the invaluable lessons of a living Christianity, to live the light and joy of her own home, and the fruitful blessing to her own generation. In conclusion, to all who seek to benefit themselves by such examinations, whether women or men, we must remind them not to rest content with making their *brains* temples of light, however brilliant, but to dedicate their *hearts* as temples to Him who has promised, if we are in Him, to dwell *in us.—The Rock.*

2.5

The Ladies' Edinburgh Magazine (1875–80) was produced by and for the Ladies' Edinburgh Literary Society and the focus was very much on educational and literary accomplishment. This piece illustrates well the kinds and level of debate encountered by groups of like-minded literary women.

'Debates of the Ladies' Edinburgh Literary Society', by Ex Cathedra, *The Ladies' Edinburgh Magazine*, vol. 4, 1878, pp. 44–45.

Our debates this year have not been less lively than usual; indeed, probably owing to the lighter subjects chosen for discussion, they have been more naturally entertaining, and a larger number of members than formerly have taken part in them. The January debate was an exception, dealing with the profound and difficult question of the supposed opposition of Darwinism to Christianity. The evolution hypothesis, supported by the negative, was not considered in itself necessarily opposed to Christianity by either the mover or the seconder of the affirmative, but the theory *as held by Darwin*, which seemed in their opinion to leave no room for a distinctive divine element in man. The voting, as influenced by this restriction of the discussion to Darwin's theory, gave a majority of one to the affirmative, *i.e.* against Darwin. The February debate on the political question, 'Would it be beneficial to Europe if the power of Russia were extended to Turkey?' was remarkable for a unanimity in the voting, which left the mover and seconder in favour of Russia in a minority by themselves, though several members declined to vote. On the one side it was urged that the Turks by their sacred laws were unfitted to govern any but Mahommedans, and that other nations, who might have protected the Christian subjects of the Porto, had left all the task to the Russians; also, that a nation so great as Russia could only be temporarily excluded from the freedom of the seas which wash her coasts; but the current of feeling seemed to be, not liking for the Turk, but jealousy of the Russian, and much anxiety about India, recalling, perhaps, Lord Salisbury's remarks that Eastern distances are apt to be studied in maps on too small a scale. The March debate, 'Does *Daniel Deronda* sustain the reputation of its author?' which produced a lively discussion, was carried in the negative by a large majority, notwithstanding a particularly well-expressed speech without notes on the other side. In April some of the best-written and most interesting papers we have ever had were read on the question, 'Is it desirable that our Government should send out another Arctic Expedition?' suggesting the thought that in no country but our own could such sympathy with nautical affairs, and such familiarity with the history of the explorations of the seas, be found in a gathering of ladies. The time of the meeting had been so taken up with the business that no discussion was possible; so the papers were re-read and the votes taken in May, when it was found that a majority of our ladies were ready to risk their countrymen in another search for the North Pole.

The June debate was a real discussion on the benefits of travel, as compared with the superior mental discipline of a home life. The papers, especially perhaps those taking the more difficult defence of a home life, were bright and original, and after discussion showed that the question was well understood by those who took part in it. In July, descriptions of pictures by several members present took the place of a debate, and the papers were much approved of. The October debate, 'Is it desirable for women to take part in field sports?' was one of the liveliest of the year, being a real practical question to many present. The mover and seconder in favour of field sports for those ladies whose taste lay that way, and who were strong enough to enjoy them, advocated fishing and hunting, but drew the line at shooting, as needing too much practice, and being too violent an exercise. The power of the negative, while disapproving of all field sports for ladies, considered them allowable for gentlemen who could not otherwise be easily amused; but some of her supporters were of opinion that she had no logical resting-place, and advanced the theory that all field sports were in their essence wrong. The voting, which probably showed the influence of town life, and might have gone otherwise in the country, gave a majority of thirteen out of twenty-five against field sports. The November debate, owing to the business before the meeting, was adjourned to December, when we had an interesting literary debate upon the relative importance of the Anglo-Saxon and Norman elements in the English language and literature. Two different aspects of our rich and many-sided English were well brought out in the speeches and papers, which were rather descriptive of different qualities of the same language than directly antagonistic. The voting gave a large majority in favour of the Norman and other grafts upon the ancient Saxon root.

While we may congratulate ourselves on the increasing interest of our debates, and especially on so many of our younger members taking a spirited and intelligent part in them, it may be well to notice here a tendency in the after discussion to let the meeting disintegrate into little knots, and the argument dissipate into small talk, adverse to the brief expression of our own ideas and careful listening to the ideas of others, which we aim at. Though we have had some fluent and excellent speaking without notes, and though, especially in reply, such speaking has special point, we are still, from the experience of last year, of opinion that, for most of our subjects, our usual practice of having at least two good written papers is best. They give, we think, closer reasoning and more orderly information than even very good extemporaneous speaking, unless where it rises into oratory.

The debates have lately suffered from the length of time taken up by the increasing business required by the magazine; we therefore hope that arrangements may be made this year to meet this difficulty.

3
The general illustrated magazine

This type of magazine carried the tradition of the miscellany for women to a wider group of readers who were more directly responsible for domestic management than those addressed by the drawing-room journal. Deploying new technologies of production as they were developed, especially in relation to illustration, this type of journal was central to the development of the popular commercial women's magazine. Like the drawing-room journal, it was usually a monthly. It differed from this earlier form, however, in that it was addressed to the middle-class rather than the upper-class woman, it was less expensive, less uniform in tone and included a greater variety of features – including advice to readers on a range of domestic and personal topics. In appearance this group also differed from the older format, printed in double, rather than single column and including a range of visual material, a feature which became more pronounced as the period went on. These magazines typically included fiction, usually serialised, general articles, poems, fashion news, and advice on domestic, romantic and personal matters, which was usually linked to readers' letters. The first truly successful example was the Beeton publication *The Englishwoman's Domestic Magazine* which came out in 1852 costing 2*d* and survived until 1879. Its price was raised to 6*d* in 1860 and this was a typical cost for the rest of the period. Titles launched in the 1880s and 1890s were often substantial, well illustrated and employed well-known writers whose names were selling points, most famously Oscar Wilde as editor of *Woman's World*, and Annie S. Swan, the romantic novelist, on *Woman at Home*, where she ran several advice columns/readers' letters pages. In the 1890s the distinction between these and other kinds of magazines was blurred by *Hearth and Home*, which was a broadsheet size threepenny weekly.

3.1

In its first two years *The Ladies' Companion* (1849–70) prefigured the general magazine for the middle-class woman. It was edited by Mrs. Jane Loudon and had a distinguished group of named contributors, including Mary Russell Mitford, Mary Howitt, Geraldine Jewsbury (whose serial is extracted below) and Eliza Acton, whose pioneering cookery column provided a model for later magazine writers including Isabella Beeton. In 1852 the contents became identical with those of *The Ladies' Cabinet* (1832–70) and *The New Monthly Belle Assemblee* (1834–70) and it became in effect another drawing-room journal.

'The Sorrows of Gentility. Chapter XII', by Geraldine Endsor Jewsbury, *The Ladies' Companion*, vol. 2, 1850, pp. 305–07.

GERTRUDE wept long and passionately upon her mother's bosom, the conflicting feelings of joy and sorrow and remorse, all the pent up speech of years were resumed into one chaotic emotion of which tears were the only utterance.

Mrs. Morley, who herself was much affected by this first sight of her daughter after so long a separation, began at length to be alarmed. "Come, my dear child, don't take on in this way! What is it that's ailing you? See, you are frightening baby, who cannot tell what to make of it all."

"O, mother!" sobbed poor Gertrude, "How ungrateful you must have thought me, the sight of you makes me feel how ill I have behaved towards you; I shall never forgive myself—I was beginning to think you had turned me off, as you never took any notice of my letter—and now I almost wish you had, the sight of you hurts me so."

"I would like to see the person who dared to say you had behaved ill," said Mrs. Morley, indignantly. "You were always the best, and kindest, and most industrious creature in the world; and if you did run away to be married, it is only what many a girl has done before, and will do after you, God help them!—so don't let that lie on your mind. I would have come to you long since, only your father was contrary and would not let me; and you have found out by this time that a husband is a master when once he takes a thing into his head. As to your letter, I only got it a fortnight ago, on account that Mrs. Slocum forgot it in her trouble. I read it to your father, and Mrs. Slocum talked to him, and the minister called, and I got him to speak. But at first your father would hear no reason . . . So then I talked to him and coaxed him, and when he saw how much I took on, and was fretting after you, he softened, and told me I might come up to London to see you, and that I might bring you back with me if I liked; and when he did come round, nothing could be more condescending than he was. He knew that I had never travelled alone, so he spoke to 'Fat Sam,' who drives the 'Dart,' to take care of me, and see me safe here. It is his off day, and he would have brought me himself; but I thought he might not just be the person to introduce amongst your grand people, for though he has a kind heart, he is a rough one to look at—"

Gertrude interrupted the torrent of her mother's discourse, to ask how long she had been there, and whether any refreshment had been offered to her.

"Oh, I never once thought of refreshment! I thought I should have dropped when they told me you were out, but I asked to see the baby, and told who I was; the boy who opened the door seemed afraid to let me in, but however he did, and I waited on the mat whilst he went into the parlour, and he came back, followed by an old lady, as high as a duchess in her manners, but with a gown on I would not have picked up in the street. I told her I was your mother, and said I had come to see you. She looked at me as if I were the dirt under her feet, and at last said you had gone out, but that if I chose to go into the nursery I might wait there till you came back, though she could not say how long that might be; and as I said that I would wait, she bid the boy show me the way, and walked off leaving me standing there. I might have been come to see one of the servants by the way she spoke. But I was too thankful to be so near seeing you to feel offended. Who is she? Does she live here? The boy called her his 'mistress.'"

"It was old Mrs. Donnelly, my husband's mother. She is very haughty in her manners. I wish I had been at home."

"Oh, I don't care for her, not I, though she is the first, calling herself a lady, who ever showed any pride to me, and I have had to speak to some of the best ladies in the land."

"But," said Gertrude, anxious to turn the conversation, "it is a long time since breakfast, let me get you something to eat."

"Ah, well, I don't care if you do get me a glass of wine and a mouthful of a sandwich, but don't let me give any trouble. I brought up a basket of 'Christmasing' with me, just a turkey of my own raising, and a pork-pie and one or two little things. I left it down in the hall. The old lady walked away so sharply that I had no time to tell her what it was. But," continued she, as Gertrude was leaving the room, "why should you go? Can you not ring the bell? I thought that was one of the comforts of living in a private house. I don't like to see you run up and down to wait on me. I can do without anything quite well until dinner time."

Her mother's patience and self-forgetfulness struck Gertrude with more remorse that any reproaches could have done.

"Oh, mother! Don't speak so kindly to me, I cannot bear it."

"Bless thee, child! How wouldst thou have me speak? I never felt so happy in my life."

At this instant the servant entered with Mrs. Donnelly's compliments, and she wished to speak to Mrs. Augustus.

"I must go to her," said Gertrude, "but she cannot want to keep me long."

Getrude found the old lady waiting for her with ill-repressed impatience.

"It is very extraordinary," she began, "that I should have to send for you, when affairs of such importance are on hand; but you are always so giddy, you think of nothing but your own pleasure. What said Lady Southend?"

"She said nothing, ma'am, except—except—that she could not agree to your proposal."

"How is that? Did she read my letter?"

"Yes, ma'am."

"And what did she say? I desire you will repeat to me every word that passed."

Gertrude hesitated. "Indeed, ma'am, nothing passed of any consequence, except that she would not entertain your proposition."

"Did she send no letter? No definite message? I insist upon your not concealing anything."

Gertrude, thus adjured, repeated the substance of the interview, though she somewhat softened the terms of Lady Southend's message; but the effect was much like that of sending a bomb-shell into a sitting room, or dropping a spark into a barrel of gunpowder, or any other experiment of a startling and explosive nature.

. . .

Whilst these events were going on at home, Mr. Augustus was rapidly drawing towards the close of his good luck abroad.

He had managed to bet heavily on the wrong dog, and the conclusion of the match found him a loser to a good amount.

As the party were going off to dinner a dirty scrap of paper was thrust into his hand, bidding him look to himself as bailiffs were on the watch to arrest him outside the door. Mr. Augustus made his escape through a window, and going through back streets and by-ways, reached his own door in safety.

A loud peal at the door-bell startled Mrs. Morley and Gertrude, as they sat by the glimmering light of the nursery fire, and immediately afterwards the voice of Augustus was heard calling impatiently from below.

"What can have happened?" said Gertrude. "Something must be very wrong to bring Augustus home at this time."

"Bless the man! He will awaken the baby," said Mrs. Morley. "Go, go and see what is the matter. Your father can never bear to be kept waiting; he will call the house down if nobody goes down."

Gertrude went down stairs as quickly as she could, with trembling limbs. There was no light in the hall; but she found her way in the dark to the dining room, the door of which was open. There she found her husband, thrown back in a large chair beside the fire-place, with his head sunk upon his bosom; the fire was extinct, and the cinders were strewn about the hearth. A single-dip candle stood on the table, with a long un-snuffed wick, and a thief on one side was guttering it away. He looked up as she entered.

"You have been a long while coming. What were you doing?—and where's my mother and Sophy?"

"Oh, Augustus!" said Gertrude, quite frightened at his sombre looks and disordered dress. "What is the matter? Are you ill? What has brought you home?"

34

"Oh, nothing; don't bother;" said he, roughly shaking off her hand. "Why do you look at me in that way?"

"Because I am frightened; you look so strange."

"It is no wonder; I am not drunk, as you seem to think; but it is all up with me. I owe more money that I can ever pay; and I shall go off to France to-night, or else I shall be inside a prison to-morrow. I wish my mother were here. Why did she go out when she knew how things were?"

Gertrude shut the door, and then returning to her husband, she said, "Augustus, if you are ruined, tell me, I have as much right to hear about it as your mother. I am your wife at any rate, and perhaps I can do more to help you than you fancy."

"What can you do?" he replied. "I suppose you did not bring a pocketful of bank-notes from the old lady this morning; and if you did, it is not a few that would help me."

Gertrude shook her head.

"Ah, I never expected you would get anything," said he. "I'll forgive her not doing anything if only she does not set her son against me."

"If only you could persuade these people to wait a little, I could work and earn money to keep myself and the baby; and then, perhaps, Lord Southend would be back, and he would advise you what to do."

"My poor Ger! What good would your work do? But you are a good girl, and it is thinking what will become of you that makes me so low. I can rough it for myself; but what will you do?—for I must off away from this."

"Oh, don't think about me," said Gertrude. "I shall do very well. My mother came to see me today; my father is quite reconciled. Won't you come upstairs and see her. I am sure she will advise us for the best. My father always goes by what she says."

Poor Gertrude knew nothing of his affairs, but she felt a pride in putting her mother into the seat of Mrs. Donnelly.

Reckless and thoughtless as Augustus was, he felt a twinge of shame at being introduced to his wife's mother under such circumstances.

Gertrude did not perceive his hesitation, he was trimming the candle.

"Remember, you must tread very softly, for baby is asleep. What a long time it is since you saw her in her little cot. She looks a perfect angel!"

The introduction between Augustus and his mother produced a mutually favourable impression, for he was extremely good looking, and had a gentlemanly address. And when he embraced Mrs. Morley and called her "Mother," all her latent prejudices against him were dispensed at once, and Gertrude stood completely absolved for running away with him. After a few moments Gertrude reminded her husband that he had come to consult her mother. Gertrude's notions of "being ruined" were extremely vague and picturesque; moreover she felt a glow of pride in the idea that she and her mother were going to advise Augustus all to themselves, and without Mrs. Donnelly; so she may be pardoned if she did not feel nearly so miserable as circumstances seemed to require.

As to Mr. Augustus he would rather have been excused entering into details, but there was no help for it. He therefore gave Mrs. Morley and his wife a rhetorical account of his affairs, making them look not like vulgar debts, but only gentlemanly embarrassments, which would disappear, and even become eventually sources of prosperity. He succeeded in talking himself into good spirits; and as Mrs. Morley promised that Gertrude and the baby should never want a comfortable home, his most legitimate source of anxiety was removed.

With all her prepossession in favour of her son-in-law, Mrs. Morley was glad that he proposed borrowing from somebody else and not from her; and she now used her influence to get him safely off . . .

Samuel Beeton succeeded in developing the relatively cheap magazine for women. *The Englishwoman's Domestic Magazine* (1852–79) which he edited jointly with his wife during their marriage, had much the same mix of ingredients as *The Ladies' Companion* (1849–70) but was smaller and cheaper. As the frontispiece indicates, it offered to do for the middle-class woman what the drawing-room journal did for her upper-class sister.

See FIGURE 6.

FIGURE 6 Frontispiece, *The Englishwoman's Domestic Magazine*, vol. 2, 1853, unnumbered page

3.3

These magazines typically included advice columns and answers to readers' letters. *The Englishwoman's Domestic Magazine* (1852–79) began with two, 'The Englishwoman's Conversazione' and 'Cupid's Letter-Bag', which were later amalgamated. Though the format was typical, Beeton's editorial persona was unusual in that it was definitely masculine and often jocular.

'Cupid's Letter-Bag', *The Englishwoman's Domestic Magazine*, vol. 2, 1853, p. 96.

LAURA B. (Camden Town).—"I have two lovers and know not which to choose. One is rich, and has given me several handsome presents; the other is poor, but so attentive and kind that I feel he would make the best husband. I have been brought up in every comfort, and dread poverty; so know not how to decide. Pray advise me."—LAURA's letter is certainly very business-like, and betrays but little genuine love for either of her admirers. For the sake of the poor lover, however, who really may be silly enough to value affection, we would advise her by all means to marry his richer rival, as, like "Pamela," the "gilt coach and Flanders' mare" has evidently its attractions for LAURA.

CYMON (Sydenham).—"In your Magazine you are always lauding the constancy of woman's affection. I am about to give you a specimen which I hope you will insert, as through your columns it may reach the eye of the lady who has played so false a part. For two years I have been constant in my attentions to a young lady who gave me every reason to believe my love was returned. Presents have passed between us, and vows of unaltered and unalterable affection. Had a serpent stung me, I could not have felt more horror-struck than when visiting the Zoological gardens a week ago, I saw a form too well known hanging on the arm of a gentleman, evidently pleased with the foppish attentions he was paying her. Being of a confiding disposition, I believed her when she told me the night before that on this particular day she should be busy with household cares, and not visible until six in the evening. This palpable deception enraged me to the degree that I could not forebear crossing their path, and raising my hat said, 'Good morning, miss; how do you do?' She immediately gave symptoms of fainting; but I was not to be so taken in, but left her to the care of her sighing swain. I have not seen her since, and do you think I should act rightly in shunning her company for the future?"—We cannot but think that this *contretemp* might admit of a milder construction than CYMON seems to have put upon it. Had the lady no brother or cousin expected from sea, and no acquaintance in the country that required chaperoning about town? However, failing in these suggestions, we advise him to call on the lady, who, no doubt, will easily explain away this slight mistake, and all will go merrily as a "marriage bell."

CLARA MARIA.—"I have been for some time very much attached to a young gentleman. I fear my love is un-returned, Formerly he paid me marked attention, so that my friends supposed his intentions were sincere. For the last six months a visible change has taken place in his conduct which, as you may well imagine, annoys me extremely, and I am quite at a loss to know in what way I have given offence. When I happen to meet him, which is a very infrequent occurrence, he manages to attract my attention quite to himself. Do you consider his intentions honourable? Please kindly advise me in what way I ought to conduct myself in his company."—The old adage in this case proves true, "Love is blind," or CLARA MARIA would not for a moment nourish the hope that her love is returned. We begin to think, after all, our grandmothers understood the art of courtship better than the ladies of the present day, for they introduced buckram into their manners as well as their dresses, and thus became objects of pursuit instead of pursuer. Can CLARA MARIA see a good-natured hint in these remarks?

MARY L. (Burton-crescent).—"Some time back I met a young gentleman at a friend's house, and in the course of the evening he flirted a great deal with several ladies, and in the end wished to transfer his attentions to me. I exhibited a marked coolness towards him, which seems to have inspired him with a sincere attachment, as he has ever since been constant in his inquiries after me, the friend at whose house I met him believes he is sincere, and wishes me much to see him again. Shall I be doing right?"—We think Mary should be very guarded in the way she receives the advances of so fickle a gallant. Her friend, we presume, is a married lady.

3.4

The Ladies' Treasury (1858–95) edited by Mrs Warren, was the most long-lasting of Victorian general illustrated women's magazines. It was typical not only in its mix of genres but also in that it offered both to entertain and to instruct. The general article was the main medium for that element of general education which persisted into these magazines from the drawing-room journal. Though some articles were illustrated, usually with woodcuts, the example from which this extract is taken was not.

'Social Employments of Women', *The Ladies' Treasury*, vol. 1, 1858, pp. 21–23.

SINCE Florence Nightingale went out on her mission of charity to the East, it has become matter of consideration in this country, whether the services of refined and educated women might not be made available in our ordinary hospitals, and in reformatories and workhouses. As the presence of such women in the military hospitals was found to be of the highest advantage in the relief of bodily suffering, and as an instrumentality for imparting religious consolation, why then, it is asked, should not the same benefits be extended to institutions at home, which are manifestly defective in these respects? There is good reason to believe that there would be no lack of the required agency, if the government and public opinion could be brought to sanction its employment. In continental countries this agency has been long at work, and, according to all reliable accounts, with the most complete success. Here, in England, it would not be desirable, or even practicable, to copy the system pursued in Roman Catholic states; above all things, we should object to any formal setting aside of the individual under the obligation of a *vow*, or to any conditions of arrangements affecting personal liberty. Such conditions would not assert with English views and sentiments; and besides, we are persuaded that they are perfectly unnecessary. The common feelings of humanity, sanctioned and sustained by religious principle, would be found to be sufficient. There being numbers of women almost wholly unconnected with home or family relations, who require nothing so much as a sphere of honourable activity for their faculties, it is not to be doubted that many of them would gladly enter upon a work affording them opportunities of doing good among the suffering and depraved of their fellow-creatures, and would engage in it under impressions of earnest sense of duty.

Some experiments have already been made, which show that this proposed labour of love and money is within the range of practicability. A staff of volunteer lady-nurses, with paid and trained nurses under their orders, has been now for some time employed in King's College Hospital. Respecting them, it is observed by Mrs. Jameson:—"I have the testimony of one of the gentlemen filling a high official situation at the hospital (and who was at first opposed to the introduction of these ladies or, at least, most doubtful of their success), that they have up to this time succeeded; that strong prejudices have been overcome, that there has been a purifying and harmonising influence at work since their arrival." There appears to be no difficulty about the ladies and the medical men working well together; nor is it likely that if the experiment were judiciously extended, there would be any fear of its failure.

Among the facts collected by Mrs. Jameson, bearing upon the salutary effects of feminine influence in the continental hospitals, there are some which are very striking. "One of the directors of the great Military Hospital at Turin," she says, "told me that he regarded it as one of the best deeds of his life, that he had recommended, and carried through, the employment of the Sisters of Charity in this institution. Before the introduction of these ladies, the sick soldiers had been nursed by orderlies sent by the neighbouring barracks—men chosen because they were unfit for other work. The most rigid discipline was necessary to keep them in order; and the dirt, neglect and general immorality were frightful. Any change was, however, resisted by the military and the medical authorities, till the invasion of the cholera: then the orderlies became, most of them, useless, distracted, and almost paralysed with terror. Some devoted Sisters of Charity were introduced in a moment of perplexity and panic; then all went well—propriety, cleanliness and comfort prevailed. 'No day passes,' said my informant, 'that I do not bless God for the change which I was the humble instrument of accomplishing in this place.'

. . .

On the subject of our own military hospitals in the East, Mrs. Jameson says: "All to whom I have spoken, without one exception, bear witness to the salutary influence exercised by the lady-nurses over the men, and the submission and gratitude of the patients. In the most violent attacks of fever and delirium, when the orderlies could not hold them down in bed, the mere presence of one of these ladies, instead of being exciting, had the effect of instantly calming the spirits and subduing the most refractory. It is allowed also that these ladies had the power to repress swearing and bad, coarse language; to prevent the smuggling of brandy and raki into the wards; to open the hearts of the sullen and desperate to contrition and responsive kindness.

. . .

The gentleness, the sympathy, and constancy of the ministration had efficacy to soothe even intolerable pains; and how strongly this was felt and experienced, is shown in the story of the poor soldier, who said that the very shadow of Florence Nightingale passing over his bed seemed to do him good!

The presence of women of refined habits and education, shown to be thus effective in the wards of hospitals, has been found to be of no less service in the cells of prisons, and in those reformatory institutions which are designed to reclaim the criminal. On this point it has been remarked, that there are many persons who would receive with a laugh of scorn or a shudder of disgust the idea of having virtuous, religious, refined, well-educated women brought into contact with wretched and depraved prisoners of the other sex. It would be even more revolting than the idea of a born lady—a Florence Nightingale, or a Miss Anderson, or a Miss Shaw Stewart—nursing a wounded soldier appeared only two years ago. Yet this is precisely what we wish to see tried. Captain Maconochie mentions the influence which his wife exercised over the most hardened and horrible criminals, the convicts at Norfolk Island: because she was fearless, and gentle, and as a *woman* these men respected her,—they who respected nothing else in heaven or earth. In other places more favourable for the experiment, the uses of disinterested feminine influence have been proved by admirable results. In a report on the conditions of prisons in Piedmont, furnished by the authorities, it is stated as "an indisputable fact, that the prisons which are served by the Sisters of Charity are the best ordered, the most cleanly, and in all respects the best regulated in the country." This statement is confirmed by the Minister of the Interior, who adds: "Not only have we experienced the advantage of employing the Sisters of Charity in the prisons, in the supervision of the details, in distributing food, preparing medicines, and nursing the sick in the infirmaries; but we find that the influence of these ladies on the minds of the prisoners, when recovering from sickness, has been productive of the greatest benefit, leading to permanent reform in many cases, and a better frame of mind always: for this reason, among others, we have given them every encouragement.

. . . Facts, however, such as the above, when we remember what Mrs. Fry accomplished by mere visiting, ought surely to convince us of the usefulness of feminine influence as an agency towards reforming the class of criminals. There cannot be any reason why English ladies, duly trained and organised, should not be able to effect as great an amount of good in this direction as has been effected in other countries under a system of Christianity which we must regard as far less perfect than our own. To be sure, the work requires to be entered on as an express vocation, and as such demands peculiar feelings and capacities; but the same demand has to be met in the continental countries, and we have no doubt the means of meeting it are as abundant here as there.

On the management of poorhouses, the writer from whom we have already quoted has made many observations, and attributes the existing defects of these establishments mainly to the want of a refined womanly sympathy and superintendence. Of the workhouses which she has visited, she says:—"Some are admirably clean, and, as far as mere machinery can go, admirably managed; some are dirty and ill-ventilated; and one or two, as we learn from recent disclosures, quite in a disgraceful state. But whatever the arrangement and condition, in one thing I found all alike— the want of a proper *moral* supervision. I do not say this in the grossest sense, though even in *that* sense, I have known of things I could hardly speak of. But surely I may say there is want of proper moral supervision where the most vulgar of human beings are set to rule over the most vulgar; where the pauper is set to manage the pauper; the ignorant govern the ignorant; where the aged and infirm minister to the aged and infirm; where every softening and elevating influence is absent; or of rare occurrence, and every hardening and depraving influence continuous and ever at hand. Never did I visit any dungeon, any abode of crime or misery, in any country, which left the same crushing sense of sorrow, indignation, and compassion—almost despair—as some of our English workhouses."

. . . In one of our large London parishes, a committee of lady-visitors has latterly been allowed to look over the wards, in the character of occasional inspectors. This will do good in individual cases; but what is wanted is a domestic, permanent, ever-present *influence*, not occasional *inspection*. Lady-visitors, to do good, must be properly authorised and organised—must work in concert, lest they contradict and interfere with each other.

Touching the system or course of training that would be necessary for these lady-workers, to qualify them for their vocation, many sensible remarks have been made by the writer already named, all of which, however, may be passed over as being, for the present, beside the purpose which we have in view. What we desire, by means of this paper, is to call popular attention to the principle which she sets forth and illustrates—the principle of communion of labour between men and women in the work of governing, reforming, guiding, succouring the depraved and the unfortunate. We think we have made out a sufficient case to justify some practical effort. In what particular way sisterhood of charity could be found in this country, we do not pretend to say, but who can doubt that among Protestant Englishwomen as much devotedness, energy, skill, judgement, and compassion could be found, as is found among the women of Catholic countries?

. . . Let the reflective mind of England ponder well the matter, and there will be hope of its being, sooner or later, wrought out to some worthy and serviceable result.

3.5

In the 1880s and 1890s, these magazines retained the general article as a staple but the topics discussed began to include some of the new pastimes, sports and occupations which women were taking up. *Woman's World* (1887–90), from which this extract comes, had begun as *Lady's*

World (1886–87) (see Bibliography of titles). However, when the publisher, Cassells, persuaded Oscar Wilde to take over the editorship in 1888 he agreed but on condition that as a magazine for the modern woman it should become *Woman's World*.

'Pastimes for Ladies. On Three Wheels', *Woman's World*, vol. 6, 1887, pp. 243–44. See also FIGURE 7.

ONE can well imagine the general feeling of shocked consternation which would have pervaded all sections of the community some ten or twelve years ago at the mere suggestion that women would ever take to cycling as a means of recreation and amusement; yet within the last half of that period it has become a recognised fact that women have an equal share with men in what is certainly one of the most health-giving and delightful institutions of this age; and tricycling, with all its attendant joys, is daily gaining in popularity with women of all ages.

At first, there is no denying the fact, tricycling for women was somewhat doubtfully regarded by the majority. Mrs. Grundy was disposed to raise her eyebrows and cough slightly at the mere idea of gentlewomen taking part in what had hitherto been regarded as exclusively the sport of men. There was also a certain amount of very reasonable prejudice, caused, it must be confessed, by the highly conspicuous and far from graceful appearance of a certain set of novices while endeavouring to fathom the mysteries of the new art; terrible warnings in the way of costume, and other details, which made many a parent and guardian of feminine youth fervently express their feelings on the tricycle question, and hastily nip in the bud any young desires which pointed in the direction of three wheels.

But all good causes conquer in the end; and tricycling for women has won its way steadily, through prejudice and opposition, to its present acknowledged station among the favourite exercises of nineteenth-century maids and matrons.

Now, Englishwomen of almost every class have adopted the new pastime. The young Princesses are devoted tricyclists, and there is a goodly show of machines in the Royal stables. Women of the middle classes ride very largely: using their machines for amusement, as a means of health, or as a help in their daily work. More than one daily governess has blessed the means of swift and easy locomotion which takes her to and from her daily task with such quickness and comfort; and there is every reason to believe that the time is coming when shopwomen, and even operatives, will be enabled to share in the convenience and pleasure of what has been not inaptly called "the poor man's steed."

Surely no form of exercise has ever opened up so delightful a vista of enjoyment to women as tricycling! . . .

But it is not alone as a pleasant pastime, it is as a health-giving exercise, that tricycling takes its highest stand. Medical men are agreed that, for the majority of ills that feminine flesh is heir to, there is no medicine like

FIGURE 7 'Pastimes for Ladies . . .' illustration, p. 244

41

regular doses of the three wheels. Of course, like all other physic, it requires to be taken judiciously, with moderation at first; and, even after long practice has increased the length and duration of rides to an almost incredible extent, still with a resolute avoidance of over-fatigue, chills after over-heating, &c. With these slender precautions there are few women, even the most fragile and delicate, who may not ride regularly with pleasure and benefit to themselves.

And to those who seek in the tricycle a means of health, how great is the reward! Headache, rheumatism, neuralgia, and a thousand kindred pains disappear as by magic: strained and tortured nerves are soothed and strengthened; the circulation, quickened and regulated, begins to start afresh the run-down machinery of the tired frame. To the sickly woman, bent beneath a load of nameless aches and wearinesses, her life darkened by formless shadows, terrible though intangible, I would give but the one word of advice, "Tricycle." To the girl who is devoid of every charm of brilliant complexion and of sparkling eye, who longs in vain for the loveliness she sees in those about her, I would say, "Try tricycling."

To the tyro in the art of tricycling there are many difficulties which to her timid fancy appear as lions in the way. It is in the hope of proving how imaginary most of these puzzles are, that I offer a few practical hints to the beginner.

First of all, it is always best to learn upon a hired machine before starting one of your own. Nothing is really simpler than the motion of pedalling, and the steering is merely an affair of practice. Any woman of average intellect ought to manage the whole science in half an hour sufficiently to make her feel at home in the saddle. Take great care at first, and do not try to ride fast. Give plenty of room to passing vehicles, and avoid sudden swerves. In time steering will become purely involuntary; and the rate of speed may be indefinitely increased. As you grow used to your machine, learn to know its various parts and their use. Never start for a ride without an examination of nuts and screws, to see that they are all in proper condition, and be careful that your machine is well oiled, and the brake in good working order . . .

Having mastered the art of riding, you will not long be content without your own mount. Never buy a tricycle without a previous trial, and get some friend who understands the subject to thoroughly examine the machine before you finally make it yours. Of course every maker will tell you his own machine is the best, but popularity is the truest test of merit, and among the favourites of the day are the "Royal Salvo" (the tricycle specially patronised by Her Majesty the Queen), the "Premier," the "Royal Crescent," and the "Cripper."

Having procured a machine (which should always be obtained from a good maker, economy in the matter of make being very false policy), the next question will relate to costume. The vast amount of absurd and valueless advice on this point volunteered by writers who have merely a theoretical knowledge of the subject, is melancholy to the practical rider . . . Practical experience has taught that the prettiest and most suitable dress is a skirt of tweed or flannel of some dark shade, made ordinary walking length and width, with a deep kilting, well taped down, and drapery stitched down to prevent its blowing into the wheels. This skirt should be worn with neither steels nor dress-improver, but be well tied back with elastic, and fastened with buttons to the round bodice, to throw all the weight upon the shoulders. Shoes must be worn, not boots; and the hat should be a plain sailor straw, or a felt hat, without more adornment than a wing or a club ribbon. Neatness and simplicity are the beauties of a cycling costume, and there must be no loud colours, no floating ends, artificial flowers, ribbons, or feathers. A plain Norfolk jacket for cold weather completes the whole. A linen collar, or tiny frill, fastened by a plain brooch, finishes this pretty and trim costume. Let me add that corsets should never be worn; they are both inconvenient and injurious. One of the many modern substitutes should take their place . . .

For, machine and dress comfortably supplied, it will certainly not be long before our novice ceases to be content with gentle exercise over well-known roads close at hand, and begins to sigh for a bolder flight. There is no question that touring is the most delightful of all cycling pleasures. Even with a limit of a few miles a day, a tour of two or three weeks can cover long distances either at home or abroad, and it is at once the most economical and most enjoyable mode of modern travelling. Enough luggage can be carried on the machine to supply immediate wants, and heavier *impedimenta* may be sent on from point to point by rail.

In conclusion, let me offer a few short pieces of advice to the would-be tricyclist. Begin with runs of half a mile or so, increasing the distance as one can stand it. Never start directly after a heavy meal, nor sit down to eat as soon as a long and tiring ride is finished. Dress as lightly as is compatible with warmth. Dr. Jaeger's sanitary under-wear is perhaps the best, and a fur shoulder-cape, or an extra wrap of some sort, should always be carried to put on in case of a sudden change of weather, or of "coasting" a hill when over-heated . . . Never ride carelessly, or forget that it is possible for a lady to be as graceful and elegant in the saddle of a tricycle as in any other position in life. Never attempt to ride up a hill after the effort becomes severe; and remember to put on the brake before dismounting on an incline.

If these rules be conscientiously adhered to, even the most complete novice may take her rides abroad without the slightest fear of accident or risk, and her enjoyment and comfort will be almost certainly insured. It is hardly too much to prophesy that, once having tasted the joys that attend the tricycle and its use, she will part with her most cherished earthly possession sooner than forsake the pleasures which come "on three wheels."

FIGURE 8 Fashion plate, *Hearth and Home*, vol. 1, 1891, p. 676

3.6

Illustration including the fashion plate remained a crucial element in the visual appeal of most women's journalism. *Hearth and Home* (1891–1914) was a new kind of general magazine. It was a broadsheet weekly like the ladies' newspaper but with a mixture of contents more like the general illustrated magazine and a price between these and the cheap domestic. The illustration here was directly linked with an advertisement on another page of this issue.

See FIGURE 8.

3.7

By the end of the period, general illustrated magazines combined the traditional mixture of fiction, articles, domestic advice, fashion news, poetry and competitions with newer genres like interviews and with more 'modern' topics and more features attributed to named authors. Ella Hepworth Dixon's *The Englishwoman* (1895–99) looked over her shoulder back to Samuel Beeton's mid-century formula and title, while she represented the confident new woman.

See FIGURE 9.

FIGURE 9 Cover, *The Englishwoman*, vol. I, 1895

4
The religious magazine

This group of magazines were all published by religious groups that aimed either to convert to or support women in the evangelical, missionary or other Christian cause. Many, such as *The Mother's Friend* and *The British Mother's Magazine*, were aimed at working-class women but a significant number, such as *The Christian Lady's Magazine*, were aimed at middle-class women. Almost all had denominational backing and so were pre-eminently non-commercial ventures, but they were significant because they were so pervasive. Those aimed at a working-class readership were cheap, often penny monthlies that were didactic in tone and spartan in presentation. An exception to this is *The British Workwoman* which added stunning visual narratives and elegant typography to the otherwise conservative blend of instruction and devotion. Most were mothers' magazines and long-running examples include *The Mother's Friend* and *The Mother's Treasury* which instructed mothers on the gospel and on taking their position in the family and society. Others such as *The British Workwoman* and *The Servant's Magazine* were for working women and provided instruction and advice on domestic, moral and religious life. They were considered ideal reading for servants and were typically bought by employers for their staff or distributed free on the streets. Those aimed at a middle-class readership were more expensive but included the usual attention to scripture and to general moral issues; they also assumed a relationship of equality between editor and reader, something which was absent in those addressed to working-class women. By the end of the century the women's sections of missionary societies such as the Anglican Church Missionary Society began producing magazines for women in Britain describing work with women overseas. These were not commercial magazines but they did use some of the new journalistic devices such as photography.

4.1

This is the first article to appear in *The Mother's Friend* (1848–95). It delineates the general aims of the new publication, the style and tone of which is typical of the didactic religious magazine aimed at the working-class woman.

'Our First Word to Mothers', *The Mother's Friend*, vol. 1, 1848, pp. 1–2.

THIS little magazine is prepared for your benefit, busy mother; it is very cheap, only a farthing a week, so you will not miss the cost of it. It is sent forth to the world by the friends of mothers, and no labour will be spared in trying to make it interesting and useful to you. Come, sit down a minute, aye, take your boy on your lap if you like, he will not hinder your reading a page or two. We have seen mothers many a time sitting down to hush the young ones to sleep, with a book in their hands, from which they have gathered thoughts to cheer and help them amidst their daily toils. Thus, while the father has been labouring for the daily bread, the mother has been trying to elevate her own heart and the hearts of her children to the love of God and man. I fancy I see you looking with deep interest upon your infant boy. You call him "precious", "noble", "beautiful." You hug him to your heart. You feel you could die for him; so perhaps you really could; but did you ever reflect that your child can never die? Those bright eyes now beaming on you shall see the heavens pass away with a great noise, and the elements melt with fervent heat, the earth also, and the works that are therein burned up. Those very eyes shall see the Judge sitting upon his great white throne, and before Him he shall see all nations gathered together. Yes, and YOU will be there!—all your family will be there! This little book comes to aid you and them in making ready to meet with joy and not with anguish that great gathering day. Remember, mothers, IMMORTALITY is written upon you and yours. Oh, do try to bear in mind, as you look at your young ones, growing up into life, there is a world beyond the grave, a world where all we love shall live again. This is the very reason why we feel so deeply interested in you and your dear children; we can, we do sympathise with you in your cares and anxieties, and we hope to render you aid and encouragement in your great work. We know you can find little time for reading, therefore the papers admitted into this Magazine will be short, so that while resting from your labours, or nursing your infant, you may gather a few thoughts to help you amidst your important duties. We intend—

> To explain and enforce the varied duties of the mother and endeavour to awaken a deeper feeling on the subject of a mother's responsibilities.
> To advocate kind and proper treatment of children—to promote the cultivation of the affections, and encourage a right discharge of duty.
> To show the importance of making every thing connected with the child, from its earliest infancy, tend to the reception of true Christianity.
> To give the history, and make known the designs and results of Maternal Associations.
> To offer such practical suggestions as shall contribute to the health and happiness of the family—in short to aid the wife and mother in her endeavour to make HOME HAPPY.

4.2

The Christian Lady's Magazine (1834–49) was produced for the middle-class woman. The following abridged article deals with the potential clash between fashion and the religious life.

'A Word Upon Dress. By the author of "Not at Home" and "The First Dissenter" ', The Christian Lady's Magazine, vol. 10, new series, 1855, pp. 337–41.

> ". . . The bonnet to its right use;
> 'Tis for the head."—SHAKESPERE

["]Take no thought what ye shall put on," is a command which—to say nothing of obeying it in the letter—it would seem to be very difficult to carry out even in the spirit. In an ever varying climate like our own, health and comfort demand the exercise of some consideration on the subject of raiment; nor are the claims of custom and propriety to be disregarded by the Christian woman. The careless disuse of a cloak or a boa, may cause serious or even fatal illness; and by arraying herself on a showery day in a dress or bonnet suited only to summer sunshine, the unguarded wearer, although by no means a votary of fashion, may bring upon herself the loss of money which she would have desired to spend to better purpose. A certain kind and degree of attention, therefore, to the subject of attire, is proper and necessary; and cannot be inconsistent with the command, "Take no thought what ye shall put on."

. . .

There never has been, however, and there probably never will be, a period presenting, in the matter of dress, no extreme of fashionable folly to be avoided by "women professing godliness;" nothing to excite, with regard to such women, the wonder of the world, in that they "run not with them to the same excess of riot." At the present day a fashion so ludicrous as to form a subject for the satire of "Punch," is not only followed, but even carried to the utmost extreme by Christian ladies. Need I say, that I speak of the bonnet worn, during the past and present year, not *upon* but *behind* the head? In order to judge of the utter unseemliness, the absurdity, of this head gear, let any candid-minded person cast a glance over a well-filled church. Such a person will surely be ready to adopt the words of my motto, and exclaim—

> ". . . The bonnet to its right use;
> 'Tis for the head;"

if indeed, he or she be not rather disposed to expostulate in the earnest language of St. Paul, and say, "Judge ye for yourselves; is it comely for a woman to pray to God with her head uncovered?" Surely if there be any meaning in the first half of 1 Cor. xi.—if we are to believe, that though manners and customs may be changeable, principles are of constant and universal application— we must feel that the absolutely uncovered heads of some of our young ladies are unsuitable now as they would have been of old, in a Christian congregation; that the fashion in question is ill-suited to the retiring character, which becomes women in every age; and that when followed to the full modish extent, it is utterly at variance with the modesty and decorum of dress and demeanour by which English women have hitherto been distinguished.

The gauze or tiffany hat, placed horizontally over the eyes, as described in the early part of Mrs. Sherwood's life; the coal-scuttle or poke-bonnet, worn by English ladies before the Peace; and the various forms of head attire since in use; ungraceful, unclassical, and unpicturesque, as several of them were, had still, in common, one small merit; they *did* cover the head; and, in part, the face; they did not leave the wearer as completely exposed to view as is a Milanese or Roman peasant girl! Surely it is impossible to contemplate young persons belonging to families professedly religious exhibiting themselves in church, to all intents and purposes unbonneted; with their hair dressed for display, and having a braid which seems to be purposely so placed as to render it impossible that the bonnet *should* cover the head; without feeling that it cannot be *thus* that their parents can wish them to appear in the house of God. The solid countenance, the immovable look, which generally accompanies this style of dress, is perhaps the natural com- pliance with a fashion which suffers no emotion to pass over the face unperceived; but it is not on that account the less inconsistent with a devotional spirit, and with that broken and contrite heart which becomes those who confess themselves to be "miserable sinners".

Christian young women! Were I willing to suggest to your consideration, with respect to this subject, motives lower than the highest, I might observe, that the fashion upon which I am animadverting, is, generally speaking, as unbecoming as it is unseemly; and, moreover, that when it shall have passed away, permanent traces of it will be found to have impressed themselves upon complexions reddened or bronzed, as the case may be; that if the projecting bonnet and lace or gauze veil of other days ministered less effectively to *present* vanity, they at least tended to preserve the charms which they partly concealed, and which are, in any case, sure to vanish *quite as soon* as the owner can desire; and, finally, that if sacrifices affecting personal appearance be indeed demanded from you, it is desirable that they should be offered in a better cause than in that of a ridiculous, and unbecoming, and, as it may be hoped, a transient fashion.

47

The British Workwoman (1863–96), companion paper to *The British Workman*, was a broadsheet which was generously illustrated, something quite rare in the religious magazine. This piece utilises the dialogue which was a form particularly popular with the religious magazines and adopts a self-consciously didactic tone, also typical of this group.

'Trials of a Complaining Wife. (A Conversation between Mrs. Fretwell and Mrs. Candid.) By the Author of "Good Servants, Good Wives, and Happy Homes," &c., &c.', *The British Workwoman*, vol. 1, 1864, p. 47.

Mrs. Candid.—I have called to enquire after your child that got burnt yesterday. I hope he's going on well.

This was said by a decent tidy working-man's wife, to one of her neighbours.

Mrs. Fretwell.—Thank ye, he's doing nicely; he's far better than he desarves to be, a plaguy brat, that he is, he's allas in mischief. I've been nursing him till I'm fairly tir'd out, what wi' one thing an' another, I'm jaded almost to death. I wur just resting mysel' a bit when you came in, an' I'll tell you what I wur thinking as well; I wur pondering over the many hardships we poor women ha' to endure. I declare, our life's nout but toil, an' care, an' trouble; our lot is a very hard one. I wur thinking, too, how much better off our husbands are than us poor wives.

Mrs. Candid.—I must say I think otherwise. 'Tis true they are not tried in the same way that we are, but they have to rough it as well as their wives, and often a great deal more so. We couldn't bear what they have to endure.

Mrs. Fretwell.—Don't tell me so. Just think, in a morning they've nout to do but get up an' go straight their work, an' attend just to one thing all t'day through; then when meal times come, they expect to have everything ready in their hands, an' if one has getten anything that's not just to their liking, dear me! there's much glumping and grumbling as is quite sick'ning. Then at six o'clock their work is done, an' they can go out and enjoy themselves i' all manner o' ways, just as they like, spending t' money, too, which they ought to bring home; but they think o' nout but their own pleasure; precious little do they care about their poor wives who are drudging at home, fag, fag, fagging at it, from getting up to going to bed. Then think how it is wi' us women slaves. How often do we have to tell o' toilsome days an' sleepless nights, wi' sickly and tiresome bairns, an' perhaps at the time we're badly ourselves; but it matters not, sick or well, we must attend to our daily toil, and from morning to night, its nout but cleaning an' cooking, washing an' scrubbing, nursing an' toiling. O dear! it makes me bad to think about it. With all this, one is teased an' worried almost to death wi' bad unruly childer, allas getting into mischief o' some sort or another, like that lad there, because I wur away to have a bit o' gossip wi' a neighbour, began to light some matches, an' set his sel' on fire. So you see, besides doing for 'em i' all manner o' ways, one has to watch 'em as a cat watches a mouse, an' even then, however one may scold and storm, they will get into mischief, an' are ever kicking up some shindy or another. But whatever comes across, or has to be done, our unreasonable husbands expect one to have everything to be clean and tidy to be sure, to have their meals allas ready to t'minute, an' to be waited upon hand an' foot. If this isn't slavery I don't know what is. Talk about t'niggers o' America, can they be worse off than us poor working-men's wives. I often wish, I know, that I'd never been born.

Mrs. Candid.—You have made out a pitiable case, Mary, certainly; but it is very clear you are suffering your feelings to blind your judgement. It is true that as wives and mothers we have many cares, toils, and sorrows; but then they are inseparable from married life, especially with us working people. They are only what all who enter upon it should look forward to, and reckon upon, as what in the nature of things may be expected. The promise and vow you made when you went to church to have the marriage knot tied, had certainly a reference to many of those things you complain of, for did you not pledge yourself "to obey your husband, to serve him, to love, honour and keep him, in sickness and in health until death should you part?"

Mrs. Fretwell.—Oh, as for that, I said just what t'parson bid me. I knew I couldn't be married if I didn't, but yo' may be sure I've never thought about it since; as for t'other things, its sartain, I never reckon'd o' half of what I've had to do, an' pass through, or else I should never have been a wife to drudge as I do.

Mrs. Candid.—What, did you not reckon on keeping your house clean and tidy, on attending to your husband's wants and comforts, and on nursing your children, and minding their health and welfare?

Mrs. Fretwell.—O, as to childer, I hop'd I should never have any. I'm sure they came before they were wanted, an' for other matters, I thought but little about 'em. The fact wur, I wur tired o' sarvice, mistresses were so bad to please, this wur wrong, an' that wurn't right, besides, one wur kept allas a going; of one went to the door to have a chat, or to look about a bit, the bell was sartain to ring, summit or other was sure to be wanted; an' there was so much bother if one wanted to dress up and show off like other girls, that I might as well have been i' prison, i' else confinement, so I made up my mind to marry t' first man that offered that could earn a living. . . .

Mrs. Candid.— . . . and here we have the reason why there are so many unhappy marriages, and so much misery and disorder in society. It must ever be the case where love is not the principle of the marriage union—a sincere respect for, and attachment to each other. Love is the life and soul of marriage, without which it differs from itself as a dead carcase differs from a living body. Let this be wanting, and marriage is degraded in the way you have spoken of, and becomes a mere selfish compact. . . .

Mrs. Fretwell.—But if one doesn't feel this love, how then?

Mrs. Candid.—You must remember that the Bible commands it as a duty; you must love your husband, or sin against God, and as we pray for grace to fulfil every other duty, why not pray for grace to fulfil this also. There are many things for which a wife and a mother has special need to pray; she should pray that she may set a good example to her family, that she may be able to instruct and discipline her children, and train them up in the way they should go; she should pray that she may be enabled to regulate her temper and her words; but next to her own salvation, she should be concerned to obtain grace to discharge aright the important duties to which she solemnly pledged herself at the marriage altar, and the first of these was to reverence and love her husband.

Mrs. Fretwell.—Ah! but prayer is what I know little about. I us'd to pray when I wur a girl, and went to t'Sunday School, but it's been neglected ever since.

Mrs. Candid.—This is a sad confession to make. No wonder I found you so desponding, and so full of dissatisfaction and complaints. An acknowledgement of error is, however, the first step towards amendment, and if you will only be prevailed on to begin the exercise, I will tell you what will follow; you will be led to think over *why* you *ought* to love your husband, you will dwell upon your own sacred and public promise to do so, on his just claims to your affection, on the influence of love in exciting love, and how happily this will operate in promoting your own happiness and welfare, and that of your family. . . . One other result will also follow: by prayer you will place yourself in communion with the great God; you will think of *His* claims, and of your duty to *Him*, and you will think also of your spiritual state, of the solemn realities of a future world, of your personal and relative responsibilities; and who can tell but the issue may be the salvation of yourself, your husband, and your children. But I must now leave you; our conversation has got strangely prolonged; I hope you will kindly receive my remarks, for by them I am sincerely seeking your welfare.

Mrs. Fretwell.—I believe you are; you have done me a great kindness; you have really opened my eyes, so that I begin to see things very different to what I did; but let me beg of you to come again an' instruct me more fully how I may go on.

Mrs. Candid.—I will see you again. I hope brighter and happier days are before you. Good morning.

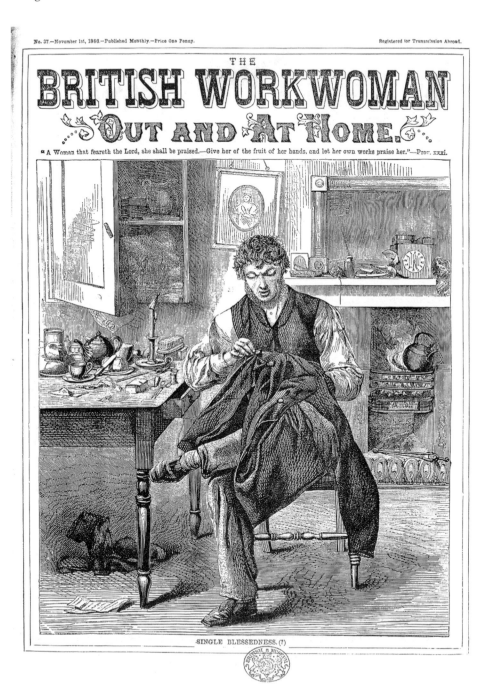

FIGURE 10 Cover page, *The British Workwoman*, vol. 3, no. 37, November 1866

4.4

The cover pages from *The British Workwoman* (1863–96) illustrated appeared on consecutive issues.

See FIGURES 10 and 11.

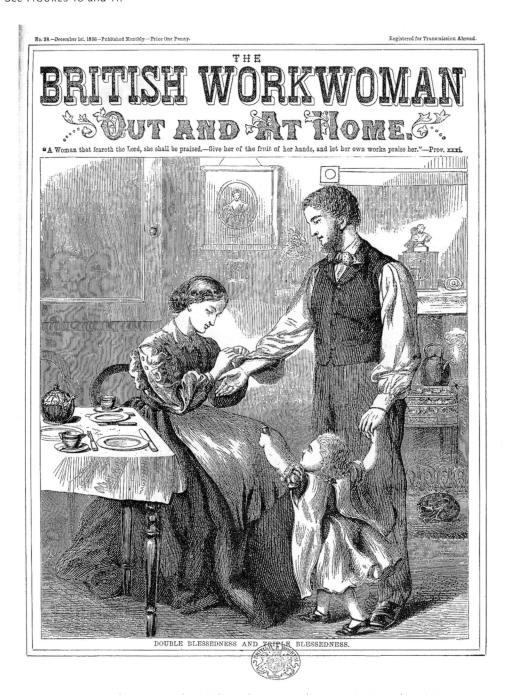

FIGURE 11 Cover page, *The British Workwoman*, vol. 3, no. 38, December 1866

This short piece from *The Servant's Magazine* (1838–69) illustrates well the tone and approach of religious publications aimed at servants.

'Plain Questions Worth Asking One's-Self Daily', *The Servant's Magazine*, vol. 1, new series, 1867, p. 21.

1. Have I this day behaved myself as a Christian servant ought to do?
2. Have I been diligent, remembering that my time belongs to my employers?
3. Have I in every circumstance told the *plain truth*, though it might be to my own disadvantage?
4. Have I governed my temper, not giving way to passion, sulkiness, fretfulness, or any spirit of revenge against anybody who has offended me?
5. When found fault with, was I careful not to answer again, but behaved humbly and meekly?
6. Have I been patient under vexations?
7. Have I taken all care of my master's property, using with economy what is intrusted to me as if it was my own?
8. Have I been free from wastefulness in my eating and drinking, not taking more than could do me good, or leaving on my plate, or putting in the grease-pot or the pig-trough bits that hundreds of my fellow-creatures would be thankful for?
9. Have I been strictly honest—honest even in little things?
10. In every thing have I acted as under the eye of my mistress, but above all as under the eye of God?
11. Have I served Him, who is a Spirit, in spirit, while I have been occupied in my lawful business?

5
The ladies' paper

This group of journals shared many of the characteristics of the general illustrated magazines. However, what distinguished them was that they called themselves 'newspapers' and were registered as such, that they attempted to define a feminine 'news', came out weekly rather than monthly and were printed in what we would now call 'broadsheet' format, usually in three columns. From the first these ladies' newspapers were also distinguished by their lavish use of illustration and their reliance on advertising, two characteristics which became even more marked in the 1880s and 1890s. The first example, *The Lady's Newspaper*, was launched in 1847 as a generously illustrated broadsheet costing six pence and dedicated to Victoria. It ran until 1863 when it amalgamated with the most famous and long-running of the ladies' newspapers, *The Queen*, which had been founded by Samuel and Isabella Beeton in 1861. *The Queen* kept much of the format, the weekly appearance and price of *The Lady's Newspaper* but defined itself as an upper-class journal. It carried extensive high-quality engravings of fashion plates and reproductions of contemporary paintings, court news, advice on manners and dress and reviews but it also informed its readers of advances in women's education, suffrage meetings and other aspects of women's advance into public life. By the mid-1880s half its page were devoted to advertising and it, along with *The Lady's Pictorial* and *The Gentlewoman*, became a site on which some of the twentieth-century practices of women's magazine advertising were developed, especially the 'advertorial'. These papers also carried extensive small advertisements, especially *The Lady* which still does so.

5.1

The Lady's Newspaper (1847–63) mixed short articles and comments on contemporary affairs with the traditional elements of 'female journalism', brief biographies of notable women, fashion, and needlework patterns. Most of it, however, was devoted to short articles on a wide range of topics, printed in three columns in broadsheet format with numerous engravings. These two extracts from the editorial page were part of a campaign fought by the paper to make the streets safe for women and give an indication of its lively style.

'Mrs. Perryan and Mr. Hardwicke' and 'The Protection of Women', *The Lady's Newspaper*, vol. 1, 1847, p. 361.

MRS. PERRYAN AND MR. HARDWICKE.

Since our last number another instance of magisterial regard for women and their privileges has occurred, against which it is our duty to protest. Bad as the previous cases have been, we think Mr. Hardwicke has, by an extraordinary effort of his genius, out-heroded them all.

A certain Mrs. Perryan, residing in a court in which two of her lodgers were wrangling, endeavoured to restore peace betwixt them, and for so doing was pounced upon by a brace of policemen; dragged through the court; knocked down with a blow from a truncheon; kicked, beaten, and bruised, till the blood poured from her nose and mouth—for the heinous offence of endeavouring to keep the peace.

Mr. Hardwicke, after severely *rebuking* the two constables, remarked that they had not even a "pretext" for their behaviour; that, had Mrs. Perryan and her husband, who was also concerned in the affair, been in the wrong, their duty was, knowing them to be housekeepers, to come to that court and procure a summons against them. After which flourish of justice, the worthy magistrate, seemingly regretting that he had spoken with so much severity, fined the policemen forty shillings each, or one month's imprisonment.

Of course the alternative part of the sentence will not take effect; and, therefore, we may regard the judgment as confined to the forty shillings; by which wretched penalty two public peace-officers are held, on the authority of a police magistrate, to have sufficiently expiated their offence—cowardly, brutal, and disgusting as it was!

So that what we some time ago apprehended, out of the excess of our alarm, is actually coming to pass; and if affairs continue to progress in this way—if the *Hardwickian* estimate of female value is to become the general standard—to kill a woman by-and-by will not be murder; but, judging by the late police decisions, it will be competent to a constable, his inspector, or a magistrate himself—for these are the only sort of persons who would think of such transgressions—to hang, drown, or beat into a mummy any female individual he may take his peculiar fancy to, for something not exceeding five pounds.

THE PROTECTION OF WOMAN.

THE annual meeting of the Associate Institution for Improving and Enforcing the Laws for the Protection of Women will be held at the Freemasons' Hall on Monday next, B. B. Cabbell, Esq., M.P., in the chair. Bound as we are, as much by inclination as our duty, to watch with ceaseless anxiety every movement whose object is to procure that proper estimation of women from society which they have never yet received, we shall not fail in our next number to lay a full report of the proceedings before our readers.

Ladies, it is to be observed, are especially invited to attend, and the chair will be taken at twelve o'clock precisely. It is to be hoped that the meeting will not alone be numerously but influentially attended; and that a cause which has received less attention than any other of its importance will find advocates worthy of its merits.

For our own part, our efforts are ceaseless to obtain for women the respect due to them. Hardly a day passes, and certainly a week never, which does not produce some extraordinary manifestations of indifference—and often worse—to the claims of women upon society. Insisting at all times on greater EXCELLENCE from them—and getting it—instead of rewarding that excellence by unusual privileges, the endeavour of the world appears to be to cut female privileges down to the smallest amount of concession. In fact, the aim of society with respect to women seems to be to obtain the best possible article at the lowest imaginable price; and, in many instances, without paying for it at all.

5.2

The Lady's Own Paper (1866–72) though comparatively short lived, developed the tradition of the large size ladies' paper. It offered good quality large illustrations, usually woodcuts, and included poems and some fiction as well as articles on general social issues and the position of women, of which this is an example.

'Un-mental Women', by Fanny Fern, *The Lady's Own Paper*, vol. 5, 1871, p. 289.

SAYS a modern, and, need I add, *male* writer: "Marry a woman's heart, not her head." I wonder are there no men extant who can stand both! Are there no women possessed of both? Will stupid people never be done with divorcing the two? And did you ever take note of the married life of the man who was so afraid of marrying a woman with a head? Well, I have. I meet them in all my wanderings by sea and shore. These are the men, tired of darning-needle twaddle about broken teacups and Johnny's shoes, who say soft things to their respective Joannas and Maries, but, to avoid the terrible tedium of their vapid presence, are often called away "on business." These are they who, when they want conversation, seek it out of the house. It never occurs to them that it is a duty they owe this limp being of their choice to help her to a higher place of companionship. Not at all. Having made so fatal a mistake, they leave their wives to the inanities and the consequences. Now, as I've remarked elsewhere before, there is no animal so hard mouthed to drive as a fool; therefore these Maries, over every little obstacle, are full of their petty snivellings and whinings, and their hypocritical Johns say – "Yes, it is a shame," without caring a penny about it, and call them "little dears," and then run away from them as fast as they can.

It is a perfect union, that of head and heart in a woman. It is a blessed thing when, at his own fireside, a man may talk intelligently and be understood. It is a blessed thing when his wife has taste and refinement, with culture added, and when, in addition to all this, she "looks well to the ways of her household," and knows its daily outgoings and incomings. And mark, the higher a woman's culture, and the broader her understanding, the less she will despise or underrate that personal supervision and oversight which is due to the comfort and happiness of those dependent upon her. It is only your *sham* intellectual women who utterly sniff at such obvious duties. And in saying this let me not be misunderstood. If intellectual women can safely delegate the *details* of work to others, let them always do it. But until their means are adequate to this let them stand, like true women, to their posts, bearing the postponement of their heart's desire as *second* to this, and, perchance, as possible by good management in the happy future.

Charlotte Brontë made good bread, and went patiently through household work, for the sake of her household. So could I cites cores (*sic*) of instances among our modern literary women, whose very best utterances have been evolved from the kitchen, from over the mending-basket or cradle, or while tenderly watching by a sick-bed.

Oh, believe me, *brains* never interfered with obvious duty. It is the *want* of brains, the *pretence* of erudition in men and women, like the hypocritical church members who pray on Sunday and give us short measure on weekdays, that brings discredit on this question to the unthinking. And *only*, I am happy to add, to the unthinking. Hypocrisy is not to be confounded with religion, any more than is dictionary talk with true culture.

Men without brains, or with a little of the article, are naturally afraid of women who have them. They don't like "to be seen through," as they call it, or, worse than all, to be "answered back!" which translated means that a woman is to be only an echo, or keep silence, no matter what her honest convictions on any subject. Did it ever occur to such men that to teach and insist on hypocrisy in one thing is not to *limit* it? The pupil will not always ask her marital teacher to define the occasions for its practice, and "serves him right" will be the just verdict.

I have always found that men of the broadest culture and intelligence are they who are most earnest in raising women to their own intellectual plane. Therefore we can afford to let the others go. Only when they are sick of the vapid companionship they have chosen, it is very funny to see them fly for relief to the women "with heads."

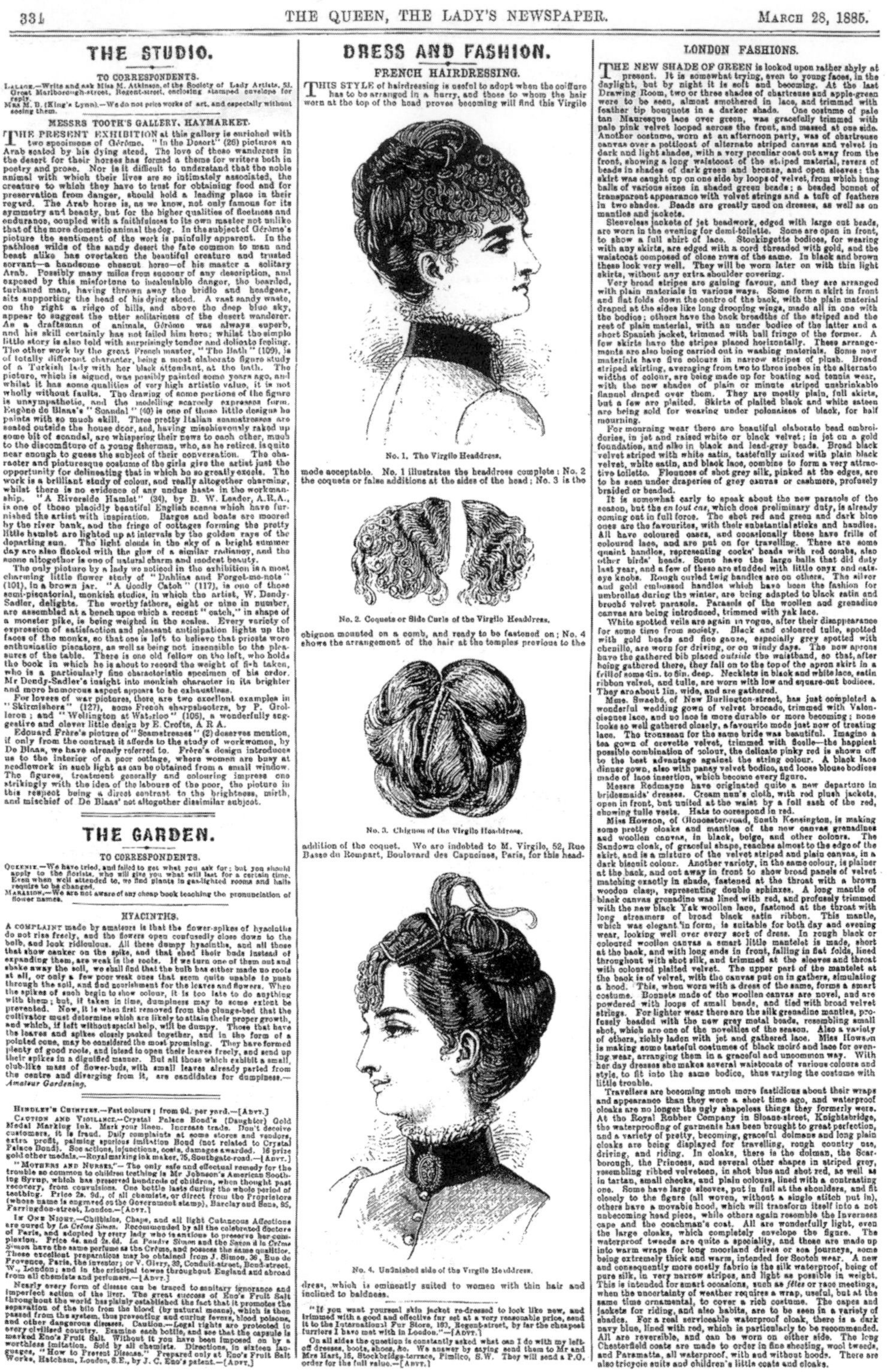

331 THE QUEEN, THE LADY'S NEWSPAPER. MARCH 28, 1885.

THE STUDIO.

TO CORRESPONDENTS.

LALAGE.—Write and ask Miss M. Atkinson, of the Society of Lady Artists, 51, Great Marlborough-street, Regent-street, enclosing stamped envelope for reply.

MRS M. D. (King's Lynn).—We do not price works of art, and especially without seeing them.

MESSRS TOOTH'S GALLERY, HAYMARKET.

THE PRESENT EXHIBITION at this gallery is enriched with two specimens of Gérôme. "In the Desert" (26) pictures an Arab seated by his dying steed. The love of these wanderers in the desert for their horses has formed a theme for writers both in poetry and prose. Nor is it difficult to understand that the noble animal with which their lives are so intimately associated, the creature to which they have to trust for obtaining food and for preservation from danger, should hold a leading place in their regard. The Arab horse is, as we know, not only famous for its symmetry and beauty, but for the higher qualities of fleetness and endurance, coupled with a faithfulness to its own master not unlike that of the more domestic animal the dog. In the subject of Gérôme's picture the sentiment of the work is painfully apparent. In the pathless wilds of the sandy desert the fate common to man and beast alike has overtaken the beautiful creature and trusted servant—a handsome chesnut horse—of his master a solitary Arab. Possibly many miles from succour of any description, and exposed by this misfortune to incalculable danger, the bearded, turbaned man, having thrown away the bridle and headgear, sits supporting the head of his dying steed. A vast sandy waste, on the right a ridge of hills, and above the deep blue sky, appear to suggest the utter solitariness of the desert wanderer. As a draftsman of animals, Gérôme was always superb, and his skill certainly has not failed him here; whilst the simple little story is also told with surprisingly tender and delicate feeling. The other work by the great French master, "The Bath" (109), is of totally different character, being a most elaborate figure study of a Turkish lady with her black attendant, at the bath. The picture, which is signed, was possibly painted some years ago, and whilst it has some qualities of very high artistic value, it is not wholly without faults. The drawing of some portions of the figure is unsympathetic, and the modelling scarcely expresses form. Eugène de Blaas's "Scandal" (40) is one of those little designs he paints with so much skill. Three pretty Italian sempstresses are seated outside the house door, and, having mischievously raked up some bit of scandal, are whispering their news to each other, much to the discomfiture of a young fisherman, who, as he retires, is quite near enough to guess the subject of their conversation. The character and picturesque costume of the girls give the artist just the opportunity for delineating that in which he so greatly excels. The work is a brilliant study of colour, and really altogether charming, whilst there is no evidence of any undue haste in the workmanship. "A Riverside Hamlet" (34), by B. W. Leader, A.R.A., is one of those placidly beautiful English scenes which have furnished the artist with inspiration. Barges and boats are moored by the river bank, and the fringe of cottages forming the pretty little hamlet are lighted up at intervals by the golden rays of the departing sun. The light clouds in the sky of a bright summer day are also flecked with the glow of a similar radiancy, and the scene altogether is one of natural charm and modest beauty.

The only picture by a lady we noticed in the exhibition is a most charming little flower study of "Dahlias and Forget-me-nots" (101), in a brown jar. "A Goodly Catch" (117), is one of those semi-piscatorial, monkish studies, in which the artist, W. Dendy-Sadler, delights. The worthy fathers, eight or nine in number, are assembled at a bench upon which a recent "catch," in shape of a monster pike, is being weighed in the scales. Every variety of expression of satisfaction and pleasant anticipation lights up the faces of the monks, so that one is left to believe that priests were enthusiastic piscators, as well as being not insensible to the pleasures of the table. There is one old fellow on the left, who holds the book in which he is about to record the weight of fish taken, who is a particularly fine characteristic specimen of his order. Mr Dendy-Sadler's insight into monkish character in its brighter and more humorous aspect appears to be exhaustless.

For lovers of war pictures, there are two excellent examples in "Skirmishers" (127), some French sharpshooters, by P. Grolleron; and "Wellington at Waterloo" (105), a wonderfully suggestive and clever little design by E. Crofts, A.R.A.

Edouard Frère's picture of "Seamstresses" (2) deserves mention, if only from the contrast it affords to the study of workwomen, by De Blaas, we have already referred to. Frère's design introduces us to the interior of a poor cottage, where women are busy at needlework in such light as can be obtained from a small window. The figures, treatment generally and colouring impress one strikingly with the idea of the labours of the poor, the picture in this respect being a direct contrast to the brightness, mirth, and mischief of De Blaas' not altogether dissimilar subject.

THE GARDEN.

TO CORRESPONDENTS.

QUEENIE.—We have tried, and failed to get what you ask for; but you should apply to the florists, who will give you what will last for a certain time. Even when well attended to, we find plants in gas-lighted rooms and halls require to be changed.

MARATHON.—We are not aware of any cheap book teaching the pronunciation of flower names.

HYACINTHS.

A COMPLAINT made by amateurs is that the flower-spikes of hyacinths do not rise freely, and the flowers open confusedly close down to the bulb, and look ridiculous. All these dumpy hyacinths, and all those that show canker on the spike, and that shed their buds instead of expanding them, are weak in the roots. If we turn one of them out and shake away the soil, we shall find that the bulb has either made no roots at all, or only a few poor weak ones that seem quite unable to push through the soil, and find nourishment for the leaves and flowers. When the spikes of such begin to show colour, it is too late to do anything with them; but, if taken in time, dumpiness may to some extent be prevented. Now, it is when first removed from the plunge-bed that the cultivator must determine which are likely to attain their proper growth, and which, if left without special help, will be dumpy. Those that have the leaves and spikes closely packed together, and in the form of a pointed cone, may be considered the most promising. They have formed plenty of good roots, and intend to open their leaves freely, and send up their spikes in a dignified manner. But all those which exhibit a small, club-like mass of flower-buds, with small leaves already parted from the centre and diverging from it, are candidates for dumpiness.—*Amateur Gardening.*

HINDLEY'S CHINTZES.—Fast colours; from 9d. per yard.—[ADVT.]

CAUTION AND VIGILANCE.—Crystal Palace Bond's (Daughter) Gold Medal Marking Ink. Mark your linen. Increase trade. Don't deceive customers, it is fraud. Daily complaints at some stores and vendors, extra profit, palming spurious imitation Bond (not related to Crystal Palace Bond). See actions, injunctions, costs, damages awarded. 16 prize gold other medals.—Royal marking ink maker, 75, Southgate-road.—[ADVT.]

"MOTHERS AND NURSES."—The only safe and effectual remedy for the trouble so common to children teething is Mr Johnson's American Soothing Syrup, which has preserved hundreds of children, when thought past recovery, from convulsions. One bottle lasts during the whole period of teething. Price 2s. 9d., of all chemists, or direct from the Proprietors (whose name is engraved on the Government stamp), Barclay and Sons, 95, Farringdon-street, London.—[ADVT.]

IN ONE NIGHT.—Chilblains, Chaps, and all light Cutaneous Affections are cured by *La Crème Simon.* Recommended by all the celebrated doctors of Paris, and adopted by every lady who is anxious to preserve her complexion. Price 4s. and 2s. 6d. *La Poudre Simon* and the *Savon à la Crème Simon* have the same perfume as the Crème, and possess the same qualities. These excellent preparations may be obtained from J. Simon, 36, Rue de Provence, Paris, the inventor; or V. Givry, 39, Conduit-street, Bond-street, W., London; and in the principal towns throughout England and abroad from all chemists and perfumers.—[ADVT.]

Nearly every form of disease can be traced to sanitary ignorance and imperfect action of the liver. The great success of Eno's Fruit Salt throughout the world has plainly established the fact that it promotes the separation of the bile from the blood (by natural means), which is then passed from the system, thus preventing and curing fevers, blood poisons, and other dangerous diseases. Caution.—Legal rights are protected in every civilised country. Examine each bottle, and see that the capsule is marked Eno's Fruit Salt. Without it you have been imposed on by a worthless imitation. Sold by all chemists. Directions, in sixteen languages, "How to Prevent Disease." Prepared only at Eno's Fruit Salt Works, Hatcham, London, S.E., by J. C. Eno's patent.—[ADVT.]

DRESS AND FASHION.

FRENCH HAIRDRESSING.

THIS STYLE of hairdressing is useful to adopt when the coiffure has to be arranged in a hurry, and those to whom the hair worn at the top of the head proves becoming will find this Virgile

No. 1. The Virgile Headdress.

mode acceptable. No. 1 illustrates the headdress complete; No. 2 the coquets or false additions at the sides of the head; No. 3 is the

No. 2. Coquets or Side Curls of the Virgile Headdress.

chignon mounted on a comb, and ready to be fastened on; No. 4 shows the arrangement of the hair at the temples previous to the

No. 3. Chignon of the Virgile Headdress.

addition of the coquet. We are indebted to M. Virgile, 52, Rue Basse du Rempart, Boulevard des Capucines, Paris, for this head-

No. 4. Unfinished side of the Virgile Headdress.

dress, which is eminently suited to women with thin hair and inclined to baldness.

"If you want your seal skin jacket re-dressed to look like new, and trimmed with a good and effective fur set at a very reasonable price, send it to the International Fur Store, 163, Regent-street, by far the cheapest furriers I have met with in London."—[ADVT.]

On all sides the question is constantly asked what can I do with my left-off dresses, boots, shoes, &c. We answer by saying send them to Mr and Mrs Hart, 15, Stockbridge-terrace, Pimlico, S.W. They will send a P.O. order for the full value.—[ADVT.]

LONDON FASHIONS.

THE NEW SHADE OF GREEN is looked upon rather shyly at present. It is somewhat trying, even to young faces, in the daylight, but by night it is soft and becoming. At the last Drawing Room, two or three shades of chartreuse and apple-green were to be seen, almost smothered in lace, and trimmed with feather tip bouquets in a darker shade. One costume of pale tan Mauresque lace over green, was gracefully trimmed with pale pink velvet looped across the front, and massed at one side. Another costume, worn at an afternoon party, was of chartreuse canvas over a petticoat of alternate striped canvas and velvet in dark and light shades, with a very peculiar coat cut away from the front, showing a long waistcoat of the striped material, revers of beads in shades of dark green and bronze, and open sleeves; the skirt was caught up on one side by loops of velvet, from which hung balls of various sizes in shaded green beads; a beaded bonnet of transparent appearance with velvet strings and a tuft of feathers in two shades. Beads are greatly used on dresses, as well as on mantles and jackets.

Sleeveless jackets of jet beadwork, edged with large cut beads, are worn in the evening for demi-toilette. Some are open in front, to show a full shirt of lace. Stockingette bodices, for wearing with any skirts, are edged with a cord threaded with gold, and the waistcoat composed of close rows of the same. In black and brown these look very well. They will be worn later on with thin light skirts, without any extra shoulder covering.

Very broad stripes are gaining favour, and they are arranged with plain materials in various ways. Some form a skirt in front and flat folds down the centre of the back, with the plain material draped at the sides like long drooping wings, made all in one with the bodice; others have the back breadths of the striped and the rest of plain material, with an under bodice of the latter and a short Spanish jacket, trimmed with ball fringe of the former. A few skirts have the stripes placed horizontally. These arrangements are also being carried out in washing materials. Some new materials have five colours in narrow stripes of plush. Broad striped skirting, averaging from two to three inches in the alternate widths of colour, are being made up for boating and tennis wear, with the new shades of plain or minute striped unshrinkable flannel draped over them. They are mostly plain, full skirts, but a few are plaited. Skirts of plaited black and white sateen are being sold for wearing under polonaises of black, for half mourning.

For mourning wear there are beautiful elaborate bead embroideries, in jet and raised white or black velvet; in jet on a gold foundation, and also in black and lead-grey beads. Broad black velvet striped with white satin, tastefully mixed with plain black velvet, white satin, and black lace, combine to form a very attractive toilette. Flounces of shot grey silk, pinked at the edges, are to be seen under draperies of grey canvas or cashmere, profusely braided or beaded.

It is somewhat early to speak about the new parasols of the season, but the *en tout cas*, which does preliminary duty, is already coming out in full force. The shot red and green and dark blue ones are the favourites, with their substantial sticks and handles. All have coloured cases, and occasionally these have frills of coloured lace, and are put on for travelling. There are some quaint handles, representing cocks' heads with red combs, also other birds' heads. Some have the large balls that did duty last year, and a few of these are studded with little onyx and cats-eye knobs. Rough curled twig handles are on others. The silver and gold embossed handles which have been the fashion for umbrellas during the winter, are being adapted to black satin and broché velvet parasols. Parasols of the woollen and grenadine canvas are being introduced, trimmed with yak lace.

White spotted veils are again in vogue, after their disappearance for some time from society. Black and coloured tulle, spotted with gold beads and fine gauze, especially grey spotted with chenille, are worn for driving, or on windy days. The new aprons have the gathered bib placed *outside* the waistband, so that, after being gathered there, they fall on to the top of the apron skirt in a frill of some 4in. to 5in. deep. Necklets in black and white lace, satin ribbon velvet, and tulle, are worn with low and square-cut bodices. They are about 1in. wide, and are gathered.

Mme. Swaebé, of New Burlington-street, has just completed a wonderful wedding gown of velvet brocade, trimmed with Valenciennes lace, and no lace is more durable or more becoming; none looks so well gathered closely, a favourite mode just now of treating lace. The trousseau for the same bride was beautiful. Imagine a tea gown of crevette velvet, trimmed with ficelle—the happiest possible combination of colour, the delicate pinky red is shown off to the best advantage against the string colour. A black lace dinner gown, also with pansy velvet bodice, and loose blouse bodices made of lace insertion, which become every figure.

Messrs Redmayne have originated quite a new departure in bridesmaids' dresses. Cream nun's cloth, with red plush jackets, open in front, but united at the waist by a full sash of the red, showing tulle vests. Hats to correspond in red.

Miss Howson, of Gloucester-road, South Kensington, is making some pretty cloaks and mantles of the new canvas grenadines and woollen canvas, in black, beige, and other colours. The Sandown cloak, of graceful shape, reaches almost to the edge of the skirt, and is a mixture of the velvet striped and plain canvas, in a dark biscuit colour. Another variety, in the same colour, is plainer at the back, and cut away in front to show broad panels of velvet matching exactly in shade, fastened at the throat with a brown wooden clasp, representing double sphinxes. A long mantle of black canvas grenadine was lined with red, and profusely trimmed with the new black Yak woollen lace, fastened at the throat with long streamers of broad black satin ribbon. This mantle, which was elegant in form, is suitable for both day and evening wear, looking well over every sort of dress. In rough black or coloured woollen canvas a smart little mantelet is made, short at the back, and with long ends in front, falling in flat folds, lined throughout with shot silk, and trimmed at the sleeves and throat with coloured plaited velvet. The upper part of the mantelet at the back is of velvet, with the canvas put on in gathers, simulating a hood. This, when worn with a dress of the same, forms a smart costume. Bonnets made of the woollen canvas are novel, and are powdered with loops of small beads, and tied with broad velvet strings. For lighter wear there are the silk grenadine mantles, profusely beaded with the new grey metal beads, resembling small shot, which are one of the novelties of the season. Also a variety of others, richly laden with jet and gathered lace. Miss Howson is making some tasteful costumes of black moiré and lace for evening wear, arranging them in a graceful and uncommon way. With her day dresses she makes several waistcoats of various colours and style, to fit into the same bodice, thus varying the costume with little trouble.

Travellers are becoming much more fastidious about their wraps and appearance than they were a short time ago, and waterproof cloaks are no longer the ugly shapeless things they formerly were. At the Royal Rubber Company in Sloane-street, Knightsbridge, the waterproofing of garments has been brought to great perfection, and a variety of pretty, becoming, graceful dolmans and long plain cloaks are being displayed for travelling, rough country use, driving, and riding. In cloaks, there is the dolman, the Scarborough, the Princess, and several other shapes in striped grey, resembling ribbed velveteen, in shot blue and shot red, as well as in tartan, small checks, and plain colours, lined with a contrasting one. Some have large sleeves, put in full at the shoulders, and fit closely to the figure (all woven, without a single stitch put in), others have a movable hood, which will transform itself into a not unbecoming head piece, while others again resemble the Inverness cape and the coachman's coat. All are wonderfully light, even the large cloaks, which completely envelope the figure. The waterproof tweeds are quite a speciality, and these are made up into warm wraps for long moorland drives or sea journeys, some being extremely thick and warm, intended for Scotch wear. A new and consequently more costly fabric is the silk waterproof, being of pure silk, in very narrow stripes, and light as possible in weight. This is intended for smart occasions, such as *fêtes* or race meetings, when the uncertainty of weather requires a wrap, useful, but at the same time ornamental, to cover a rich costume. The capes and jackets for riding, and also habits, are to be seen in a variety of shades. For a real serviceable waterproof cloak, there is a dark navy blue, lined with red, which is particularly to be recommended. All are reversible, and can be worn on either side. The long Chesterfield coats are made to order in fine sheeting, wool tweeds, and Paramatta, all waterproof, with and without hoods. There are also tricycle suits and children's little coats and cloaks.

FIGURE 12 *The Queen*, vol. 77, 1885, p. 331

"LIBERTY" ART FABRICS.

"Liberty" Srinagar Serge.

A new Indian Cashmere, introduced by LIBERTY and CO. It is the outcome of a long series of experiments to produce, with fine yarns, an Artistic Costume Cloth, which should be within the reach of the most economical, can be obtained *by the yard*, 25 inches wide. Price 1s. 9d.

"Liberty" Umritza Cashmere.

A proved success. New Colours are constantly being added, making an everchanging variety.

In pieces of 9 yards, 25 inches wide. Price 21s. and 25s.

"Liberty" Arabian Cotton.

Very fashionable for Spring Dresses. Made specially for LIBERTY and CO. In ever-increasing variety of artistic colours. In pieces of 30, or half pieces of 15 yards, 30 inches wide. Price, per piece, 42s., half piece, 21s.

"Liberty" Corah Silk.

A native hand-woven Fabric, made from the finest yarns, and in the natural colour, viz., Cream. A most useful Silk, washes perfectly. Price 17s. 6d. to 40s. per piece of about 7 yards, 34 inches wide.

"Liberty" Tussore Silk.

Is made from the *Wild Silk of India*, strongest and toughest known. For washing dresses surpasses all other silk fabrics. Price 21s. to 42s. per piece of about 9½ yards, 34 inches wide.

"Liberty" Soft Ivory-White Rumchunder Silk.

A beautiful Draping Fabric, in a variety of different makes. Price, from 21s. to 70s. per piece of about 7yds., 34in. wide.

"Liberty" Coloured Rumchunder Silk.

A Soft Fabric, woven to meet the demand for a heavier Silk, in the Artistic Colours. Price 50s. per piece of about 7yds., 34in. wide.

"Liberty" Hoonan Damask Silk.

A beautiful Fabric, made and dyed in China. In rich colours. Price 45s. per piece of about 7yds., 34in. wide.

"Liberty" Nagpore Silk.

Woven by hand in India from the finest Bengal Yarns. The irregularity of the weaving produces a play of colours rendering it unequalled for Art Drapery. Price 25s. per piece of about 7yds., 34in. wide.

"Liberty" Mysore Silk.

Is similar to the Nagpore Silk, and in addition is printed with quaint designs in the same class of colours. Price 25s. per piece of about 7yds., 34in. wide.

"LIBERTY" ART FURNISHING FABRICS

At prices which shall not make them simply *articles de luxe*.

New Designs,
New Materials,
Fast Colours,
Soft Finish, and
Sterling Value,

Complete Sets of Patterns Post Free.

JAVA COTTONS FOR DRESSES.

Messrs LIBERTY and CO. have now received the whole range of designs in these new dress materials, samples of which can be forwarded on application.

The patterns are almost exact reproductions of the original Java "Sarongs," which are probably the most artistic styles of cotton printing the world has ever seen.

The Java Cottons are in pieces of about 9½ yards, 32 inches wide. Price 12s. 6d. Half-pieces, 6s. 6d. Every piece bears the stamp,

"LIBERTY" JAVA FABRICS.

CHILDREN'S SMOCKS, complete, as above, from 15s. 6d.
Special Price List Post Free.
ARTISTIC COSTUMES on View.
Coloured Sketches Post Free.

NEW PATTERNS AND CATALOGUES POST FREE.

LIBERTY & CO.

CHESHAM HOUSE—For Furniture, Carpets, and Curtains.
EAST INDIA HOUSE—For Dresses and Jewellery.
2, ARGYLL PLACE—Artistic and Historic Costume Studios.
*Manchester Agents—*GOODALL and CO.

REGENT ST.
LONDON, W.

FISHER & SON,
219, REGENT-ST., W.,
LADIES' TAILORS.

THE PARK COSTUME,
£7. 17s. 6d.

PATTERNS AND SELF-MEASUREMENT FORM SENT FREE ON APPLICATION.

RÖHRS' PATENT.
THE SOCIETY CORSET.

The simplicity of the entirely new pliable and strong features employed in the make of these New Corsets ensures a free and perfect fit and good figure without the aid of the usual stiff whalebones. This Corset readily expands and contracts with every movement, giving freedom of action to the vital organs, the injurious effects of tight lacing being entirely dispensed with in these New Corsets (*which have never before been made*). Pronounced by all wearers a Perfect Corset. Medically recommended. Price in Silk, from 2 to 3 guineas.

MADAME GOUGH,
COURT DRESSMAKER
AND
CORSETIERE,
78, NEW BOND STREET,
LONDON, W.

Patented on the Continent and United States.

MRS ROSS.

WARDROBE PURCHASER to any amount for Cash. Twenty years at 45, Praed-street Paddington—Mrs ROSS, having a large connection for the sale of good LEFT-OFF CLOTHING can give good prices for them. Ladies waited on. P.O.O. per return for all parcels, boxes, &c. Please Note this address. 45, PRAED STREET, LONDON, W.

STOCKBRIDGE'S
SPRING NOVELTIES.
COSTUMES.
NEW DEPARTMENT NOW OPEN.

Novel and Original Designs in Costumes, Tailor-made Cloth.

Wedding and Dinner Dresses, Ball Dresses, Court Trains, Tea Gowns, Riding Habits, Boating and Tennis Dresses. Reasonable Estimates Given for Household Mourning.

THE COUNTESS.

An Elegant Dress, made in Silk, Satin, or Veloutine, with Brocade,
5 GUINEAS.

Also in Faille Francais and Brocaded Velvet, Black or Colours,
10 GUINEAS.

W. P. STOCKBRIDGE,
MANTLES, COSTUMES,
AND
FANCY DRAPERY,
204, 206, & 262,
OXFORD STREET, W.

THE
ST. MARGARET SPECIALITIES.

Ladies' Jerseys and Jersey Jackets,
Girls' Jersey Costumes, Boys' Jersey Suits.

Ladies' & Children's Cashmere Ribbed Hose.	Yachting, Boating, Running, and Football Jerseys.
Ladies' & Children's Empress Black Cotton Hose.	Lambswool, Merino, and Cotton Underclothing.
Gentleman's & Boys' Knickerbocker Hose.	

THE ST. MARGARET JERSEY SPECIALITIES are made from the celebrated ST. MARGARET'S CLOTH, which is warranted to wear splendidly, is beautifully silky in appearance, and, like all the St. Margaret Specialities, are guaranteed to be free from poisonous dyes. Gold Medals have been awarded at the Health Exhibition and the Crystal Palace International Exhibition for superior Hose, Jerseys, and other Specialities. To be had only of the principal Drapers, Hosiers, &c., in London and country.

COOPER, CORAH, AND SONS,
ST. MARGARET'S WORKS, LEICESTER.

ELVERY
Waterproofer.

ELVERY'S
WATERPROOF
DOLMAN

**MANUFACTURER OF
LADIES' WATERPROOF
DOLMANS,
ROTONDES,
AND
ULSTERS.**

In Navy Blue, Brown, Black, Grey, and Tartan Checks.
"Warranted to stand all climates."

31, CONDUIT ST.,
LONDON, W.

One door from New Bond Street.

LEFT-OFF CLOTHES WANTED.
MRS GILLEMAN,
31, HINDON-STREET, PIMLICO, S.W.

(late Miss Graham, of Thomas-street, Grosvenor-square) gives the highest value for Ladies', Gentlemen's and Children's LEFT-OFF CLOTHING, Linen, Jewellery, and Property of every description. P.O.O. promptly remitted for parcels received from town or country. Ladies waited upon at their own residence. Terms, READY CASH.

FIGURE 13 *The Queen*, vol. 77, 1885, an unnumbered advertising page

5.3

The Queen (1861–1967) remained the leading example in this field. Although it specifically addressed 'the upper-ten-thousand', it was almost certainly read by a far larger group. Its full-page fashion plates continued the tradition of using high-quality engravings to provide detailed models for women's clothes but it also included visual illustration in the text. The first page illustrated is typical. It includes a review of an art exhibition, advice on gardening, advice on dress and fashion and an article on London fashions and some small advertisements. Advertising continued to be important in these papers. Full pages of display advertisements took up half this number.

See FIGURES 12 and 13.

5.4

From the start the ladies' papers had specifically addressed women's public role alongside their role in society. *The Queen* (1861–1967) never openly advocated the causes espoused by the feminist journals but it carried news items on women's employment, higher education and suffrage meetings alongside news on the arts and theatre and advice on etiquette and dress. The mixed form of the periodical enabled such apparent contradictions to persist.

'A Woman's Work at the Docks', *The Queen*, vol. 87, 1890, p. 414.

A VISIT to the East-end of London is sometimes more attractive than to the West. Certainly it was so the other day, for our bourne was the Scandinavian Sailors' Home, and the occasion was the birthday of its foundress and director, Mrs Hedenström Welin. The dining hall was decked out in festive array with flowers and palms and banners. The table was spread with a meat tea of the most abundant character, to which the sailors did ample justice. Mrs Welin was overwhelmed with presents and congratulations, and offerings of flowers that a ball-going dame might envy poured in upon her throughout the day. A tour of inspection revealed spotless cleanliness every-where, and, what is more unusual in an "institution," an air of sunny cheerfulness, which Mr and Mrs Welin appear to infuse into the home by their presence. In addition to the dormitories, fitted up cabin-fashion, there are snug little single bed rooms, and the public rooms include, besides the dining hall, a large smoking room and library. In the course of conversation we were glad to learn that the home is now for the first time free from debt, thanks in great measure to generous help from the Dowager Lady Ashburton and the late Mr David Carnegie. But the directors would like to do a great deal more if the funds were forthcoming. Sickness has been rife amongst the seafaring population, and at the home it has been almost impossible to afford invalids the nursing and attention they require. Moreover, the atmosphere of the West India Docks is not conducive to the recovery of health and strength. Mr and Mrs Welin earnestly desire to possess a small convalescent home in the direction of Epping Forest or Buckhurst Hill, where the air would be bracing and the spot easily accessible by the Great Eastern Railway. Will any of our readers help the home now as they have done so liberally upon former occasions? There is no doubt that whatever is given will be spent to the utmost possible advantage.

Mrs Hedenström Welin has waged an incessant war against intemperance, and in this, as in all her other efforts towards the rescue of the poor from sin and suffering, she has had since her marriage a powerful helper in her husband. Mr Welin finds that it is difficult to preach and practice temperance within the home when the sailors, the moment they step outside its threshold, are assailed by the temptations of numberless public-houses. A small coffee shop has been established in connection with the home, but it is not, of course, sufficient for this thickly populated district. It is much to be desired that the managers of some of the cocoa-rooms in London could see their way to open an establishment near the home. Mr and Mrs Welin are at all times pleased to see anyone who is interested in the home, the address of which is Garford-street, West India Docks, E.

5.5

Like the general illustrated and cheap domestic magazines, the ladies' papers at the end of the century often carried illustrated interviews. As this example from *The Gentlewoman* (1890–1926) shows, in these papers the subject was often an aristocratic woman and the interview was as much about the decor and furnishings of her home as about her own achievements. These interviews blended with the advice on furnishing and house decoration which became an increasingly popular feature in all kinds of magazines for women at this time. They also exploited the techniques of the new journalism to suggest an intimacy with the great and famous into whose most private rooms the reader was allowed to look.

'Gentlewomen "At Home". No. XXVI. The Countess of Cottenham at Queen's Gate.', *The Gentlewoman*, vol. 1, no. 26, 1890, pp. 1–2. See also FIGURE 14.

A RAY of the welcome sunlight, which visits us so rarely at this time of year, illumines with the sheen of gold the Venetian-tinted hair of Lady Cottenham as she sits before her writing-table, placed at an angle with the windows which look over the wide area occupied by the Natural History Museum and the Imperial Institute. And as you enter the room she turns her well-poised head from the contemplation of her correspondence to receive you with a re-assuring grace of manner, and with a smile of such peculiar sweetness, that it is regarded as quite a proverbial charm by her special *coterie* of friends, who value the privilege of her acquaintance all the more, perhaps, because, since her widowhood, she has withdrawn herself to a great extent from general society and from much entertaining, while devoting herself to the bringing up of her young family. It is on that topic that Lady Cottenham more willingly converses than of herself, who, she archly declares, "is a very uninteresting personage." Photographs of her children face her on the writing-table, around the silver-gilt inkstand presented by Sir Gerard Noel, Bart., to Charles Pepys, in acknowledgment of signal professional services in the Court of Chancery before he was successively Solicitor-General, Master of the Rolls, and afterwards first Lord Cottenham, Chancellor of England.

FIGURE 14 'Gentlewomen "At Home".'
An illustration from p. 2,
'Lady Cottenham's Boudoir'

On the wall opposite to her, as she converses with you hangs the portrait of the late Earl of Cottenham, by Bompiani, and just below are the pretty faces of their three children, wearing broad lace collars, taken some few years ago by Edward Taylor. The portraits depict the present Lord Cottenham, the Hon. Everard Pepys, now a lad at Harrow, and the Lady Mary Pepys, who again smiles at you at the maturer age of ten years, from another picture of her placed on an easel draped with red silk, and painted by the late young painter Baldry.

. . .

Affection for her children is a delightful trait in Lady Cottenham's disposition, and it is therefore with pride quite pardonable that she leads you to the Turkish divanned apartment, at the end of the large drawing-room, which as admirably serves as a lounge with its Eastern draperies and coloured lanterns, as a stage where, as Lady Cottenham tells you, the tableaux were posed in which her daughter, with the Countess of Crawford, the Hon. Mabel Hood, Lady Ridgway, Mrs. Algernon Law, and others have at times taken part. No less than two hundred and fifty pounds were the net result of one of these entertainments, when there have been represented Millais' "Princes in the Tower," "St. Augustine," and "Joan of Arc," "Marie Antoinette," "Hagar and Ishmael," &c., which enabled the children of St. Peter's parish, London Docks, to enjoy three weeks of invigorating country air amongst the fields and flowers. With some it may seem but a duty to do acts of charity; with Lady Cottenham, kindly deeds are a continual source of pleasure. With her keen sense of sympathy in all cases of pain and poverty, her great interest in that devoted band of ministering angels, the Nursing Sisters of St. Margaret, East Grinstead, can be well appreciated, and she derives especial satisfaction from her connection as an Associate with that order. And while she is describing to you the various objects and successes of this noble charity, she incidentally draws your attention to the pretty screen embroidered with peacock feathers, the handiwork of the sisterhood.

There are many other objects worthy of notice scattered through the pretty drawing rooms, draped with Japanese needlework on the walls, decorated with rare china, *objets d'art*, nick-nacks and photographs, amongst which you notice those of Lady Abergavenny, the "beautiful Nevill Twins," General Gordon, and Rustem Pacha. A marble bust of the late Lord Cottenham is suitably placed, and gains an additional interest from the fact that it was the work of the "ghost"-ridden sculptor, Richard Belt; and you cannot fail to be enchanted with the exquisite miniatures of Lady Cottenham and Lady Mary, by Edward Turrell, whose manner reminds one much of that of Cosway. It is interesting to know that Lady Cottenham herself is a delicate miniaturist, and you may see an example of her talent represented in the enamel of Lady Harriett Warde, which hangs below the engraving of that lady in the boudoir, which is situated beyond the Turkish lounge. Here you may find, too, on either side of the mantelpiece, portraits of Lady Cottenham's father and mother, Sir Robert Dallas, Bart., and Lady Dallas; of her uncle, the second Lord Ellenborough, formerly Governor of India; a lovely water-colour, by Edward Taylor, of the late Lord Cottenham and his daughter, and a miniature of the Lord Chancellor Cottenham, by Ross. But most of the family heirlooms, souvenirs, and much of the family plate is in the custody of the Court of Chancery, of which Lady Cottenham's children are wards during their minority; while the family seat of Tandridge is let, and the estate is being generally nursed, until Lord Cottenham comes of age, in 1895.

. . .

6

The feminist journal

Although the term feminism is an anachronism in this period it can be usefully applied to this group of periodicals that all attempted to provide a critique of contemporary culture and women's place within it. This type of publication falls into two main groups, the campaign journal and the more general feminist journal. The campaign journals were committed to single issues such as work and education, or specific campaigns like the reform of the Married Women's Property Act and the claim for suffrage reform. Titles such as *Women's Education Union* and *Women's Suffrage Journal* fall into this category and were aimed primarily at activists involved in the particular cause. Related to these publications is a group of titles related to women's professions which began to appear in the mid-fifties, *The Governess* and *The Sempstress* are two such titles. By the end of the century the number of titles dedicated to specific professions had proliferated in line with the growing opportunities for women's work. The general feminist journals represented here offered a much broader perspective on women's issues and titles include *The Englishwoman's Journal, Woman's World* and *Shafts*. Whilst they often covered the progress of individual campaigns they also discussed a whole range of issues affecting Victorian women. The staple diet of the general feminist journal was articles on reform, general interest features, letters, short or serialised fiction and reviews. The use of firm editorial control lead to a uniformity of tone and address absent in their more commercial competitors. The articles and features in the first generation of titles tended to be long and the sparing use of illustrative material made for a sombre layout that complemented the earnest nature of the contents. These journals were not primarily commercially ventures but *The Englishwoman's Review* did have a long and apparently successful run. The fact that women dominated the process of publication from the role of editor, to contributor and sometimes even printer, of a number of titles, was significant, particularly for *The Englishwoman's Journal* and *Women's Penny Paper*.

6.1

The Englishwoman's Journal (1858–64), backed and produced by members of the Langham Place Circle including Barbara Bodichon, Bessie Parkes and Matilda Hays, was an early pioneer of what was to become a tradition of feminist periodical publishing.

Contents list for *The Englishwoman's Journal*, vol. 1, 1858.

62

The feminist commitment to the amelioration of the condition of women consisted very largely in engaging in debate around the woman question. The following article from *The Englishwoman's Journal* (1858–64) presents a discussion about male and female intellect.

'Are Men Naturally Cleverer than Women?', *The Englishwoman's Journal*, vol. 2, 1859, pp. 333–36.

MANY persons, even many women, believe that the female intellect is naturally inferior to the male, and that under no circumstances whatever could it be equalised, and it is against this theory that we enter our protest, for it is of such a discouraging nature that it tends to realise itself. If we are convinced that our condition is hopeless, that the Creator himself has fixed on us the stamp of inferiority, why should we struggle against our inevitable doom? Let us rather bear our lot with resignation, and making no opposition to the decrees of Providence content ourselves with hoping that in another world we may be promoted to a more honorable position. But though we utterly repudiate this creed, we are not going to contend that as affairs now stand men and women are generally on an intellectual equality. Far be it from us to make an assertion which the experience of almost every one must prove to be untrue; for to whom do we turn for assistance in an affair of difficulty, to our male or female relatives? When we want a good investment for our money, do we ask the advice of our aunts or of our uncles? A stout asserter of the present equality of the female intellect will say, "Yes, but we apply to our uncle instead of our aunt, not because she is his inferior in intelligence, but because he has had the most experience in money matters and has studied the subject of investments for years, while she has never turned her mind that way;" and this is exactly the point at which we wish to arrive. Men are superior to women because they know more, and they have this knowledge because they have three times the opportunities of acquiring it that women possess.

Let us now see by what means women could acquire more knowledge. First by a more practical education. We think that there exists in many minds a confusion between knowledge and the means of acquiring it, though there is in fact a broad distinction between the two. For instance reading is a good means of acquiring knowledge, but if a man who can read never opens a book nor takes up a newspaper he will be no wiser than he was before he learnt his letters.

Languages likewise are a great means of obtaining knowledge. If a person can read books in two or three foreign tongues, and does read them, he will doubtless gain much information, but the mere power of reading them unless it be exercised will obtain him no information whatever. Now girls of the upper classes of society almost invariably, and those of the middle class very generally, are instructed in two and often three foreign languages, and as their education extends over a period of only ten years (for before eight the education that can be given is trifling) it is plain that the greatest part of their time will be spent in attaining not knowledge but the means of acquiring it; means which are seldom if ever made use of, for what do young ladies read in after life in German and Italian save ballads, poems, or plays? and few even do as much as this, but the moment that their governess is dismissed or they are released from school and allowed to enjoy the pleasures of the world, they put their foreign books aside and never open them again, and thus the whole labor of childhood and youth is thrown away. If during these ten years three languages have to be learnt, how little time can be bestowed in obtaining what really is knowledge. Real knowledge strengthens the understanding and improves the judgment. The learning of languages strengthens the memory, while drawing and music refine the taste. Now observe, women are never accused of being inferior to men in memory and are confessedly superior to them in taste; thus in that particular point wherein they have received an equal education with men they are mentally their equals, where they have received a superior education they are their superiors, and it is only where they have received no education at all or a very slight one that they fall short of the male standard. We would therefore advocate that girls be restricted in their accomplishments to one foreign language, and either to drawing or music as their taste inclines, and that the rest of their time be spent in studying that which will strengthen their understandings and improve their judgment, such as history, arithmetic, mathematics, and logic. This last may appear useless, but we assert that women are often ignorant of the principles of reasoning, and that the perverse and crooked use which they sometimes make of arguments tends to bring the female understanding into contempt more than any other circumstance whatever.

They should learn also things of practical use,—how to get a post-office order, to write a cheque on a banker, etc., and should be taught the meaning of various business terms such as "discount," "above and below par," and what funds and securities are, for at present young ladies know far more of the course of the planets than they do of these useful mundane institutions. This elementary instruction would enable those scholars who had any natural intelligence to learn more hereafter, and thus give them the power of protecting their own interests, while even the stupid ones would be made capable of understanding the conversation of men.

Had this kind of instruction been universal, the unhappy lady whose case we have all so lately read in the newspapers, who left her money-securities with her broker from ignorance of their value, would still have been in the possession of her fortune. The advocates for a graceful ignorance of business in women ought to subscribe and provide for the declining years of that unfortunate victim to their theory. Were this reform in education carried out, women would be found to possess more reasoning minds and greater powers of calculation than they now get credit for, and something would have been done towards raising them to a mental equality with men.

But even then men would still remain in a superior position with regard to the means of acquiring knowledge. The world is after all the best school-master, and women cannot move in the world as freely as men. From some professions they are debarred by their own feebleness, from others by the prejudices or interests of men. The man who spends his life from twenty to thirty in idleness at home, becomes inferior to another who has passed those years working in a profession; or rather the latter rises superior to the former, though originally their abilities may have been equal. We need not therefore believe that the present intellectual inferiority of women arises from any natural cause while there are so many artificial ones to account for it.

Let us not despair, but set to work with hearty good-will to break down whatever impediments to the mental improvement of women it may be in our power to remove, while we endeavor to train from the rising generation a body of reasoning, thinking, practical women who will be ready to take advantage of every favorable opening, and before whom those barriers of prejudice may disappear which hitherto have proved insurmountable.

6.3

The following abridged article from *The Englishwoman's Review* (1866–1910) presents a discussion of the richness and diversity of female experience as represented in literature and history and was written by a key figure in the mid-Victorian women's movement, Bessie Parkes.

'Types of Character', by Bessie Parkes, *The Englishwoman's Review*, vol. 1, 1866, pp. 5–12.

IN one of Mr. Ruskin's lectures, notice is taken of the effect of sub-divisions in increasing the apparent size of a wall; many windows in a frontage giving the beholder an impression of a large house. In the same manner the limited number of stars discernible by the human eye, convey to us the undefined notion of an illimitable firmament, each starry point occupying a sphere of its own in our imagination, of which, though scarcely separate to our consciousness, the sum total is far greater than if they were flung together in nebulous confusion like the sands of the sea.

Or to take another simile:—when an artist wishes to give an idea of a wide and various horizon, he does it by sharply isolating the objects of the foreground; he darkens and defines a tree, or throws in a bright bit of scarlet and white upon a woman's figure standing by a well. Then the mind which has firmly seized upon the colour, form, and texture of this near object, carries the impression of reality back into the blue mountains or sweeping plains; feels that the foliage so faintly indicated in the middle distance is really full and delicate with multitudinous leaves; that the silver strip of winding river ripples under the wind, and that even the viewless air is spaced by the motes golden in the sunbeam, and the rapid pinions of the flying bird.

This principle of art applies equally to written description. An historian gains his chief triumphs by his portraiture of the men who made the history of their time. Carlyle's wonderful drama of the French Revolution is a series of *tableaux vivants*, with France for the back-ground; Macaulay painted political parties by throwing forward their representative men; in Henry Taylor's "Philip Van Arterwelde," the heroic brewer gives clearness and consistency to the stormy crowd of citizens, who without him would be a mere seething mob; and when we picture to ourselves the triumph of a principle, as, for example, that of absolutism or democracy, it must always be associated with the image of a Bismark, a Jack Cade, a Washington, or a Mazzini, a Cobbett, or a Louis XIV. For this reason I have at all times believed that the most effectual help which could be rendered by literature toward advancing the education of women, or extending their capacities of usefulness, was that of presenting numerous conceptions of what they really are in some few of their innumerable types, showing that the stuff out of which it is desired to create a better average, is not a dull or even a beautiful uniformity of nature, but something extraordinarily diverse in its kinds, and capable of infinite modification by circumstances. And, indeed, though little inclined by habit or principle to any sort of satire or bitterness in dealing with these questions, and habitually avoiding either, as a measure of taste and prudence, yet, if any arguments might fairly be allowed to rouse a strong sense of the absurd in the listener, they would be those which are based upon the supposition that all women possess (or ought to possess) a fixed type of nature, from which any deviation is a sin against true beauty and true strength.

It is perhaps less to be wondered at, that readers are so often blind to the contour of the images in history; because, unless these have been seized and pourtrayed by a master hand, it is a difficult thing to realise what people were like who lived and died long ago, and under conditions which we imperfectly appreciate; but it *is* remarkable that the great diversity of the heroines of fiction should not make more impression than it does, because we have these pictures presented to our eyes with every advantage of careful composition, and framed with the most judicious attention to their form and meaning. Books have been written, it is true, about the women of Shakespeare, and certainly Charles Lamb and Mrs. Jameson realised, to the fullest extent, every delicate shade of difference in that wonderful gallery. But popular writers upon woman's life wield the pen with an entire forgetfulness of Shakespeare's practical declaration of what *he* saw in women, when he drew the loving Cordelia, the ambitious Lady Macbeth, the queenly Constance, the saucy Kate, the lively learned Portia, and the noble, sensible, eloquent Isabella; and such of his female characters as are depicted exclusively in their relation to men, as mistresses and wives, are yet quite different in their way of experiencing or fulfilling those relations; what likeness is there between Miranda and Desdemona, Rosalind and Juliet, Hermione and Cleopatra?

Leaving Shakespeare, from whose writings it is as difficult to point a fresh conclusive moral as it would be from the Gospel of St. Matthew, let us look to Scott, the great master of narrative fiction. He was not remarkable for his discrimination of female character; too many of his ladies are mere charming conventionalities—motives for the action of his delightful tales, and no more. But when he quitted the region of lovemaking, pure and simple, for the more complicated emotions of human existence, who, except Shakespeare, ever gave such vivid and totally distinct descriptions?

. . .

Then I think of Miss Austen, and her two delightful specimens of young English womanhood; wilful Emma Woodfall and bright Elizabeth Bennett, women who would not have been dull or stupid in the meanest or the most heroic sphere of life. And I think of Charlotte Bronté, whose "Jane Eyre" is eclipsed by the far more complicated "Shirley;" then, crossing the Channel, there are the extraordinary rich creations of Balsac and George Sand . . .

Any one who cares to pursue the train of thought thus indicated, may easily collect many more examples from famous works of fiction. Between the epoch of the Greek Tragedians and that of George Elliot, the varieties of female character are plentiful, and comparisons might be instituted which would be very interesting, as bearing, not only on the nature of the specimens, but on the art displayed in their treatment. It will be more profitable to us now to turn to the reality of life, and to the types of humanity which it affords to us.

Take, first, the women who have been distinguished in the annals of Christianity. It may, perhaps, be suggested that these are all much alike;—not so; look at the Carthagenian St. Monica, mother of St. Augustine, a sort of incarnation of *human* maternity spiritualised by ardent faith . . .

Again, let us take a political period,—that of the French Revolution. The terrors and distresses of that great convulsion brought out most peculiar results. An aristocracy popularly supposed to be utterly vicious, turned to bay with supreme courage and profound resignation, and a number of women were thrown up to the stormy surface of the time, of whom very little is known in England, but who are to be traced in their memoirs and correspondence as memories whom the world should not willingly let die. First of all there is the queen. It has been perhaps the misfortune of Marie Antoinette, so far as regards the due appreciation of what she really was, that her beautiful figure stands out with such dramatic intensity. People disbelieve in her because she is so poetical, so pathetic, was the dear daughter of so great an empress, and bowed to her doom with such truly regal resignation. It is like being asked to admire Joan of Arc, or Spenser's Una, or any other half or wholly legendary figure. The democrats accused her of every vice, and our great Burke defended her with passionate eloquence, insomuch that on that one subject he was thought to be hardly master of himself. But when I look carefully at what we do know of her during those bitter years, the impression made on me is that of a woman whose whole nature rose to an emergency, who utterly cast off the frivolity of her earlier years, supposing that in youth she had been frivolous when all around were of a like mind, and tried with might and main to do her duty. She could not help being handsome and stately, and having fine manners, she had been bred to these things from her cradle up, and this mere drapery should not make us unjust. Nothing in Marie Antoinette is so noticeable as her perfect simplicity; she is not half so *stagey* as Madame Roland; and whether the volumes of correspondence attributed to her, and concerning which so sharp a controversy has arisen between Paris and Berlin be true or false, their straightforward sense is a proof either of what she really was, or of what some very clever forger knew to be in harmony with the documents of undoubted authenticity which came from her pen.

. . .

Take a widely differing group of people; the philanthropists, who worked like Mrs. Fry among the prisoners, or like many of the Boston women for the slaves. Imagine Hannah More throwing herself into poor schools; Miss Dorothea Dix, the friend of the insane, whose parcels are forwarded by American railways free of charge! Take Madame Jules Mallet, in France, the indefatigable patrons of infant schools, and Mary Carpenter in England, at the head of her reformatory; these names all suggest a diversity in likeness, and while one was jested at for being so intimate with Bishops, another belongs to the head quarters of dissenting Friends, and a third to the grave circle of the French Protestants.

From these, turn in sharp contrast to the artists:—Rosa Bonheur, in her large new studio in the Forest of Fontainbleau, her short curls, black velvet jacket, and a hand free, vigorous and precise; Felicie de Faeuvau, in her Florentine home, quaint, severe, medieval, dressed in a soft brown robe, falling close to the feet; Hatty Hormer, in a Roman garden, fountains without and fountains within, and marble beauty freeing itself under the sculptor's chisel; or George Sand herself, greatly gifted and as greatly mourned; or Giulia Grisi, with her perfected power; or the splendid yet matronly figure of Mrs. Siddons, or the delicate spiritual presences of two of England's well-loved late-lost poetesses. Complete this group as you will, and ask what likeness these bear to any of the more ordinary yet most sterling kinds of people – the active farmer's wife, the faithful household servant, the sensible partner of the professional man.

To ignore the wealth of creation in any department of life, is as blind as if one saw nothing but oaks and elms in a forest, flint and chalk in a rock, or blue and green in a rainbow. The more we find to observe in external nature or in humanity, the more we find to rejoice in and to occupy ourselves about; and it is into the capacity of perceiving distinctions that all culture is ultimately to be resolved; whether such culture relate to the vibrations of music, the gradations of colour, the subleties of motion, or the infinite aspects and developments of the human being.

6.4

Feminist journals utilised the traditions of other general women's magazines in their cause and this letter to *The Englishwoman's Review* (1866–1910) reflects the lively debate that took place in the correspondence pages of this type of publication.

'Correspondence', *The Englishwoman's Review*, vol. 19, 1888, pp. 494–96.

The Editor is not responsible for the opinions of Correspondents.
[TO THE EDITOR OF "THE ENGLISHWOMAN'S REVIEW,"]

November 2nd., 1888.

DEAR MADAM—the *Standard* of this morning and the *St. James' Gazette* of this evening both print an extract from the *Hospital* (presumably a medical newspaper) headed "Women and their Victims." It is a tirade against "idle modern women of the wealthier classes" for wearing birds in their hats and bonnets. The writer begins by stating that men take mother birds from their nests, leaving the young birds to starve, "because certain women insist that it shall be so." He (or she) then goes on to argue that because some women wear birds in their hats they are "incomparably inferior to many costermongers, crossing-sweepers, and untaught African negroes," and bids them "reflect upon their worthlessness."

"Is it really, then, come to this?" he asks, "that a nineteenth century woman is so utterly selfish, so hopelessly without brains or feeling, and is so incapable of learning, even the very elements of humanity, that she must and will have birds to adorn herself with at whatever cost? At bottom, it really is want of intellect. The idle modern woman of the wealthier classes is so self-indulgent, so pandered, and so spoilt, that she can no longer be counted upon to exercise a reasoning faculty. Impulses, whims, and poutings, alternate with fits of sulkings or rage, and so she spends her life."

However, this professor of humanity presently takes "consolation" in the thought that certain of his fellow-beings "will die some day," as, fortunately, "they cannot live for ever." Here follows a delicate insinuation that for women death may mean annihilation—it is amusing to find the old doctrine that women have no souls thus cropping up again—and the extract finishes with expressing the "deepest anxiety" on the man's part about the "gradually increasing mental weakness among the prosperous," presumably prosperous women, though they are not here specially mentioned.

Now, an accusation of cruelty to animals, preferred by *men*—and Englishmen, too,—against *women*, is so ludicrously absurd, that one is surprised to find it printed, without a word of reprobation, in responsible papers such as the *Standard* and the *St. James' Gazette*. For, as Miss Miller truly remarked in one of her able lectures on "Women and the Bible"—"it has ever been Man's mission to destroy life; and Women's to preserve it." But of that more anon. With regard to the bonnets, the writer of the above strictures is altogether mistaken as to the class of women who are guilty. It is not the women of the "wealthier classes" who wear birds in their headgear. On the contrary, they have often tried hard to put down the cruel fashion; some years ago, they formed a League for the express purpose, and induced several of the first-rate ladies' milliners to join the League, who bound themselves never to use for trimmings any birds or parts of birds that had not been killed for culinary purposes or as vermin, such as pheasants, blackcock, hawks, &c. The result of these efforts was most marked; wings, birds and even ostrich-plumes disappeared, first from the windows of the better-class milliners, and then from those of a host of their imitators, so much so that even the irate censor of feminine morals, above quoted, appears to have noticed the fact and to have "hoped . . . the fashion . . . was going out." But alas! It is not of much use for women to decree sumptuary laws in the interests of humanity, so long as the interests and tastes of men are in direct opposition. Let any man who feels a sufficient curiosity on the subject go and ask in a bonnet-shop what is the reason of the reappearance of the birds as trimmings; he will be told it is due entirely to the men who gained their living by it, and who were thrown out of employment by the well-meant action of the "wealthy women" aforesaid. I have asked, sometimes, if the men could not turn to some other trade. The answer always amounted to this – that there was no trade for them *they liked so well*.

Herein, I believe, lies the key to the whole matter. Most men love killing for killing's sake. It is not the "wealthy woman"—for, the wealthier they are, and the more solicitous about dressing in good taste, the less they will be found adorned with the corpses of small birds—it is not *they* who encourage the trade; but it is the men who will not allow it to be put down. The innate cruelty of Englishmen (when not softened by the influence of their womenkind) is proverbial. From the peer who maims unfortunate pigeons at Harlingham, and leaves them to die in lingering agonies, down to the peasant boy killing rats in a barn, the taste for the murder and torture of helpless animals is almost universal in the masculine sex.

It is not the typical Englishman truly represented by our neighbours across the Channel as saying, "It is a fine day; come and let us kill something?" does he not begin by pulling the legs off from flies before he can speak? does he not, as a schoolboy, throw stones at every cat or bird he sees, and rejoices greatly if he is so lucky as to lame them for life? does he not "collect," that is, stick pins into, live butterflies, and later on, does he not crimp salmon and vivisect dogs?

If, as the writer in *The Hospital* hints, cruelty to animals makes it doubtful whether the perpetrator have a soul, the chance of a life hereafter for *men* can be but small, it is to be feared.

The only remark of our critic with which all readers of your Review will sympathise, is towards the end, where he says "The movement in favour of the emancipation of women, it may be hoped, will not only give enlargement, but a sense of responsibility and duty." Quite so; let men give us the suffrage, first, and then they will be good enough to recollect that we are legally but "chattels" and that consistently they should not expect "brains and a moral faculty" from us, any more than from their chairs or tables.

I am dear Madam, faithfully yours   "A CHATTEL"

6.5

This article on a career in journalism from *Women's Penny Paper* (1888–90) illustrates the feminist journal's consistent commitment to discussion of the question of women's role in society. The focus on the new professions like journalism reflects the gains made in the struggle to widen professional opportunities open to women. Authored by the eminent journalist and activist, Frances Power Cobbe, it provides a useful insight into the life of the journalist.

'Journalism as a Profession for Women', by Frances Power Cobbe, *Women's Penny Paper*, vol. 1, 1888, p. 5.

WELL-EDUCATED women, and those possessed of a little more than average ability, will be found, I think, to shew several special aptitudes for Journalism, which will enable them ere long to take a fair place in that potent and well-paid profession. For the good of the community at large,— which would be advanced by a larger infusion of womanly conscientiousness, tenderness and purity of feeling into the morning and evening draughts of literature,—and for the sake of our sex, which would thus obtain ready utterance for its aspirations and a career of great honour and influence opened to many of its members,—I should rejoice exceedingly in the introduction of two or three women on the staff of every newspaper in the kingdom. But together with their peculiar aptitudes, women, unfortunately, commonly bring several countervailing deficiencies to the task of a regular contributor to a public journal; and if they are ever to compete on equal terms with male journalists these deficiencies must be remedied. I propose in this paper to offer a few words of advice on this subject, dictated by considerable personal experience.

The advantages of a woman journalist are—

1. Readiness and quickness in using whatever mental powers she may possess. In other walks of literature *pace* may be of little consequence compared with strength; but in writing for a daily paper every second of time is of consequence, and to think in an instant what is best to say on a given subject, and what illustration can enrich the treatment of it, is of more utility than slowly to evolve profound reflections, which may come too late for the next issue. It is the *ready money* of the mind, not the heavy investments of erudition and science, which are available in a news-paper office.

2. Warmth of feeling and wide sympathies which will supply the woman possessed of them with the power of enlisting the pity, the indignation, or the sorrow of her readers, in the stories on which it will be her duty to comment. She will enjoy that gift of genuine pathos which masculine contributors, with very good hearts and intentions, are continually found to lack.

3. Humour,—if a woman be so exceptionally blessed as to possess it in its positive and radiant, and not merely its reflective light,—will, in her writing shine out with a lustre undimmed by the coarseness, or the malignity which too often renders the would-be facetiousness of certain journals saddening and disgusting, rather than diverting. The editor of a paper in large circula-tion once told a lady contributor that she was "the only member of his staff who could write a sub-humorous leading article without either acerbity or coarseness; and that such a gift was simply invaluable for his work."

Against these feminine aptitudes for journalism we must set the following almost equivalent disabilities:—

1. Few women possess the steady health and equable brain-power which can enable them to perform the serious mental labour of original composition on a fresh subject every day (or, let us say, every alternate day), week in and week out, through the greater part of the year. A great deal may be effected by resolution, and by foregoing exhausting amusements in the intervals of work; but it is suicidal for a woman who cannot fairly rely on her own sustained powers to offer herself as a candidate for regular office work on a newspaper. The disappointment and worry to an editor of erratic attendance and imperfect work must be enough to disgust a man with female contributors once and for ever.

Again, *young* women can hardly possess enough knowledge of the world and of life to write to good purpose on the majority of topics discussed in newspapers. Every scrap of acquired knowledge, often of the most apparently out of the way kind, fits in sooner or later into a journalist's task—history, geography, biography, all sorts of anecdotes, quotations from poets and thinkers, sciences of every description, facts of natural history, architecture, sculpture, painting, manufacture, finance, manners and customs, even heraldry and the Almanack de Gotha, all in their turn enrich and adorn the delightful work of a clever journalist. But it is not possible in youth to have hoarded these heterogeneous mental stores from whence to draw at will; and still less is it easy then to form such sound judgments of the befitting, the decorous, the expedient, as to steer clear of all the rocks which lie round the course of our navigation in social or political seas. For these reasons, and some others not to be here detailed, I would advise women intending to become journalists, not to press into the profession too early, but to prepare themselves for it by the largest possible sweep of study, and by cultivating a ready and bright style of writing, easy and clear, so that "he who runs may read," and yet never sinking below the level of pure literary composition into the vile slang and colloquialism of American penny-a-lining. If women enter largely on the profession of journalism, let us earnestly hope it will be to maintain the decency and dignity of the English press as it has existed for a generation; and not to hasten its threatened descent into miserable personalities, vulgarity and slip-slop.

In conclusion, I would fain be allowed, as an old woman journalist, to say to my younger sisters—"Respect your great profession!" Think of your office-chair as of a little pulpit whence you are going to speak to ten thousand, fifty thousand, perhaps to a hundred thousand people. For good or for evil you will exercise a larger influence than you will ever know. Never then, to oblige your editor, argue even on a small matter of political or ethical discussion against your own conviction, but tell him frankly he must choose another contributor if he desire the subject to be so treated. Never give the pain (an excessive one to a weak mind) of newspaper condemnation and scorn to any opponent save in case of real moral ill-desert. Many a life beside that of Keats has been poisoned and spoiled by the cruel review of a book, written utterly thoughtlessly. Be as humourous as your gifts permit, for harmless fun is the salt of modern existence; but turn nothing into a jest which is good or holy, pure or noble, even in feeble aspiration.

It has become a commonplace to say that the potency of the press in these days is greater than that of kings. Bear in mind then, the responsibilities as well as the glory of sharing in any measure in such royal power.

7
The magazine for young women and girls

1880 is seen as the seminal year for the girls' magazine with the appearance of the first issue of the enormously popular *Girl's Own Paper* published by the Religious Tract Society. However, the periodical for young women and girls dates back to 1838 with the publication of *The Young Ladies' Magazine of Theology*. This was to become the first in a long line of magazines aimed at a young female audience. But it is the 1860s that saw the rise of the magazine for girls in significant numbers with the appearance of magazines such as Edward Harrison's *The Young Ladies' Journal* and his rival Samuel Beeton's *Young Englishwoman*. These were aimed at the young middle-class woman who could be any age between 13 and 25 years and differed from juvenile magazines like *Chatterbox* and *Aunt Judy's Magazine* in their focus on the life of the girl and specifically female accomplishments. *Girl's Own Paper* heralds the second generation of magazines for young women, now re-defined as girls and appealing not just to a slightly younger age group but also to a time of life, girlhood, not envisaged a generation earlier. Rivals to *Girl's Own Paper* soon appeared and titles such as *Atalanta* and *Girl's Realm* catered for a mass market that had carved out specific niches for specific readerships, the audience of girls and young women being one of them. They ranged in price from the penny *Girl's Own Paper* to the sixpenny *Atalanta* but they were aimed at the middle-class girl whose range of opportunities had widened considerably. The strides of the Victorian women's movement can be seen in the definition of girlhood constructed in the pages of this type of magazine. Although still in training to be a wife and mother, late Victorian girls are seen as able to consider work opportunities, university education and sport as options for their pre-marital years. The contents were similar to those found in the general illustrated magazines but with an emphasis on a younger readership. The 1880s and 1890s also saw the proliferation of the cheap weekly designed specifically for working-class girls and young women such as *Girl's Best Friend* and *Sweethearts*; earlier cheap popular titles such as *The Young Ladies of Great Britain* and *Wedding Bells* prove that the market had been spotted a generation earlier but it is the later group that saw the most success. These titles rejected the focus on accomplishment and achievement of their rivals aimed at the middle-class girl, and focused on romance and sensationalism and were designed primarily for pleasure and not instruction.

7.1

The Young Ladies' Journal (1864–1920) was the first successful magazine aimed at a young female audience. Through its long run it remained remarkably consistent in terms of both content and style.

See FIGURE 15.

FIGURE 15 Cover, *The Young Ladies' Journal*, Sept., 1869

Most of the cheaper weeklies for girls provided a significant amount of fiction. This short story from *The Young Ladies' Reader* (1881) is typical of the type of fiction found in these publications.

'Only A Flirtation', by A. C., *The Young Ladies' Reader*, vol. 1, 1881, p. 7.

NIGHT had settled on the quiet village of S——. The sun had sunk behind the surrounding hills, and the town clock on the church had struck the hour of ten. Only here and there a pedestrian was seen on his homeward way, or strolling idly along enjoying the cool breeze of an autumn night.

Somewhat secluded from the more inhabited part of the village stood one of those vine-covered cottages that poets rave about, and the careworn man of business dreams of. The garden which surrounded it was filled with fragrant flowers while summer lasted; but now only a few late roses graced the deserted beds.

The moon shone brightly on a couple who were standing at the gate of this rustic garden. They were apparently lovers; yet the set teeth and determined air of the man, the pale face and shrinking attitude of the maiden, denoted that something more than usual was taking place. Was it a lover's quarrel? The moon stopped to listen to what they said. The man spoke first—

"You must forget me. I am not worth remembering, nor the foolish words I may have spoken. It was only a little flirtation, you know—very pleasant while it lasted; but then all such things must come to an end."

And he waited a little impatiently for her answer, never once thinking how the true heart of the maid beside him was wounded by those cruel words, "a little flirtation."

The moon rose higher in the starry heavens, and again looked down on the two at the gate. Lo! the timid maid seemed to have been transformed into a woman, cold and haughty. Drawing herself up to her full height, she replied—

"Certainly; I would not consider it in any other light than a flirtation; and, as you say, all such things must have an end, pleasant though they be."

"But, Helen," said the man, glancing at his watch, "you must not think me heartless or fickle, for if I thought you really loved me——"

"Enough!" she interrupted, "I know what you would say; but it is better unsaid; and I think it would be best to part at once."

"Perhaps it would," he said, somewhat relieved by her reply. "But," he continued, "if we should meet again, will it be as friends or strangers?"

"As friends, of course, and why should we not? For we have been only friends," and a slight bitterness mingled with the calmly spoken words of the girl. "So," she added, "I will bid you good-bye, as it is growing late."

And thus they parted. He did not take her hand, but only bowed and hurried away, and was soon lost in the darkness. Then, when he was gone, all her calmness, all her forced fortitude, gave way, and, sinking on a rustic bench near the gate, she gave way to a paroxysm of tears which came from wounded pride and love.

After a while she turned her gaze to the moon, and as she gazed, her features expressed a thought so deep that not even the moon could penetrate it. A change seemed to have taken place in the character of this village maiden; no longer timid and shy, but a strong woman, with a purpose to live for. How often a little accident, happening in the outset of life, changes the whole tenor of one's future!

The clock was striking eleven as the figure of a girl crept wearily up the garden path and disappeared within the cottage. The moon continued on in its course through the silence of the night, carrying this scene with it.

The history of these two people is short and simple. Helen Kingsly was the only child of her widowed mother, who resided in the cottage before mentioned. Her father died when she was little more than an infant, leaving a small income by which, with a little economy they managed to live tolerably well. Helen was the beauty of the village in which she lived, and no wonder Horace Beauchamp, the only son of rich and worldly parents, while resting after his college labours at S——, found it very pleasant to amuse himself by winning the heart of the village maiden.

But when the time came for his return to the city, he found, to his dismay, that the flirtation had gone a little further than he intended, for he found that Helen loved him; so, not knowing any other way to break the affair off, he resolved to strike the blow at once by telling Helen he must return immediately to his home. At first she seemed quite at a loss to comprehend his meaning when he made his farewell, which was cold and constrained; but as he talked, the truth slowly dawned upon her; then all her pride came to her aid, and he, thinking her calmly-spoken good-bye was from her heart, contented himself with the belief that he was mistaken in thinking this village maiden loved him.

Meanwhile, Horace Beauchamp had arrived at his home in the busy city, and the weeping girl at the gate was forgotten.

* * *

Five years passed away, bringing many changes. Death had visited the house of the Kingslys, and carried away the mother, leaving Helen to the care of an aunt, who was a wealthy widow living in the city. She hastened to the village, and, as soon as the funeral was over, took Helen to her own home, and tried by every means to make the lonely orphan forget the great loss which she had suffered. For four years Helen studied hard at French, music, and instructive literature. Painting and dancing were added to the fashionable accomplishments, in which she tried hard to succeed.

At the age of twenty-one her aunt introduced her into fashionable society, in which Helen shone as a star; and, although a year had passed since that event, she still reigned as an acknowledged belle. During her first season she met Horace Beauchamp quite often. They greeted one another as friends, and for some time past he had become her attendant to almost all the places of amusement that she attended. At the opera or in the ball-room he was always at her side. Her rare beauty, now fully developed, made a deep impression on the thoughtless young man, and he tried by every attention to erase from her memory the recollection of their meeting that summer five years ago.

September had come again, and the leaves presented a fine collection of autumn beauties. Evening shades were fast gathering over the busy city; the moon had already begun its course in the heavens.

Helen Kingsly was standing on the veranda of her aunt's elegant residence. She was waiting for some one, and her restless manner revealed her impatience at the delay. Suddenly a footstep sounded near her, and turning round, she beheld Horace Beauchamp. With a bright smile she welcomed him, saying—

"I expected you before, Mr. Beauchamp. Your note asked me to be at home at eight, and now it is nearly nine."

A slight reproach could be detected in her tone, and he hastened to apologise.

"A thousand pardons for thus keeping you waiting; but I was detained by an urgent business call. As soon as I was free I came immediately to see you, as much depends on your answer to a question that I am about to ask."

She bowed, and he went on—

"An old friend of my father's, from Australia, offered me the position of junior partner in his extensive business. I am to give him my answer to-morrow, but it remains with you, Helen, whether I shall go or stay. Which shall it be?"

Helen's silence filled him with hope, and he again urged his suit, ending by saying—

"You must love me, Helen, for your actions tell me so."

Then she knew that the moment of her triumph had arrived, and in a cold, scornful tone, she replied—

"You certainly are mistaken in my actions, whatever they may have been. I was only enjoying a little flirtation—nothing else, but very pleasant while it lasted."

"Oh, Helen," he groaned, as he heard his own words repeated, "am I not forgiven? I know that I deserve it. I will try and bear this punishment. Farewell; I shall accept the offer of my father's friend. I will go to Australia." And with one last look at the woman he loved so well, he turned and left her to her own reflections.

Helen sat very still. She heard his farewell words, but could not reply. His footsteps, echoing along the pavement, sent back a wail to her broken heart. Gone! And when she had gained the revenge she so craved—when she had brought him to lay his heart at her feet—when she had sent him away with bitter reproach to himself, she found only too late how passionately she still loved him.

Three days after the parting scene with Helen, Horace Beauchamp left for Australia, and his father, after settling his affairs, soon followed. Horace did not see Helen again, and how he lived, she never knew.

Helen bore her sorrow bravely. The following winter was gayer than ever, but when spring came she drooped. "A cold she had caught during the winter," they said; but it grew worse rapidly, and when June roses were all in bloom Helen Kingsly passed from this world to the one above.

Her aunt, broken-hearted by her loss, left the city, and took up her abode in the cottage in her niece's native village, and there lived until she died. Now the cottage has gone to ruin, the roses and vines are dead, the gate is broken down, and all around is deserted.

7.3

The magazines aimed at the middle-class girl dealt with what were considered to be all aspects of girls' lives. Although new activities like sport began to take up more and more space, the traditional activity of housekeeping was still dealt with and discussed. The following article on housekeeping from the regular feature 'The Brown Owl' in *Atalanta* (1887–98) advises the middle-class girl on her responsibilities in the home.

'On Housekeeping', by Eleanor Bairdsmith, *Atalanta*, vol. 4, 1890, pp. 346–48.

To theorise on the sort of housekeeping that falls to the lot of most girls is almost an impossibility. Of course there are cases in which a daughter, or a sister, has authority in the household as complete as if she were mistress in name as well as in deed. These are exceptions, and a girl usually keeps house within certain well-defined limits, rightly, and, of necessity, under the surveillance of her mother.

Some natures take to housekeeping as a duck does to water. To others it is a weariness to the flesh, and it must always remain a question if we can shine in pursuits that are distasteful. We follow them as a duty creditably to ourselves, and with good results as regards others, but to achieve brilliant success, taste and capacity must go hand in hand. There is not, however, much scope for brilliancy in housekeeping, nor is this the special mark that girls should aim at.

First of all, I plead with parents for young housekeepers that they have a free hand. Of course, during their maiden efforts, the family must make up its mind to a certain amount of discomfort, but, unless, so to speak, you give a girl her head, you cannot see the stuff she is made of. Let the limits of her jurisdiction be defined as strictly as her parents see fit, confine it to the bare ordering of meals, but she should have full authority while it last. A system of wheels within wheels is always a little difficult to work at first, both upstairs and downstairs, but that it can be made to answer is abundantly proved in many households. Until responsibility is granted, no advance is made in any occupation, however humble and necessary. Even a girl to whom full domestic power is relegated will find she must consult with her parents, but if a mother cannot resign the actual management of the reins of government, she had better retain them altogether, for no one ever gained satisfaction from an arrangement in which no one knew who held the responsibility.

I plead very strongly too, that the young housekeeper should have charge of the money. It is infinitely more interesting, as well as instructive. It gives a variety which the bare ordering of meals is sadly apt to lack, and it teaches a girl very soon the value of money. If she is fond of figures, it is not unpleasant work to keep the weekly books, and she learns by simple means to be answerable for the money of others. When girls come to be housekeepers on their own account they have to be responsible for a weekly or monthly sum of money, and the sooner they are trained to this habit the better it is for them.

To different minds, housekeeping implies a widely different sphere of duties. Some women are never content unless they do everything themselves, but to keep a dog and do all the barking oneself strikes one as rather a futile arrangement. The proper function of the mistress of the house, to superintend everything, to know that from garret to basement things are going smoothly, and to set each member of her household to their proper work. Some women spend their lives housekeeping. Even if they like it, which they do not seem to do, for they take it hard, and have many burdens, surely it is not the worthiest way of expending their strength. Concentrate all your thoughts and your best energies on your housekeeping during that part of the day when it demands your attention; but, in pity to your family and friends, watch lest it should absorb your mind and your conversation every hour of your life. A housekeeping machine is a sad kind of woman, and she is not always successful. Do your duties cheerily and well and then put them away from you. Nothing is done better because you allow it to get on your nerves.

But to the average English girl, in the average English home, housekeeping comprises the daily ordering of meals, the keeping of the weekly books, and the giving out of stores where they are kept under lock and key. This is housekeeping proper, and it is about as much as one girl, new to the work, can manage. Of course there are many other departments, which in a daughterful household, can be undertaken by other members of the family. I cannot help feeling myself that it is a more human system not to keep everything under lock and key, but that is a matter of principle which every housekeeper must think out and decide for herself. Should our aim be to live together as a family, trusting those downstairs as we would those upstairs; or shall we treat them as our natural enemies, who are biding their time to defraud us when they can? Money should be kept under lock and key on principle, and the wine cellar; but with regard to the general stores it will usually be found that if the servants are trusted they will prove themselves trustworthy.

Suppose then that housekeeping is narrowed down to the limits of the two duties of ordering meals and of keeping the weekly books; is it possible to make even this "drudgery divine?" In one case variety is the great end to aim at, and in the other, method. Method is a good thing in most cases, but in ordering dinner it is fatal. The results of variety in book-keeping are also disastrous. The two duties must be kept studiously apart. The end of method in ordering dinner is too apt to be that the household knows as well as the housekeeper what meat will appear on a certain day. When the said meat has appeared, a gloomy foreboding is felt of the exact nature of the resurrection pie in which it will turn up at a convenient season. Variety, especially in moderate establishments, is the great difficulty. Most young housekeepers have ardently longed for the invention of a new animal; but, as their sighs are unavailing, how can they best cope with the means at their command with the monotony of our daily food? Thoughtfulness is a great feature of good housekeeping. The most high-souled being amongst us has his favourite dish, and that this should be remembered is a delicate attention that seldom fails of its effect. A selfish or a slovenly housekeeper orders what first comes into her head to save herself trouble, but the tastes, and even the fads, of each member of the household ought to receive due consideration from a girl who takes a proper pride in discharging her duties well. In some houses economy has to be carefully studied, and this further complication must be bravely faced, but in no establishment, of whatever wealth or magnificence, should waste be tolerated for an instant. In the latter case, however, it is not very advisable to give the housekeeping into a girl's hands, as it only trains her up to manage a house on a scale quite out of proportion to her probable start in life, and we none of us find much difficulty in expanding; to retrench is a serious consideration with us all.

The housekeeper should give attention to a general supervision of the premises downstairs. The tidiness of the cupboards, the cleanliness and comfort of the servants' quarters are her care. She must hold herself responsible for the smooth working of all matters within the limits of her domestic kingdom, and though she has my fullest sympathy if she is harassed by perpetual interference, even this she must bear patiently as part of her life's discipline.

One word about book keeping. System, neatness and clearness are indispensable qualities. Find out the best method and keep to it. Be sure that you understand it yourself, and can make it clear to others, and you should be ready and willing at any moment to render an account of your stewardship.

Housekeeping is not attractive to all of us. Many of us have a positive distaste to it; but it must be done—and what must be done, ought to be done well. Beef and mutton, so many pounds of butter, and so many quarts of milk are not interesting compared with our most cherished occupations; but even they can have their charm, if, for the brief time of day that they must absorb our attention, we consider, not how quickly we can scramble through our duties, but how much we can minister to the little comforts of those we love.[1]

[1] This paper invites discussion. All letters or remarks must reach the Editor not later than February 20th, and must have the words "Brown Owl" on the cover.

7.4

Work outside the home had become quite common for middle-class girls by the end of the century, although some jobs were seen as more appropriate than others. Nevertheless, it was commonly assumed that marriage would mark a natural end to such work. This article from *The Young Woman* (1892–1915) details the daily life of the shopgirl.

'Life Behind the Counter', by C. J. Hamilton, *The Young Woman*, vol. 1, 1892, pp. 128–30.

A LONDON SHOP!—to be in a London shop seems to many a country girl the very summit of her ambition. To be inside those huge plate-glass windows, with beautiful new things on every side, and well-dressed people coming in and out all day, what a delightful life a London shop-girl must lead! And yet is it really so? Is all gold that glitters? Is everything rose colour when we come close up to it? Alas! No. I have had some acquaintance with girls behind the counter, and the difficulties, dangers, and temptations of such a life can hardly be overrated. Of course there are a few cases where the girls have respectable homes with their own parents to go to after their work is done, and then the dangers and difficulties become infinitely less; but, as a rule, girls are sent out quite alone into the great world of shop-life, to sink or swim as best they can.

Let us imagine a girl from a provincial town coming to London to begin life as a shop-assistant. After a great amount of advertising she obtains a situation, say in one of the large suburban establishments, for she cannot expect to get to the West End without some experience of London business. She is fortunate if she gets a salary of £25 a year, with board and lodging; sometimes she may get more, sometimes less. The time is just before Christmas, the busiest time in the year, when extra hands are taken on; she is drafted off into the bazaar to sell toys and fancy goods—work which does require much experience. She begins her duties one cold morning in December. The other "young ladies" eye her superciliously. They see at a glance that her dress is country-made, after the fashion of a year ago, while theirs, although also black, are cut after the latest fashion, and fit to a nicety. The new-comer, bashful and timid though she is, finds that she has quite enough to do to attend to all the calls that are made upon her—spoiled children, who spend an hour choosing a shilling horse and cart; exacting old ladies, who are buying penny articles for a Christmas tree, and worse than all, customers who, after tossing over dozens of things, end up by walking out of the shop without buying anything at all.

And then if the slightest mistake is made in a bill, a fine of 6d. is inflicted on the shop-girl. At one large establishment in Bayswater, I saw a list of these fines, and a formidable one it was. If the girl's number was not put down on the bill, 6d. If the amount of money given by the customer was not put at the end, 6d. If wrong change was given, 6d., and the girl to bear the loss; and so on. Incivility to a customer was charged 1s. In the hurry and bustle of a crowded shop a new hand is very likely to make numerous mistakes, and has to suffer accordingly.

At one, or half-past one, the first instalment of shop-assistants go to dinner, which generally consists of roast joints, with vegetables, and pudding. Then to work again till five, when they have tea; and at eight, supper of bread and cheese, and sometimes cold meat. The hours for closing vary very considerably. In the West End some of the large shops are closed at six, but in the City and in the large suburban districts, such as Brixton, Kilburn, Hammersmith, etc., the shops, especially at Christmastime, are frequently kept open till seven, eight, nine and even ten o'clock. In fact, the evening hours are the busiest, as servants and those engaged in offices are then able to get out to do their shopping. After the shop is actually closed, say at half-past nine, an hour is generally occupied in clearing up and setting the goods straight for the next day. At eleven, tired in body and mind, our country girl goes up to her little room, which she shares with three others; one sleeps with her, and there are two other girls in another bed. Very often some of them have needlework to do, and so they sit up gossiping and stitching, till past twelve o'clock. Sometimes there is not room for the extra hands to sleep in the house, and lodgings are taken for them outside, so that when their work is over they have to turn out and walk some distance before they find their night's lodging.

But let us suppose our country friend is safely in bed. At seven o'clock, when the grey light of a winter's morning is just beginning to dawn, she is roused from her slumbers. Now she must hurry, for there is little time to dress and snatch a hasty breakfast before the shop opens. Sometimes the girls have to wash at the end of a long passage, and to wait shivering in the cold until their turn comes. I knew a delicate consumptive girl who had a serious illness from colds caught in this way. Dressing for a London shop demands a good deal of care. The collar must be spotless, and the hair elaborately arranged.

A hasty meal, of tepid tea, with bread and salt butter, is swallowed; and then, at eight o'clock, or, at the latest, half-past eight, off to the counter again, to stand there for perhaps twelve or thirteen hours. The daily round has begun in real earnest. During the cheap sales in January and July the work is almost as heavy as before Christmas. Premiums are given on certain classes of goods in some shops; that is, if a girl sells a pair of stockings or gloves, she is allowed 2d. or 3d. in the shilling, and this, of course, makes her especially anxious to sell them, and earn something extra for herself. One girl told me that she often made six shillings a week by premiums. The system is, of course, liable to lead to dishonesty and falsehood. If a customer asks, "Is this in fashion?" or, "I think this is soiled," the answer is sure to be, "Oh, no, madam, you are quite mistaken; the goods only came in last week, they are quite fresh." And sometimes this is far from the truth.

When Sunday comes, the long hours of Saturday night (in the suburban shops) and the fatigues of the whole week are so exhausting that the girls do not feel inclined to go to church; they lie in bed late, and then stretch themselves on a sofa (if they can get one). I regret to say in some shops there is a fine of 2s. 6d. if a girl ventures to sit down during business hours—a cruel and barbarous rule.

In the afternoons the girls brighten up considerably, and set off, in their smartest clothes, to visit their friends or go to evening service; but let them take care that they are back at ten o'clock, for if they come in after that hour, without leave, they are likely to be fined 2s. 6d., and for the second offence they may be dismissed without a satisfactory character. This means waiting day after day at registry offices for many a weary month, it means advertising to no purpose, and interviewing managers only to have the doors shut in their faces, and all, perhaps, because the omnibus was too full, or the train ten minutes late.

Girls in shops are exposed to many dangers. There is the danger of making undesirable acquaintances, and there is also the great temptation to an excessive love of dress. They see and hear so much about fine clothes that it seems the whole duty of woman to be well-dressed, and the desire to set themselves off, to outshine all their rivals, and excite a full meed of admiration, becomes almost a passion. The delicate bloom is rubbed off, and they are apt to become fast.

A shop life may make a girl smart and bright, but it scarcely helps to fit her for the duties of a wife and mother. She learns to love excitement, and to crave for it. The brilliant lights, the gay colours, the new fashions, all become welcome, and ordinary home life seems dull and tame in comparison. There is no time for quiet thinking or serious reading, and true friends are few and far between. The Young Women's Christian Association and the Girl's Friendly Society are doing, and have done, most useful work, but they cannot do everything and are often powerless to grapple with the hidden evils which are found underneath the gay surface of these London shops. Those evils I am just now unable to deal with—I have only attempted to point out a few of the pitfalls and snares which London shop-girls have to meet. Thank God that so many of them bravely overcome all difficulties and temptations, and lead pure, beautiful, and useful lives.

7·5

The Monthly Packet (1851–98), edited by Charlotte Yonge and closely affiliated to the Church of England, began as a juvenile magazine but during the course of its long run became addressed to a young female readership. Although the majority of girls' magazines celebrated the achievements of modern girls, they were not all in favour. This piece from the discussion and letter section 'The China Cupboard' debates the question of the New Woman.

'The New Woman', The Monthly Packet, vol. 89, 1895, pp. 128–30.

WHETHER the new woman—the lady, in capital letters—that is put on every stage and placard exists or no, remains a matter for doubt; nevertheless, she is a character universally talked about, and most of us have her picture so vividly marked upon our minds, that to us she does exists, whether we have seen here in the flesh or no.

It must, however, be generally understood that within the last fifty years, woman has advanced by rapid strides from the quiet, stay-at-home body who constituted the female element then.

Sixty years ago in our universities a lady was a strange being, to be stared after with surprise; now we see them everywhere duennaless, riding about by fifties on bicycles; and what does the old woman say to this?

The result of women's trying to unsex themselves and strike out on lines allotted to the sterner sex cannot but injure the idealistic woman.

Who could idealise a woman riding about in clothes which, though passed by the police, were never in Nature's eye when woman was created, rushing about on a bicycle to meetings, making herself conspicuous on public platforms.

As in the days of St. Paul woman was not suited to speak in Church, so likewise in these days is it the case on public platforms; only bringing home to the minds of their hearers how unfit they are to do it.

A public life designated for the sterner sex cannot sit well on the shoulders of weaker woman; there is no room for her essential tenderness of manner and sentiment: these qualities do not develop on the public platform. The refined expressions of gentle beauty give way to an aspect of boldness; there is no room for the sympathetic gifts of woman's nature in the heart of the new woman.

The late Corney Grain 'hit the right nail on the head,' however, when he said, that there would always exist one insurmountable barrier to woman's unsexing herself—namely, Mother Nature.

Woman was made subservient to the nobler being, man; she is naturally influenced by his firmer nature, and so long as man holds his sway the world will not be annoyed by the new woman.—U.V.W.

N.B.—We believe the students of the Women's Colleges at Oxford do not use bicycles.—C.C.

7.6

Girls' Own Paper (1880–1927) played a seminal role in the development of the modern magazine for girls. The following abridged article illustrates the interest in sport and outdoor activity found in most girls' magazines and the original included a list of cycling clubs that readers could contact.

'Our Girls A-Wheel', *Girls' Own Paper*, vol. 18, 1897, pp. 220–21.

IV.—GIRLS' CYCLING CLUBS AND ASSOCIATIONS

"UNITY is strength!" with such a motto for our foundation-stone, it is wise to discuss the advantages to be gained by Our Girls A-Wheel with co-operation and organisation. It is an undisputed fact that the womanhood of the nineteenth century enjoys a more unrestricted and independent life than our foremothers. Cycling is practically the only pastime by which it is possible to make public the appreciation of athleticism. Tennis may be played in the private garden; swimming may be enjoyed in the bath, gymnastics in the obscure gymnasium, cricket in the empty field, and with an occasional row in the river, may exhaust the opportunities for physical recreation. There is a lack however of earnestness in all such achievements. So long as the science of physical development is forwarded in unfrequented corners, in a spirit of listlessness, it is supposed by many to be blameless.

But, by the aid of the wheel, a new era has commenced, and the womanhood of the twentieth century may be the eye-witness of a great revolution. To build up the physical nature according to the opportunities afforded, and to study the science of living, may be considered in a few years to be the highest duty of our girls. Today, when we allow to pass, without comment, hundreds of delicate wheelwomen, mounted on their dainty steeds, through the rural lanes, and even the most crowded thoroughfares of our cities, we reflect with astonishment what progress has been witnessed even by our own eyes. This freedom and safety along the roads of civilisation speaks volumes. It means more than self-government. To successfully steer a cycle up hill and down dale, alone and unaided, requires a certain degree of nerve, muscular and mind strength not to be despised; but before such an exhibition could have taken place, years and years of pioneer work had to be performed.

In the year 1878, the Cyclists' Touring was originally founded to combat the dogged and unreasonable opposition to the new methods of locomotion, and to protect the interest of its persistent adherents on the road. The pioneer wheelers, to whom we owe a debt of gratitude for making our paths straight and safe, were received with ill-concealed antipathy, which culminated at times with undoubted brutality.

. . .

In the cycling realm it is natural that our girls should discover that they are capable of enjoying both individual and collective life. Club life teaches the wheelwoman to be self-dependent, no matter what the obstacle, and that there is a prosperous niche for every human soul on God's earth if only folks would make up their minds to hunt till they find it. It teaches first social opportunity, then friendship and advantages of unity. It may be that our grandmothers commenced attending convivial gatherings by sipping afternoon tea and tasting the delights of an afternoon ecstatically spent in conversing on fashion, perhaps frivolity, which leads the way to books and philosophy, and by the advent of the wheel, to the delights of the glorious world outside the gardengate. So soon as our girls taste the refreshment of union, learn to like its sweets and appreciate a new understanding of the higher life that comes from freedom of action, and provides a healthy use of unconsidered moments, they will combine together to put the finishing touches to the pioneer work so ably performed by their sturdier fathers and brothers. The roads have been made both safe and rideable. It is now time for them to be utilised for the most innocent, most healthful and most fascinating enjoyment.

Buoyancy of spirit begets spirited action. It is listlessness that renders life so uninteresting, and a weak action of the heart creates languor and morbidity. Physical weakness and inferiority makes a soul cowardly, emotional, artful, untruthful, irresponsible, untrustworthy, capricious and fretful; but a physical vigour shall bequeath to coming generations a heritage of acquired health and character. Cycling may enlarge the circle of feminine graces until it includes courage, self-reliance, self-control, truth of being, spiritual freedom, and graces which will ennoble. The cycle may become a stepping-stone towards physical reformation, wherein lies the attainment of true womanhood.

But what has all this to do with clubs. That is the point I am now coming to. Without the cycle you cannot have the club. In the year 1892, to compete with the rapid growth and power of feminine cycling, the Lady Cyclists' Association was founded by Miss Davidson to encourage and keep up the tone of cycling, to bring its members in touch with one another, to foster the wearing of the reform costume, and to find riding companions, etc. During the season rides were organised, and in the winter a social gathering is arranged. Its secretary is Miss Grace Murrell, of 35, Victoria Street, Westminster. S.W., from whom all particulars can be obtained. The Countess of Malmesbury is the president.

. . .

In the past seasons the rides have been most successful, as many as from thirty-five to forty-five sitting down to tea, and it has been the experience of the association that these cycle rides have proved to be very useful (1) in inspiring the spirit of comradeship amongst the riders, and (2) increasing the riding powers of even the most delicate. Organised trips with congenial companions are the most pleasurable forms of cycling. Meeting at the trysting-place in ones and twos, the members glide up, and, with hearty and sincere handshake, the members greet each other, after which, with a merry jest and laugh, they ride along together, animated by the congenial flow of bright spirits and happy flow of chatter. The address of the M.H.C.A. (Mowbray House Cycling Association) is Mowbray House, Norfolk Street, London, W.C.

Let us for a moment reflect what an amount of character-building of the finest description is silently going on during these club rides. The moment the rider mounts the bicycle a complete change in both mental and muscular exercise is experienced. The sensitive steed exacts the attention of both the mind and the body. To the necessity of maintaining equilibrium and propulsion every muscle responds; to avoid obstacles or tough places on the road, the eye quickens mechanically, and is ever on the alert. Trouble is sure to quickly follow an error of judgement, for the bicycle is not versed in any law of self-preservation. Quick judgement, rapid thought, and prompt action, are both involuntarily and intuitively imposed upon the wheelwoman in a hundred little ways. The brain no less than the eyes and muscles of the body, comes into sympathetic action with the movements of the sensitive vehicle beneath the rider, who thus is unconsciously drawn away from herself, and the innumerable cares of her liliputian world, with the cobwebs of the brain, are swept away in the tide of quickened, oxygenated blood that courses through the veins in response to the new spirit of breath and action, whilst she is at the same time being inspired by the most glorious sense of comradeship, which is the slender tie worthy of joining all sorts and conditions of our girls together.

There are also many other clubs for ladies and gentlemen in London, among which I may mention the Trafalgar Bicycle Club and the Wheel Club, both of which cater for the society folk, not to mention the numerous local cycling clubs, which are to be found in every district. There is no doubt that advantages are to be gained from club member-ship, as the unattached rider is not the most enviable mortal to be found on this terrestrial ball. Even with a cycling chum it is possible to lose many interests which await the cyclist, for she may be more profitably employed when we most desire to go a-wheeling, she may prefer the companionship of others, or desire a quicker or a slower pace than that which pleases us, but with many companions it is easier to share our joys and cares . . .

7·7

The relationship between the advice column and the letters' page was very close in many types of women's magazine, including the cheap weeklies in the 1890s. This extract from *Sweethearts* (1898) typifies the type of advice column found in these cheaper weeklies. Although they were ostensibly aimed at young women these magazines were read by men who occasionally wrote in, as illustrated here.

'Helpful Advice. Freely given by your Editor', *Sweethearts*, vol. 1, no. 17, 1898, p. 11.

The number of letters that I have received lately to say how much the writers are fascinated with Miss Mona Delacourt's grand serial, "The Girl I Left Behind me," have given me a great deal of pleasure to read, and I must thank the writers one and all for their warm praise of our little paper.

One of them even goes so far as to say:— "I have taken in your paper from the first number, and would not be without it for anything. All my friends to whom I have given a first copy now take it regularly. The serial is just splendid, and I think all the girls have quite fallen in love with the Captain already, and the short stories are just perfection."

That's the sort of thing that does my heart good; it's everything to know that the stories suit the readers' taste, and I am very glad that those I have selected for my girl friends to read in SWEETHEARTS have hit the mark.

A man who has lost the use of one hand, "Bessie Bellwood," may be just as good a man for all that, and I am glad to see that his misfortune makes no difference to the place he occupies in your regard. But you say that he has never made you a declaration, and you want to know how you can possibly find out what his feelings are.

There, I must confess, you have set me a riddle that is impossible to answer. But if you will take my advice, "Bessie Bellwood," you will not think too much of that young man, nor allow him to address you constantly by your Christian name, as you tell me he is in the habit of doing. Make him treat you with more deference, and he will be sure to like you all the better for it. Any man would tell you that.

I suppose everyone desires a situation in London (W. B. Dundee,) but the number of clerks at present is so woefully in excess of the demand that I can't advise you to change your quarters. Still, at the same time, there's no reason why you shouldn't be on the look-out for a suitable vacancy. You should have shorthand, typewriting and book-keeping at your fingers' ends to command a good berth, and whatever you do, don't come to town to look for one, answer advertisements etc., and secure

your post first. If you are already a skilled typist, and your machine is by an eminent maker, it's possible the firm might help you.

Mind, I haven't said this to discourage you, but because I know well you have set yourself a difficult task. Drop me a line again soon. Many thanks for so kindly distributing the specimen copies I sent you.

"Apple-blossom" having broken off with her lover and acted towards him with scorn, contempt, and pride, has now found out that he was all in all to her; and, although racked by despair, will not make the slightest attempt to bring about a reconciliation. What is she, in this dreadful dilemma, to do? True love is always extremely forgiving; so the best thing she can do is to write her lover a nicely-worded letter—the briefer the better; such a letter as will not only exhibit her good sense and the natural affection of her disposition, but not compromise her independence in any way. After a quarrel it is as well not to rush all at once into an engagement. When the wings of Cupid have been once ruffled they are not smoothed again in a violent hurry.

It is evident, "Sweet Violet," that your sweetheart doesn't like the idea of your going to Australia, and no wonder when one considers the terrible state of trade there. Cannot you marry and settle down in some business here, instead of going abroad on a speculative errand? I think your sweetheart knows best, 'Sweet Violet.'

Yes ("X.Y.Z.," Wolverhampton) a Charming Present is sent to a reader of SWEETHEARTS every week, and judging by the letters I constantly receive, they appear to give great satisfaction.

Here is a nice little note from Claire, (Nottingham), that fully confirms what I have written. She says:—

"Allow me to thank you very much for the dear little present I received yesterday morning. I was very pleased with it, the more so, I think, because, strange to say, it arrived on my twenty-first birthday. I think you must have been consulting Gipsy Jess.

"I am still delighted with SWEETHEARTS, and can truthfully say I have never read a better half-penny paper."

Then she adds: "My sister and I take a copy each, because we are so eager to read the contents that we cannot wait for each other to finish the paper."

I can only say I'm very pleased indeed to hear it!

Don't forget to have a good look at our new competition on the next page. £5 a month eoming (*sic*) in with no extra trouble would do wonders for you, wouldn't it? And if you don't win the first prize, you still have a chance of one of the hundreds of others that are being offered in connection with it. So the chances of success are many in your favour.

Half a million copies sounds a large order, but with the help of my numerous friends I am hopeful that the weekly circulation of SWEETHEARTS will reach these figures before the paper is twelve months old.

"Eighteen months ago," writes "Ladybird," "my lover, like Captain Lisle in your lively new serial, 'The Girl I left behind Me,' was ordered out to India. I did, and I do, love him well. But from the day he left, I have never received so much as a line from him to say how he has fared. Do you think I had better await his return or, in the meantime, accept an offer that I have just had?"

Well, you say you care for the man still, so I shouldn't have thought there could be two opinions about the matter. Wait, by all means, "Ladybird," if your affection will stand the test of time. Your lover may have been ill, or letters easily go astray. It's strange what a number of untoward incidents may occur if only you come to think of it.

"Soldier Jim." If the young lady has been so indiscreet as to accept the pointed attentions of other young fellows when actually engaged to you, and you have broken off the engagement in consequence, I should hesitate very much before you renewed it, "Soldier Jim." At any rate don't take any decisive steps at present.

"Can you explain to me," asks "Puzzled," "why the girl I am in love with behaves so oddly? When we are alone she seems to like my society—she is as kind and nice as possible, and gives me so much encouragement that I am quite happy.

"But whenever anyone else is present, she is quite another girl. She avoids me, and seems quite uncomfortable if I come and talk to her. She hardly answers, and gets away as fast as she can. Am I to suppose she is trifling with me? I ought to mention she knows my intentions, for several people have teased her about me."

If several people have teased her, you may be quite sure that is more than enough to account for her behaviour. Of course, she is shy of showing her preference for you before others. Why don't you bring matters to a crisis, and come to some understanding about the matter?

"Julia A." wishes to know if she can with propriety break off an engagement of very short duration with a young man, when she has seen another she likes better, and who, she thinks, would make her more happy in the married state.

"Julia" must be punished. She is not only fickle, but indiscreet: She should have sounded the depths of her heart before she entered any engagement.

Still, for the sake of both parties, I think it would be best not to let it go any further.

7.8

This editorial address from *Girls' Realm* (1898–1915) exemplifies well the general mood of the girls' magazine about the progress made by modern girls and the intimate tone characteristic of the new journalism.

'A Chat with the Girl of the Period', by The Editor, *Girls' Realm*, vol. 1, 1899, p. 216.

My dear girls,—I must apologise to you for giving you a name that recalls an attack made by a woman of brilliant talents on the girls of more than a quarter-of-a-century ago. The death of Mrs. Lynn Linton, the other day, set us talking about the great article in *The Saturday Review* that made her fame. Some of us said it was deserved by the girls, others, and I was among them, vowed that there was no foundation for that savage onslaught, and that the writer had created a monster on purpose to slay it. A lover of paradox averred that there was no girl of the period. Every period has its girls and you are the girls of yours. I think that I know a good deal about you; and that I appreciate the attitude you adopt towards life. The claims that you make are the result of your reaction against the restrictions that hemmed in the lives of the girls in the days of your grandmothers. The influences that moulded and fashioned them were all negative. "Don't" was the word they were always hearing. "Do" is the word that inspires you. If the old-fashioned girl longed for active exercise, "Don't," said the voice of the monitor. Violent exercise is unfeminine. The sun and the air hurt the complexion. The modern girl is weary of this ideal of ladyhood. She is a creature of the open air; she wants to be stirring. She is tired of being taken to see her brother play football; she wants to have a kick at it herself. She glories in being a sportswoman, and in every form of physical culture. She has her bicycle, she plays cricket, golf, hockey, lawn tennis; she has her clubs for these games, and she has her gymnasiums. The result is, that she has not the appeal of feminine dependance in her deportment; and her carriage suggests that she can hold her own with her kinsmen and masculine friends, should one of them dare to contest her right to be considered a young Amazon.

If the old-fashioned girl yearned to be educated in the liberal meaning of the word, "Don't," said the warning voice. "To be learned is to be unfeminine. Innocence based upon ignorance, that is what is charming. What does a woman want with learning? Let her know how to keep house, and look after her husband's and children's physical comfort. If she never marries, let her take a back seat and play the *rôle* of the maiden aunt, and be thankful."

The modern girl shivers with indignation at such a prospect held out to be her. She is tired of living in a doll's house, and, married or unmarried, she will never take a back seat. She claims that she has as much right to a good education as have her brothers. She insists that she will be as good a housekeeper, and better, for having her judgment and her taste cultivated; that she will be as good a wife, and better, for being her husband's comrade and chum. That she will be a better mother for understanding the laws of health, and having some notions of her own about methods of education. Society has answered in the affirmative, and high schools, art schools, colleges, and conservatoires are ready to give her of their best. If the girl of a former generation wanted to enter upon some career, "Don't," was groaned, rather than uttered. It was worse than unfeminine. It was disgraceful. If a girl must earn her living, let her earn it as a governess. Teaching was the single profession that it was held a girl who respected herself could follow. "Do, do, do," cries the modern girl to the one who wants to lead a professional life. "Enter the lists with the men. Be a doctor, a journalist, a singer, a gardener, a post-office girl, a telegraph girl. The professions are being thrown open to you, and out into the world goes the girl of the period to fight her way, and the air is no longer charged with criticism, but is filled with genial good wishes.

There certainly is an immense difference between the girls brought up under the rule of "Don't" and those under the rule of "Do." It is a platitude to say that being human both have their qualities and their faults. The new standpoint towards life, the affirmative and creative, as opposed to the negative and restrictive, has its dangers, but it is not unfeminine. It is, perhaps, more essentially feminine because it is essentially human. "Don't" can never be applied to the qualities that lie at the foundation of the human soul and preserve its sanity. There can never be a "Don't" to modesty, courage, truth, or unselfishness. The "Do" attitude must be fashioned by reason, by common-sense, and chastened by the imaginative sympathy. The modern girl's demand for liberty in things lawful is a just claim. There are some "do's" that I think she had better leave alone. I shrink when I see a fresh young thing puffing away at a cigarette. What does her pure, healthy blood need with narcotics? The slang of some modern girls is deplorable; their irreverent attitude towards our dear and splendid mother tongue partakes of a certain "hail fellow well met" manner that she affects towards the world in general; towards the young and the old, towards men and women alike. That the girl of the period claims to have a "good time" as her right, is a marked characteristic of her. Ah, you little pagans, the idea of having a "good time" is no new ideal. It is as old as the history of the human race upon earth, and again and again it has proved that in and for itself, it is not a working ideal. A "real good time" is not so easy of attainment as to be secured by impatience against what is not pleasant to contemplate. Now as always a life lived narrowly, a nature that gathers without giving, sinks into gloom and disappointment.

Take her all in all, the girl of the period is a "fine fellow," breezy, plucky, quick to enjoy, and ready to stand by her sex. This quality which is being developed in her is the most hopeful of the new feminine ideals. Hitherto women have sadly lacked sex loyalty. There is forming an *esprit de corps* among girls which delights me. It sets me dreaming of a "Guild of Girls," of which THE GIRL'S REALM will be the organ. If you respond to this scheme, I will return to it in a future number.

I should like my girl readers to write to me in their own frank way, and tell me the standpoint at which they have arrived, and the measures they hope to take in order to realize the pleasing vision of a "good time." If you will write to me about yourselves—never mind how frivolous your desires are—about your ambitions, your difficulties, I will try to help you, to realise yourselves; we shall grow to know one another, and be able to work together.

Your Friend,
THE EDITOR.

8
The cheap domestic magazine

The 'New Journalism' of the 1880s and 1890s was sometimes characterised as providing cheap poor-quality journals for the quarter-educated. Although this was an over-simplification, there was a general widening of target readerships among journals for women and this included the emergence of a new kind of illustrated magazine which was cheap, chatty in tone and domestic in focus. Like the well-established penny or half-penny serials which were associated with working-class women's reading, these magazines were inexpensive (usually a penny), were usually weekly and included fiction. However, they defined themselves as healthy as against the sensational and 'unhealthy' fiction serial and they offered a mixed diet of chatty short articles on housekeeping, care of children and gossip about royalty or the famous; illustrated interviews; fashion news; chats about books, competitions, and advice columns on a range of issues, as well as fiction. They were printed on cheap paper but lavishly illustrated. Such titles as *Home Sweet Home*, *Home Notes* and *Home Chat*, signalled their domestic emphasis. These magazines wooed the large commercial advertisers and were heavily dependent on advertising, which was scattered through the magazines and mixed with editorial material. Women's journals of this kind were central to the publishing strategies of Harmsworth, Pearson and Newnes, the three publishers whose rise to power in the 1890s laid the foundations of their press dominance in the twentieth century. However, similar journals were published by smaller houses like the Woman Publishing Company which produced the penny weekly, *Woman*.

8.1

Woman (1890–1912), unlike the other penny weeklies, acquired something of a reputation for being 'advanced'. However, as its cover and motto suggest, it was a cheerful but conservative magazine which offered chatty short articles, domestic 'wrinkles' (that is advice or 'tips'), extensive fashion notes with patterns and advice on dressmaking, short fictions and tit-bitty articles under various editorial pseudonyms. It was also typical in its dependence on advertising. Arnold Bennett edited it during the 1890s writing under such pseudonyms as Sal Volatile or Barbara.

See FIGURE 16.

8.2

The cheap domestic magazines for women were at the centre of the 1890s battle for the new feminine reading public. Harmsworth set the pace with *Forget-Me-Not* (1891–1918) and *Home Sweet Home* (1893–1901) but it was not until 1894, when Pearson launched the monthly *Home Notes* (1894–1957), that the first long-running penny magazine for women began. It was a substantial penny worth and included fashion notes and free paper patterns along with domestic advice, chatty articles, and fiction.

FIGURE 16 Cover, *Woman*, no. 224, 1894

'Fireside Talks', *Home Notes*, vol. 2, 1895, pp. 193–94. See also FIGURE 17.

"BUSINESS is business" we often hear, and women who earn their own livings have special need to remember this, for we are not living in an age of chivalry, but at the end of the nineteenth century, when political economy, and the survival of the fittest are far more thought of than old-world deference and respect for our sex.

From stern necessity many women enter into competition with men, and perhaps a few do so from choice, but whatever their motive, they should all act in the same spirit. They should do their utmost to acquire business habits and methods, and to master all the details and technicalities of the trade, or profession into which they have entered. If a girl means to get on she must expect no immunity from hardships or disagreeables because of her sex, and above all she must, if well-born, expect no extra consideration because she happens to be "a lady."

Honest work, done to the best of her power, does not lessen the dignity of any woman, and a hard-working, self-respecting girl is pretty sure to make herself respected wherever she may be, and all the more so because she is modest and not self-assertive.

Men very generally have special business clothes, and I think that women would do well to follow their example in this, for certainly to be well-dressed one's clothes must be suitable. What looks worse than the shabby finery one so often sees worn by business women. Their clothes may once have been pretty but they are unsuitable for daily wear in all weathers, and soon get untidy in a way which would be impossible were they plainly made and close-fitting.

* * *

IN the bringing up of children it is very important not to lose sight of the fact that child-nature is three-sided; for if this be not considered their education will be defective.

In education, the moral, physical and intellectual sides of child-life all have to be trained and developed, to make a well-proportioned human being, and neither side must be developed at the sacrifice of the others.

How often one sees mothers who ignore this principle in the education of their children! Some, for instance, thinking too much of their bodily health, fall into the error of giving them excellent physical training, but treat the intellect as if it were almost unworthy of consideration. Then again, the ambitious mother, who wants to see her boys rise in the world, is liable to make so much of the intellectual side of education that she almost loses sight of that which has to do with morality. On the other hand, a religious, simple-minded woman in her desire that the

FIGURE 17 'Fireside Talks', masthead, p. 193

child may be good, perhaps cultivates the moral side of his nature, and lets the intellectual and physical sides take care of themselves.

Now all these systems are wrong, for each of the three sides of the child needs careful training; that all may be developed simultaneously and harmoniously into a perfect whole.

* * *

ENGLISH lady cyclists have not the daring of their American sisters. Knickerbockers are but little worn over here, but I hear that in New York hundreds of women wear them when on wheels.

* * *

THE Queen keeps a birthday book at Windsor, Osborne and Balmoral, and any artist who appears before her is requested to sign his or her name in it. In this way Her Majesty gets an interesting collection of autographs of artists who have in one way or another contributed to her pleasure, and no doubt they are all very willing to gratify her wish.

* * *

THE third number of *Dressmaking at Home* is now on sale, and by its large circulation I am sure that a large number of readers of *Home Notes* must already know it. I would, however, draw the attention of new readers to this most useful publication. It is published on the first of every month, and contains sixteen pages, profusely illustrated by the best fashion artists of the day. No expense or trouble has been spared to make this paper the best of its kind . . .

The price of *Dressmaking at Home* is only 1d. a month, an absurdly low rate when it is remembered that, besides all of which I have spoken before, it contains every month a paper pattern of a new and fashionable garment . . . Any lady can follow our free patterns, for not only are they accurately cut, but with each is given a diagram showing how to lay the pattern on the cloth.

* * *

The demand for our paper has been so great that I would advise readers to order their copies early, or better still, to place an order for a year with their newsagent for this will ensure their getting a copy each month.

8.3

Harmsworth responded to the launch of *Home Notes* (1894–1957) with *Home Chat* (1895–1958) perhaps the most successful of all the penny papers, though Newnes' *Woman's Life* (1895–1934) also had huge sales. *Home Chat* made available information about fashion and advice on appearance to a wider readership than ever before. However, it also offered to help the reader in her work as a domestic woman with care of children and housework, concerns addressed in advice columns, children's pages and also in the now ubiquitous advertisements.

'Toilet Queries', *Home Chat*, vol. 5, 1901, pp. 510–11. See also FIGURE 18.

"MY teeth will remain yellow-looking, though I clean them very regularly, and I cannot get them to look white, try as I will."

Some teeth are much yellower than others, and, do what you will, they will never become white. But they may have become this colour from taking iron or steel medicines. In this case, take your medicine in future through a tube. To clean the teeth, try powdered charcoal mixed with salt. This will often succeed where other things fail, and use tooth-powders in preference to pastes.

* * *

"I suffer terribly from cramp in my feet; the pain is making me look very old. What is the cause, and is there anything to stop it?"

FIGURE 18 Facing advertising and children's pages, *Home Chat*, vol. 4, 1900, pp. 118–19

The cause is usually some disorder of the liver, or a gouty, rheumatic tendency. Consult a doctor about it. Avoid carefully everything sweet, and drink lemonade with your dinner. When the cramp comes on, move your big toe about, however painful. Rub below the knee hard with the hand, and stand on your bare feet, and take a little strong carbonate of soda and water.

* * *

"After dancing or exertion in a close room my face gets red and spotted very much, besides having a greasy look. Can you give my a simple remedy? I use powder on it, but that does not cure it."

The use of the powder is what makes the face in the state it has got into. Don't wear too tight a bodice, and wash your face in tepid water before you go to your dance, and take a light meal, not a heavy one, before you start. Be careful what you eat for supper; avoid ices and wine, and rub on a face-cream at night.

* * *

"Can you recommend me simple exercises for the muscles of the face? My face seems too full, and I have criss-cross lines all over it. Should I use almond-oil at night, rubbing with a loofah?"

If you use a rough loofah on the soft, delicate skin of your face you will quite ruin it. Night and morning relax the muscles of the face by gently pushing the skin upwards on the cheeks. Rub in a little face-cream with the fingers across the lines, and gently wipe off with a bit of chamois leather. Almond-oil is good. Diet carefully, avoiding cream, much milk, sugar, bread, pastry, and cake, or fat meat. Take plenty of exercise of all kinds, and avoid close, hot rooms.

* * *

"My hair never seems to be nice or smooth and glossy after washing. What should I use as a shampoo that will not hurt the hair?"

A very good shampoo is to beat up a fresh egg in a pint of tepid water and use that. The water must not be hot, or the egg will set and be useless. Add a few drops of rosemary to the shampoo. Soap-and-water can also be used. Dry well and brush for some time after it is dry. You need a tonic, change of air, and to drink plenty of milk for a time.

* * *

"Is cold or hot water best to use in one's bath if one is troubled with rheumatism? and does hot water or cold make you grow fat soonest?"

It is always best, unless you are strong and robust, to use tepid water in your bath entirely, and most certainly if you are at all rheumatic. Very hot baths are apt to make you grow thin, as they are very weakening, and make you feel ill as well.

* * *

"I am a literary women and have begun, I fear, to suffer from 'writers' cramp,' as I begin to have a great pain in my right arm. Is there any cure?"

You must cease writing entirely with the right hand in this case. The pain and weakness is a sure forerunner of "writers' cramp," and there is no possible cure except entire rest. Use a typewriter for your work, and write with your left hand. You must give up sewing, and tennis, golf, &c., and use electricity and massage to the arm itself.

* * *

"What can be done to entertain wedding guests at a hotel reception after a very quiet wedding?"

You need not entertain then at all. Give them light refreshments, and let them look at the wedding presents and talk to each other. Under the circumstances, the bride should change her dress and start on her wedding journey as soon as possible, so as to allow the party to break up.

* * *

"We want to be married from home. What steps must we take to do this legally?"

One of you must live for three Sundays in the parish you wish to to be married in, while banns are put or a licence is procured. If you wish to be married by a registrar and not in church, you must still put in twenty-two days of residence in the same parish before your marriage can be performed.

* * *

"Is it allowable to send P.P.C. card by post to people with whom I have only a slight calling acquaintance who live at a distance?"

It is perfectly permissible to do so where people live near, and yet you have no time to spare to call on them. Send the cards in an addressed envelope by a servant, or merely leave the cards yourself at the door. This can be done two weeks or so before you leave the neighbourhood. Those by post can go a few days only before.

* * *

"I am living in Berlin, and would like full particulars as to how to get my son in the English Navy as an officer."

He must be of pure European descent and the son of either natural-born British subjects, or of parents naturalised in the United Kingdom. He must have a nomination from the First Lord of the Admirality, or from those naval officers who hold the right of giving them, and must not be less than thirteen. He must be in good health, and free from all physical defects and hereditary disease, and be well-developed and active for his age. And besides producing certificates of birth and good conduct, he must pass an examination before he is permitted to become a naval cadet on the "Britannia."

8.4

This cover from Newnes' *Woman's Life* (1895–1934) shows all the classic features of the penny domestic magazines, including the stress on illustration and on being 'bright and attractive' – adjectives applicable to the reader as well as her magazine. It carried the well-established mixture of magazine genres and also put side by side the domestic and the fashionable, the conservative and aspects of the 'New Woman'.

See FIGURE 19.

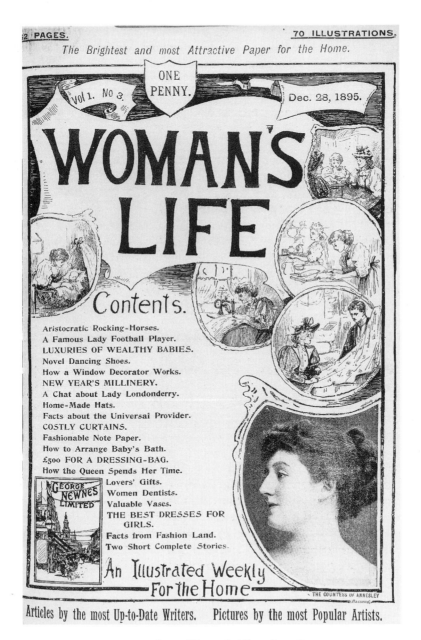

FIGURE 19 Cover, *Woman's Life*, vol. 1, 1895

Above all, the cheap domestic magazines offered themselves as entertainment. Fiction remained a crucial element in the attractions they offered. Unlike those from the mid-Victorian era, these magazines tended toward short complete fictions or series of linked stories rather than long serials. This complete short story from *Woman's Life* (1895–1934) was illustrated in the original. It gives the typical romance theme a new twist.

'Madge Smith's Revenge', *Woman's Life*, vol. 1, 1895, pp. 76–78.

THE west was all aflame with the autumn sunset ere Cora Smith and her little twelve-year-old sister Madge closed the cottage door behind them and ran down the garden path towards the stile, where hazel-eyed, sweet-faced Cora Smith's lover was waiting for his lady-love, as she had many a night waited for him.

Almost every evening they met there at the stile—their "trysting place," he said—just half way between her home and his rooms. He had proposed it, and she was nothing loth to accede, it was so pretty and romantic.

Aunt Smith was not at all pleased with this dark-eyed young fellow, and though she had not forbidden Neil Rowan the house, both lovers knew that she preferred "his room to his company."

"Neil, Neil," she said, almost unconsciously, aloud; and little Madge clasped her sister's hand closer and looked up in her face.

"Do you love him so very much, sister Cora?"

"Better than all the world; better than my life. And I am to be his wife, little Madge, when the beautiful spring comes. I shall leave you all to be his. But this is our secret, and only you can share it."

They were almost nearing the edge of the wood, and the stile was but a few steps away. Another step forward and then Madge held her sister back.

"Wait!" she whispered; "I see two men on the seat, Cora. We do not want to meet strangers there."

"No," she said; "it is Neil's friend, Willis Dean. We will wait until he goes, for I do not care to meet him."

Even as she spoke the figure rose, and the sound of his voice came on the twilight air distinct and clear.

"And what of this love affair, Neil? When is it to end, and how? Are you really in earnest, and do you mean to marry the girl?"

Cora Smith's hand closed upon the arm of Madge till she shrank in pain while they waited for the answer. Neil Rowan laughed softly.

"Marry her!" he repeated. "She is just the subject for a splendid flirtation, and I assure you I have done the thing well; but for anything further—bah! I am going back to town to-morrow, and this is our last meeting; so be off, old fellow, for I expect her every moment."

Just for one moment Madge Smith's heart stood still in awful fear, for she thought Cora would faint. Without a word she rose and glided away, and Madge followed her in silence.

Neil Rowan waited for some time.

"She isn't coming to-night," he said to himself, "that is certain. The scheming aunt no doubt managed to prevent it this time. Oh, well, it saved a scene. I will drop a loving farewell note, and so it ends—a summer's amusement."

The farewell note came to Cora Smith the following night. Meantime she fell ill, and fever ensued. Ere the insane light gave place to reason again death sealed the white eyelids.

Day by day, week by week, month by month, so sped the time until eight years were counted.

Eight times the grass had grown over the little grave in the lonely country churchyard, and again the October winds rustled the autumn leaves over the narrow mound.

Wonderful changes had the eight years brought. Side by side with this grave were two others, and the headstones bore the names of both Aunt and Uncle Smith. They had rested there six years, and every summer beautiful Madge Smith came down from her house in town and lingered in the old home a week, trimming the grasses and planting bright flowers on the graves. Bright, beautiful Madge Smith, the heiress of all Uncle Smith's hidden wealth, the wealth he guarded so well during that toil-worn life.

Three years before, Madge Smith left school to reign queen of society. Beautiful, strangely beautiful, with that cold, white, high-bred face, those wide, fathomless, glittering amber eyes, a figure matchless in symmetry and grace, accomplished, polished, and the heiress of great wealth —no wonder that lovers, old and young, knelt at her shrine. Strange wonder, the world said, that all were scorned—not gently and with words of pity and apology, but spurned from her very feet with scornful lips and blazing eyes.

Never were those lips seen to smile, or those wonderful eyes to soften in response to any lovers; no glacier was more frigid than she to all men. All, did I say? Only a few weeks since a new rival appeared on the scene of action. Neil Rowan, merchant and millionaire, entered the list of Madge Smith's adorers—not for her wealth, but, he said, for her beauty alone. He had enough wealth. It was genuine love that this man felt for beautiful Madge. A wonderful change had come over the fair lady since his appearance. Bright before, she was brilliant now—sparkling, witty, bewildering; and the world looked on in amaze to see the flush stain her white cheek, and the bright smile light up her eyes at his approach.

And did he not recognise her? you are wondering. How should he? Cora Smith and the summer in the country were forgotten things with this man. He had broken half-a-dozen silly hearts since then, and left them all with Time, the great healer. He had flirted and left the past all behind him. And now he came and laid the first pure, real love of his lifetime at this woman's feet. So he told her, one autumn night, in the grand saloon of her stately home.

How her hands trembled and her eyes shone as she listened.

"Wait," she said, "I will give you my answer to-morrow night; it is my birthday, and I shall give an entertainment. You will come? I will answer you then. Be in the library at ten, and you shall hear my answer."

And the night came, and he was there, waiting. He paced the room impatiently. Would she ever come, this girl who was dearer than life? The world had seemed stale, flavourless, until he met her, the woman who alone, of all her sex, had ever stirred the slumbering passion of his heart.

Just then he heard the light ripple of a woman's laugh in the adjoining room. Her laugh; he knew it among a thousand; and her voice—she was speaking loud and clear.

"There, now, you must let me go. Mr. Rowan is waiting for me in the library. You know I am to give him my answer to-night."

And her guardian's voice, speaking tenderly, replied:

"And that answer—I can guess it, Madge. You are going to marry him and leave us all."

She laughed softly.

"Marry him! No, indeed, sir. He is just the subject for a splendid flirtation, and I assure you I have done the thing well; but for anything further—bah! But he is expecting me, so bye-bye till I come again," and she tripped lightly through the half-open door, ere the amazed guardian could utter a syllable.

A white, ghastly, shivering figure stood by the library window.

"For mercy's sake, Madge Smith, tell me you were jesting!" he cried, as glowingly beautiful she glided into the room.

"Not so, Mr. Rowan," she answered, "I spoke the truth. If you overheard my words I need not repeat them. It is my decision."

"But you gave me hope; you led me on; you have given me reason to think you loved me!" he cried passionately. "It is the one love of my life! I have centred every hope and thought in you, Madge, and for my sake, for mercy's sake, do not wreck my life!"

She was very pale now, and her eyes were black and glistening.

"Neil Rowan," she said, slowly, "I have prayed for this hour for eight years, but never in my wildest dreams did I think my prayer would be so fully answered. When I saw the hue of death, the white agony on my only sister's cheek, when I saw her writhe in speechless agony at the words she heard eight years ago to-night, I vowed to avenge her. Again, when I heard the thud of the earth upon her coffin, I vowed that vow. Fate has brought it about even sooner, more completely than I expected. If I have given you one hour of such agony as she suffered I am content; if you could live and suffer it for countless ages I should be better content. Good night!"

Shortly afterwards the sharp ring of a pistol rang with startling distinctness through the crowded drawing-room. All sprang to their feet, save Madge Smith. Perhaps her cheek paled a little—I cannot tell—but the light of her eye never changed, her smiling lips never relaxed as she gazed upon the blood-stained corpse in the library. Neil Rowan had taken his own life, and Cora Smith was avenged.

PART II

in which we represent the range of genres featured in women's magazines of the Victorian period

9
Mastheads and covers

Though it is often difficult to find copies of magazine covers, some do survive, particularly from the end of the century. Some kinds of magazine especially ladies' papers and general magazines had elaborate mastheads. Later magazines began to use attractive covers. These were designed to induce the reader to buy as well as give her an idea of the magazine's character and contents.

9.1, 9.2

Mastheads: see FIGURES 20, 21.

FIGURES 20, 21 Mastheads: *The Lady's Own Paper*, vol. 2, 1866; *The Queen*, vol. 87, 1890

9.3, 9.4, 9.5, 9.6, 9.7

Covers: see FIGURES 22–26.

FIGURE 22
Cover, *The Servant's Magazine*,
vol. 1, new series, no. 4, 1867

FIGURE 23
Cover, *The Barmaid*, vol. 1, no. 1, 1891

FIGURE 24
Cover, *Home Notes*, vol. 2, no. 26, 1894

THE
SERVANTS'
MAGAZINE.

NEW SERIES.

1867.

LONDON:
S. W. PARTRIDGE & Co., 9, PATERNOSTER ROW.

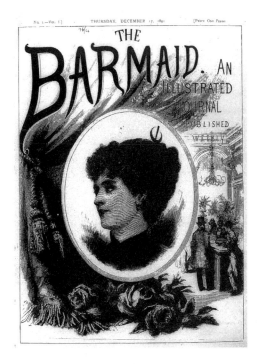

"SHAFTS": Monthly, 3d.; post free, 3½d.
Annual Subscription, Country and Abroad, 3s. 6d.
Offices: 11, Westbere Road, West Hampstead, London, N.W.

APRIL,
1897.

Vol. 5. No. 4.

SHAFTS

A PAPER FOR WOMEN

& THE WORKING CLASSES

LICHT COMES TO THOSE WHO DARE TO THINK

WISDOM
JUSTICE
TRUTH

CONTENTS

EDITED BY
MARGARET SHURMER SIBTHORP.

OH, SWIFTLY SPEED, YE SHAFTS OF LIGHT
WHILE HOSTS OF DARKNESS FLY:
FAIR BREAKS THE DAWN: FAST ROLLS THE NIGHT
FROM WOMAN'S DARKENED SKY.

"SHAFTS" is published to the Trade by Messrs. Dawbarn & Ward, Limited,
6, Farringdon Avenue, London, E.C., on the 15th of each month.

FIGURE 25 Cover, *Shafts*, vol. 5, no. 4, 1897

THE NEW ½d. STORY PAPER FOR BRITISH GIRLS.

SWEETHEARTS ½d

SIXTEEN PAGES OF LOVE, COURTSHIP, AND ROMANCE.

"OUT OF THE WAY—RUN FOR YOUR LIFE," HE SHOUTED. (SEE PAGE 2.)

| FULL OF THRILLING LOVE STORIES. | "A Lover of High Degree" "In Cupid's Toils" "Roma's Reward" BEAUTY SECRETS: ADVICE TO LOVERS LOVERS' DREAMS, Etc., Etc. | A MOST FASCINATING SERIAL NOVEL. |

FIGURE 26 Cover, *Sweethearts*, vol. 1, no. 2, 1898

10

Discursive prose: the article

Sharp distinctions between the different categories of prose in magazines cannot be drawn. There was a general tendency in most types of magazine for the article to fall easily into the mode of the advice column. Some articles deployed narrative techniques which made them close to fiction. However, it is still useful to distinguish the general article as a genre, which, together with fiction, was the crucial element in all magazines. Sometimes articles were simply fillers separating the more important elements of the magazine. However, the general article – informative and usually authoritative in tone – could and did offer instruction and social comment on a range of topics. Certain broad subject areas recurred in different magazines: historical narratives, travel writing, discussion of domestic and social issues particularly those which affected women. There were also certain themes which kept returning in different journals, the relationship of mistresses and domestic servants was one such. Other topics became the focus of a flurry of articles at one particular moment and then disappeared. Unlike the newspapers, magazines did not always carry editorials but instead offered a range of different kinds of editorial comment, sometimes in answers to correspondents, sometimes as a puff for the magazine, sometimes as a piece of discursive prose on a topical issue which might be indistinguishable from another general article.

10.1

Religious and evangelical magazines relied heavily on the article together with reports of meetings or accounts of work in the mission field, either at home or abroad. Printed in close type and unillustrated, these articles were unrelentingly serious in tone and didactic in intent.

'Hints to Young Ladies. No. IX. Habits of Conversation', *The Mothers' Magazine*, vol. 4, 1838, pp. 158–63.

OUR habits of conversation are sometimes understood to embrace our entire intercourse with one another. This is a very natural application of the term, since our whole intercourse is held and conducted through the medium of speech. The powerful influence we exert on one another, is a sufficient reason for all the cautions expressed in the word of God on this subject, and may well justify the place we now assign it in these hints.

But it may be asked—"Why address young ladies *particularly* on such a subject as this?" They are at liberty, then, to presume that I would say nothing to them, which I would not also say to all others. Yet I will claim the special attention of young ladies for one reason, which conveys a compliment:—their controlling influence, and their acknowledged powers of conversation, impose a weight of responsibility on *them*, which attaches to no other class. These very circumstances, too, surround them with peculiar temptations as well as responsibilities. A sword may be harmless when kept under bolts and bars, or when wielded by a man of prudence and peace. But in the hand of a maniac, or of unprincipled ambition, who would not fear it? Without a figure, young ladies can kill with their tongues; and the chivalry, which would resent a rude affront, yields its feelings, and even truth and life itself, to gallantry. Weapons capable of such a use, you will say, ought always to be true, and controlled by stern principle and prudence.

. . .

How much we are influenced by conversation, all can testify. What we hear makes a direct impression on the mind. We carry it home, think of it, repeat it, converse upon it. We do not readily expel the image it has formed in the mind, whether of pleasure or of pain. We attend a social party. What was said there forms the object of attention which we carry with us: what *we* have said is carried away by others. We hear of it again. It is ours. It must be maintained. It decides our course, and controls our characters. If it be wrong, we try to persuade ourselves it is right. It is right in our premises. We cannot recede. If it be a sword, which has entered deeply into the reputation of our neighbour, we hold the hilt, and our reputation becomes involved also. If it be a fire kindled on our neighbour's dwelling, we have struck the spark, and must justify the deed.

Passions become flagrant by indulgence. Speech is one of the channels of gratification. Bad tempers, restrained, are more easily controlled than after they have been permitted to express themselves and come abroad through the organs of speech. They have then pervaded another portion of the body, and claim all the territory they thus acquire. Malignant passions may be stifled in the bosom; but, like combustible gases, they explode when exposed to atmospheric air, and in contact with the fire of the tongue. Such is our experience; and hence it is not, perhaps, without a reason in the constitution of human nature that the sin, which has no forgiveness, employs the tongue to reach its transcendent enormity. Our words are our own only while they remain unexpressed. When published, they are common property. They present our character, and we must be judged by it. An eminent Roman, surnamed Silentius, condemned himself to silence for nine years, because he had been imprudent in his speech. Better thus to be silent for ever; yes, better to cut out the tongue as well as to pluck out a right eye, than to make them the instruments of our condemnation to hell.

. . .

The first rule we should prescribe to ourselves will teach us not to talk too much. The mind is strengthened by reflection. But great talkers are rarely deep thinkers. They advance shallow opinions diluted by a flood of words. As words are the signs of ideas, a tongue that can never be silent must use thoughts as they rise, without selection or maturity. Such is the language of the maniac, between whom and a perpetual talker the resemblance is too striking not to have been remarked by all.

. . .

Avoid all profaneness in conversation. Profane expressions are too common even among ladies, where profanity, as that term is commonly understood, is excluded. All is profane which weakens in the mind a reverence for God, and which, either in word or sentiment, associates unworthy thoughts of him. How often do we hear from a thoughtless tongue the exclamation, "O Lord!" If it be not used malignantly or profanely, yet it borders on profanity, and indicates the absence of that high reverence which should always be associated with every name we apply to Jehovah.

. . .

There are yet two or three practical rules which belong to this subject, and which my limits only allow me to allude to. First, let me say, never interrupt others while speaking. To do it, is the height of impoliteness. A true *gentleman*, you may have observed, never does it. A real *lady* will not do it. If she does, her character is yet incomplete. When I see two young ladies talking at the same time, and in the same circle, and on the same subject, in a contest of words to see which shall outrun the other, I say to myself, there has been some mistake in their education.

Do you know any such young ladies? And what are you compelled, in sober reason, to think of them? Let your answer to this question furnish you with a rule for your own direction.

Another rule, which good sense and propriety will dictate, is not to talk too long. This error naturally leads to the former. After stating our opinion, common civility requires that we should wait for the opinions of others. When the subject has been suitably discussed, or is exhausted, dismiss it. The introduction of a new one will impart the charm of novelty, and awaken fresh interest. Never monopolize the conversation, especially if others are engaged in it. After they have heard *you*, listen to *them* without impatience. Even if their conversation is not as interesting to you as your own has been, it is a gross self-compliment and a breach of good manners to yawn through their reply, or be inattentive to it.

Talk not too loud. This is rude; and nothing but endurance, sometimes extended towards it too far, prevents it from being despicable. It certainly is inconsistent with true modesty; it offends delicacy; it is an annoyance to all sober thinkers, and is in very bad taste. You never heard a lady talk on a sober subject, nor make a sensible remark, in a loud, overreaching, or boisterous tone. A subdued manner is suited to rational conversation. It is the soft tones which attract the surest attention. Gentlemen may be *amused* by a great talker and forward manners, but they will reserve their *affections* for the modest and sensible young lady, who speaks in an under tone, with the confidence which knowledge inspires, and amid the blushes of that natural modesty so absolutely necessary to female influence and dignity . . .

10.2

Articles in the drawing-room journals were often educational and serious in tone but broader in their range than the religious magazines, and appeared in well-produced formats, sometimes with engraved illustrations. Historical writing was a favourite as in this abridged article from *Mrs. Ellis' Morning Call* (1850–52).

'The Women of England in Olden Times. The Anglo-Saxon Ladies', *Mrs. Ellis' Morning Call*, vol. 1, 1852, pp. 27–33.

No theme can be more welcome to our readers of every class than "the women of England,"— that sex to whom *we* especially among nations owe so much of our happiness, of our domestic character, even of our national glory. "The women of England" is a theme which belongs not exclusively to the present—it is also eminently a theme of the past; for our fair countrywomen have in all ages of history held a conspicuous place for their private and public virtues, as well as for their personal charms. If, as is no doubt the case, there be a national distinction even in women, it must be an interesting task to trace that distinction historically, either in one country by itself, or in several comparatively; and thus to investigate the origin or reasons of the distinctive character, and view woman's position at different periods, and under different aspects of society. Woman possesses naturally a mind perhaps more uniform than that of man—it is the harder and harsher sex which gives the character to an age or a people—womankind receives the impression, but, modified as it is in the transfer, she perpetuates it, and probably exercises a greater influence on the character of the succeeding generation than man himself. Under no circumstances is the powerful though gentle influence of woman on the national character more visible, than in the various branches of that great stock of nations which has peopled Western Europe; no doubt because amongst them, from the remotest period to which history carries us back, the female sex has been treated with that respectful devotion which shows a conviction of its true share in the happiness and civilization of mankind. In no case is this more true than when applied to "the women of England," and it is our intention in a series of papers, to trace their condition and manners at different periods, from the moment when they first accompanied their Saxon fathers and husbands over the wide waters to these shores. We shall devote this first paper to a hasty sketch of the state of female society under the Anglo-Saxons, during a period which unfortunately has left us but little exact information relating to domestic manners.

During the whole Anglo-Saxon period, the position which the gentler sex held in English society appears to have undergone very little change, and we trace in it those characteristics which are still considered to be the best traits of English domestic life. The Anglo-Saxon woman was the attentive housewife, the tender companion, the comforter and consoler of her husband and family, the virtuous and noble matron. Domestic life was in that age simple in character, and scarcely differed in its forms and sentiments from the palace to the cottage. The queen attended to her domestic duties equally with the wife of the burgher.

. . .

The Anglo-Saxon ladies bore the character of being superior workwomen, and especially of being skilful embroiderers. A foreign chronicler, who wrote in the eleventh century, assures us that "the French and Normans admired the beautiful dresses of the English nobility; for the English women excel all others in needlework and in embroidering with gold." And we are told by another writer of the same age, that their work was so peculiar that it was well known on the continent by the appellation of "English work," (*opus Anglicum*). Work of this kind formed the usual occupation of ladies even in the most exalted station in life. The four princesses, sisters of king Athelstan (early in the tenth century) were celebrated for their skill in spinning, weaving, and embroidering; and Editha, the queen of Edward the Confessor, the last of the Anglo-Saxon monarchs, was also known as an accomplished needle-woman . . . In the correspondence of the earliest Anglo-Saxon ecclesiastics, the ladies also took a part by writing letters, and they are frequently spoken of, and they always appear with the same amiable character. In the various vicissitudes of their country, ravaged by intestine (*sic*) wars, and often depopulated by the invasions of the ferocious Danes, the ties of society were at times loosened, and evil and violent passions, with their usual concomitants, selfishness and licentiousness, spread their corruption around; yet, in spite of all this, the women seem to have escaped censure far more universally than the men; and even at a later period, when the Anglo-Saxons are accused of aping the vices and extravagances of the Normans, which were introduced at the court of Edward the Confessor, it appears that the ladies mostly preserved their old simplicity of manners and dress, while their husbands sought after novelty in both. The women remained at home exercising their domestic duties with unostentatious virtue, while the men went abroad to indulge their vanity and pride.

It is to be lamented that we know so little of the domestic economy of the Anglo-Saxons. . . . Here and there history has preserved an anecdote which gives us a glimpse, though slight, of the interior of the Saxon mansion. Every reader will remember the story of the Saxon queen Osburgha, the mother of the great Alfred, how she sat in her room, surrounded by her children, and encouraging them in a taste for literature, when her illuminated volume of Saxon poetry rivetted the attention of the young Alfred, and first gave him that thirst for learning which distinguished him ever after . . .

The Anglo-Saxon women, left, as we have said, much at home, frequently found leisure for literary occupations, and it appears from many circumstances that they were much less deficient in learning even than their husbands. The male children, up to a certain age, were left entirely to their care. We see that it was to his mother, and not to his father, that king Alfred owed his love of learning. We will conclude our notice of the Anglo-Saxon ladies with another anecdote of an accomplished princess, Editha the queen of Edward the Confessor. Ingulph, a monk of Croyland was her contemporary, and, as it appears, her personal acquaintance. There is a chronicle attributed to him, but of the authenticity of which some doubts have been expressed. He is there made to give an account of his younger days, when he went to school at Westminster, and he says of this amiable princess—"I have very often seen her in my boyhood, when I used to go to visit my father, who was employed about the court. I often met her as I came from school, and then she questioned me about my studies and my verses; and willingly passing from grammar to logic, she would catch me in the subtleties of argument. She always gave me two or three pieces of money, which were counted to me by her handmaiden, and then sent me to the royal larder to refresh myself."

This anecdote, gives us a notion of the great simplicity of domestic manners among our Anglo-Saxon forefathers even in the palace of royalty.

10.3

Fashion magazines also carried short articles, which were often lighter in tone than those in the drawing-room or even the general illustrated magazines. This satiric account of the bloomer comes from a magazine which, with various name changes and mergers, lasted from 1824 to 1891.

'The Adventures of Isabel Fitzbloomer. Narrated by Herself. In a Confidential Communication to Mrs. Kate Norton', *The World of Fashion*, vol. 27, 1850, p. 125.

> "Yes, once there was a form thus heavenly bright,
> But now 'tis veil'd in everlasting night;
> Each glory which that lovely form could boast,
> In graceless aids and hopeless aims is lost."
>
> ANON.

I LISTENED to sweet voices, that were wafted upon light and western breezes over the Atlantic. I said in my dreaming that the rights of women would never be acknowledged until we demonstrated the fact, to lordly man that we are as capable of wearing with dignity similar garments as well as exercising the same intellectual faculties, as himself. It is universally admitted that woman does not receive justice from her (so styled) "lord and master," the right of mastery being incapable of proof. I therefore resolved to put on the costume which some ladies in America have adopted, and as I possess what may be termed a fine figure, I believed that I should exhibit that costume to advantage!

I was not dismayed by the doubts of my friends of the propriety of this resolution, because my friends all happen to be short of stature, and some of them inclining to the order of figure which is called "dumpy;" and I observe that people in general have strong objections to things that exhibit any particular want of grace or personal deformity which they themselves may happen to possess. Long dresses, for instance, are enthusiastically admired by ladies who can make no pretensions to the slipper of Cinderella, whilst short dresses are as earnestly recommended by those whose feet are small. "Chacun a son gout!" said I to myself, and resolved to be a Bloomer.

I fancy that I looked particularly smart in the new costume. My Roman outline of countenance told well above the black silk Joinville which I wore round my neck; and as I have always dressed my hair in the fashion of Young France, my appearance, I flattered myself, as rather manly and commanding.

I was amusing myself at the piano one morning, when a friend of my brother's Capt.— of the Guards who came in accidentally and was conversing with Fred at the other end of the room, came up and offered me his case of cigars—believing that I was really a man!

I was rather annoyed at this, because, although a champion of women's rights, I hope always to enjoy the high and noble prerogative of my sex, and to obtain the respect that is due to women.

It was a rainy day, and my maid, who had been out on some commission, returned in a public vehicle, the extortionate driver of which created some confusion at the door. I went down into the hall, to see what was the matter, when the very vulgar fellow exclaimed to the young woman (who can be impertinent when she pleases, and who had, no doubt, exasperated him) "If you was a man, I'd knock you down; and as you a'nt, I'll give it to young master there, in your stead!" Forthwith he rushed at me, and I quite believe he would have struck me, if John the porter had not stepped between us, and thrown the impertinent fellow over the threshold. The worst remains behind. I knew that I had made a decided impression upon Algernon Harrowby. He had, in fact, told me so. I was happy! Suddenly he discontinued his visits. I could not imagine the reason. I set my brother Fred to inquire. It was long before Fred could meet with him; and when he did, it was in a railway carriage, and Algernon's destination was the Continent! Judge of my consternation, when Fred returned to tell me that Algernon Harrowby was shocked by my inconstancy—my perfidy! He had seen, as he rode past my house, a gentleman kissing me in my own room!

Terrible mistake! The "gentleman" was myself! The individual mistaken for me was my cousin Mary, from the country, who is rather like me in point of figure; and to who I had made a present of my English dresses, when I adopted the American.

Algernon has not returned to England. But I renounced the "Bloomer" costume directly the mistake was discovered.

10.4

Travel narratives and accounts of other lands were a perennial favourite throughout the period. They were a feature of the drawing-room journal but persisted into the ladies' papers, religious, general illustrated and girls' magazines. *The Ladies' Treasury* (1858–95) was the most long-lasting of the general illustrated magazines. It retained some features of the drawing-room journal alongside the lighter tone and stress on illustration of the newer types. This abridged article was illustrated in the original.

'Persia and the Persians', *The Ladies' Treasury*, vol. 5, 1859, pp. 135–38.

PERSIA is one of those countries which history, romance, and poetry have invested with a peculiar charm. The great events which have marked its history, the imposing magnificence of the details, perplexing the imagination with images of countless multitudes of people, of exhaustless wealth, and of almost boundless power, have led to the conclusion that Persia must abound in all the elements of prosperity. But this charm is dispelled by personal observation. In Persia, absolutism exerts its most powerful influence. The Oriental vocabulary is exhausted to supply titles of honour and dignity for the monarch. We behold, in imagination, the mighty potentate, seated in a costly divan, his robes glittering with jewels, his court crowded with obsequious attendants, from the spendidly attired officials, comprising the executive government, to the Georgian and Circassian slaves, who, with dance and timbrel, amuse the leisure of the Shah. We gaze with the "mind's eye" on cities lifting their sunny domes and gilded minarets into the azure sky, surrounded by orchards and groves of trees. We look upon streets in which every object indicates the wealth and prosperity of the merchants, the taste and ingenuity of the architects, the religion and piety of the faithful. . . .

But the dazzling light of romance, and the gorgeous colours of history, have thrown over the whole country a delusive brilliancy which rapidly vanishes before the eye of the actual spectator.

Persian power has been declining since the days of Nadir Shah, and it seems impossible that this ancient monarchy should ever again assume that important rank which it formerly occupied amongst the countries of the East.

Two centuries ago, Chardin, who resided a long time in Persia, estimated its population at forty millions. At the present day, it does not exceed eight or ten millions. This decrease in the population is characteristic of the general decline of the country. Its military strength has changed considerably, and the army now is rather a species of police than a body of regular soldiers. The physical character of the people has also degenerated, so many migratory nations having settled in the country, that it contains only a fragment of its native race.

The despotic principle of the government is still ostensibly recognised, but some rude limits restrict the royal authority. The khans, on whom the defence of the country really depends, enjoy so many privileges that they exercise a most important influence over the absolutism of the Shah. In his own family only, the monarch is actually supreme, and he is allowed to nominate his successor. He may, if he pleases, instead of his legitimate son, choose the offspring of a slave, and set him on the throne of the empire. In former times this often occurred, and in order to secure the realm from civil broils, the Shah cut off the heads, or put out the eyes, of the rest of his progeny. His right to decapitate any individual, at his pleasure, is still recognised. In conversing with the British envoy, Futeh Ali pointed out the difference between Oriental and European sovereigns. "There," said he, "stand Solyman Khan Kajar, and several more of the chiefs of the empire—I can cut off their heads if I please. Can I not?" he added, addressing them. "Assuredly," they replied, "O Point of the World's Adoration!" "Now that," said the Shah, "is what I call real power."

It is to be questioned, however, whether Solyman Khan Kajar would have quietly submitted to the delicate operation of beheading, so long as he had a troop of mail-clad warriors at his back, and might with his sword strike off the monarch's crown.

. . .

Family influence is carried to a very great extent at the Persian court. Nepotism flourishes in the East as well as in the West. This is illustrated by the following anecdote:—Hajee Ibrahim was a noble of Ispahan. A shopkeeper of the capital went one day to the brother of Ibrahim, who was governor, to request exemption from a tax which he was unable to pay. "You must pay or leave the city," replied the governor. "Where shall I go?" asked the shopkeeper. "To Shiraz," was the reply. "Your nephew rules that city, and all your family are my enemies." "Then go to Cashan." "But your uncle is governor there." "Then complain to the Shah." "But your brother Hajee is prime minister." "Then go to the lower regions," exclaimed the governor, in a passion. "But your pious father is dead," retorted the shopkeeper. The nobleman burst into a laugh at the witty impudence of the man, and said, "Then I will pay your tax myself, as my family keeps you from all redress in this world and the next."

Persian ladies are not often seen in public; they dwell in those strictly Oriental habitations which Persians, as well as Moslems, recognise as appropriate to the married state, and the secrets of the harem seldom transpire. When they leave the house, they put on a cloak, which descends from the head to the feet, and their faces are carefully veiled, holes only being left for the eyes. "It is curious," says a recent writer, "to see a number of tall and elegantly formed figures walking in the streets, and presenting nothing to your view but a pair of sparkling black eyes, which seem to enjoy the curiosity they excite." The ladies are said to be exceedingly fair, of good complexion, with handsome features, and elegant figures. . . .

Marriage in Persia is celebrated with great magnificence. The parties are often betrothed in infancy, though they never see each other till they stand before the priest. "The nuptial ceremony must be witnessed by two men, or by one man and two women. When the bride is carried into the room allotted for her reception, the bridegroom appears, and sees her face for the first time in a looking-glass. He then takes a piece of sugar-candy, and, biting it in halves, eats one himself, and gives the other to his bride. He then takes her stockings, throws one over his left shoulder, places the other under his right foot, and the ceremony is complete." The feasting and rejoicing often last forty days. A man may divorce his wife at pleasure, and the only check to his arbitrary power is the scandal which attaches to the measure, and the necessity of returning the dower.

10.5

Articles on the press in general or specifically on the periodical in which the piece appeared became increasingly common as the century went on. This extract is from an article which acts not only as an editorial for the new feminist journal, *The Alexandra Magazine* (1864–65), but is also as an explanation of why the magazine as a genre was perceived as important to campaigners for women's rights.

'The Use of a Special Periodical', *The Alexandra Magazine*, vol. 1, 1865, pp. 257–63.

IN publishing the first united number of the two magazines whose names appear on the title page, the editor has asked me to write a few prefatory remarks, addressed to the friends of both; giving some of the motives for amalgamation, and the reason why it behoves those who care for the interests of working women of all classes to rally towards this joint effort.

The *Englishwoman's Journal* was started many years ago, at a time when very few people cared or wrote anything about the education or the work of our sex. The funds were contributed by people whose views differed in detail, but who were united in a desire to investigate the great mass of female misery and indigence existing in England ... That a very considerable change has been wrought in public opinion will hardly be denied, when the numerous pens now employed on these subjects are considered. This change has, of course, been far from solely due to the *Englishwoman's Journal*; but that periodical threaded the separate parts of the movements, brought the thinkers and the workers together, and, though never distinguished for intellectual excellence, it preserved a uniform tone of serious and sensible discussion, never degraded by frivolity, nor stained with a single sentence implying laxity of principle.

The time has come when it appears desirable to secure the diffusion of practical principles over a larger class of society, and in a cheaper form.

The starting of the *Alexandra Magazine* on a plan which, if not absolutely identical, was at least in close connection with the working aims of the older journal, has afforded this opportunity; and the two have been merged into one with an earnest hope that the change may be mutually advantageous;—that the joint periodical will, by reason of its greater cheapness, reach many homes into which the *Englishwoman's Journal* could not penetrate; and that the writers who have long contributed to its pages may bring an accession of thought to those of the *Alexandra Magazine*.

Of the use of a periodical in working these questions I have never entertained any doubt. It has been frequently urged, why not trust to the diffusion of ideas through the general press, now that editors and readers are so much more willing to accept them than they once were; and while each article thus written is certain to circulate far more widely than anything printed in a special magazine? But I am convinced there is something in a re-iterated effort which far outweighs the effect of the separate thoughts. It is not this or that number of a magazine, this or that article from a given pen, which does the work; it is partly the effect of repetition—line upon line—and partly the knowledge that there is in the world a distinct embodiment of certain principles ...

With regard to the particular principles on which such a journal should be conducted, it seems to me that the programme should be as wide and as general as may be. It is not possible to erect consistent water-tight theories upon the duties and interests of half the human race; the subject is too large, the details too various. The ground which each individual, and each writer or reader will feel to be *sure*, will be precisely that involved in his or her religious creed, but beyond that it appears to me a field for tentative excursions, and for the gathering of facts.

During the years that I conducted the *Englishwoman's Journal*, I tried, as far as possible, to admit both sides of the controversy with regard to the management of benevolent institutions; as, whether they should be managed by a carefully selected paid agency, or by those religiously dedicated to such work; or, by a mixture of the two? And so of the question, whether women should study and practise medicine; what branches they might reasonably and legitimately go through, what abjure? nor did I refuse letters denying the suitability of the study for them altogether; though most of those who started the journal were strongly in favour of it. As regards education, no editorial limit was imposed; nor any as to the introduction of women into business. The only subject which I steadily refused to discussion was the political one, believing it too impractical, in the present constitution of the world, to make it worth while to risk very vital and practical interests by the introduction of so unpopular an element.

Such were the main topics of the *Englishwoman's Journal*; those of the *Alexandra*, as I understand them, are to bring these still closer into practice, and to place them before women who are actually working for their livelihood—how to set about doing this or that, whom to apply to, what choice to make under various circumstances. Whereas the elder journal originally leant to the side of theory, largely interspersed with practical considerations, so the younger one leans to the side of practice without quite ignoring the underlying theories.

Such a journal ought, as far as possible, to be *organic*; not a mere machine used for the purposes of propaganda, but a living link between human intelligences. It does not matter that it be clever so much as it matters that it be honest. It should be worked out not by one but by many, under a certain supervision by one. It should not so much guide towards a definite end, for I do not believe that such can at present be discerned in the chaotic disorganization of feminine work which now afflicts us; but it should gather together all wholesome suggestions, all sound advice, all pertinent facts. Lastly, it should never be taken as a sample of what women can do. Those who have achieved prominent excellence in literature, whether prose or poetry, those who have struggled up to a remarkable or respectable position in art, are usually too much engrossed to devote much time to such efforts as this journal is destined to embody . . .

In resigning the practical control of the old journal, and in looking back over the years of editorship (and the two last years during which I have not actually occupied the post), it gives me joy to reflect that the estimate of women's capabilities, with which we began the periodical, has never seemed a deception. I believe it more difficult than I once did for a girl to attain special professional excellence, more difficult for her to be artist, author, tradeswoman; but my conviction of the strong common sense and moral excellence of Englishwomen, and of those American and French-women with whom I have been brought in contact, is greater than ever. The efficient organization of work is immensely more difficult than I once believed; the snares of life are far more frightfully dangerous than could ever have been divined by those who had then scarcely dived beneath the smooth surface of social *convenances*; but all the multiform experience of seven long years has only served to reveal the sterling stuff, the honest conscience, the substantial value of the great majority of those with whom we have been brought into connection. No effort, even on purely mortal and temporal grounds, would be too great to secure them maintenance, honourable professional status, or happy domestic life. For a few, or at least for the small minority of our sex, I would always crave an open possibility of intellectual advancement and creative toil. In the large majority, the duties and the happiness of domestic life will ever be the ideal lot . . .

The department which might be of the most special interest in relation to all such matters is that of correspondence—"Open Council," as it was called in *the Englishwoman's Journal*—and I can hardly understand why it never rose to greater literary excellence. Women are generally allowed to write good letters, and to give the reigns to expression, with great ease and elegance. We had plenty of sensible, well-expressed epistles, but the opportunity of uttering suggestions and ideas, of touching abuses with satire, or cheering the worker with sympathy, was not as largely used, as we had anticipated. Perhaps the habit of writing letters, as such, is gradually disappearing. Notes supply their place, and, except in foreign correspondence, we shall hardly leave to the next generation those models of familiar thought, applied to lively observation, which delight us in the epistolary literature of the 18th century. It is, however, a great loss in such a journal, when the lighter and more various element is sacrificed to solid articles. The lives of women are necessarily more broken up into details than are the lives of men. The existence of the house-wife comprises a perpetual adaption of skill to the exigencies of the moment . . .

This *variousness* makes it particularly difficult to write elaborate papers on the subject of their lives. If one mounts the hobbyhorse of a theory, cherished in the closet, it is of course easier to ride off on a straight line through the air; but if one wants *truth* and to do some good in the world as it is, it is necessary to allow for limitations and hindrances at every turn

. . .

10.6

Discussions of the servant problem appeared in every kind of magazine from the ladies' papers through general illustrated to feminist. This abridged article from one of the ladies' papers is only unusual in its humour and in the solution it suggests.

'Our Domestic Woes. The Servantgalism of the Period or The Alphabet of Woes', *The Lady's Own Paper*, vol. 5, 1870, p. 335.

A was the advertisement.

B stands for the Brown family, who sent the advertisement. A ship in mid-ocean without a rudder, a drowning man with his hands tied behind him, only imagine the condition of these good people, for

C was the cook, who had left them the previous evening and breakfast was wanted for five—mama, the two girls, papa and Harry. With miserable aspect did the members of this unhappy family survey each other. Bread could be bought at the baker's and tea at the grocer's, but who knew anything about the mystery of an omelete (*sic*)? . . . For the kitchen it was a howling waste. There were potatoes in the best China soup tureen, cabbages in the China closet, pickles in the wine glasses. The shelves were covered with sugar, salt and ants. An iron pot stood on one of the best damask table-cloths. The beefsteaks were wrapped in some of the finest napkins. The China towels had all too plainly been used as floor cloths. The floor cloths lay in suspicious proximity to the glasses.

D stands for the day; dreary and interminable. Thirty-six hours in it, mama and the girls were sure, as they dragged their trained skirts up and down the stairs, wearily consoling themselves that the new servant would arrive tomorrow. Papa and Harry took meals at a restaurant; and they bought cakes and ate them standing, and waited for tomorrow. For who among them would clean the closets and sort the towels and empty the bowls and find the place for the rubbish. Manifestly it was impossible and the Brown family waited.

E stands for the elegant person who arrived on the morrow. She wore a lady-like bonnet and a trimly-fitting dress. She had beautiful hair smoothly braided. Her politeness was perfect.— so was her dinner. Nobody could find fault with the fish or the roast. The dessert melted in the mouth. The sidedishes were a constant surprise. The Browns looked at one another proudly. "See," they said to one another, "there need be no trouble securing really good servants. All that is needed is firmness." Ten days after she came they repeated this little speech all the more emphatically because . . . her dinners and her manners were altering fast . . .

F stand for the fracas to which the elegant female shortly treated them. Being ordered to obey, she flatly refused. Being ordered to leave, she refused that also, "unless you give me a month's wages, ma'am." This was the crisis. Papa was in the City. Meantime the torrent of her eloquence carried all before it. "They might send for as many constables as they liked. 500 men couldn't stir her till she chose to go and that would be soon enough, when she got her wages. Call them ladies! They was working women like herself—common working women. She had been deceived. She took them for first-class ladies and they did their own serving and one of them wrote for a newspaper". All this delivered with shaking of fists and many contemptuous laughs. Mama and the girls went about, trying not to feel as if a bear was baiting or a bull worrying them; but when help came and she departed with the constable, the revulsion came also. And let

H stand for a fit of hysterics, while the letter **G** must be content to wait, being wanted at the end of our story; and let it wait with all the more patience since it will be called upon to represent one of the most powerful and dignified potentates in the world.

I stands for inquiry offices, where the Brown family went for their dinner—that is for a cook to cook their dinner; for what is a dinner raw? There was the half-crown office, the five-shilling office and the seven and sixpenny office . . . At the seven and sixpenny office was a manufactory for supplying trustworthy servants. However, the manufactory got hold of them in the raw, it turned them out trustworthy. The article was not on exhibition; but you paid your money, left your order, were booked and ticketed all in one breath, and the next morning the article was delivered at your door, warranted with all the virtues—that is, so the manufactory declared—and was very cross indeed with the Browns, who, after waiting, uselessly ventured to apply a second time . . .

J stands for James, the next-door neighbour's man, who knew "a likely girl as was wanting a place."

K stands for Kate, the likely girl, who looked likely enough to bring about worry and vexation of spirit. The dinner was an insult to the human stomach; the china had come to its day of doom; and though, **L** may stand for the lies she told, no numeral can properly represent them . . . Any attempt at following her only unsettled one's equilibrium, and induced symptoms of softening of the brain; and, awful as looked the alternative, the family saw nothing for it but to send her adrift . . .

M stands for the marauders, in whose footsteps the Brown family now followed, astonished; that mighty, unknown host, devouring like the swarms of Egypt, before whom tubs of butter and gallons of syrup were as nothing, for whom were made whole fruit-cakes—to whom the servants handed, through the window, fresh loaves of bread, tea, sugar, preserves, by the wholesale . . . The expense was astonishing—not to mention the turmoil, breakages, insolence and daring outrages on the human stomach perpetrated by the likely girl. And still the Brown family had no dinner.

N was the neighbour who came to console Mrs. Brown and who told her how she had seen the provisions handed out at the basement windows and how her cook had served her in the same manner.

O! was what the family said continually at every fresh revelation.

P stands for the perplexity in which they found themselves. They had eaten standing; they had not eaten; they had trembled before the elegant female; they had sent down untasted the combinations of the likely girl; they had advertised; they had contributed their mite to the servants' inquiry office; they had been bullied, sneered at, cheated, lied about, nauseated! Their backs ached; their legs were weary; their hearts sank within them; they were in despair! And still no dinner.

Q was the queerity which Harry brought home, being tired of feminine mismanagement. The ladies declared that she was grand, gloomy and peculiar. She was, at any rate, peculiar . . . Like a meteor she shot across the horizon, and disappeared suddenly, together with a bottle of fine whisky.

R stand for the references. In those days they stood the family in place of light reading. Hosts of ladies, their hands on their hearts (in pen and ink), solemnly assured the ladies of the Brown family that the bearers of the references were honest, sober and capable; the best of cooks, the neatest of waitresses . . . And still the family had no dinner, for one can't dine on references. If so, how luxuriously could the Browns have existed.

S should be painted in black lines, for it stands for the situation. The family discussed it with all their friends and read satires and songs on the subject, whose name is legion . . . They were the victims of a tyranny.

T stands for this tyranny, none the less real because wearing a humble shape. The father of the family grew haggard in trying to support it. The mother grew haggard in grimly enduring its necessary but intolerable vexations; but she bore it; and when she criticised, it was in whispers in the drawing room with some other martyr in silk and velvet. . . . Reading an article in his pet magazine on servants, paterfamilias grew rabid. Her skill, her moderation were therein extolled and proved beyond a doubt. And there is no knowing what reforms might not have been inaugurated but for one objection. The said servant was not to be found—no, not even when specially advertised for, and humbly entreated to appear, and receive good treatment and large wages.

U stands for you, the army of martyrs, more or less in the same predicament.

V stands for the variety of strange appearances now conjured by the Browns, still dinnerless. They were little more than appearances. They rose, elf-like, on the hearth in the morning, and disappeared by night . . .

W stands for wages, governed by some mysterious inverse law; as a rule, the more worthless the servant, the more unreasonable her demands . . .

X represents the family's temper in those days of trial.

Y stands for the youth who, knowing no better, spoke his mind thus:

"What is the use of waiting for a cook? Why don't you three stout women apply for the place yourselves and get your own dinner?"

When the ladies heard that, they were seized with amazement. It had never occurred to them. A cook was promised them in a fortnight; meantime, they resolved to try the youth's suggestion. There is all the difference in the world between determining to carry a basket home and dragging it by one handle till help arrives. Our ladies had the basket now in good earnest. They took off their trained skirts, and put on short gowns and divided the work between them. And it is quite astonishing how easily these ladies disposed of this dragon, this ogre, this constant terror, that cost double their own living and was appeased only by worry, dirt, noise and robbery; how simple, how very simple, when resolutely taken in hand, became this woeful, entangled, complicated, involved, mysterious, process of house-keeping; and how much shorter grew the bills, in spite of the fact that their bill of fare was much improved!

Z stands for the zest with which the ladies soon entered into the undertaking. Washing dishes *per se* is disgusting: sweeping is not amusing; cooking is tiresome. But there is a certain honest pleasure in the work of your own hands, at which idlers scoff but which workers realise. To see order, system and neatness result from your labour is many times more delightful than a morning call or a walk down Regent-Street. The ladies grew rosy. They were not overtired, but they had exercise enough—what they never had before in their lives. They were no longer perpetually fretted and perpetually bottling up their temper. The blood circulated better; the liver had its own way at last. Mrs. Brown got rid of her headaches. Her daughters—one of whom was recommended to the lifting cure, while the other had a pain in her side—by degrees forgot the doctor. And there was no more trouble about dinner. They got it themselves and it was worth eating. But that neglected letter **G** stands for Mrs. Grundy, who all the time had been lying in wait for them; and now she put them on trial.

If they could receive her in a dingy parlour swept by a dirty Mary Ann or Bridget and entertain her with complaints of the kitchen, she would unhesitatingly style them ladies; but to usher her into a drawing room swept by themselves—no matter how tasteful, how pure, how cheerful—she is doubtful. To keep a maid of some order, no matter how wretched, is the line of distinction between a lady and a woman—an insignia of rank, so to speak!

10.7

Articles on paid work for middle-class women became a favourite subject for articles across a range of magazine in the 1890s, especially those aimed at girls and young women. Journalism was an expanding profession and one which was becoming more visible through the growing use of by-lines, the development of a more personalised journalism and such new genres as the interview. It was not surprising, therefore, that journalism became a profession to which many magazine readers aspired and the topic of articles such as this.

'Young Women and Journalism', by W. T. Stead, *The Young Woman*, vol. 1, 1892, pp. 12–14.

. . . Some months ago I wrote in THE YOUNG MAN a paper on "How to become a Journalist," which applied equally to young men and young women. There is no royal road to journalism specially smoothed for either sex. There is a road which either man or woman may travel without being even so much as asked about the great petticoat or trouser differentiation which, as an American lady recently remarked, seems to make some people imagine that woman is not a sex but a species. Of course, human prejudice counts for a good deal even in journalism. There are many editors who, other things being equal, would give a journalistic commission to a man rather than to a woman, and, for my own part, I must plead guilty to the opposite prejudice, for I would never employ a man if I could find a woman who could do the work as well. But, taking the profession as a whole, there is not very much sex prejudice one way or the other. Even the most hidebound old editor is now beginning to see that his staff is incomplete without women, just as the most bigoted opponent of woman's suffrage has learned that he cannot carry his election without the support of Primrose Dames or their Liberal counterparts.

 Nevertheless the first thing I would like to impress upon young women who aspire to be journalists is that they must not presume upon sex, and imagine that because they are women therefore they have a right to a situation or an engagement whenever they choose to apply for it. To be a woman confers many privileges and inflicts many disabilities; but if you were a hundred times a woman that would give you no right to a niche in the journalistic profession. One half of the thousand millions of human beings in the world are of your sex, and any claim therefore that you can set forward, on the basis of your sex, applies equally to five hundred million other human beings. If you want to be a journalist, you must succeed as a journalist—not as a woman or as a man. All that you need expect, and all that you should ask for, is a fair field and no favour, to prove that you can do the work you ask should be allotted to you. You have a right to ask that your sex should not be regarded as a disqualification; but it is monstrous to erect that accident of your personality into a right to have opportunities denied to your brother.

If women are to get on in journalism, or in anything else, they must trample under foot that most dishonouring conception of their work as mere woman's work.

You must not think that because you are a woman chivalry and courtesy demand that your work should be judged more leniently than if you were only a man. I am sorry to say that such is too often the case, and I admit that I have often been an offender that way myself. But it is unkind and unfair to women to let them feel that they will be excused because they are women, that they will be allowed to scamp work for the same reason; and that after all their work will be accepted, not on its merits, but because it is women's work. That kind of kindness is most unkind . . .

Next, after the false kindness and undue consideration on the part of some editors which after all, at the beginning, may be excused for the sake of encouraging the timid to do their best, the chief foe that women have to contend with in journalism is their own conventionality, and the fantastic notion that a lady cannot be expected to do this, that, or the other disagreeable bit of work. That such and such a duty is not the thing to ask from a lady, that a lady must not be scolded when she does wrong, or that a lady ought not to stay up late or go about late,—all that is fiddlesticks and nonsense, as our good old nurses used to say. Ladies with such notions had better stay at home in their drawing-rooms and boudoirs. The great rough real workaday world is no place for them . . .

Of course women can do as they please. Only if they please to do what does not fit in with the general working of a newspaper office, the editor will be pleased to dispense with their services. It is not ladylike, you say, to go to report a police court case. It is not proper to be out on the streets at midnight, and so forth. Well and good. If so, no women need apply for journalistic work on even terms with men. They may do odds and ends of work, they may have the fringes and the leavings of men, and be paid accordingly. But, if a girl means to be a journalist, she ought to be a journalist out and out, and not try to be a journalist up to nine o'clock, and Miss Nancy after nine.

I don't want girls to be unladylike. The unwomanly woman is a hideous thing in any profession, and one of the chief advantages women have in journalism is, that they are more pleasant and therefore better liked than men. They throw all that away when they ape men. There are departments of journalistic work in which a young lady with good manners and womanly tact can beat any man on the staff out of sight, but the woman who is mannish and forward and generally aggressive, simply throws away her chances and competes voluntarily at a disadvantage. For no editor in his senses wants either mannish women or womanish men on his staff. What he does want is a staff that will do whatever work turns up without making scenes, or consulting clocks, or standing upon its conventional dignities.

. . . If you go into journalism, in order to make a living, do not object to begin at the beginning and to learn the business before expecting that it will keep you. Learn shorthand and, having learnt it, keep it up and don't forget it and lose speed. And whatever else you do or don't do, get to write a neat, legible hand, or if that is beyond your reach make yourself proficient on the type-writer. Remember that if your copy is difficult to be read it simply won't get read at all, but will go into the wastepaper basket. If, by rare good luck, it should be accepted, it will puzzle the compositors and the readers, and there will be a loss of time all round, where time is valuable; finally, there will be many mistakes which will make you gnash your teeth, but for which you have only yourself to blame. You may not be a genius, but you can be neat and accurate, and you can make yourself write a legible hand.

Don't think that secretaryships grow on every gooseberry bush. There are very few secretaryships, and they are usually given to those who are known and proved to be faithful, and also to have general acquaintance with the business in which their chief is engaged. As for contributions to the papers, remember that articles are accepted much more because they are "on the nail," and bear directly upon the subject of the hour, than because of any exceptional literary merits which they possess . . .

Finally, let me conclude this little homily by reminding all young women who are or are going to be in journalism, that they have the honour of their sex and the reputation of one half the human race, more in their keeping than any other women of equal numbers. For the newspaper is the educator of the public, and the people who write in newspapers have the best opportunities of creating public opinion. You who are on the newspapers are on your trial. Not merely does the public judge your work as work, and not as mere women's work, but your colleagues of the other sex watch you with an attention that is always critical and sometimes not sympathetic. For the sake of all we hold dear, don't make fools of yourselves, and don't give the enemy occasion to blaspheme by pointing to your work or your behaviour as conclusive reasons why they will never again, if they can help it, have a woman on their staff. If, on the other hand, you can hold your own level with any man, and besides can add—as you will do, if you are really womanly women—to the pleasantness and interest and general efficiency of the staff, you may rely upon it that you will stand in much greater danger of being spoiled by over kindness than of being treated with surly or grudging respect.

Discursive prose: the short paragraph or 'tit-bit'

Towards the end of Victoria's reign, as part of what was dubbed 'The New Journalism', many women's magazine's adapted the shorter, snappier prose style associated with the weekly general magazine called *Tit-Bits*. Serious commentators were concerned that the tit-bit was a concession to those who were incapable of serious reading. Not surprisingly they were widely used in the cheap domestic magazines. However, this kind of style was neither entirely new in the 1880s nor confined to cheap journals. Short pieces of prose as fillers between other elements of the magazines were standard practice throughout the period. From the mid-century in the ladies' newspapers and fashion magazines short paragraphs of news, gossip or comment were a regular feature and were often strung together to take the place of an editorial. This practice was taken up in general illustrated magazines and in other kinds of journal in the 1880s and 1890s. In cheap domestic magazines like *Home Chat* or *Home Notes*, the 'article' consisting of a series of disconnected items was standard.

11.1

The short note, often satiric or comic, was a feature of several kinds of magazines including the fashion journals. Such items were clearly fillers but they contributed to the general tone of the journal.

'Flighty Girls and Good Wives' and 'Frivolity', *Townsend's Monthly Selection of Parisian Costumes*, no. 142, 1864, unnumbered page.

Flighty Girls and Good Wives.—The gay, the rattling, and laughing, are, unless some party of pleasure, or something out of domestic life, is going on, generally dull. Some stimulus is always craved after by this description of women; some sight to be seen, something to see or hear other than what is to be found at home, which, as it affords no excitement, nothing "to raise and keep up the spirits," is looked upon merely as a place to be at for want of a better. A greater evil than a wife of this description, it would be difficult to find. The mopers are all giggle at other times; the gaiety is for others, and the moping for the husband, to comfort him, happy man, when he is alone: plenty of smiles for others, and for him to participate with others; but the moping is reserved exclusively for him.

Frivolity.—A fop, who had annoyed by his frivolous remarks his partner in the ballroom, among other empty things asked whether "she had ever had her ears pierced?"—"No," was the reply, "but I've often had them *bored!*"

11.2

A feature of the ladies' papers and fashion magazines was the practice of stringing together a series of short paragraphs with no apparent relationship between the items. These were longer than the usual tit-bit and shorter than the article. The two paragraphs extracted here were in a series of these. The double-page, three-column spread included similar or slightly longer pieces under headings which included 'A Tale of Romance', 'How to make a Young Wife out of an Old Maid', 'A Beautiful Island' and 'Diamonds'.

'Crossing a River in South America' and 'Ladies' Thin Shoes', *The Ladies' Gazette of Fashion*, Oct., 1866, p. 77.

CROSSING A RIVER IN SOUTH AMERICA.

The mode of crossing a river, which is far from inconsiderable, is of a very peculiar kind, whenever the height of the flood renders the ordinary method of fording impracticable. On both banks of the river are men, whose occupation it is to conduct travellers through the bounding torrent, which in some places breaks violently over concealed rocks. These men are called *Vaqueanos*; they are peasants, who take pride and pleasure in their dangerous occupation, and are in general remarkable for their great bodily strength and for their large and well-trained horses. The preparations are soon made: as soon as the party plunge into the stream, the guides press themselves close to the travellers on both sides, and fasten him between them in such a way that, even if he were to lose his balance, he cannot easily fall from the saddle. These men govern the horses with such unerring skill, that they remain constantly pressed together. Wherever the depth is so great that the horses must swim, the guides seize the reins of the middle horse and bid the traveller shut his eyes lest his head grow dizzy. The water rushes by with astounding rapidity and deafening noise, and, in our case, was cold enough to make all three complain of the bath, since even the horse that swims best plunges so deep into the stream as to wet the rider to the hips. It is not until after being freed from the tight grasp of the two guides, that one perceives that they hold the lasso always ready, in order to save the traveller, if, in spite of their precautions, he should be snatched away by the waves. On the coast of Peru, between Lambayeque and Truxillo are many broad mouths of rivers, or rather arms of the sea, which can be crossed in this way alone, since, though generally too shallow to admit of boats, they have many deep places through which it is necessary to swim. There the *Chimbador*, who takes the office of the Chilian *Vaqueano*, makes the traveller mount behind him, while he manages the horse. It said that those men, (the Chimbadors) who are almost always men of colour, and who ride into the water in a state of nakedness, always carry with them a long knife for the purpose of stabbing the passenger, should the latter fall off, and, grasping his guide in the agony of despair, threaten to involve both in a common destruction.

LADIES' THIN SHOES.

Thin shoes, as an article of female dress, I am sufficient of a Goth to wish to see disused; and I would replace them with shoes having a moderate thickness of sole, with a thin layer of cork or felt placed within the shoe and over the sole. Cork is a very bad conductor of heat, and is therefore to be preferred: if it is not to be had, or is not liked, felt may be substituted for it. I think thin shoes ought not to be used, unless for the purpose of dancing, and then only to be worn while dancing. The invalid or dyspeptic ought assuredly never to wear thin shoes. And as to the common practice of changing thin shoes for warm boots, it is a practice which I know to be replete with danger, and therefore to be rash and almost culpable. There is another custom, or habit, or usage, in the dress of my fair countrywomen, which must be noticed here; it is that of covering the head with a cap in the morning, and leaving it uncovered in the afternoon or evening. It is indefensible, useless, absurd, and dangerous.

In the 1880s and 1890s this technique of the series of short unconnected paragraphs became a feature of a range of periodicals. This example comes from the threepenny *Hearth and Home* (1891–1914) which combined the format of the ladies' newspapers with the contents and interests of the general magazine.

'People, Places and Things', *Hearth and Home*, vol. 2, 1891, p. 136.

"He that uttereth slander is a fool." – Solomon.

Miss Annie H. Blomefield, who gained a first-class in Part I. of the Moral Science Tripos at Cambridge, is from Newnham, which she entered three years ago, having won a Cobden Scholarship. She is a daughter of the Rev. John Blomefield, and was educated privately, studying under Miss Leifchild before going to college. Her age is twenty-seven, and she was born at Leeds. Our promising students are finding openings now, not only at home, but in the colonies. Miss Alice Taylor, after gaining distinction in History and English in the Cambridge Higher Locals, went out to Melbourne, where she has received the appointment of Vice-Principal of Trinity College, Dostel.

* * *

In the mathematical list at Cambridge, published on Saturday, Miss Read, of Girton, was placed equal to 26th, and in the Natural Science Honour List at Oxford Miss Kirkaldy and Miss Pollard, both of Somerville Hall, gained their Firsts. Before this time only one lady, Miss Seward, of Holloway College, had obtained this coveted distinction, so I am glad to chronicle this addition to our scientific strength.

* * *

At the recent medical examination at the Royal University in Ireland, the lady students who presented themselves obtained high places. Miss Hester Russell, of the London School of Medicine for Women, carried off the only honour awarded in the degree examination. Miss Anna Church, of the College of Surgeons, Ireland, was in the upper class division; Miss Frances Dick, of the London School, passed for degrees of M.B.B.Ch. and B.A.O. In the second examination in medicine Miss Emily Winifred Dickson, daughter of Mr. T. Dickson, M.P., was bracketed second class with Mr. M'Math, and obtained an exhibition of £15.

* * *

It will be remembered that Miss Abbott's request to be admitted to the General Hospital at Montreal, to study clinics, was refused by sixteen votes to fifteen. In consideration of the bare majority, the committee has since decided to pass Miss Abbott, but will issue no more tickets to ladies till the question has been settled by the governors. The dean of the medical faculty of Bishop's College is strongly on the women's side, and desires to prevent any necessity for resorting to inferior universities by building a new wing to Bishop's College Women's Hospital. In Austria a lady doctor is practising in a hospital as Serajevo (*sic*), but the Mussulman patients do not take kindly to her presence. They cannot be *very* ill, haply! France, long justly renowned for the superb training it offers to women in medicine, is now considering a measure which will admit them to the profession of pharmacy.

* * *

The Annual Meeting of the Somerville Club was held on June 6th. The Chairman, in her opening remarks, alluded to the action taken by the *Daily Telegraph*, in a leading article which appeared some weeks ago, with reference to a lecture delivered at the club. She stated that the said article had grossly and calumniously misrepresented the facts, and that the replies to it, sent at the time by members of the committee, had been refused insertion. She remarked that the writer of the article had evidently taken advantage of an opportunity to throw mud at all women who have the courage to inquire into those important, legal, and social questions which most deeply concern them. In conclusion, she appealed to the members of the club not to swerve from their path on account of such false and cowardly statements and insinuations, but to pursue their progressive policy with unabated vigour. A resolution calling upon the committee "to exercise increased vigilance in their choice of subjects for lectures, so as to avoid any chance of unpleasant notoriety arising from adverse comments in the Press," was unanimously rejected by all the members present with the two exceptions of the mover and seconder.

* * *

LIMERICK County has been *en fête* on account of the marriage last Wednesday, of Miss Anna Josephine Barington, daughter of the late Sir Croker Barington, Bart., of Glenstal, with Mr. Pollock, of Mountainstown, county Meath. The ceremony took place at Abington church, the officiating Clergymen being the Rev. Lewin Weldon, D.D., brother-in-law of the bride, assisted by the Rev. Mr. Seymour, rector of the parish. Sir Charles Barington gave his sister away, and Mr. G. Fowler, of Rawlinstown, acted as best man. Among the valuable wedding presents is a silver tray, presented by the congregation of Abington church, as a token of their appreciation of the bride's kindness in conducting the music for so many years.

11.4

The 1890s cheap weeklies, whether aimed at women or girls, practised the art of the 'Tit-Bit' in various ways. This extract from the halfpenny *Sweethearts* (1898) shows the tendency at its most developed.

'Little Bits that Girls Like', *Sweethearts*, vol. 1, 1898, p. 7.

HOW TO RETAIN A MAN'S LOVE.

MAN is the most easily flattered animal in creation.

Life without flattery is to him a barren waste.

Let the woman who wants him to go on loving her flatter him consistently and habitually.

Not in great vulgar doses, which disgust and repel, but delicately, insinuatingly—more by hint and suggestion than by open show.

She must not tell him he is clever, and strong, and admirable; she must let him see she depends on his opinion and his judgement, and goes to him for information; that she trusts herself to his protection in preference to anyone else's; that she finds a charm in his society that no other man's can afford her.

As long as she impresses this upon him, he will adore her.

She has only to keep on impressing it, and he will never want to leave her side as long as he lives.

MANIFEST YOUR FRIENDLINESS.

WE have all heard of those people whose "natures are so deep" that they never betray emotion! We have met with a number of that class, and we take them at their true value.

It is my honest opinion, supported by considerable observation, that the person whose nature is so very, very deep that no emotion ever rises to the surface and finds expression, is generally the one who is incapable of emotion.

If you love your wife why not tell her so? You can't tell her of it too often, and then back up your statement by *deeds*. If you love your husband, why not say so, and show it in every word, look, and act. Do *your* part in friendships. Do not expect your friend to do it all. *Manifest* your friendliness. Life is short. Crowd into each day all the brightness and blessedness that the twenty-four hours will hold, and you will receive one hundred per cent interest.

MUCH TOO SWEET.

"Do you love me?" said the paper bag to the sugar.

"I'm just wrapped up in you," replied the sugar.

"You sweet thing!" murmured the paper bag.

GEORGE'S BLUNDER.

HE: "If you'll give me just one kiss I'll never ask for another."

She: "George, it is bad enough to tell a falsehood without insulting me at the same time."

12

Prose fiction

Nearly all women's magazines published fiction in the form of serialised novels or short stories. Serialised fiction, the mainstay of much journalism in the period, was an important way of getting and keeping readers. The quality and length of serial fiction varied enormously from title to title. Some routinely ran serials for as long as a year, while others favoured short runs. At the end of the period, complete short fictions became more popular. In terms of quality, much of this writing was formulaic and mediocre but some titles, like L. T. Meades' *Atalanta* and Annie S. Swan's *Woman at Home*, prided themselves on their quality fiction, including 'the editors' own. Most of the fiction was by anonymous writers who produced mainly romantic and sentimental fiction centred on the home and marriage. Occasionally well-known writers were published in these magazines and occasionally a magazine would be adventurous in its fiction. In its first year, *The Englishwoman's Domestic Magazine* serialised Hawthorne's controversial *The Scarlet Letter*, but this may partly have been because there was no copyright payable on American work at this date. From the 1860s sensation fiction appeared in general illustrated magazines as it did, along with gothic tales, in the cheap magazines of the 1890s. In this latter part of the period the new educational and work opportunities for women gave magazine fiction a different territory on which to work out its traditional themes. Serial fiction is difficult to represent in a collection like this. Our choice, which is mainly of complete short works, may therefore give a false impression of the relative importance of serialised novels and short fictions in the magazines.

12.1

Fiction became increasingly important in the general illustrated magazines, particularly in the form of serialised novels, which were often the lead item. We have given the opening page of one such novel from *The Englishwoman's Domestic Magazine* (1852–79) as a reminder of the vast range of serial fiction we have not included here.

'Wayfe Summers. Chapter 1. My Guardians', *The Englishwoman's Domestic Magazine*, vol. 3, new series, 1861, p. 1.

WHAT a strange life is that of a friendless child! To have all the great capacity for loving, all the craving desire for dependence, crushed back into a young heart, left only to its own morbid fancies and unfulfilled longings! Yet this life was mine.

My guardian, as he was called, I saw but seldom. Once a quarter I was told to put out my white frock and the blue sash, kept specially for these occasions, and underwent the awful infliction of "a thorough wash," in which strong yellow soap was freely applied to my burning ears, that I might make a becoming appearance in the dingy parlour, there to await his formal inspection. My recollections go no further back than this, except in such vague glimpses of a still more wretched life, as I can never recall, save in a momentary remembrance—like those strange delusions of a former state which sometimes visit us, of which the actual experience is wanting, and the memory is but another name for fancy.

He was a small, spare, erect, neat old gentleman—my guardian—with a well-set bald head, the polished bumps of which always diverted my attention from his calm grey eyes; a face regular, and not unkind, but formal and unchanging as his manner—all his dress, from the stiff white uncreased stock to the neat black gaiters over his polished shoes, so smooth and spotless, that I used to wonder, as I gazed at him, whether it would be possible for him to keep so clean and trim if he came to live in Perram-street, under the superintendence of Mrs. Bradley.

He never stayed long. At the first "rat-tat" at the door, at half-past three, I left the window, where I had been waiting his arrival; and by the time the last "tap" which ended the *crescendo* summons on the knocker had died away in the hollow echoes of the passage, I had climbed up-stairs, where I waited on the landing till the bell rang to call me to his presence. One description of these interviews will serve for all . . .

12. 2

The religious and evangelical magazines carried some moralising and religious narratives. These usually purported to be true accounts but we have chosen to include a typical example here for reasons which we hope are obvious. The extract has been cut.

'Poor Meggy; or, The Wages of Sin', *The British Workwoman*, vol. 3, 1866, p. 275.

In a fever-haunted den, in one of the lowest districts of the metropolis, lay a dying woman.

She was literally a moral and physical wreck, steeped to the very lips in vice and infamy, her spirit polluted with almost every crime that can cast disgrace on womanhood, and her form, which had been beautiful, branded with sad traces of her dark career.

The scene of her exit from the world in which she had helped to diffuse so much of the poison of sin reeked with ill odours, arising from filth and neglect; and still more with the sickening miasma exhaled each moment from the pestilential breath of the loathsome disease which was destroying her.

She moved, or rather writhed, uneasily on her pallet, and passing her arms wildly above her head, poured forth the most fearful blasphemies. No minister of religion was there, for it was one of those localities so signally dedicated to the darkest crimes, that, unless specially sent for, such seldom visited it . . . A haggard-looking girl, who had once been beautiful, alone tended her, and though only pity forbade her departure in this extremity, it was evident she shrank in repugnance and terror from the awful imprecations and terrible cries of despair to which ever and anon the sufferer gave vent. She kept as far from the bed as possible, and ran back into the darkest corner, whenever a fresh burst gave evidence of renewed mental disquiet.

"Come here, Meggy," the sufferer shouted, in a furious voice; "why do you keep snivelling out there? I want you: come near me, I say."

"What can I do for you?" asked the girl, half timorously, half soothingly, making a step forward.

"I won't hurt you," said the woman, in quieter tones; "only come near me."

The girl drew near cautiously. "What is it you want?"

"I want you to look at me," she replied, fixing on the trembling creature a look so piercing and so full of unutterable meaning that it entered her inmost soul,—"to look at me well, so that you will never forget the sight to your dying day."

The girl shuddered, and half averted her face.

"Look at me, I say," the woman vociferated again, "and let the remembrance haunt you till it scares you from vice. It's the only reparation I can make you for the ruin I have brought upon you. I'm going to my account. The torment has already begun within;—don't you see it? Don't you read it?"

"Hush, hush! Oh, pray forbear. There's mercy yet."

"Mercy for me? None—never. I'm lost—hopelessly, irremediably. When you think of me, think of me as burning *there—there*, for ever and for ever."

"It's never too late," said the poor young woman. "I remember my dear Sunday-school teacher used to say——" She could not proceed, but, sobbing forth, "Oh dear, oh dear!" wept convulsively.

The dying one regarded her with an expression of countenance to which only the shadows of the eternity which were so darkly gathering on her spirit could afford the clue. At length she cried, almost springing from the bed: "Sunday-school teacher! Do you want to madden me? Oh, *that* Sunday-school, *that* pastor, *that* mother! *How* lost, how doubly damned!'

"No, no, no!" sighed forth the poor girl; "don't say so, for mercy's sake."

"Hark ye, Meggy," said she, in accents so terrible that the girl felt it was almost more than she could bear,—"there's mercy for you, but none for me. As soon may God blot His sun out of heaven as forgive such a wretch. I've ruined you, yet you talk to me of mercy—poor innocent! But that's not all I've done. Only a small part,—ha! ha!"

She laughed so wildly that the sound seemed superhuman.

"Once more, come near me. I want to talk to you. I won't harm you, as I live. I want but to convince you there is no hope for me."

Meggy went to her bedside.

"Stoop lower," she said, in a strange whisper.

Involuntarily the girl bent down to her.

She grasped her hand, as though to prevent its withdrawal, till the whole she wished to say had been said; then, in a tone so preternaturally distinct and thrilling that it seemed almost like the hiss of a serpent in her listener's ear, she said: "Twenty years I've been following this life of crime. You're only one of scores that have been destroyed through my means. Some are gone quick into hell. Others are going there as fast as guilt or misery can take them. O, the scenes I have witnessed, the infernal wrong I have done. No verier slave of the devil ever walked the earth. And do you think he'll be cheated of his own? Won't he pay me my wages?" A loud shriek rang through the miserable room, as she concluded; and releasing her grasp of Meggy, she fell back upon the pillow, in strong delirium. For a time it was awful to gaze upon her, and still more fearful to listen to the frenzied ravings which poured from her lips. The wretched young creature began to meditate flying from the scene, when the door was opened, and a stranger entered. She was a woman, seemingly in the prime of life, in vigorous health, and of showy exterior. It was apparent at a glance the class to which she belonged. Whatever she was, however, Meggy evidently welcomed her. It was a human face, and helped to mitigate the weight of the horror, so closely allied to the supernatural, which was pressing on her spirit. Very different was the greeting of her dying sister in crime. She regarded her with a countenance of such fixed hate, and grinned at her with an expression so almost demoniacal, that the strong woman, inwardly quailing, turned from her to Meggy, addressing to her some words of inquiry, and encouragement also, such as it was. She need not have feared the reproaches and menace that the looks promised, however. Power of utterance was fast failing the miserable departing one. The excitement of the last hour was rapidly giving place to utter exhaustion, and even while the stranger spoke to Meggy, the death damps gathered heavily on her brow. The whole visage swiftly changed.

"See, see," said Meggy, pointing fearfully with her finger; "she is going."

The visitor turned to look, and while she gazed, the eyes closed, and the spirit passed to the bar of the Judge of all the earth, *"to give an account of the things done in the body."*

. . .

For the next two days Meggy strove hard, but unavailingly, to forget the scene we have depicted.

During this time the mistress of her present abode had been making preparations for the funeral, which was to take place on the third; for as there is said to be honour amongst thieves, so the wretched adept in vice would not subject her former accomplice to the indignity of a parish burial. To this end, indeed, chiefly, she had possessed herself of what remained of the proceeds of her guilty career.

She had been busy all day, and unusually wearied; night arrived at length, and with it an unexpected visitor.

A spectre grim and gaunt knocked loudly at her door for admission. Fain would she have said him, nay; but he told her, in tones not to be mistaken, that *her* hour was come, and, willing or unwilling, she must go with him to that unseen bourne whither he had already introduced her whose obsequies she was preparing to celebrate.

Trembling with fear, she remonstrated, pleaded, promised:—all in vain. Then, sick with mortal terror, and racked with anguish indescribable, she called for Meggy. She came, and knelt by the bedside, her white lips striving in vain to utter a single word.

Long, more vainly still, did she from whom the scenes of earth were now for ever receding struggle to give expression to the emotions which were raging within. At length, at intervals, she slowly ejaculated, while her clammy hands despairingly clutched at all within her reach: "Judgment!—Hell!—Eternity! The worm that never dies! Lost, lost! Fly!—fly for your life."

Life departed with the words; and rising from her fearful proximity to the corpse, in the dead of night, that young girl did fly:—from the room, from the house, from the neighbourhood. Unconsciously and aimlessly she wandered through street after street, square after square, turning after turning, knowing and heeding not whither she was going. It was cold; she was thinly clad, and the pavement was sloppy. She thought not of it. One idea alone possessed her,—that of flight; flight as far as possible from the scenes of her former guilt and misery. At break of day she stood on Blackfriars-bridge.

As she gazed on the water, she realised for the first time that she was now literally a houseless wanderer, absolutely shelterless. True, the streets had long been her principal home, but *this* in its uttermost extent was new to her. She shivered and moaned audibly. "One resolute leap!" whispered an inward voice, "and all is over." She pauses. Ah, tempter, art thou about to prevail?

Praise God, no! "Judgment! Hell! Eternity! the worm that never dies!"—still ring in her ear, in the accents of the dying. She starts, rouses herself, and hurries from the spot, pausing not, till faint from exhaustion, she sinks upon a door-step, in a somewhat secluded street. The arrival of a stranger, ere long, obliges her to rise; when, looking up, she perceives written over the portal, "Refuge for the Homeless." What music! Without a moment's hesitation, she closely follows the stranger, and enters with her. Her tale is soon told, and admission willingly accorded, for nature's own voice spoke eloquently, and no other pleader was needed.

Here we will leave her, in the hand of Him who so mercifully wrought her deliverance; earnestly supplicating that she may ultimately prove to be "a brand plucked from the burning."

Does my reader say, "What a sad narrative!" Sad it is; but, alas! in its darkest incidents, no less sad than true. The awful deaths of the two women, partners in guilt too horrible for more than the barest intimation of its character to sully these pages, were related to me for fact by an exemplary lady, whose life mission it is to reclaim the lost and erring of her sex. The escape of one of the victims of their evil machinations I can bear witness to, for I have conversed with her in the Refuge to which I have alluded.

Seeing, then, the narrative is true, shall the impression of its sadness be the only one left on the mind of the reader? Shall it not prove a beacon to some, and encouragement to others? A beacon to warn off the dangerous ground poor Meggy suffered her unwary feet to tread, and encouragement where the first false step has been made, whispering that there is yet hope out of the depths—yet resource, if they are whole-hearted in seeking it.

E. R.

12.3

Fashion magazines also used fiction, usually short complete stories, like this one.

'Margaret; or The Word "Obey" ', *Townsend's Monthly Selection of Parisian Costumes*, Dec., 1865, pp. 5–7.

"I NEVER would say it," cried Grace Carislee, tossing her curly head; "I never would, if I died an old maid."

"All very fine, Grace," answered Constance Gower. "Wait till your turn comes, and rather than remain a spinster for life, see if those rosy lips will not murmur the word as sweetly as possible. For my part," she continued, half scornfully, "I have never yet seen the man I could obey. As a matter of form we must use the word; but whether it is kept, remains to be seen after marriage."

"Margaret, what say you?" inquired Grace, bending over the graceful musician who completed the trio round the piano in a country drawing-room. "Let us have your opinion. Ought the word 'obey' to be used in the matrimonial service, or not?"

"Used, most certainly," was Margaret's quiet reply, accompanied by an earnest look into the earnest blue eyes which were questioning her.

"Your reason?" was the next impetuous question from Grace, while Constance Gower raised her eyebrows into a more decided arch than Nature had given them. "I give the best reason," she replied, "because it is right."

"Well," remarked Grace, pettishly, "we know that; but then, why is it right? I'm sure it is the men's place to obey. You would like your husband to obey you, I know, in everything. Now, should not you?"

"No!" was Margaret's almost abrupt reply. Such a remarkable assertion called from both her companions a volley of questions, which Margaret allowed to be asked, and then with a slightly flushed cheek, answered, "I think that every woman with true feeling must recognize that one word as the sweetest, as well as the most important, in the ceremony which so entirely changes her life. She is glad and proud to yield her obedience where respect and love have gone before."

"All very fine," put in Grace Carislee; "and how many men are there in the world, now-a-days, that your true feeling woman could respect and love as you so romantically describe? I'm sure I cannot think of one."

Margaret Gainsborough thought of one, and with the feeling that memory brought for inspiration, she proceeded even more earnestly than before.

"You are wrong, dear Grace, in your last remark; for I heard you say, not long ago, that a certain gentleman—not far from us now—merited the love and respect of the best woman in the world."

A rosy flush dawned on Grace's cheek, and the wayward eyes softened as she answered in a lower tone—

"Well, my cousin Guy Earlsland, is the best and dearest fellow alive, I know; but then it would be very horrid to promise to do everything he said."

Margaret's reason had to say a few proud words to her heart, ere its throbbing was hushed, and that one loved name could be spoken with calmness.

"Such a man as Mr. Earlsland is scarce likely to exact from anyone, more especially from one dear to him, any service that would be unwillingly rendered; therefore, how could a woman's happiness and well-doing be otherwise than safe in his keeping?"

"Oh, I know you and cousin Guy are great friends," replied Grace Carislee; "and if you meet his counterpart, you would no doubt be fully prepared to give him your obedience."

"Yes," answered Margaret Gainsborough: and her heart's silent homage to Guy Earlsland's truth, honour, and manliness, fully ratified her answer.

The sudden entrance of the gentlemen, Guy Earlsland among them, brought the interesting discussion to a close.

. . .

Truth to tell, Margaret Gainsborough had at last met her master. To none save him could she bow—with none save him could she be happy. Love, to her, meant as much worship as one creature may give to another without infringing on the sacred rights of the Creator—a long story of homage paid to a superior being—such as Guy Earlsland appeared to her now. But the happy musing was interrupted by the entrance of Grace, with flushed cheeks and dancing eyes. Her volatile nature had never learned to keep a secret; and what Margaret would have treasured in her heart till necessity published it, Grace told ere she was fairly in the room.

"Maggie, darling, what do you think? I am going to be married to Cousin Guy Earlsland!"

At one blow the dream of years was struck down; and with a smothered sob, that cherished dream's requiem, Margaret turned with the old sweet look, in which, however, a careful, interested observer might have seen a strange, startled look of suffering only half understood by herself, she murmured words of congratulation, which, though commonplace in themselves, were sweet from her lips.

Grace, full of her new happiness, talked on, unconcious (sic) that her friend was silent.

Long after Grace was asleep, Margaret stood still, dressed as she had been in the evening— not even the scarlet geranium was taken from her black hair, nor the bracelet unclasped from the round white arm. Silently, tearlessly, she was digging the dead hope's grave in the palace where it had lived—her true, throbbing, passionate heart. And when all was over, when the last flower Affection had to spare was laid on the new-made grave, to wither there, cool reason and stern will closed and locked the door of the sepulchre, and Pride flung away the key.

Till then, she had not dared to think of Guy Earlsland; and when she did, she looked on Grace Carislee's sleeping face and said to herself, "If she was only more worthy of him! God grant he has made no mistake."

* * *

Margaret and her father went abroad . . . when after four years of absence, Margaret Gainsborough returned to England, not one other image had usurped Guy Earlsland's image in her too true heart.

* * *

One evening, in a crowded reception room, she was brought face to face with the two people who had so unconsciously changed her life. Guy Earlsland was walking listlessly and silently through the crowd of people, when a sudden move in the throng revealed Margaret Gainsborough to his pleased eyes. Eagerly he joined her, and was delighted to renew the acquaintance so pleasantly commenced four years before. A long talk they had. Margaret told of her travels and their pleasant associations; the strange, beautiful things she had seen, and which he could speak of, too, having seen them also. When he left her—unwillingly, indeed—he wondered what strange sympathy there was between them, and vaguely asked himself why he had never discovered all this before. Scarcely had he quitted her side, when her attention was claimed by Grace Carislee, fresh and blooming as when they last parted. As they talked together of old times and recent adventures, Grace suddenly said—

"Ah! when I last saw you, I was engaged to Cousin Guy. That's all off now, you know."

"Indeed!" said Margaret, vaguely.

"Yes," laughed Grace, "we quarrelled about that word 'Obey.' You remember what I once told you about it? Well, I gave my ideas to Guy on the subject—his did not agree with mine. We quarrelled, and parted—not literally, you know, because we are cousins; but we shall never marry. I was very vexed, but Guy seems to have got over it nicely."

. . .

Three months afterwards, Margaret Gainsborough was visiting again at Carislee Park. Constance Gower had said the word *obey*, and also found that she was obliged to keep it. She and her husband were of the party—Grace's new swain, Charles Devereux, and Cousin Guy Earlsland.

The summer days passed quietly and pleasantly to all. Margaret was dreaming again; perhaps this time not so vainly, if Guy's devotion might mean anything. One night, as they stood together listening to a duet played by Grace and Mrs. Coningsby, Guy Earlsland commenced a conversation in a low tone. They talked of many things—their visit, now drawing to a close; their friends; and finally, their graceful young hostess.

"Ah!" said Guy, "when we last met here, Miss Gainsborough, my cousin Grace and I were engaged. We made a mistake, you see, and were allowed to rectify it, ere too late. You know the story," he added, in a still lower tone.

"Were not you rather hard on poor Grace?" she asked, looking fearlessly up in his face, but dropping her eyes again before the expression that she saw there; "She was only joking."

"I dislike jests on such subjects," was Guy Earlsland's answer. "I am going to ask you a question, if I may."

He took her silent bow as an answer, and went on—

"What is your opinion on the word in question?"

Her upward look was his best reproof; and with deep humility in face and tone, he added—

"Margaret, may I ask your love—and your respect?"

One moment she paused, ere her reply was made. It was characteristic when it came.

"You have them, Mr. Earlsland," she said.

"I can trust the rest then," he replied.

When Grace Carislee and Margaret met alone that night, Grace said quietly—

"Margaret, I think that word *obey* is a very good one, after all. I suppose I could not get married if I did not use it; and Charles Devereux is so very nice, and has such fine houses and carriages, and diamonds, that really I—— Why, Margaret, that is Cousin Guy Earlsland's ring; it was his mother's! However, did——"

Margaret's look answered her.

* * *

Grace became Mrs. Charles Devereux, a leader of fashion, and was—as the world goes—a happy woman. Luckily, her husband required very little obedience from her, and thus she never knew the full beauty of the word *obey*.

Of three fair girls who in the beginning of the story discussed its use so earnestly, only Margaret knew how necessary a thing it is for a wife's happiness to sweetly, conscientiously, and gracefully *obey*.

Even the ladies' papers, like *The Queen* (1861–1967), ran some short fiction. This is part two of a two-week serial.

'How She Repented', *The Queen*, vol. 78, 1885, p. 313.

ROMAN SOCIETY had enough to interest it for the next few weeks; and the Villani-Lawrence affair was food for the gossips of a rich and succulent kind. Of course the young men went out, and of course Mark, being the aggrieved, and the other the aggressor, was dangerously wounded in the chest, while that other escaped scot-free without so much as a scratch. Everything was exaggerated in the telling. The scene at the ball; Carry Caine's insolent coquetry and Count Villani's more insolent triumph; the manly bearing of Mark Lawrence, according to some—according to others, the brutality of his reprisals; the deadly enmity shown in the duel, and the character of the wound—all got that extra touch which transformed the one little white feather lost in preening to five stark-stripped hens lying dead on the hen-house floor. Without exaggeration, however, there was plenty wherewith to feed that love of gossip and scandal which seems interwoven with the thread of life. And added to the things of the past were now speculations on the meaning of Count Villani's radiant looks, with Carry Caine's wild spirits and anxious almost haggard face, which somehow did not match her words nor answer to her bold and defiant bearing. Yes; there was enough and to spare of causes for talk at the five o'clock teas on hand, and to set speculation flowing at all four corners. But during all this time of frivolous chatter and ill-natured exaggeration the poor young fellow's life was trembling in the balance, and with his life—his reason. Strong as he was, the strain had been more than he could bear; and now the question was, not only: Would his life be spared? but, if it were spared: Would it be worth the while? Would not death be preferable to a life-long mental darkness?

. . .

One evening Mrs Lynes was standing close to the great coquette. It was in the house of the lady who thought Mark inconsiderate for having brain-fever consequent on a severe wound and much mental anguish.

"I want to introduce to you my friend, Miss Caine," said the lady, suavely.

She knew of Mrs Lynes' objection, but it seemed to her that a bold move like this would maybe win the day, and that Mrs Lynes would scarcely refuse an introduction to one who stood within earshot.

"Miss Carry Caine?—the girl who has played with an honest man's heart, and perhaps sacrificed his life to her shameless vanity?—introduce me to her? No, I thank you!" said Mrs Lynes, aloud. "I would not touch the hand of a heartless coquette whom I regard as little better than a murderess."

She spoke in a clear voice, then turned away abruptly; and for the first time in her life Carry Caine was seen to shrink and cower, like a flower over which has passed the hot breath of the simoon. Presently there was a stir and a rapid running to and fro of feet, a pressing forward of curious heads and cries for cold water and fresh air. Carry Caine had fainted; and for a long time lay as if dead.

"See what you have done by your cruelty!" said the lady to Mrs Lynes, reproachfully.

"What have I done?" the other answered. "If anything at all, I have broken up the ice of vanity that had encrusted her heart, and have made a woman out of a moral *fille de marbre*."

This was the last evening at which the girl appeared in public. Society resented this sudden eclipse of its brightest star, and felt disposed to organise a revolution which should drag her back to the throne she had vacated—to the world she had left desolate and leaderless. But the beautiful American was inflexible. No prayers moved her, no entreaties stirred her. She simply refused all invitations and kept herself invisible to all callers. No one knew when she went out nor where nor how she had fresh air and exercise. She withdrew like a snail into its shell, and there was no spell which could compel her to come forth.

. . .

One day Mrs Lynes was sitting in her cool room, where the pleasant plash of the fountain in the court-yard was heard, and the scents of flowers came in with the sound—like a partsong braided into one divinest harmony. It was the month of May, when Rome is at its most beautiful and life is at its best, and when all the gentler feelings are to the front and the darker and harsher have sunk into the background. It was a day when even Mrs Lynes might be found capable of forgiving vanity and dealing with coquetry as a minor fault, not altogether destructive.

There was a ring at the bell of her apartment, and, without waiting for the customary permission to enter on demand of the servant, a girlish figure pressed close behind old Giovanni, and a young voice, a little veiled, said: "May I come in, Mrs Lynes? I am Carry Caine."

"Good heavens!" said Mrs Lynes, starting from her seat. Had it been Circe herself, she would not have been more astonished. "Miss Caine!" she repeated, "what brings you here?"

"My sorrow," said Carry, always in that veiled voice, "and my wish to atone for my sin."

In a moment Mrs Lynes had her hands on the girl's arms.

"Is this really true?" she said, searching her face keenly. "Have you indeed got this grace of sorrow—this penitent desire of atonement?"

"Yes," said Carry quietly, a few tears falling silently, without sobs or wailings, from her eyes. "I have been frightfully wicked, I know, but now I am sorry, and I wish to do what I can to show that I am sorry."

"I am glad it is so," said Mrs Lynes; and with this she lifted her hands from the girl's arms, and put them round her waist, drawing her to her bosom and kissing her.

"Thank you," said Carry Caine quietly; but immediately after her quietness left her, and, clinging to her new friend like a child, like a child she sobbed out her pain on the breast which, once so hardened against her, was now as a pillow of down for the aching head—a refuge in time of trouble for the throbbing heart. It was a strange foundation for the friendship that sprang up between these two. Public, hard, indignant repudiation to be the base of a tender, sympathetic, faithful affection!—Yes, it was indeed a strange foundation; but it was none the less true; and the American-Romano society had now another subject wherewith to occupy its idle hours— the intimacy between Carry Caine and Mrs Lynes, the woman who had publicly refused to know her.

Time, youth, and care healed Mark to a certain degree—healed him enough to let him take his place once more in the world. He came back to society, but he came back a changed man. Pale, worn, hollow-eyed, and haggard, with the look of one who has just escaped death, and even now is not quite free, he confronted those who had made merry over his fatal love, and hazarded a return to the presence of the woman who had so ill-requited his devotion. But he came back always what he had been, the true-hearted gentleman who had failed because he had measured another's vanity by his own simplicity of intention and singleness of heart—because he had interpreted her falseness by his own truth . . .

It was in the same ball-room which had seen his fatal discomfiture and Count Villani's sorry triumph that Mark Lawrence and Carry Caine met for the first time since his return to life. She had heard of his intention to be present, and she broke through her rule of seclusion that she might meet him in public, and before all the world make her submission. Never had she looked so beautiful as she did then. She was more than ever the Star of society, the Beauty of the world of Rome; and all watched her, curious, anxious, on the tiptoe of expectation. It was in the air that something was to take place; and the eyes which watched seemed to be multiplied as groups stood drawn a little apart, and all looked at Carry Caine and Mark Lawrence, the two who were to make pastime for the rest. When Carry came in, Mark was standing at the upper end of the room talking to the Minister. They were discussing his speedy departure for America.

As white as her own dress, the girl walked slowly up the room—Mrs Lynes by her side—slowly, slowly, until she came to the Minister and Mark. He stood there, fronting her, blanched but resolute, half-expecting some new wrong but believing himself so far cured of his folly as to be able to bear it. Carry went straight up to the young fellow—her former toy and victim, and now her judge. She held out her hand.

"Forgive me, Mark," she said in a clear voice, her eyes fixed, her lips drawn and tense; "I want to apologise to you publicly for the shameful part I played the last time we met. I want to say that I am sorry—more sorry than I can express—and to ask you to forgive me. Can you forgive me enough to take my hand?"

What followed on this speech no one ever knew. It was a confused and chaotic little scene, where no one saw exactly and no one heard correctly; but all did see that Carry Caine had tears in her eyes; that Mark Lawrence had taken her hand, and lifted it to his lips; and that Mrs Lynes and the Minister were talking together with smiles, the Minister being heard to say: "And I will be her father, and give her away."

12.5

The cheap domestic magazines offered romantic and sentimental fiction in serial form or as complete short stories like this, which filled exactly one page of the magazine:

'His Brown-Eyed Maiden', by Sarah Capp, *Home Notes*, vol. 1, 1895, p. 187.

"And it was a case at first sight?" I queried.

My old school chum, Norman Arkwright, also in the army, puffed sorrowfully at his briar-wood a moment or two. Then he nodded his head by way of answer.

"And you have never seen her since?"

"Never!" in a minor key.

Norman was home from India on sick leave. As he had no near relative in England, Bee begged me to invite him to stay with us, and thus it happened that our little home received a third inmate.

To make matters clear, this was July. Lionel Davenport had proved such trumps in releasing Bee from her engagement to him—she confessed that she was feeling so wretched when he proposed to her, that she accepted him out of sheer desperation—that there was no need for our marriage to be postponed, and Bee made me feel the happiest of men before April. My regiment had been shifted to Shorncliffe, so that we were not so very far away from Bee's people.

A few days after Norman's arrival he unbosomed himself of a secret sorrow. He had fallen desperately in love with some unknown maiden, and declared that he should go back to Calcutta a wretched man if he never met her again.

"It happened like this", he said. "I ran down to Hampton on the chance of seeing a fellow I used to be friendly with. To my intense surprise I found that he had been away from there several months. As it was early afternoon, I decided to go for a row on the river before returning to town. Then I saw her. She was accompanied by a small girl and a lad, and was taking an oar. Our boats got side by side in the lock, and our eyes met. Such eyes, Geoff, old man.

There was an utter "Arry in a canoe at the same time, and he was no more able to manage his craft than the merest infant. Being the laughing-stock of the place did not contribute to inspire the fellow with confidence. He floundered and splashed about, and finally ran into her craft, nearly upsetting it, but for my being able to avert the catastrophe in time. Of course, she expressed her gratitude, and that sort of thing, and we began to talk. Then the lock was opened, and our boats got separated by that idiot of a Johnny pushing his canoe in between. When I finally got out of the lock, I could espy her boat nowhere, and, though I rowed up stream in a manner that created consternation, not a trace of the dear little girl was visible. I haunted Hampton every day for a whole week, but I never caught a glimpse of her again."

"Advertise," I suggested.

Norman looked angry.

"It's no laughing matter, Geoff. If I don't marry that brown-eyed maiden I'll die a bachelor." I could afford no sensible suggestion, so I changed the conversation, but later I asked Bee's advice. I have noticed that women can generally see a way out of the difficulty.

"You think he is really serious, dear?"

"Positively."

"It's very sad," sighed Bee, sympathetically. Then her eyes brightened.

"I say, Geoff!"

"Well, little woman?"

"It's a hundred chances to one if he ever sees that girl again, and really it is a pity for such a nice fellow to waste his life over an illusion. I have just thought—"

"Go on."

"Don't you think he might take a fancy to Marjorie? you know, dear, she behaved like a little brick in putting Aunt Mary up to inviting you to that dance; and I should be so glad to see her happily married."

I saw the drift of Bee's meaning.

She was actually turning matchmaker.

"What is Marjorie like?"

"Deceiver! As if you don't remember, considering that she was my best bridesmaid."

"I only wanted to see the bride."

"Flatterer, too! Marjorie is little, looks very demure, and is what most people call a 'sweet little brown mouse'."

"Just Norman's style! Invite her here at once."

And Bee did so without delay.

The day we expected Marjorie, Bee announced in an indifferent tone that her cousin was coming to stay for a few days. I went with Bee to station, and on the way the Colonel and his wife buttonholed us. One cannot be plain spoken with one's chief, so Bee and I had to listen to a weary dissertation from the Colonel, knowing that we should miss the train. And, when we finally got away, we found that the express had come in to time, and we were more than twelve minutes late.

"How annoying," said Bee. "Marjorie will be home already."

"And have had to introduce herself to Norman."

"Poor Norman!" laughed Bee.

When we got home the maid informed us that "Miss Nugent had arrived and was in the drawing room with Captain Arkwright."

Bee and I exchanged gla[n]ces as we repaired thither.

Then an unexpected sight greeted us. The sofa was occupied by two people, sitting in close proximity. They darted apart on seeing us, and Marjorie's face went the colour of a peony.

Then Norman said—and I thought of my own experience some months earlier:

"Let me introduce you to the future Mrs. Arkwright, Geoff, old boy; and Mrs. Powys, a thousand thanks! But you might have told me that your cousin Marjorie was my little brown-eyed maiden of Hampton."

Sweethearts (1894), like *Forget-Me-Not* (1891–1918), combined the new format of the cheap domestic weekly with the type of halfpenny novelettes associated with working-class women's reading. Costing a halfpenny, it was illustrated, printed on cheap paper and offered a complete and 'madly exciting' novella in each number. It advertised itself as a purveyor of stories of 'Love, Courtship and Marriage' of which this abridged example is typical.

'A Lover of High Degree: or, How Norah Flynn Became a Duchess. A Romantic Story of Unswerving Affection and Mad Passion. By Lorna O'Reilley. Author of "A Splendid Crime," "One Summer's Flirtation," "Jilted," "A Strange Wooing," "Her Heart's Lord," etc., etc., etc.', *Sweethearts*, vol. 1, no. 2, 1898, pp. 1–6. See also FIGURE 27 (the cover of this number is FIGURE 26).

FIGURE 27 'A Lover of High Degree', p. 1

I. In Rotten Row.

It was like fairyland.

So thought Norah Flynn as she gazed for the first time on the riders in Rotten Row in the height of the London season.

Norah had passed the eighteen years of her life in a gamekeeper's cottage in Dedlington in Somersetshire, until her father's second marriage deprived her of a home.

Sorry as Dick Flynn had been to part with this daughter, the only child of his first wife, he could not fail to see that it was the only way to attain peace and quietness.

Norah was a very fair hand at dressmaking, and with the wondrous faith peculiar to the country-bred, he saw her off to the great city with thirty shillings in her pocket, never doubting that a suitable situation would present itself.

She had now been in town three days, when she had lost her way, and had wandered on until she suddenly found herself in Rotten Row.

A gentleman, on a powerful black horse, arrested her attention. He was a tall, dark handsome man; he stopped nearly opposite Norah to speak to two ladies, with whom he was evidently acquainted.

All at once a cry arose of "Mad dog! Mad dog!"

Norah looked up, and saw the people on the path rushing helter-skelter in all directions, leaving the way clear for a fierce-looking, black-and-white dog, which was rushing along with its tongue lolling out of its mouth, and its eyes rolling wickedly.

Terribly alarmed at the idea of being bitten by the animal, she exerted herself to the utmost to get away.

She looked eagerly for means of escape.

Unless she crept under the railings, and went into the area set apart for the horses, there was no chance for her.

If she resolved upon this course, she ran the risk of being ridden over.

There was a choice of evils, what should she do? She was not long before she was decided.

She stooped down, passed under the railings and ran across the Row.

The powerful black horse she has noticed before was frightened by the shouts and cries of the spectators. It bore on the curb, and pulled at the rein.

As its rider was not at that moment holding it well in hand, the animal took the bit between the teeth, and with a wild snort started off.

In spite of its rider's efforts, the horse ran at full speed.

Norah was directly in his path. She might have saved herself; but she stood in the middle of the road as if fascinated by the fine dark flashing eyes of the rider who was doing his utmost to check the horse, and so prevent an accident.

"Out of your way!—run for your life!—out of the way!" he shouted.

"Hi! Hi!" cried the spectators. "You'll be run over!"

But Norah did not move the eighth of an inch.

Nothing but a miracle could save her.

More than one person turned away, to shut out a sickening sight.

On came the horse, which was altogether beyond the control of the rider.

The fiery blood of the well-bred Arab swelled in its veins, and, with nostrils dilated, it rushed upon the defenceless girl, and hurled her violently to the earth.

Fortunately, she fell some distance from the animal, so that she escaped the cruel fate of being crushed and mangled beneath his iron hoofs.

It was quickly apparent to the sympathetic bystanders that she was not much injured. The shock to the system was, no doubt, great; but, happily, no bones were broken. She was instantly surrounded by a crowd, and carried to a quiet spot, and laid upon the grass. The stranger, who had been the innocent cause of the accident, succeeded in reining in his horse after the excited animal had gone some hundreds of yards up the Row.

He instantly alighted, and threw his reins to his groom, who promptly rode up.

Having done so, he hurried to the place where Norah was, and pushing on one side of some bystanders, found the girl sitting up, having her forehead bathed with some water hastily procured from the neighbouring lake.

Norah raised her eyes and encountered the gaze of a very handsome man.

There was an air of quiet dignity about him which sat well upon his finely-chiselled features. He was as dark as the night; an eloquent fire flashed from his expressive eyes, and his black moustache was the silkiest she had ever seen.

"I trust you are not in any way hurt?" he said.

"I feel a little faint; but I am not seriously injured."

"I am thankful to hear you say so! I was afraid that I had done you some great injury. My horse is a restive animal, and it was out of my power to restrain him. I shall be happy to do anything I can for you. I am at present staying at my cousin's. Here is my card. If you will take the trouble to call at 74, Cradlemont Terrace, the Countess of Adullam will, I know, be glad to render you any assistance in her power."

When he had gone, Norah looked at the card, and on it was written, "The Duke of Conway."

Soon after she walked home on air; she had had an adventure, and had talked with real gentlefolk. The next day she decided to go and see the Countess. Life was beginning for her.

* * *

. . . [Norah gets a job as maid to the jealous Evadne.]

III. An Unexpected Meeting.

TIME passed on, the London Season waned, and August saw the Countess of Adullam and Evadne at Bessborough.

Norah had scant leisure. Her time was fully occupied in dressing the two ladies, and making such alterations as were necessary to their numerous gowns.

She grew paler daily, and found that the only means to snatch a little sea-air was to go out early in the morning before anyone was stirring.

Those walks on the glowing sands, shimmering from the kisses of the sun and waves, were the greatest enjoyment of her life. Then she had time to think, and small wonder that her girlish thoughts centred themselves round the tall dark nobleman, who, ever since the day of her accident, had been her hero.

She was seated upon a seaweed-strewn rock one morning, wondering vaguely if she should ever speak to him again, when a familiar voice fell on her ear:

"What an early bird it is, my pretty one." . . .

Norah rose, and flushed to the tips of her tiny shell-like ears.

"Your Grace," she stammered, "I did not know you had come to Bessborough."

"I only arrived last night," he said, and seating himself upon the rock, he drew the girl down by his side.

"I have been looking for you vainly in town," he began, "and it was only the day before yesterday that I learnt that my cousin was here."

Norah nervously plucked a long strand of deep-brown seaweed from the rock, and bent her crimson face closely over it.

He placed his hand gently over hers. Her whole being thrilled with delight at his touch. Then, with a sigh, she rose.

"It's getting late, I must be going, your Grace."

"Not yet," he answered. "See," and he drew his watch and shewed her the face, "it is only quarter-past seven. Miss Chester never rises before nine."

"No, but—"

"But what?" he insisted.

"I have some work to do," said Norah, growing more confused with every minute.

"Are you so very fond of work?" queried the Duke, with a smile, as he gazed on the lovely face before him.

Norah's beautiful hazel eyes looked straight into his through their long dark lashes as she answered:

"I do not like to work so much as to continue working if I were independent."

"You do not?"

"No. Sometimes I have almost wished that your horse had killed me, for then I should have been at rest."

"Have you been miserable?" he asked, anxiously.

"Yes, very, at times."

"What was the cause of your misery?"

"Ah! That, your Grace, I am unable to tell you," replied Norah, shyly.

"Pray indulge my curiosity!"

"On no account."

"I beg of you!"

"I cannot; indeed, I cannot! I spoke thoughtlessly. I am sorry that I spoke at all."

"My dearest, I must have an answer," said the Duke, respectfully, but firmly.

Norah made no reply.

She hung her head like a guilty school-girl, detected in the commission of some offence.

The Norah uttered a sudden exclamation of surprise. The Duke's glance followed the direction of her eyes.

Evadne Chester stood before them, and her expression was that of a fiend.

. . .

V. One Woman's Jealousy.

BEFORE she had reached the hotel, Evadne had decided on her course of action. She knew that the Duke would be fully occupied that day, with matters concerning his cousin's estate. She went straight upstairs to her room, ordered Norah to pack her boxes, and be out of the house before breakfast was over.

Tears and entreaties were alike useless, and Norah, pale and tearful, left that morning— without a character.

The girl was friendless and desperate. She knew not where to turn, and as she walked slowly along, she determined to take her courage in both hands, and beg the Duke's aid to procure her another situation.

She did so by letter, with many misgivings, after she had hired a lodging for one night, to which a reply could be addressed.

This missive was handed to the Duke just as he was in the midst of his work, and he put it, unopened, into his pocket without another thought.

About five o'clock, Evadne called to the Duke that she would give him some tea in the garden. Her aunt, she said, was resting.

And the Duke, ignorant of the tempest that was raging in Evadne's heart, made his appearance in a few minutes.

As he did so, he unwittingly drew the letter Norah had written from its resting place with some cigarette papers. It fell on the grass.

The direction was uppermost, and Evadne—stern, proud, haughty ambitious Evadne—caught sight of the handwriting, which was evidently a woman's.

"Oh," she thought, "whatever happens I must see that note."

To obtain possession of it was no difficult matter, for the Duke was ignorant of its loss.

When Evadne allowed her handkerchief to drop upon the note, he failed to notice it, nor did he know that in taking up the fluttering cambric she had also grasped the letter from one in whom he was interested.

With outward calm she made tea and handed him a cup, and even said, with a meaning smile, that she hoped he'd have news for her ere long.

"How overpowering the heat is!" exclaimed Evadne, in a languid tone, a few minutes later.

She was dying to read the letter, and could not rest until she had done so.

"Do you think so?" said the Duke. "Since the wind rose the heat has been much less, I fancy."

"I shall go and fan auntie, one must be dutiful, you know. In the meantime you can smoke a cigarette," she continued.

"If you wish, certainly," he replied politely.

As soon as she was safely out of sight, Evadne tore the letter open, and read it from beginning to end.

"How dare she?" she breathed. Then with a cruel smile of mingled triumph and defiance, she tore it into a thousand pieces and burnt them there and then.

Long she sat in anxious thought, but when she rose from her chair, her mind was made up.

At all costs, Norah should be removed from her path, once and for all.

Accordingly when she had gained her room, Evadne tore a leaf from a pocket book and wrote with a pencil, in a well-defined, masculine hand:—

"I have received your note, and thank you for it. I have much to say to you, and at once. I am waiting for you at the corner of the street in which you live. Pray come. Don't be afraid.—Conway."

This she sent at once by special messenger, then thickly veiled, and wrapped in a long cloak, she glided out of the hotel in the same direction.

VI. The Duke to the Rescue.

Norah had been waiting for an answer to her letter to the Duke ever since she had sent it, and she had almost given up all hope of receiving a reply. She consoled herself a little with the thought that he was probably out when her letter arrived, and had not as yet returned.

When, towards nine o'clock in the evening, a servant brought her a letter, she took it joyfully, and eagerly tore it open.

She had never seen the Duke's handwriting, so she could not tell whether or no (*sic*) it was genuine.

She did not stop to think. It had every appearance of being his, and she was inclined to consider it so.

To her simple mind, there was nothing suspicious in the fact of his requiring her to go to the corner of the street. Perhaps he did not wish to compromise her in the eyes of the people with whom she was lodging by calling there. This was just the sort of delicate attention she expected from a gentleman, and a man of honour, like the Duke.

No one but Conway could have answered her letter as it had been answered without reading it, and who but the man to whom it was addressed was likely to read it?

Hastily dressing herself, she fearlessly left the house, and walked towards the corner.

She had not taken many paces before she was stopped by hearing a familiar voice:

137

"Are you out so late at night with the permission of your mistress?"

She looked at the speaker, and recognised the Duke.

"I am here to meet you," she replied.

"Me?"

"Yes: and I thank you for answering my letter in person."

"Your letter!" replied the Duke, in surprise. "My child, I have received no letter from you. I am here by the purest accident. I felt uneasy and restless, and I could not rest within doors; so I came out here for a walk."

"Are you serious?" said Norah.

"Perfectly so."

"Will Your Grace permit me to speak to you?"

"Say what you will."

"Miss Chester overheard our conversation this morning, and she immediately discharged me."

"Indeed!"

"She gave me some money, and commanded me to go back to London at once," continued Norah. "But instead of doing so, I wrote a letter to you, asking your advice, and laying the whole case before you."

"That letter I must have lost," said the Duke. "Ah, yes! Now I remember. A note was give to me as I was going to work this morning, but what became of it I cannot tell."

"That is strange!" replied Norah. "For only five minutes ago I received a letter, in answer to mine, telling me to meet the writer at the corner of the street, and the letter was signed 'Conway'."

. . .

Norah's heart thumped violently at the words. Was she dreaming?

"Norah, dearest," he began—

"Your Grace, I must speak to you. The matter is of vital importance."

The speaker was Evadne Chester.

"One moment," said the Duke, with a shade of annoyance in his tone. Then turning to Norah, he said, "will you be good enough to await my return? I will not keep you long."

Norah signified her assent, and she watched his tall form following Evadne into the darkness.

"Well, Miss Chester," he said quietly, "what can I do for you?"

The woman's face was turned appealingly to his. "I am in great trouble, Duke," she said, in trembling tones, "and I have come to you to help me."

"I am entirely at your service," said he.

"If I could but think so," she sighed. "Duke, you must, you shall have pity on me. I love you dearly—I cannot live without you."

A fit of trembling seized her when she had spoken these words.

The Duke made no reply. Truth to tell, he was much perplexed to find the best way to refuse this over-fond lady, and, at the same, time, spare her the humiliation that such an act would entail.

"I am more sorry that I can say for what you have told me," he said, quietly. "Believe me, Miss Chester, that had my affections been disengaged, I should have been happy to fall in with your wishes. But now it is beyond my power. I gave you my confidence the other day because I feared that you might have made a mistake."

"Then you mean to say you love that slip of a girl?"

"With all my heart and soul," answered the Duke.

A spasm passed over Evadne's face. "Goodbye!" she cried, hoarsely, and lifted his hand to her lips.

The Duke caught her hand and shook it in silence, and turned on his heel. No words of his could heal Evadne's wounds, he knew.

Suddenly, a wild shriek rent the air.

It was the death cry of Evadne.

The miserable woman had laid violent hands on her own life.

She had taken a revolver with her, for what reason is unknown, and by some accident it went off, and she fell, shot through the heart, with the smoking weapon still clasped in her stiffening hand.

The Duke hastened toward the spot.

He feared a dreadful tragedy.

Already was there a crowd around Evadne's body, gathered from heaven only knows where.

The Duke pressed forward, and took a hasty glance.

"Alas!" he said to Norah, when he returned to her side, "she has killed herself. Rash, unhappy girl! You must not stay here any longer. I shall take you back to the Countess at once."

And as Norah walked silently by his side, the Duke wondered whether the same terrible suspicion oppressed her—that possibly the revolver had been intended to secure her own removal from the scene.

VIII. The Happy Ending.

SOME days later, the Duke had another important interview with Norah.

"Dearest", he said tenderly; "you must not shun me any more, as you have done lately. I am thankful that the Countess has needed your services, otherwise I believe I should have lost my little grey mouse altogether."

"Oh! don't," cried Norah, with tears in her eyes. "Don't make it harder for me, please. I am going away as soon as possible, as soon as the Countess is able to travel and I hope you will never see me again."

"*I* don't," answered the Duke, bluntly: "we must put matters on a different footing at once."

He stepped forward, caught Norah in his arms, and she was soon leaning her head upon his shoulder, and sobbing with joy, as if her heart would break.

"Will you be mine—my own?" asked the Duke, in tender accents.

She could only smile assent through her tears.

"Do you love me?" her noble lover asked, kissing her as he spoke.

"With all my heart and soul," she whispered. "If that were all, I should fear nothing. But what will your friends say?"

"What they like," answered the Duke, boldly. "Don't trouble your pretty little head about them. *They* are not going to be married after all."

Norah smiled.

"And the Countess?" she faltered.

"That will be all right," said the Duke. "Let's forget all about everything else just now and enjoy ourselves. I'm quite tired of having no name. You must learn to call me Ronald."

There was an interval filled up to their own satisfaction.

. . .

There was no reply to his remarks save a slightly additional pressure of the slender fingers about his neck.

"Speak to me, dearest," urged the Duke. "Tell me that you think so, too!"

"Yes," came the low response, as Norah kissed him of her own accord, "the future matters nothing, now that I have found you, my king, my lord."

13
The fashion plate and the fashion feature

With the exception of the religious and the feminist journals, fashion plates and fashion features appeared in all of the types of magazine dealt with in Part I. Coverage varied in frequency, variety and quality and this section aims to represent a sense of this. The fashion plate was issued as a separate part and could be detached and kept. Details of the clothes and accessories represented in the plate were provided in the main body of the magazine, together with information on how to obtain patterns. The fashion feature was an integral part of the magazine and stood alone as a full-page spread or was part of a page dealing with a range of different material.

FIGURE 28 Fashion plate, *The Ladies' Treasury*, vol. 6, 1858. (The original is in colour)

13.1

This fashion plate from *The Ladies' Treasury* (1858–95) is typical in that it provides detail, not only of the colour, shape and texture of the dresses, but also of the setting; in this case a sumptuous interior.

See FIGURE 28.

13.2

This plate from the fashion magazine *The World of Fashion* (1824–79) is of higher quality than the preceding one in that the detail of the design of the dresses is more intricate. This quality was reflected in the price of the publication.

See FIGURE 29.

FIGURE 29 Fashion plate, *The World of Fashion*, vol. 40, 1864. (The original is in colour)

No. 2. FRENCH HAIRDRESSING (Front).

This style is to be adopted with a high morning dress. The front hair is curled as a fringe, and torsades form a coronet at the back. Tortoise-shell pins.

No. 3. THEATRE SHOULDER CAPE.

Seal-brown plush, with velvet plastron and embroidered appliqués; the fringe is silk and chenille. The front fastens with an artistic agrafe. Pattern, 1s. 2d., by post only, The Editor, The Queen Office, 346, Strand.

No. 1. GIRL OF FIFTEEN.

Cashmere *frisé* with velvet, plain cashmere, and plain velvet, all in shades of blue. The skirt is of alternate plaitings of the two materials. The sash is velvet, and the yoke and cuffs consist of plain cashmere and velvet. Pattern of costume, 3s. 7d.

No. GIRL OF FOURTEEN.

Cashmere and woollen guipure in two shades of prune. The skirt is bordered with two plaitings, and the tablier is likewise plaited and trimmed with two bands of guipure. The waistcoat to the jacket bodice corresponds. Pattern of costume, 3s. 7d.

No. 5. VELVET AND FAILLE COSTUME.

The colour is mousse, the velvet being of a darker shade than the faille. The silk foundation is edged with a kilting, headed with a deep faille flounce, plain in front and plaited at the back. A second flounce forms a double skirt at the back, and a draped tunic in front. The basque bodice has a demi-velvet plastron fastened with velvet buttons. The cuffs and high collar are both velvet. The pouf at the back of the skirt is attached to the bodice with a hook. Bodice, 2s. 7d.; skirt and tunic, 3s. 1d.

o. 6. INDOOR COSTUMES.

Fig. 1. Striped and plain woollen. The striped skirt is plaited, and the round tablier of the plain material is draped high at the sides. The jacket bodice has a striped waistcoat, fastened above with cordelieres and velvet buttons. Bodice, 2s. 7d.; skirt, 3s. 1d.

Fig. 2. Plain and frisé cashmere, or shot silk and cashmere can be used. The bodice is made with a waistcoat, and has velvet revers and collar to match the frisé. Bodice, 2s. 7d.; skirt, 3s. 1d.

FIGURE 30 Fashion page, *The Queen*, vol. 77, 1885, p. 327

13.3

In the 1880s and 1890s the ladies' papers devoted whole pages to representations of the latest fashions. In *The Queen* (1861–1967) in particular these were high-quality engravings which rendered the clothes in sharp detail. This was ostensibly so that the reader could reproduce the clothes for herself but it also added to the visual appeal of this paper.

See FIGURE 30.

13.4

This extract from 'Home Dressmaking' a regular feature in *Home Notes* (1894–1957) demonstrates the way in which the cheap domestic magazine covered fashion. The emphasis is on the practical, with hints on how to make the clothing surrounding the poor quality illustration. The magazine also provided free patterns as an inducement to buy.

See FIGURE 31.

FIGURE 31 'Home Dressmaking', *Home Notes*, vol. 1, 1895, pp. 212–13

In the later Victorian period alongside the anonymous fashion model represented in the plates and the illustrations were similar pictures of aristocratic women who were represented as the epitome of fashion and style. This full-page spread from *The World of Dress* (1898–1908) illustrates the interest in the lives of the rich and famous, the icons of fashion and sophistication.

See FIGURE 32.

FIGURE 32 'Lady Falmouth and Lady Helen Vincent Skating at New Niagara', *The World of Dress*, vol. 2, 1899, p. 41

14
Poetry

Poetry was included in all women's magazines but its status in the magazine varied from title to title, in that there is a difference between the inclusion of poetry as filler and the inclusion of poetry as part of a magazine's overall literary or ideological endeavour. Whilst it is not always easy to distinguish different types of poetry in different types of magazines there are a number of exceptions. For instance, the drawing-room journals attempted to publish work of high quality and those devoted to particular causes or beliefs such as the feminist journals and the religious magazines tended to print poetry that complemented the broader aims of the publication. Outside of these two instances the majority of poems published deal with the themes traditionally associated with popular women's poetry of the period.

14.1

The religious magazines for middle-class women did not confine themselves to religious poetry but included poems covering a range of general themes.

'Lines Suggested by Hearing the Blackbird Sing in Early Spring', by E. M., *The Christian Lady's Magazine*, vol. 10, 1855, p. 301.

> O SING once more! Now, from yon budding spray,
> Give back the music of thy gushing lay,
> And charm my heart. Sweet things are shadow'd forth
> In thy loved song; e'en in our stormy north,
> When Nature wakes from her stern, wintry sleep,
> Thy well-known tuneful haunts we fondly seek.
> Thou wilt not sing? With look so startled, coy,
> Thou seem'st to bid me for each summer joy
> To watch and wait. Ah! I would gladly hear
> Thy note, sweet bird; yet not with anxious fear.
> I find thee mute; there shall no season fail;
> But heat and cold, soft rain and wintry gale,
> Succeed in turn; so to Faith's earnest eye,
> Are seen, afar, the joys that wait on high.

14.2

This poem which appeared in *Blackwood's Lady's Magazine* (1836–60) reflects the popularity of sentimental poetry much of which centred on filial attachment.

'To My Sister', *Blackwood's Lady's Magazine*, vol. 40, 1855, pp. 149–50.

145

THEY tell me, Jane, that we must part,
  That seas and lands will soon divide
Thy brother's fond, yet cheerless, heart
  From all that late hath formed its pride;
They tell me you are soon to leave
  The scenes, the home, where first we met,
And though awhile your heart may grieve,
  Perhaps those scenes you will forget.

If e'er a thought has cross'd my brain,
  That I should live to watch thy fate,
Alas! the thought has been in vain,
  And I have known that truth too late;
For, ere a few short years have passed,
  How chang'd will be thy girlish mind,—
Without a thought, perhaps, to cast
  Upon the home you left behind.

Yes! I must see thee soon depart:
  And though, perhaps, a transient sigh
Will issue from thy sadden'd heart,
  That sadness will ere long pass by.
I know not if I wrong thy love,
  But scarcely do I think that thou
Wilt feel that grief which now I prove,
  Such sadness as o'erwhelms me now.

While both were young, we lived awhile
  Unconscious of life's ills to come;
And, whilst we watch'd our parents' smile,
  Our thoughts ne'er wander'd from our home.
We parted—and I often dwelt
  With fondness on a sister's name,
And hoped the love for her I felt
  Might sway her youthful mind the same.

We met again—I found thee chang'd
  In form, in features—yet I thought
That time could never have estrang'd
  The sister's love for which I sought;
And if those ardent hopes were vain
  I had thus cherished ere we met,
Oh! do not think I mean to pain
  Thy heart, because it could forget.

Ah! no; for whilst I yet behold
  That graceful form, that gentle face,
And mark each day and hour unfold
  Thy tender mind, thy girlhood's face,
Ah! think not I could harshly blame;
  But when thou 'rt gone, oh! sometimes dwell
With kindness on thy brother's name,
  And think upon his fond farewell.

14.3

The feminist journals printed a range of poetry but there were a significant number of poems that dealt with social or political issues and this is one such example.

'Italian Patriotic Song', by E. H., *The Englishwoman's Journal*, vol. 4, 1860, p. 170.

SONS of Italy arouse ye!
  Now's the hour to strike the blow!
Burst the hated chains that bind ye—
  Lay the Double Eagle low!

Lift on high the flag of Freedom,
  Rally round your gallant king;
Wills united, hearts unflinching,
  To the shock of battle bring.

Let "Sardinia" be the watchword—
  She, the valiant and the free,
She that never to a tyrant
  Deigned to bow the dastard knee.

Be but firm—the proud usurper
  Shall be humbled in his might!
On! the God of battle's with ye:
  'Tis for Freedom that ye fight!

14.4

Humorous poetry was particularly prevalent in the general illustrated magazines. The following poem is from *The Girl of the Period Miscellany* (1869), a rather spontaneous and short-lived satirical response to the 'Girl of the Period' controversy initiated by Eliza Lynn Linton in *The Saturday Review.*

'The Fast Smoking Girl of the Period. Described by Herself', *The Girl of the Period Miscellany,* vol. 1, 1869, p. 137. See also FIGURE 33.

I'M a filly just rising eighteen,
  Lots of life I'm determined to see;
Stow "Markham and Mental Improvement"—
  No more of such rubbish for me.
Balls, concerts, 'drums, sensation-novels,
  Are the cheese for us girls of to-day:

FIGURE 33 'The Fast Smoking Girl of the Period', illustration

And I'll do a mild weed on the quiet,
  For that is the new-fashioned way.

Slow Sophia may sew herself blind;
  With Herr Trompette I'll try the duet
We have practised so many times over,
  But never sang perfectly yet;
"Come, let us be happy together,
  For where there's a will there's a way,"
In the Lost One or La Traviata
  He'll make me quite perfect some day.

The weekly accounts may be filed:
  How can I have time for one glance,
When dear Monsieur Chassez is coming
  To teach me that jolly new dance?
He says: "Mees, you must *élever votre jupe*
  Vos très-petits pieds to deesplay."
When he twirls me about in the *trois temps*
  From earth we seem floating away!

Oh, bother the children! You know
  At South Kensington, Ma, I am due,
That exquisite cast of Apollo
  To draw with my master till two.
"Draw landscape, fruit, flowers." No, thank
you;
  Such tame subjects are not in my way:
The glorious masculine figure
  Is the model *I* study all day.

Shut up, and don't preach about marriage;
  Of spoons you well know I've a host;
When I come to your old fogey age
  I sha'n't have to mourn over time lost.
The neighbours may gossip, and welcome;
  I don't mind two pins what they say;
I'll hook a rich stupid old husband,
  And *I'll* promise—but *he* shall *obey!*

14.5

Readers' letters often appeared in the magazines and this poem which appeared in the letters section 'Our Drawing Room' in *The Young Englishwoman* (1864–77) is a comic response to the controversy about tight-lacing that had been taken up by the magazine and its sister publication *The Englishwoman's Domestic Magazine* (1852–79) during the 1860s.

'To the Slaves of Fashion', by Chestnut, *The Young Englishwoman*, vol. 3, 1869, p. 110.

You must try and lace me tighter, lace me tighter, mother dear;
My waist, you know, is nearly half the size it was last year;
I will not faint again, mother, I care not what they say,
Oh! it's sixteen inches to-day, mother, it's sixteen inches to-day.

There's many a wee, wee waist they say, but none so wee as mine;
I'm five-foot-five-and-a-half in height; my inches forty-nine;
Last year my waist was—oh, it's size I'd be afraid to say,
But it's sixteen inches to-day, mother, it's sixteen inches to-day.

You must lace me tight to-night, mother, I must try and keep this size,
I know the doctors tell you it is dangerous—*unwise*,
And they call me vain and foolish, but I care not what they say,
For it's sixteen inches to-day, mother, it's sixteen inches to-day.

I stay so quiet all day, mother, afraid the cords might burst,
I can breathe quite freely now, though it hurt me so at first!
At first it hurt me very much, but now I'm happy and gay,
For it's sixteen inches to-day, mother, it's sixteen inches to-day.

You remember the first month, mother, what agony I bore,
But I went through it without flinching; the corsets then I wore
Measured seven-and-twenty inches; oh, I care not what they say,
For it's sixteen inches to-day, mother, it's *sixteen* inches to-day.

14.6

The following poem from *The Mother's Friend* (1848–95) illustrates the religious and moral themes found in many magazines, but which were particularly prevalent in the cheap religious monthlies.

'The Rights of Women', *The Mother's Friend*, vol. 6, 1888, p. 100.

"THE Rights of woman—What are they?—
The Right to labour, love, and pray;
The Right to weep with those that weep;
The Right to wake when others sleep.

"The Right to dry the falling tear;
The Right to quell the rising fear;
The Right to smooth the brow of care,
And whisper comfort in despair.

"The Right to watch the parting breath;
To soothe and cheer the bed of death;

The Right, when earthly hopes all fail,
To point to that within the veil.

"The Right the wanderer to reclaim,
And lure the lost from paths of shame;
The Right to comfort and to bless
The widow and the fatherless.

"The Right the little ones to guide,
In simple faith, to Him who died;
With earnest love and gentle praise,
To cheer and bless their youthful days.

"The Right the intellect to train,
And guide the soul to noble aim;
Teach it to rise above earth's toys,
And wing its flight to heavenly joys.

"The Right to live for those we love;
The Right to die that love to prove;
The Right to brighten earthly homes
With pleasant smiles and gentle tones.

"Are these thy rights?—Then use them well;
The holy influence none can tell.
If these are thine, why ask for more?—
Thou hast enough to answer for!

"Are these thy rights?—Then murmur not
That woman's mission is thy lot.
Improve the talents God has given:
Life's duties done—thy rest in heaven!"

14.7

This poem from *Home Chat* (1895–58) is a good example of the type of verse which appeared in cheap magazines and which was often by popular writers.

'Defeat', by Ella Wheeler Wilcox, *Home Chat*, vol. 6, 1900, p. 100.

DEFEAT should never mean despair;
Fate leads us here and leads us there.

Through chequered paths, through shade and sun
Our early pilgrimages run.

In climbing to the mountain's crown
Full oft the road seems winding down.

In search of goals, we find a wall;
But God's large wisdom rules us all.

Fate's cruellest hindrance and delay
Is but to guide a better way.

Who strives his noblest toward an end,
And fails, may call defeat his friend,

And know behind his loss must be
Some hidden good he cannot see.

In life's experience book I read
This motto for each soul to heed—

Emblazoned there in lines of light:
The unavoidable is right!

15
Political journalism

Political journalism appeared in a wide range of different types of women's magazines. It was crucial to the feminist press but was also important in the drawing room and general illustrated magazines, and occasionally even in the ladies' papers. Not surprisingly the emphasis was on women's issues; debates on married women's property, and the suffrage. Articles ranged from the pithy to the extended and polemical. They utilised the general rhetorical skill of debate and therefore differed from the factual accounts of government debate and legislation or brief reports on meetings which were typical of the ladies' papers particularly *The Queen*.

15.1

The broadly liberal politics of the drawing-room journal made it a suitable space in which such issues as married women's rights to property could be discussed. Bessie Raynor Parkes and others associated specifically with the feminist press also wrote for other kinds of women's journal, as in this extract.

'The Laws of Property as they Affect Married Women', by Bessie Raynor Parkes, *The Ladies' Cabinet*, vol. 8, 1856, pp. 295–96.

So much public discussion has lately been aroused on the subject of these laws, that perhaps a short review of the arguments used on either side, and a summary of the steps hitherto taken towards effecting an alteration, may not be uninteresting to the readers of this periodical . . .

> "A man and wife are one person in law. The wife loses all her rights as a single woman; and her existence is entirely absorbed in that of her husband. He is civilly responsible for her acts."
> "What was her personal property before marriage, such as money in hand, money at the bank, jewels, household goods, clothes, &c., become absolutely her husband's; and he may assign or dispose of them at his pleasure, whether he and his wife live together or not."
> . . .
> "Money earned by a married woman belongs absolutely to her husband."

This is the law. But since the humane civilization of Old England objects to throwing one human being thus into the power of another without the chance of redress, certain devices and intricate machinery is resorted to, limiting the irresponsible power of the husband among the *upper classes*. Such are trusteeships; such is the operation of the Courts of Equity.

> . . .

. . . But we will quote no further, since the details of the law contrived alternately for consolidating and softening the marital authority, as though parents and husbands had for centuries been prosecuting a sort of legal combat, would take up far too much space. We will proceed to the arguments used on the one hand by those who wish to retain, on the other by those who wish to abrogate, this mass of inconsistent legislation.

An article in "Blackwood" for April . . . gives a very fair and kindly idea of the sort of argument employed on the stand-still side of the question. It is much as follows: That the man and the woman are so far made one in marriage that any attempts to allow them separate interests endangers the God-ordained moral unity of the relation; that since in the matter of children they *must* possess a joint and indivisible interest, it does not much matter what becomes of so secondary a point as that of property; that the tendency of all ages and of all legislation has been to subordinate the woman to the man; that women are incapable, by character, by position, and by education, of dealing wisely with their own pecuniary interests; that the laws of the land follow the laws of Nature, and therefore that it is no good to try and overturn them; that any change would result in a general disorganization of society (also it is not unfrequently asserted that any change in *law* would leave *practice* just where it is!); finally, that all women would be arrayed against all men; and lastly, that women don't want any alteration.

The opponents of the law declare, on their side, that the moral unity of marriage is a deep and subtle thing, not dependent in any way on exterior legislation; nay, rather, that in the words of Emerson's noble essay, "there must be very two before they can be very one;" that the crippling of the woman's powers in depriving her of free action and responsibility, unfits her to be a noble mate to a noble man; that although the joint parentship to children be indeed a bond of union, and a partnership in which no limiting principles of justice can prevail (since neither Solomon's principle of division, nor any theory giving sons to the father, daughters to the mother, or *vice versâ* (*sic*), will ever compensate *either* parent for loss of or separation from any one child); yet that for the very sake of the children themselves, the mother ought to be able to retain and use her own earnings. Whatever marriage *ought* to be, it is actually certain that the moral ideal is oftentimes broken by the ill-conditioned use of the poker or a great stick; that it is drowned at the gin-palace and insidiously destroyed by strychnine; and that therefore, although in those unions wherein a true love reigns, father and mother would work harmoniously in feeding, clothing, or educating their children, it is well and advisable that where that blended influence reigns not, the mother should be independently enabled to provide schooling, &c., instead of being forced to see her little ones picking up crime in the gutters.

The argument . . . denies that the sex which produced Florence Nightingale and Mrs. Chisholme (we take them as specimens of *practical* ability) is incapable of dealing with pounds, shillings, and pence; it denies that any disorganization of society would ensue from a change, or that men and women would fly asunder like chemical non-affinities, unless held together by the combining power of law; and finally it denies, emphatically, persistently, and with the testimony of a thousand witnesses, that women themselves desire no change . . .

15.2

General illustrated magazines sometimes included political journalism alongside their fiction, advice and fashion tips. While Beeton, of *The Englishwoman's Domestic Magazine* (1852–79), was a liberal and supporter of women's suffrage, this was by no means true of all such journals or of all who contributed to the debate in their pages, as this abridged article shows.

'Should Women be Permitted to Vote? By a Woman', *The Ladies' Treasury*, vol. 4, 1868, pp. 171–74.

MUCH has been said for and against women being permitted to have a voice in the government of the country, but the argument on each side, like a proverb, cuts both ways. To women who have themselves accumulated property by their industry it seems hard to have no recognised individual *status* beyond the right to control and manage that property, and which having known the getting they well know the best ways of spending; the suffrage in such hands would not be misused. But money-getting women, whether as farmers or traders, are in the minority. Not so those who possess inherited property, but who know nothing of its working value. Women at the age of twenty-one are no longer "infants" in the eye of the law; but as regards the management of their wealth, hitherto under trusteeship as infants, they know nothing more than the spending of their income in a manner agreeable to themselves. Nor are they educated for anything better. Business women are a separate genus—are, in fact, more like educated men. A habit of considering consequences, of battling with difficulties, of exercising self-possession, of foresight, and of order, gives them a vigilance almost unmatchable even in men, and to such women a vote should be given if it were possible. But it is not. The weak of the sex are in the majority. Most women above the lower class seem born into the world to lean upon others; they repeat the thoughts of others, see with the eyes of others, and have no notion of self-responsibility. Are these the women to whom the franchise should be extended? Certainly not, and until a very different moral and mental education is bestowed on them from that now in practice, it is vain to look for women's progression in political, intellectual, and ethical matters.

Moreover, women rarely argue with coolness of temper. They can contend, but not argue a point, or look at it in all its bearings, and give a judgment unbiassed by prejudice. Their intellectual capabilities may be as great as men's, but they want men's training and experience. Their foresight is often greater, but it wants the balance of caution. Their reticence is less than men's, their impulsive faculties in excess; their patience infinitely greater, and, when interested by love or charity, inexhaustible; and, as a class, women are utterly unselfish. All these qualities render them exceedingly open to prejudice, and unfit to influence, otherwise than through the legitimate means of husbands, fathers, or brothers. Women as widows or unmarried may in some, perhaps in numerous instances, be more capable of voting with judgment than men; but for them there are duties which only women can perform, and of infinitely more importance to the general well-being of society than chattering about politics, but loosely understood, attending public meetings, or recording their votes in public. The safety of the country is better lodged in men's hands than in women's, by reason of sex and education. There is no equality between the sexes, mentally or physically. Not all the training in the world will make men and women equal . . .

15.3

Political journalism was the life blood of the feminist press along with reports of meetings and other activities of a political nature. The long discursive essay on political or social topics was widely used and the following abridged extract represents the serious erudite voice of reform.

'Women and Politics', *The Englishwoman's Journal*, vol. 12, 1863, pp. 1–6.

WHY may not women take an interest in politics? Many will reply at once, "Is it worth while to make suggestions, and propose changes when things are going on very comfortably as they are." Yes, it is better to have a good reason for every existing state of things, because there is such a continual natural change in the phases of domestic and social and political life that if a thorough investigation is not every now and then set on foot, we are likely to find ourselves often in no very pleasant plight, and sometimes, in a very deplorable condition.

Suppose, we were never to say, "has it given over raining?" how long we might hold up umbrellas! When we have once had a thorough clearing in our houses, we find that a similar overturn must soon take place again; old curtains must be mended, broken furniture repaired;

the carpet that was an excellent covering for the floor, at one time, ceases to be so when continuous treading has worn it into holes; the paint that was a protection when it existed, is only a disfigurement when the sun has blistered it nearly away. Then we find that one kind of manufacture answers a purpose better than another; we talk about it, we discuss it with our friends and neighbours, in short we ventilate the subject as well as the house. By some such course as this it has come about that we are no longer living in rooms covered with rushes. Is this an advantage or not? the cleanly housekeeper would answer that it is. Somewhat the same process takes place, or ought to take place with regard to social and political as well as domestic institutions. Frequent ventilation is a necessity for every healthy condition of things whether physical or mental.

Allow us to repeat the question then, why women should not take an interest in politics? A ready answer is, they cannot understand such subjects, owing to their infirm mental constitutions. We will take it so—we will not deny their weak-mindedness—we believe in it. But we will not accept that reason for their exclusion from privileges which are vouchsafed to all men without any mental test beyond mere sanity. However foolish women may be, it cannot be denied that there are many men who not only hold political opinions, but who register those opinions in votes and are encouraged to do so, who are far more weak-minded than many women.

Again, because the minds of women are weak, especial pains ought to be taken to strengthen them. They are occupied with small matters, trifling and unimportant, if such words can be rightly applied to any link in the great chain of events. They are not accustomed to grasp large ideas, they cannot take comprehensive views. But we know when a child's hand is filled with a small toy, that if we place a large one before him, he drops the first and attempts to grasp the great one—it is too large for his small fingers, so he brings out his other hand and strains every nerve, and succeeds in holding it. Compare a weak mind with the child's hand. When some noble subject of thought is placed before it, not only will it open for its reception, but will positively seem to increase twofold.

What course is pursued with those nations whom nature or circumstances lead us to call inferior, or with those classes amongst civilized people who are habitually degraded? with negroes? with ragged school children? with shoe black brigades? It is said "give them higher aims"—place them in positions of trust—waken them to a sense of their responsibility. Only by such means can it be fairly tested whether they possess the intelligence which may be merely undeveloped. Why should we not apply the same treatment to ourselves, and because our minds are weak, place a high endeavour before them and perhaps find out that we have powers which neither we nor others dared to hope were our portion? As surely as the negro slave rouses to new action when the fetters fall from his limbs, as surely as the untaught children in our own land behold another world in their every-day existence when knowledge shines out of their eyes, so surely shall we behold a new glory in our being when we bend every energy we possess to grappling with those large schemes of thought and enterprise which at once exalt and lay low the soul, but in which men are too apt to rejoice alone. We should take nothing from them—from men—by so doing. There is space and to spare in the mental world. We should no more interfere with their privileges by sending our minds through the realms of thought, than by lifting up our eyes to the daily marvel of the setting sun, we should darken to their gaze its mysterious beauty.

But should we not spoil ourselves—should we not make our own minds rough and masculine by making them so large and strong? That is the same sort of question which Chinese women put, as they look down smilingly upon their little feet. But development increases natural tendencies, it does not alter nor destroy them. And a little mind is a more serious evil than a little foot.

Well, but why choose politics as a means for obtaining this wonderful expansion so much to be desired?

153

Because the beautiful and wide-spread charities of wise legislation seem to render the science of political economy peculiarly fitted for the kindly nature of a woman. It bears upon the well-being of our species more directly than any other science. Think for a moment of the sin and misery one unjust law produces. That law, for instance, which made it legal for one man to hold another in bondage; the groans, the shrieks, the wails that pierced the calm air of our Indian isles have scarcely yet ceased ringing in our ears. A life-time devoted to freeing individual slaves would but have liberated a few; a life-time spent in altering the law which bound them, enfranchised millions . . .

15.4

Ladies' papers routinely carried reports on meetings and brief accounts of women's achievements in various spheres. They sometimes also included political journalism as this extract makes clear.

'The Petticoat in the Politics of England. By Justin McCarthy. Author of "My Enemy's Daughter," "The Waterdale Neighbours", &c.', *The Lady's Own Paper*, vol. 5, 1870, p. 20.

THE late Madame Emile de Girardin it was, I think, who described some provincial microcosm where every man was governed by his wife except one, and he was governed by another man's wife. It would be rather too much, perhaps, to say that the ways of this place precisely resemble those of the English political world; but it is certain that the soft, low voice of woman has long governed the politics of England to a degree whereof probably most people, even in go-ahead America, have but little notion. Woman suffrage, I believe, is likely to become a fact in England sooner than in the United States. The difficulties in the way are less complicated. In England, even under the late Reform Bill, the franchise is given only to the occupier of a house or separate lodgings—the person who pays the rent. Therefore, were the sexes placed on a political equality, in regard to the vote, there would still be none of the complications and the confusion which, reasonably or unreasonably, are so much dreaded in America—the discord between husband and wife, the swamping of intelligence by the myriad votes of impetuous maid-servants, and so forth. The husband, mother, or son who pays the rent would have the vote, just as now; only where a widow or spinster was the recognised and responsible occupier would the woman have the vote, as indeed she already has in various parochial and other such elections. Probably the time will come when universal suffrage will be demanded for England, but that time is not just yet; and meanwhile woman will be allowed to ascend by gradual elevation towards what Mr. Mill considers her legitimate sphere, or be permitted, if you prefer to look at the subject with Mr. Carlyle's eyes, to descend an inclined plane towards that bottomless pit whither womanhood suffrage is to be followed by doghood suffrage.

I am not, however, about to write an essay on Woman Suffrage; whereon, whether in England or elsewhere, there has perhaps been a sufficiency of writing already without my help. My purpose is rather to speak of that kind of influence which women have long exercised in English politics, and which may be described as the irresponsible and illegitimate influence—the petticoat influence. I grieve to have to speak ungallantly, but I am compelled to say that in the overwhelming majority of cases it has been a corrupt and almost as often a corrupting influence. Nor need the advocates of woman's suffrage (I am one of its sincere and candid advocates myself) take alarm at this, or attempt the futile task of disproving it. Irresponsible, illegitimate, and subterranean influences nearly always are corrupt. The fact is rather an argument to establish, than an argument to disprove, the necessity of the political enfranchisement of women.

Corrupt, however, the political influence of the petticoat in England assuredly is. Let us begin at the base of the social pyramid. The influence of the wives of uneducated or half-educated voters in the smaller boroughs is immense. The wives are almost always to be reached by bribes or presents or promises or flatteries. An election agent of experience once told me that when he had secured the wives he cared nothing about the husbands. The eloquent and judicious candidate always pays special attention to the task of flattering and winning wives. In almost numberless cases detailed before election committees, the business of bribery was carried on directly with the wife, who undertook, plain and square, to manage her husband . . . Of course there is bribery which is done not with four shekels of the tested gold. Where the electors are of a somewhat higher class than those whom I have just been describing, there are influences of a more delicate order brought into operation. There are, of course, the agent's flattery, the candidate's flattery; sweeter and more seductive than all, the flattery brought to bear by the candidate's gracious wife. So pray do not mistake the meaning of the kind of influence to which the virtuous and corrupt spouse of the British elector commonly yields. It is the sweet condescension of higher rank which conquers her; and this is far more sweet and conquering when it comes from the candidate's wife or sister than from the candidate himself. For although it is an exquisite sensation to Mrs. Plumper to see the honourable candidate, son perhaps of a peer, take off his hat to her and bow and smile, to hear his winning voice and feel his shake of his hand, yet it is a prouder moment by far when the candidate's wife or sister calls upon her and recognises with gracious courtesy her social existence. Here we have the power of the petticoat controlling politics by a double-acting influence. Of course, however, the demeanour of the candidate himself, and even his personal appearance, will count for a great deal. A handsome face, a pleasant tongue, and a noble name are almost irresistible with the class of wives who are above the money bribe or the green parasol . . .

All this, however, is a kind of influence which may be regarded as elementary and obvious. Given the system of personal canvass, and it follows that the results are inevitably placed more or less in the hands of the women of a family. Given the system of bribery, and it follows that the irresponsible wife will be a willing and a convenient medium for the corruption of her husband. But the illegitimate influence of women over English politics takes a much higher range, and finds far subtler modes of operation than this . . . Many an honest British Philistine beyond the middle age yawns or dozes for hour after hour every night on the back benches of the House of Commons, weary of speeches he does not care to hear, and having no desire whatever of making a speech himself, who would be quietly at home in his obscure and happy bed but for the energy and ambition of his wife and her girls. This poor man is sure to be the victim of a clever minister.

Social influence is a tremendous power in English politics. The drawing-room often settles the fate of the division in the House of Commons. The smile or the salute of the peeress has already bought the votes which are necessary to secure her husband's triumph. The late Lady Palmerston was a perfect mistress of this kind of policy, and was, in her way, a sort of ruling, cajoling queen of society.

. . .

Woman in England, then, although she has not yet a voice in the public administration of politics, can certainly not be said to have had no share in the practical rule of the country. Indeed her influence has been far too great, because it has been irresponsible and illegitimate. There is not an injustice known to the political system of England which has not been favoured, abetted, struggled for, begged for, wheedled for, intrigued (sic) for, by women. And in nine cases out of ten the women who thus misuse their influence would repudiate with utter indignation any proposal to confer the suffrage upon their sex, and would as soon adopt Mary Walker's pantaloons as Helen Taylor's political professions.

I cannot refrain from saying a few words in praise of the ability, moderation, discretion, and gracefulness with which the English women of a very different class—the English women who, like Helen Taylor (John Stuart Mill's stepdaughter) demand the vote for their sex—have conducted their agitation. These ladies have done but little speaking, and absolutely no spouting or screaming. They have not troubled themselves or the world with weary disquisitions on the natural equality or inequality of the sexes; they have not concerned themselves to prove that woman is the superior creation and the last work of Nature; they have not said anything about the tyranny of man, and I do not believe that they even regard man as very much of a tyrant. The tyrant man has to a very considerable extent recognised the justice of their cause, and fought their good fight for them; and now the fight is all but won.

16
Advertising

Advertisements tended to get stripped out of magazines when they were bound into volume form. It is therefore sometimes difficult to know precisely how much advertising some of these magazines carried. However, we can be confident that throughout the Victorian period most women's magazines carried at least some advertisements. For most of the period these were confined to end-papers, that is the sheets immediately inside covers. Advertisements in the 1830s and 1840s were relatively unimportant, lacked visual appeal and had a limited relationship to the contents of the rest of the magazine. Until 1853 advertising was heavily taxed, part of a series of taxes on print which were gradually lifted in the first half of Victoria's reign. The 1853 change in taxation was significant but it was not until the 1880s and 1890s that the growth in new kinds of magazines, changes in print technology, and the arrival of a new kind of journalism transformed advertising in women's magazines. These changes in turn were related to more general developments in marketing and the growth of brand images, such as Bovril or Pears Soap. Some types of magazine, particularly the ladies' papers became famous for advertising and relied on it to keep down their cover prices and fill their pages. *The Queen* by the mid-1880s gave more than half its pages to advertisements. These were still mainly printed on separate pages from editorial matter but they were visually more exciting than in the past and there was a strong relationship between advertisements and the advice given in the editorial sections of the press. The 'advertorial' had been developed in general illustrated and fashion magazines like *The Englishwoman's Domestic Magazine* and *Myra's Journal* but it now became more widespread. In the cheap domestic magazines of the 1890s, advertising was not only financially and visually important, it was completely integrated into the editorial matter, appearing opposite or on the same page as articles and advice columns.

16.1

The Lady's Newspaper (1847–63) was the earliest weekly broadsheet for women. It was merged with *The Queen* (1861–1967) in 1863. From the start it carried pages of advertisements, laid out like the rest of the paper in three-column unillustrated format.

See FIGURE 34.

16.2

Advertisements appeared even in feminist journals and other kinds of magazine whose main purpose was not commercial. This was to become a feature of the specifically suffragette press of the early twentieth century. These advertisements appeared opposite the article on 'The Use of a Special Periodical' (see 10.5 above.)

See FIGURE 35.

378 THE LADY'S NEWSPAPER.

GINGER WINES.

EDWARDS' celebrated Old Ginger Wine, highly recommended for its purity, strength, and excellent stomachic qualities, 18s. per dozen. Observe: To prevent imposition each bottle is capsuled, and the cork branded. To be had of most dealers, and of the manufacturer, JOHN EDWARDS, 39, Holborn-hill, London.

THE AUSTRALIAN PALE ALE.

CHIDELL and JONES, Wine and Spirit Merchants, 40, Lime-street, City, and Agents by special Appointment for the Sale of ASHBY'S celebrated AUSTRALIAN PALE ALE, beg to inform their Friends and the Public, that this season's Brewing is in splendid condition in Bottle, and also in 9 gallon and 18 gallon Casks.

N.B. Strongly recommended by the Faculty.

E. J. DENT'S Manufacture of Watches and CLOCKS is protected by three separate patents. Ladies' elegant Gold Watches, with gold dials, and jewelled in four holes, Eight Guineas; Gentlemen's ditto, enamel dials, Ten Guineas; Youths' Silver Watches, Four Guineas; substantial and accurately-going Silver Lever Watches, jewelled in four holes, Six Guineas.—Dent, 82, Strand; 33, Cockspur-street; and 34, Royal Exchange (Clock Tower Area).

CHILDREN'S Beaver and Felt Hats.—PERRING has a most extensive, varied, and fashionable assortment of Children's Beaver and Felt Hats in various colours, elegantly fitted up, for the inspection of the Nobility, Gentry, and Public. Also, some new and superior Velvet Hats for Gentlemen, suitable for winter wear, in a variety of shapes, from 12s. to 21s.; Ventilating Beaver Hats, 16s. to 21s.; Livery Hats, 8s. to 16s.; Youths Hats, 6s. 6d. to 12s. Youths' and Children's Caps of every description. Gentlemen's Shooting, Fishing, Lounging, and Travelling Caps.

Cecil-house, 85, Strand; and 251, Regent-street.

THE Crystal Spectacles of Thomas Harris and SON are of well-known excellence for strengthening weak sight and preventing its decay; being accurately fitted to the face, they neither disarrange ladies' hair, mark the nose, nor in any way disfigure the countenance, but combine every quality for the wearer's comfort. Best blued steel Crystal Spectacles, 15s.; silver, 20s.; Solid Gold, 42s.; Glass Spectacles from 2s. 6d. the pair. Thomas Harris and Son, Opticians to the Royal Family, No. 52, Great Russell-street (opposite the Old Gate of the British Museum, London); established 70 years. Caution—To avoid mistakes, recollect the number of the shop is 52! T. Harris and Son have no other.

ROBINSON'S Patent Drying Machine. Mr. W. E. JENKINS, Proprietor of the Patent, has had the pleasure to receive (among many others) the following Testimonial from the Laundress of a highly-distinguished Private Establishment:—"I have had one of Mr. Robinson's Drying Machines in use for some time. It has entirely abolished, in this Laundry, the destructive system of wringing, hitherto necessary, and I can confidently say, from ample experience, that it could never injure a thread of the finest material. I consider it a most valuable invention, and all who use it will find, as I do, not only that the work of the Laundry can be done in a far more rapid and satisfactory manner than before, but, above all, the saving in wear and tear will be very considerable."

Manufactory, 27, Charles-street, Berners-street, London.

FOR Indigestion, Bile, Sick Headache, Giddiness, Loss of Appetite, Lowness of Spirits, with sensation of fulness at the pit of the stomach, pains between the shoulders, and all the distressing feelings arising from debility and indigestion, STIRLING'S STOMACH PILLS are the best remedy; they can be taken at any time, without any danger from wet or cold, requiring no restraint from business or pleasure. They act mildly on the bowels, without pain or griping, giving strength to the stomach, and promoting a healthy action of the liver, by which they prevent and cure the Jaundice and Dropsy, clear the skin, remove sallowness and pimples, purify the blood, brace the nerves, and invigorate the whole system. Females at a certain period of life should never be without them. Prepared only by JOHN WILLIAM STIRLING, 86, High-street, Whitechapel. Sold in boxes at 1s. 1½d., 2s. 9d., and 4s. 6d. each, in every town.

*** Caution.—Ask for "Stirling's Stomach Pills," and see that the name is on the stamp.

J. W. S. is also Agent for Lefay's Grand Pomade; a certain cure, by rubbing, for all painful affections of the Nerves; giving instant relief in the most severe paroxysms of these tormenting maladies, Tic Douloureux, Lumbago, Gout, Acute Rheumatism Sciatica, &c. &c. A Post-office order for 5s. will pay for a 4s. 6d. case and its conveyance to any part of the Kingdom.

MESSRS. LEA and PERRINS, Proprietors of the WORCESTERSHIRE SAUCE, beg to submit the following Testimonials, as a guarantee to the public of the superior qualities of this Sauce, and also to caution the purchasers against worthless imitations, by observing their names are affixed to the metallic capsule which secures the cork of each bottle, to imitate which is fraud.

"Witley Court, Feb. 28, 1846.

"Gentlemen,—I have great pleasure and satisfaction in bearing testimony to the rare qualities of your celebrated Worcestershire Sauce, which has long been an accompaniment to the Royal table, and from its peculiar piquancy, combined with exquisite flavour, is now an established favourite. It is often inquired for by families of the highest rank, who have the honour of visiting the Royal residence.

"M. MALARET, Chef de Cuisine.

"To Messrs. Lea and Perrins, Worcester."

"Conservative Club, Feb. 27, 1846.

"Gentlemen,—At the request of several members of this club I introduced your Worcestershire Sauce, and have great pleasure in saying that it has given universal satisfaction.—I am, gentlemen, your most obedient servant,

"SAMUEL HALLAM, Steward.

"To Messrs. Lea and Perrins, Worcester."

"Fladong's Hotel, 144, Oxford-street, London, March, 1846.

"Gentlemen,—I have much pleasure in testifying to the good quality of your Worcestershire Sauce as applicable to all kinds of meat and made dishes, fish, game, &c., considering it to be, without exception, the best sauce in use.

"WILLIAM LOVEGROVE.

"To Messrs. Lea and Perrins, Worcester."

Sold, wholesale, retail, and for exportation, by the proprietors, Lea and Perrins, 6, Vere-street, Oxford-street, London, and 68, Broad-street, Worcester; also by Messrs. Barclay and Sons, Messrs. Crosse and Blackwell, London; and generally by the principal dealers in sauce.

70, CORNHILL.

JOHN B. CROSS respectfully solicits from the public an inspection of his Stock of Watches, comprising every variety in modern use, of the best workmanship and at the lowest remunerating prices. Ladies' elegant Gold Watches, with gold dials and jewelled in four holes, eight guineas; Gentlemen's ditto, enamel dials, ten guineas; Youths' Silver Watches, four guineas; substantial and accurately-going Silver Lever Watches, jewelled in four holes, six guineas.

Manufactory, 41, Charterhouse-square.

H. WALKER'S Needles (by authority the "Queen's Own"), with the new large eyes, are easily threaded (even by blind persons), and work with great ease, having improved points, temper, and finish: they are made of every length or substance, and for every purpose: the labels are correct likenesses of her Majesty and his R. H. Prince Albert, in relief on coloured grounds. Sent free by post, by any respectable dealer, on receipt of thirteen penny stamps for every shilling value.—H. Walker's Improved Crochet Needles, all sizes, on large wire, Hooks and Eyes, Fish-hooks, Steel Pens, &c., are recommended.—H. Walker, Manufacturer to the Queen, Gresham-street West (lately called Maiden-lane), New Post-office, London.—Two of Miss Linwood's Pictures for sale.

ELASTIC Boots.—The Queen's Boots.—J. SPARKES HALL informs ladies and gentlemen that he has brought his ELASTIC BOOT to the highest state of perfection, and having recently effected several important improvements in that excellent article, which have rendered it the easiest, best fitting, and most elegant boot ever offered, he has manufactured for the present season a stock of more than 2000 pairs. He begs to announce that this assortment comprises double soles, treble soles, and cork soles, all made on an entirely new principle, and warranted to be the most durable as well as the most beautiful workmanship. The shape and form are peculiarly his own, and, from the extensive patronage he is honoured with, he believes the only true form that has ever been adopted to secure at once both ease and neatness. Every article is, in respect of material, workmanship, fit, and style, the best; and all workmen and workwomen at this establishment have good wages and regular employment throughout the year. A printed circular, with full particulars of the prices of the following articles, with instructions for taking measure in the readiest manner, will be forwarded with great pleasure free to any part of the world. Elastic boots, elastic clogs, and goloshes for ladies, gentlemen, and children, without straps or fastenings; elastic shoes, elastic ankle bands, elastic beaver soles, and elastic gaiters.—J. SPARKES HALL, Maker to her Majesty the Queen and the Queen of the Belgians, 308, REGENT-STREET, opposite the Polytechnic Institution.

TO THE CARPET TRADE.

ROYAL Victoria Felt Carpeting, manufactured without spinning or weaving.—Patronized by her most gracious Majesty, and used in the Royal Palaces. This description of Carpeting has now become one of the established manufactures of this country. Its advantages are beauty of design (equal to Brussels), imperviousness to dust, durability, and more especially economy, as it can be purchased for less than half the price of Brussels.

The Patent Woollen Cloth Company, who are the sole Manufacturers under the patent, having availed themselves of the rapid strides now making in the arts of design in this country, inform the trade that their Patterns for the present season are now out, and that they will be found far in advance of all hitherto produced, and suitable for every description of room and decoration. The public can be supplied through their Agents in nearly all the provincial towns in England, Scotland, and Ireland, and at every respectable Carpet House in London and its suburbs. They also manufacture Table Covers and Window Curtains, embossed and printed in a great variety of elegant and novel designs; Plain Cloths suitable for Upholsterers; Cloths admirably adapted for Coach and Railway Carriage Linings, Waistcoatings; Thick Felt for Plate Glass and Marble Polishing; Gun Waddings; and of all thicknesses suitable for Pianoforte Manufacturers, at a very considerable saving as compared with those made by hand; D'Oyleys, &c. &c.

Wholesale Warehouses: 8, Love-lane, Wood-street, Cheapside.—Manufactories: Elmwood Mills, Leeds; and Borough-road, London.

PURE Castor Oil. Administered by means of the PATENT CAPSULES.

This valuable Medicine can now be taken by persons of delicate habits without their experiencing that nausea which is so often an obstacle to its being administered at all. A small quantity of the Castor Oil is enclosed in a flexible capsule or envelope, formed of thin membrane. One, two, or more of these Capsules constitute a dose, according to age and other circumstances. They are swallowed without any difficulty, and are wholly tasteless. Other medicines of a nauseous kind are equally capable of being thus pleasantly taken when enveloped in the membranous Capsule. These Capsules may now be had of Evans and Lescher, Patentees, London; and of John Bell, Squire, Sanger, Oxford-street; Waugh, Regent-street; Dinneford, New Bond-street; Butler, Lucas, Jackson, Cheapside; Johnston, Cornhill; Stamper, Leadenhall-street; Baildon, 73, Princes-street, Edinburgh; and of all chemists and medicine venders throughout the kingdom.

*** Ask for the Patent Flexible Capsules.

NERVOUS OR MENTAL COMPLAINTS, TIC DOULOUREUX, EPILEPSY, PARALYSIS, AND INSANITY SPEEDILY CURED.

THIS Great Discovery, which has been used in private practice upwards of eighteen years in thousands of cases of the most unpromising description without a single failure, will now be available to all classes. The Proprietor, being urged by common sympathy and a desire to promote the welfare of his fellow-creatures rather than any covetous motive, offers to cure all sufferers at the ordinary

COST OF THE MEANS EMPLOYED.

Low spirits, mental debility, exhaustion, delusions, giddiness, blood to the head, groundless fear, failure of memory, stammering, disinclination for society, study, &c., wretchedness, blushing, thoughts of suicide, paralysis, epilepsy, and insanity permanently cured.

Patients generally recover in from three to five weeks. No fee. Unequalled references and testimonials in all parts of the kingdom.

"GIVEN AWAY," a PAMPHLET explanatory of the above treatment, which will be cheerfully franked to any address on the receipt of one stamp. Remedies forwarded to any distance.

Address, Dr. Anderson, 26, Arundel-street, Strand. At home, 11 to 5 and 7 to 9.

HOUSEHOLD Fuel, 26s. per Ton.—The PATENT FUEL COMPANY (Warlich's Patent) now deliver their superior and much-approved HOUSEHOLD FUEL within Four Miles of the Works at Deptford, or the Company's Depôt, Shot-tower-wharf, Commmercial-road, Lambeth, at 26s. per Ton, for Cash. This fuel is 20 per cent. more economical than coal, ignites easier than coal, and is made up in blocks varying in weight. Orders to be sent to the Secretary, at the Company's Offices, 15, St. Mary Axe; or to Mr. Walstab, at the Depôt, Shot-tower-wharf, Commercial-road, Lambeth. WILLIAM NICHOLAS DE MATTOS, Sec.

CABINET Furniture, Carpets, Bedding, UPHOLSTERY, &c.—The GREAT WESTERN FURNITURE BAZAAR, 30, 31, 32, and 99, Crawford-street, Marylebone, JNO. DENT and CO., Proprietors. An inspection is respectfully solicited of actually the largest stock of furnishing requisites in London, the whole warranted, and price marked in plain figures, whereby parties can make their own estimates and a selection at once of the whole of the articles suitable for any class of house. Any article purchased and not approved of will be exchanged, it being their firm resolve to conduct their business on strictly honourable principles. Second-hand Furniture of every description constantly on sale.—N.B. No connection with any shop or place called "Furniture Bazaar."

JENNY LIND'S Voice Lozenges, for improving, strengthening, and clearing the Voice, and relieving all affections of the Throat; strongly recommended to Clergymen, Singers, Actors, and Public Speakers. The Proprietor begs to call the attention of the Public to the following flattering testimonial:—

"Birmingham, August 26, 1847.

"I certify that I have used Mr. Charles Belton's Voice Lozenge, and that I have found it very useful in strengthening and clearing the voice.

(Signed) "JENNY LIND."

The above are prepared only by CHARLES BELTON, Chemist, High-street, Birmingham, and sold retail by all respectable chemists, &c., throughout the kingdom, in boxes at 13½d., 2s. 9d., and 4s. 6d. each. Wholesale agent, W. Edwards, 67, St. Paul's Churchyard; Dicey and Sutton, 10, Bow Churchyard; Barclay and Sons, 95, Farringdon-street, London.

STOOPING of the Shoulders and Contraction of the CHEST are entirely prevented, and gently and effectually removed, in Youth, and Ladies and Gentlemen, by the occasional use of the IMPROVED ELASTIC CHEST-EXPANDER, which is light, simple, and easily applied, either above or beneath the dress, and worn without any uncomfortable constraint or impediment to exercise. To young persons especially it is highly beneficial, immediately producing an evident IMPROVEMENT in the FIGURE, and tending greatly to prevent the incursion of PULMONARY DISEASES; whilst, to the invalid, and those much engaged in sedentary pursuits, such as reading or studying, working, drawing, or music, it is found to be invaluable, as it expands the chest and affords a great support to the back. It is made in silk; and can be forwarded, per post, by Mr. ALFRED BINYON, Sole Manufacturer and Proprietor, No. 40, Tavistock-street, Covent-garden, London; or full particulars, with prices and mode of measurement, &c., on receipt of a postage-stamp.

SKIN DISEASES.

DISPENSARY for the Cure of Diseases of the SKIN, Hampstead-street, Fitzroy-square.—Physician, Dr. INNIS, No. 33, Fitzroy-square.—This Dispensary is opened for the treatment and cure of those most troublesome and vexatious complaints, skin diseases. Whether we take into consideration the frequency of the complaints, or the disfigurement caused by them, we are equally surprised at the little attention and study paid to them in England. There are no classes of disease that come under the care of the medical man so difficult of treatment as those of the skin: the study of them in this country is but in its infancy, for up to the present time there has been no opportunity for the surgeon to study them, and it is only from the experience of medical men, exclusively devoted to this branch of medical science, that these distressing complaints can be expected to be relieved. No practical good can arise, either to the profession or to the unfortunate patients, until hospitals and dispensaries are established for the exclusive treatment of these diseases. It is with this view that Dr. Innis, after devoting much attention and study to these diseases, and having proved most successful in his treatment, has complied with the requests of numerous friends and patients, and opened the above institution. The Dispensary is open daily from ten to one o'clock.

Dr. Innis may be consulted daily until two o'clock, at his residence, 33, Fitzroy-square.

BY Command of her Majesty's Government.—I, WILLIAM GRIMSTONE, Sole Inventor and Manufacturer of the celebrated Eye Snuff, manufactured of British Herbs only, under the authority of the Lords of the Treasury, bearing date the 16th day of February, 1825, do hereby acquaint all wholesale and retail venders and consumers that the Commissioners of Stamps have commanded that in future all canisters bearing the label as corrected by their late solicitor, Mr. Godfrey Sykes, in the year 1827, shall have a medicine-duty stamp affixed upon each canister. That the above order has been issued in consequence of the undoubted and proved curative qualities of this herbaceous eye snuff in all cases of disease affecting those delicate organs, the eye, the ear, and the head. In consequence of the above order, each and every canister of Grimstone's Eye Snuff bears the Government Stamp. The price is now 9½d., 1s. 6d., 2s. 7d., 4s. 6d., 9s., and 17s. 6d.; but for the better accommodation of the consumers the dealers can be supplied with Grimstone's Herbaceous Snuff, at wholesale prices, with boxes or bladders of 10 lb. and upwards, so that it may be sold at 6d. per ounce loose by the venders. The Eye Snuff forwarded through the post for money orders only. A 2s. 7d. canister will cost 3s. 6d., postage and stamp included. To William Grimstone, Herbary, Highgate.

MRS. DISNEY, Chiropodist, 18, Newman-street, Oxford-street, has the honour to announce to the nobility and gentry her EFFICACIOUS and EASY MODE of EXTRACTING CORNS, removing Callosities, and counteracting the Malformations of the Toe-nails, without cutting or causing the slightest pain; as also her successful treatment of Bunions, which has hitherto gained her the confidence and patronage of many families of distinction, to whom references can be given.—Patients attended at their residences, giving one day's notice.

FIGURE 34 Advertisements, *The Lady's Newspaper*, vol. 1, 1847, p. 378

FIGURE 35 Advertisements, *The Alexandra Magazine*, vol. 1, 1865, p. 257

16.3

Personal advertisements of the kind illustrated here continued to form a staple of women's
magazines, including the ladies' newspapers, throughout the period. Indeed, *The Queen's*
(1861–1967) personal and small advertisement section was so successful that it led to the
creation of a separate journal, *Exchange and Mart*, and *The Lady* (1885–) built its success on
such advertisements, as it still does into the twenty-first century.

Advertisements, *The Queen*, vol. 20, 1867, p. 13.

TEETH.—Avoid exorbitant charges. No fee accepted unless perfect satisfaction is given. Good sets from £2 10s. to £5; a tooth from 5s. Partial sets equally moderate by Mr. POOL, the old established surgeon-dentist, 21, Holles-street, Cavendish-square.

ARTIFICAL TEETH and PAINLESS EXTRACTION

Mr. DAY, Dentist 291, Regent-street Every description of artificial teeth supplied upon moderate terms compatible with pure materials and first class workmanship.

Mr DAY

(late principal assistant to Mr. Rakell of 8. Grosvenor-street), 291, Regent-street (three doors from the Polytechnic).

SINGING,—A superior and pleasing style of Italian and English SINGING LESSONS given by a lady teacher of high respectability; music taught; country families and schools attended. Terms moderate:— Address A.J. Hastings, Stationer, Duke-street Manchester-square.

LADIES WANTED to execute embossed wool work at their own homes from Toohey's ABC patterns, which are a new and superior invention to the Berlin patterns. The work is liberally paid for. Terms for instruction. 10s. 6d. Apply by letter, or, if personally, between ten and five to Mr TOOHEY, Soho-square, next to the Bazaar. Work is guaranteed and can be sent to any part of the country.

LADIES are earnestly entreated to ASSIST the GRAND FANCY SALE to be held at the Hanover Square rooms, on the 18th and 19th of June, in aid of the Extension Fund of the NATIONAL HOSPITAL for the PARALYSED AND EPILEPTIC, Queen-square, Bloomsbury. Ladies contributing goods to the amount of six guineas or disposing of five

guineas' worth of tickets will become life members of the charity. Clothes for the Poor and useful articles for the Patients' Stall will be gratefully received.—Address JOHANNA CHANDLER, Hon. Sec. 43 Albany-street, Regents Park, N.W.

A WIDOW LADY, the daughter of a clergyman, residing at Kensington, wishes for two or three LITTLE GIRLS to EDUCATE with her own, under a clever and experienced governess. They would be taken to the sea-side in the holidays or the Continent if desired. Address "G.C." 21 Upper Phillimore-place, Kensington. The highest references can be given.

A LADY, the daughter of a clergyman, desires RE-ENGAGEMENT as GOVERNESS in a family. Qualifications: English, French, German, the rudiments of Latin and Italian, music and singing. Salary required, £50. Address "P.S." Post-office, Sutton-at-Home, near Dartford.

AS GOVERNESS, HOUSEKEEPER or COMPANION—A Lady wishes to meet with either of the above SITUATIONS. Acquirements: English, Music, French. & Good references.—Address "Y.Z." No. 20, Dorset-street, Portman-square.

LADY'S MAID or UPPER MAID in nobleman's family; experienced in all her duties, excellent character; not object to country, or travelling.—"A.B.", Queen's-row, Pimlico.

THE Advertiser will be very grateful to any lady who can RECOMMEND her a trustworthy and experienced NURSE for her first baby.—For further particulars, address Mrs. WILSON, Redgrave Hall, Bolesdale, Suffolk.

16.4

The Lady's Own Paper (1866–72), like all the other ladies' papers, carried fashion news and advertising alongside its articles and reviews. Though the three or sometimes four columns of print remained standard for most advertising, the arrival of display advertisements linked the interest in readers as 'shoppers' with the stress on visual attraction which characterised these papers and – by implication – their readers. This is an early example.

See FIGURE 36.

FIGURE 36 Advertisement, *The Lady's Own Paper*, vol. 9, 1872, p. 541

16.5

More typical of advertising throughout the 1870s and 1880s was the mixture of print with small illustrations which can be seen in these pages of *The Queen* (1861–1967). In the 1880s and 1890s the link between women's journalism and advertising was strengthened as advertisers began to quote from advice columns in support of their products.

See FIGURE 37.

FIGURE 37 Advertisements, *The Queen*, vol. 77, 1885, unnumbered page

16.6

General illustrated magazines and magazines for girls carried advertisements in their endpapers throughout the period, but here, too, solid blocks of print became broken up with eye-catching visual material.

See FIGURE 38.

FIGURE 38 Advertisement, *The Young Ladies' Journal*, vol. 7, 1885, unnumbered page

16.7

Cheap domestic magazines depended as much as the up-market journals on advertising and they depended on brand-name advertising. The distinction between advertising and editorial matter began to dissolve both in terms of organisation of the page and in terms of content. Advertisements were often printed opposite advice columns – as was our example from *Woman* (1890–1912) – and addressed readers' anxieties about their appearance or physical health.

See FIGURES 39 and 40.

FIGURE 39 Advertisement, *Woman*, 5th Feb., 1891, p. 21

FIGURE 40 Advertisement, *Home Chat*, vol. 6, 1901, p. 317

17
Advice columns and readers' letters

Advice was a staple of the women's magazine and encompassed a range of different constructions of femininity. Whether on fashion and appearance, reading, or domestic management, the advice column was an important element of the magazines' general discursive prose. From their inception, magazines for women had invited readers to write in seeking advice and the relationship between these two elements, advice columns and readers' letters, is complex and tangled. Almost every kind of magazine we represent here had an 'Answers' section dealing with readers' enquiries. For most of the Victorian period, it was usual to print the answers without the readers' letters, a practice general in all kinds of journal. However, many different kinds of magazine also offered a space for readers' letters which offered opinion rather than sought advice. In addition, some, particularly the general magazines, ran competitions with prizes for the best letter. The ladies' newspapers and fashion journals tended to confine themselves to 'Answers' but the general illustrated magazines from early on also printed some extracts from readers' letters and quite separate advice columns, which nevertheless often referred indirectly to readers' enquiries. By the 1890s, some of these general magazines had correspondence columns which included long extracts from readers' letters, as did Annie S. Swan in her column 'Over the Teacups' for *Woman at Home*. Alongside these features in which readers were represented as exchanging views, the older pattern of advice persisted, often with a more informal tone and a strong but friendly editorial persona. At the end of the period, most magazines but especially the cheap domestic ones ran a range of specialised advice features on health, appearance, household management, care of children and house furnishing. Girls' magazines advised on work and appearance and general knowledge. The ladies' papers gave advice on etiquette and dress but not on personal matters. *Myra's Journal* and other fashion magazines concentrated on advice on dress and appearance.

17.1

In Beeton's *The Englishwoman's Domestic Magazine* (1852–79) the advice and letters section, called 'The Englishwoman's Conversazione', became more important as the magazine developed. In the 1860s the Conversazione gained some notoriety because of a series of letters on tight-lacing and on the disciplining of young women.

'The Englishwoman's Conversazione', *The Englishwoman's Domestic Magazine*, vol. 3, 1854, p. 168.

SOPHIA ANDERSON.—What a happy thing it is that those who know least and are capable of achieving the smallest results are those who cry out the loudest about the tools they have to work with, and complain the most unreasonably of that which is most likely right in itself, but which they are not able to understand or appreciate! Now, hear our good friend and subscriber, SOPHIA

ANDERSON. She says, ferociously enough, "It is my opinion, and that of my friends, that if you undertake to offer patterns to the public in your ENGLISHWOMAN'S DOMESTIC MAGAZINE, you should offer *correct* ones, not lead people to waste their time, and perhaps material, in endeavouring to manufacture articles of clothing from your incorrect patterns. I should like to know how it would be possible to make a little boy's jacket with a back piece, such as you have depicted in this month's (June) number? There is no place for the arm-hole. I was fortunate in fitting and testing the *paper* copy I took before I ventured further and so spared my holland if wasted my time." Commotion in the office of ENGLISHWOMAN when this missive was opened—the Editor and his staff looking like so many monuments of despair. Recovering himself, however, our chief bravely put the bomb in his pocket, and delivered it, duly and impressively (with other most kind and compensatory letters, be it gratefully said) to the Editress, the responsible person in this instance. Undismayed, but evidently hurt at the ingratitude of Sophia and her friends, she calmly, and before the chief's very eyes, traced the pattern on to some whitey-brown paper; first pinned it together and then tacked it, showing us triumphantly a little boy's jacket in paper, with arm-hole, sleeve, and cuff, as complete as possible. So when SOPHIA ANDERSON "would like to know how it would be possible &c." she has only to write to the Editress, who will have great pleasure in taking her out of any difficulty she may find herself in with respect to the patterns. Moreover, in this special instance, the Editress is anxious to send to her, on receipt of the address, this very pattern, exactly as she put it together when its correctness was impugned. The chief trusts that SOPHIA ANDERSON will make the *amende honorable* by sending a handsome—well, he will leave the choice to a committee of taste, composed of herself and friends.

KATE, AGNES, FLORA, &c., &c.—We have received several letters touching the long-promised series of articles on Wayside Weeds and Forest Flowers. Our fair correspondents complain that we have allowed the flowers of spring to come and go without saying a word about them: and have not even condescended to notice the arrival of the flaunting beauties of summer. We have never forgotten our promise, and though we may be accused of slighting those "pretty daughters of the earth and sun", by whom our hearts are linked to Nature, we are really over head and ears in love with them. We have for some time been considering how we ought to introduce them to our readers and have at length resolved to reject our original plan for one much more comprehensive. Instead of a few desultory papers on wild flowers, we mean to give our readers a course of familiar lectures on Botany—not the botany of schoolmen, with its forbidding nomenclature and terrible array of physiological facts, but the botany which may be studied in the garden, the wood, or the meadow, by any flower-loving English-woman. Though our series, when complete, will form a systematic treatise on the most delightful branch of Natural History, we shall take care to exclude all technical terms and dry details. We love the simple names which the poetic instinct of mankind has given to flowers far too well to exchange them for those which pass current among men of science. We intend to give the first of our botanical papers in our next number, or at latest in September.

CONTESSA wrote some time since a pretty letter to us—and if we had not so *many* pretty letters we should like to take notice of every one of them—and said. "You may, perhaps, be pleased to know that I have worked the Oriental Slippers given in the January number, and they look superb. The officer (Oh, happy son of Mars!) who has become their fortunate possessor is obliged to keep them under lock and key when not in use, lest they should be feloniously abstracted by his envious comrades. I can safely recommend to your lady readers to follow my example if they wish to charm either father, brother, or *fiancé* with a birthday gift. And for those unfortunate damsels in such trouble about their complexions and strait (*sic*) hair, I may, perhaps, have a secret worth knowing—do you think I ought to tell them? Perhaps if they ask me very prettily, I will. Chorus of ill-complexioned ladies—" Come, charming Contessa, tell us, tell us the secret you possess."

Blue Bell.—"Are ices dangerous to the health?" and "Do we recommend summer balls, not extemporised *al fresco* assemblies, but *bona fide* balls where taste should reign triumphant?" To the first question, we say "Yes", but we eat them moderately, it is true, because we like them; and to the second question we answer "Yes", in our *most decided* manner. By a *little* ingenuity and some taste, a ball on a July evening, with the windows down, doors open, flower-garden and lawn apparently extending the area of dancing space, not too much light within to spoil the beaming moon without, vases of mignonette, sweet herbs and one or two Eolian harps placed where the zephyrs can play upon and through then, will charm those subjected to their influence in a manner which persons who have never tried them believe only Eastern lands can boast.

Contributions Respectfully Declined from A. Hartley, Anon, Z.Z., H.B., E.H.B., Miss M'Kinndo, J.W., Matilda Hillhouse, "Pauline", "Just in Time", "What the Stars Say".

Special Notice to Correspondents.—*Communications arriving later than the 10th of the month preceding that of publication cannot be replied to in the forthcoming number of "The Englishwoman's Domestic Magazine".*

NOTICE TO SUBSCRIBERS

Covers for Vols. I. and II. of the Englishwoman's Domestic Magazine (New Series) with title-page, preface, index, envelope for holding the pattern sheets, Berlin patterns, etc. and directions for binding are now ready, price 1s. each. Sent free by post to any address on receipt of 12 postage stamps.

Volume I. of the Englishwoman's Domestic Magazine, elegantly bound in green and gold, is now ready, with the six Coloured Berlin and other patterns and 129 Designs of Embroidery and other needlework. Price 5s. free by post on receipt of postage stamps for this amount.

Volume II., uniform with Volume I., now ready, price 5s.

Our subscribers are respectfully invited to give their orders at once to their bookseller for the regular supply of the Numbers of this Magazine, so as to be certain to receive them as soon as published, with the Fashion Plates and Berlin Wool Work Patterns complete, the Publisher begging to notify that he cannot guarantee the supply of the Fashion Plates and Coloured Berlin Patterns beyond a month after their first issue.

London, 248, Strand, W.C.

17.2

The feminist papers sometimes carried letters with general advice for readers. More importantly, they were committed to using the periodical as a space in which the debates in which they were engaged could be openly carried on. This is made clear in the article, 'The Uses of a Special Periodical' which sets out the editorial policy for *The Alexandra Magazine* (1864–65) the magazine from which this extract comes. (See 10.5 above.)

'Open Council', *The Alexandra Magazine*, vol. 1, 1864, pp. 382–83.

[As these pages are intended for general discussion, the Editor
does not hold herself responsible for the opinions expressed.]

To the Editor of the Alexandra Magazine, and Englishwoman's Journal.
Female Middle Class Emigration Society, 12, Portugal Street, Lincoln's-Inn, *September 6th*, 1864.

Madam,

The enclosed extract may prove interesting to some of your readers; it is from the letter of a lady who went out from this society to the Colonies rather more than a year ago, and took an engagement two days after landing at a salary of eighty guineas per annum.—I remain, &c.,

J. E. Lewin. *Hon. Sec.*

Madam,

As you expressed a wish to hear from me again, I send you this letter, containing the little experience I have gained since writing last. In the first place, I will repeat, that I am more than satisfied with the step I took in coming to Australia. I never was so well off before—so little to do with such good remuneration; and I should add that my English experience was a singularly happy one. I am in the midst of my own friends, whom I can visit when I like; I have made some nice acquaintances beside. When this reaches you I shall have completed my year's engagement here. It is an understood thing at present that I am to remain after the completion of the year, with the new arrangement of our contract terminating with a quarter's notice on each side. . . . Unfortunately, nowhere is youth more valued than here; I know not why, but so it is. From instances I have heard of, and from every-day conversation, it is evident that a moderately qualified young woman would have every advantage over a middle-aged one, however accomplished. So impressed am I with this fact that I am using all my efforts to be as economical as possible, laying by all I can, as a means of support when work is no longer to be had.

I am aware there is an idea in England that young and accomplished governesses soon marry in this land; that is a mistake, at least now-a-days. In the early years of the colony it did so happen, for educated women were very rare then. Mrs. D. tells me she knows but one instance of a governess marrying. I, however, have heard of several, still it should be looked on as the exception and not the rule.

Music is an indispensable qualification, German a great accessary, on the strength of which any one may expect from eighty to one hundred guineas per annum.

Of course, it is but few can expect to find situations in the city, the majority must expect to go to the country. The country ladies have an advantage over the town ones, in one particular, they need very little change of dress. There are many moderate-sized towns, where schools could be opened, in which two ladies with a little capital might safely embark. According to statistics, men greatly out-number women in this land, yet it seems to me that the women find it nearly as difficult to get their daily bread here as in London. Many are the sad tales I have heard of the straits to which educated women have been driven. A new opening for female industry has been opened here in a cigar manufactory, which employs mainly women and children; this is the only new track for female labour that exists at present. Were I in the position of the third and fourth rate governesses (I was almost going to say second) in England, (*sic*) would unhesitatingly become a *domestic servant* in Australia, in preference. Here housemaids have from £25 to £30 a year; good cooks, £35 to £40. It is pitiable to think of young women, nominally governesses, yet little more than nursemaids, toiling for perhaps only £10 a-year—£20 would be quite a large sum. I have known, and still know, some cases in Wales, where respectable, decently educated young women only earn those sums. I have no doubt it would require some common sense and humility for such a governess to become a servant; but she would find herself infinitely better off (salary apart). Servants are more considered, there is more freedom and independence here than at home. If my words could reach some of my toiling sisters at home, I would say, "Be sensible, undergo a little domestic training, and come out here to take your chance with others, with a certainty of succeeding withal." For respectable, well-trained *Protestant* servants, there is always a demand; people are often obliged to take Catholics, as they can get no other good servants.

Though most of the ladies' papers concentrated on answers to enquiries under such categories as Fashion, Etiquette etc., some of them occasionally also carried letters from readers. The first extract below is the lead letter of the day. The series of short 'Answers', our second extract, is more typical of these papers.

'Correspondence', *The Lady's Own Paper*: 'Plea for Boys', vol. 5, 1870, p. 369; 'Letter basket', vol. 7, 1872, p. 332.

"PLEA FOR BOYS."

To the Editor of the Lady's Own Paper.

Sir,—On this subject, and in reply to the mother who complains of her untoward boy, I would advise her to read the remarks of a young gentleman in the supplemental conversazione of the *Englishwoman's Domestic Magazine* for April last, and then she will find a cure for her troublesome son. After innumerable whippings had failed, the governess took it into her head to dress him in his sister's clothes, which, though the feat was accomplished after much kicking and plunging, had the desired effect; and he tells us that whenever he transgressed or failed in his lessons, if his governess rang the bell, and desired the housemaid to bring some petticoats, &c., he either begged pardon for his offences or set to diligently to learn his lesson. He afterwards went to Eton, and he affirms that the whippings there were not half so severe as those of his governess.—Yours obediently,

M. Walker.

P.S.—It is all very well to talk of reasoning with untoward boys, but in many cases nothing short of a good whipping or what I have recommended will answer.

[Though the treatment seems to have answered in this case, it is one that should surely not be commended for general application. Were one asked for the most effectual plan to make a high-spirited lad despise his sisters as "only girls," he could perhaps scarcely do better than recommend our correspondent's.—Ed. L. O. P.]

LADIES' CONFIDENCES

Marian.—Your hair is light brown. The handwriting indicates carelessness and a quick temper.

Miriam.—We are very far from laughing at your story, but it is not quite up to the mark. You had omitted punctuation altogether. If, as you say, it is a bit from a friend's life, we pity poor Nelly, and think her cousin George a great scoundrel for whom hanging would be too good.

Charlie's Darling.—The handwriting is pretty; it indicates cultivation, decision, exactness and neatness. The hair is light brown with a golden shade. There is no meaning to the name of Nelly, it is an abbreviation of Ellen. Ellen means light.

Marian says: "I have frequently had calls from fashionable ladies who have sent their card in, or left them, with one or more corners turned down. Can you tell me the meaning of it? Pride prevents my asking any one else. By answering the above, through the *Lady's Own Paper*, you will much a oblige a friend." The turning down of the corner of the card means that the ladies or gentlemen, as the case may be, left them in person, instead of sending them by messenger or otherwise.

Adele says: "Be so kind as to inform me if there is any difference between a hot-house, a green-house and a conservatory. My son and I have just had an argument about it, and we leave it to you to decide." A hot-house might be for cucumbers, and not a conservatory, which need not be a hot-house; and a green-house may be only a place for sheltering plants in the winter. But a conservatory is, in common language, a green-house for exotics and tender plants.

CONSTANT READER says: "I have found such valuable information in your answers to correspondents that I cannot refrain from confiding to you and asking your advice on a matter in which I feel most intensely interested. I am twenty-four years old, and profess to be of a philosophic turn of mind, and believe that I have never yet experienced love as I have heard and read of it, although I am not positively assured that such is the case. Three years ago I met a young lady, and enjoyed her society for a year afterwards, who is physically my opposite, and whom I admire for her gentle and unobtrusive demeanour, her pure and pious example, and who I think would love me . . . I want to marry. I do not feel satisfied in my present condition. Being of a sympathetic nature, I long for someone to love, and when I think of married life as compared with the life I now live, my thoughts seem to associate *her* with my ideal of a future companion. I think of her every day, and yet I cannot persuade myself that I love her as I should. I am in trouble, and if you will please be kind enough to tell me what to do under the circumstances, and to answer through the columns of your excellent paper, you will greatly relieve and more than oblige." The philosophers always puzzle us—and themselves; and they are never more unintelligible than when in love. You doubt if you love enough. Do philosophers ever love enough? Is love consistent with the true philosophic temper? She is quiet—the very quality for a philosopher's wife. A woman of spirit would often be obliged to tell her philosopher too plain truths— e.g. Xantippe and Socrates. Next to a good talker is a good listener, and that is exactly what is most agreeable to all philosophers we have met. Propose at once; and if we may venture a suggestion to a philosopher, propose not as a philosopher, but as a man.

BRUNETTE: "Being in a dreadful state of agitation, I appeal for your advice. I feel myself deeply in love with a young man, a clerk by profession. He is rather nice looking. The obstacle [is] that I am engaged to a gentleman abroad, who has a good income of his own, besides a profession. Which am I to marry? The one abroad is extremely handsome and I like him very well." You are bound in honour as well as good sense to keep your engagement with the gentleman abroad. Do not see the clerk again. Absence and Time are wonderful specifics. You will thank us sincerely in years to come if you follow our advice.

17.4

The cheap domestic papers each ran several kinds of advice column. 'Answers to Correspondents' in *Woman* (1890–1912) was subdivided into Health and Appearance, Dress and Coiffure, Toilet, Furniture, etc. 'Medica' answered medical questions. Much of the rest of the magazine consisted of chatty columns which mixed advice with short prose tit-bits, attributed to various editorial personae, notably 'Marjorie' and 'Barbara'.

'Answers to Correspondents', *Woman*, 5th Feb., 1891, p. 21.

E. C. ST. M.—I have no choice but to put your initials in full, as I conclude from your erasure of an evident *nom de plume* on your letter you wish me to answer to your signature. What you complain of is difficult—nay, impossible—to cure all at once, but they can be subdued in the manner given below; although, I tell you honestly, you have to be patient, and allow time to help you. They do not arise from a bad circulation, as you surmise, but are due to the blocking up of the sebaceous glands of the skin. On rising in the morning, fill two basins with water as hot as you can bear it; bathe the face, and lather it with Castille soap from one basin, and wash the soap off quickly in the second basin, drying the face with a common jack-towel, using plenty of friction over this latter process. Three mornings a week, rub into the spots, after drying the face, a little powdered calomel with the tip of the finger; and on the alternate mornings, drink a wineglassful of the following mixture: Dissolve in a quart wine-bottle of water two ounces of Epsom salts and half-an-ounce of carbonate of magnesia. Take plenty of exercise, use plenty of friction to the parts where the spots principally appear, and take every day at meal-time two glasses of any of Christie's red wines.

PANCAKE.—You might try the hot lemon-water, which I wrote about in the issue of the 8th ult. If you have not a copy of WOMAN of that date, you will get one by writing to the office for it, and sending the large sum of $1\frac{1}{2}$d. Or else, on awakening in the morning, drink a tumbler of warm milk; and directly after breakfast take a teaspoonful of "Bynol" for three days, at the end of which time increase your dose to a teaspoonful after each of your three principal daily meals. Do not worry yourself about trifles; take rest after your meals; and eat plenty of roast meat and light puddings, and drink at your midday meal a tumbler of good stout. Either of these two simple treatments ought to help you to recover your bemoaned possessions.

A SILLY GIRL.—1. If the claret and iron lotion makes your hair dirty as you say, it is because you apply it carelessly, and too often. To begin with; night-time is not the time to apply any treatment to the hair, as at night the head is tired and the light is bad; daylight is the proper light for an application on this sort. Have your head thoroughly shampooed, and the ends of your hair cut and singed; and try permanganate of potash as an application. Buy an ounce in crystal, and dissolve a small quantity, say eight grains of crystal, in warm water; when the water becomes a rich red-brown colour, apply it with a brush to the hair, parting it carefully, so as to touch every grey hair, but taking care not to touch the skin of the head, as it will be discoloured if you do. Do this by daylight, standing before a good glass which is set in a bright light. 2. You may safely use hot water to your face, as wrinkles do not come from the use of such harmless stuff as that. 3. No, Matthews's Fuller's Earth is not injurious.

SOFT HANDS.—Your second letter, just received, made me feel quite sad, to think that any mother lived who is so foolish and so wicked as your sister seems to be. Doubtless she errs from ignorance, but please tell her, when next you write out to her, that she is doing her best, by her senseless vanity, to ruin her daughter's future chances of maternity and health. The treatment you say she insists on, and her silly daughter submits to, bids fair to deform and displace her internal organs, cause permanent fœtor of breath, and ruin future chances of maternity. Surely these weighed in the balance with a slim waist cause the latter to be but a feather in the scale. The other piece of vanity you refer to is pardonable, but what a senseless doll of a woman such an up-bringing means! No, I certainly do not advise you to let your daughter emulate her cousin in one single particular you mention; nor do I think that her "being constantly with a beautiful and very much admired girl will naturally tend to give her the same groove of thought," but rather the reverse.

WHITE WINGS.—I wish I could help your poor mother as easily as I can help you, but unless you write to me privately I cannot very well enter so minutely as I should like to into the matter, not only because I cannot give the space, but because the subject-matter requires too delicate a handling for the public columns of a paper. This much I can say, however, that either a proper surgical support, or better still, if your mother is able to bear it, an operation should be resorted to at once, as otherwise, under the circumstances which you describe, ulceration may set in, and then there is great danger. "Mason's Wool Fat," which you ask about, you may safely use. As regards your own hair, I should advise the plentiful use of Brilliantine, and that you should pay a monthly visit to the hairdresser, to have it cut and singed.

MERON.—Buy at the Stores one pound of quassia wood chips, and put one ounce of them into a china teapot, with a pint of *cold* water and a tablespoonful of common salt. Let this stand for four hours, and then pour the decoction thus formed through the spout of the teapot into a basin. By the help of an enema inject yourself every morning with a freshly made decoction of this sort, retaining it for five minutes in a reclining position. Write to me again at the end of a fortnight, when I shall be able to recommend a pill which you should take.

ADA (Twenty-one).—It would require minute questioning and examination to ascertain if your fears are well founded, but you can help yourself very much by abstaining from all wine, beer, and coffee, and taking only tea or cocoa. Leave off all aperients for the next fortnight, and take twice a day, before meals, half a teaspoonful of cream of tartar in a tumblerful of water. In spite of what you say in your letter (and I sympathise with you very much), I should certainly advise your seeing a doctor. Eat a piece of bread and drink some milk before starting for church.

YOUTHFUL ACTRESS.—Your ingenuous letter made me hope I should certainly see you ere long doing something better than a "walking-on" part only. To help the drooping shoulder, I should suggest your asking Mrs. Steele, of 38, Upper Berkeley Street, Portman Square, to make your stays specially for you, and that you should be careful always to stand straight, walk with your shoulders well back, and sit in chairs that have high backs. The thumbnail which you describe is a sign of malnutrition, and you should take cod-liver oil or Bynol three times a day, and every other day rub the thumbnail quite dull with powdered pumice and a piece of wood, and polish it bright again with a piece of soft wash-leather. For fencing lessons you should go to Stempel's Gymnasium, Albany Street, as the course of twelve only costs a guinea. It is close to Portland Road Station.

A WORKING WOMAN.—As I conclude from your letter that you do not want any but the simplest and least expensive of remedies, I think if you eat plenty of fat, drink plenty of milk, and take cod-liver oil for a few months, you will find that you will gain flesh, and not feel so tired. The ulceration you speak of accounts for both the thinness and the fatigue.

STELLA.—You must apply friction to your lips, and be continually moistening them slightly and biting them. I do not recommend you to tint them, as it is always unmistakable, and by the above simple method the skin of the lips becomes thinner and the blood shows through. Seawater is injurious to the hair, and you should certainly wear an oilskin cap when bathing.

SEVENTEEN NAN.—In answer to your five questions, I shall take them in the order you place them in your letter. 1. Be very careful what you eat; use plenty of hot water, friction, and Mrs. Fairbanks' "Cremoline" Soap. 2. Avoid all stimulants and hot soup, and always eat something before drinking. Abstain from tea, and substitute cocoa in its place. Do not sit over the fire, or in draughts, and on going out to evening entertainments cover the troublesome feature from the air while driving or walking. 3. Either Ivorine or Vinolia are equally good, and harmless. 4. No powder at all, but use oatmeal instead. 5. No, certainly not. If you are able to walk for an hour, you should certainly walk five or six miles a day, and you will find that the more brisk exercise you take the less you will have to fear your enemy—the red nose.

MIGNON.—I am really sorry for you, because I know nothing more cruelly helpless than nerves such as you seem to have. Get your chemist to make off into pills a quarter of a grain of opium, and take one pill three times a day, beginning the day before your examination. It stimulates the brain, and I have always found it a great help. I heartily wish you success. You had better abstain from tea, and drink Kola instead.

17.5

Forget-Me-Not (1891–1918), like the cheap domestic weeklies with which it shared many characteristics represented itself as healthy home reading. However, it did not run extensive

173

advice columns but concentrated on romantic fiction. Its 'Confidential Chat' in its second number epitomises the new kind of journalism which offered a friendly chat rather than authoritative advice.

'Confidential Chat', *Forget-Me-Not*, vol. 1, no. 3, 1891, p. 16.

I CANNOT sufficiently thank all of you for the generous support you have accorded to FORGET-ME-NOT. By making the journal an instantaneous success you have enabled me to make arrangements for the future of the journal on a most extensive scale. FORGET-ME-NOT has already a larger sale than any other ladies' paper, and the great difficulty now is, not to obtain readers, but to get the journal printed fast enough to supply those who want it. So vast has been the demand that hundreds—nay, thousands—have never yet been able to obtain a copy.

Moral: Order the paper in advance from your newsagent.

* * *

"CLYTIE" asked me: "To what kind of woman will FORGET-ME-NOT appeal?" FORGET-ME-NOT is intended, my dear "Clytie," for the womanly woman.

I have no sympathy with the "woman's-right" ladies, the blue-spectacled, short-haired, and untidy-gowned specimens of our sex who make themselves ridiculous and objectionable at public meetings. Our little paper is for the sisterly and the motherly of our land, without distinction of class or creed. It is a home paper, and is meant for those who love their homes, or are ambitious of making some good man happy. FORGET-ME-NOT will always be full of sympathy and affection for those whose lot it is to sweeten the lives of others and to brighten the world. We desire the support neither of the "blue-stocking" nor of the brainless, chattering society girl. Our chief desire is to please the wife, the mother, and the daughter who one day hopes to have a husband of her own. FORGET-ME-NOT believes that every good woman was meant to be the chief ornament of some home circle; that every Jill shall have her Jack. It is our mission to bring pure and bright amusement, good advices for the house, and as much happiness for all as is in our power. FORGET-ME-NOT would like you to regard it as a personal friend, to whom you can turn for comfort in your hours of dulness and trouble. But enough, as we must turn to practical things.

* * *

PEOPLE living in small houses, or managing on small incomes, often find wardrobes inconvenient absorbers of both space and money when furnishing their bedrooms. It is particularly easy to supply the place of this cumbersome piece of furniture at a very small cost. If there is a niche in the room, as sometimes happens, so much the better; if not take a corner, or the space between the chimney and the wall, and have a shelf made, which must be securely fastened on wooden slats nailed to the wall, about seven feet from the floor. A frill of art chintz should edge this shelf, upon which light articles, such as pottery, will make a good show. From it to the floor should hang long curtains of the same chintz, edged with a narrow frill, and hooks should be driven into the supports of the shelf to hang up the frocks, which are then kept free from dust. This simple substitute for a wardrobe can be made at the cost of a few shillings.

* * *

WHY should not well-brought-up girls become nurses? I won't say the word "nursemaid," because that might be objected to. As a rule nurses are quite as well paid as governesses, and in the upper circles many of them receive as much as 6*ol*. or 8*ol*. a year. There can be no more charming work than the care of children. I am very glad, therefore, to notice that a "House of Education" is about to be opened at Ambleside for the training of young ladies to become children's nurses. A fee of 10l. will be charged for a year's training, and the cost of living will be only ten shillings a week. Lots of people now prefer ladies for their children's nurses.

* * *

I saw a very pretty and effective table-square the other day made simply from a bit of white material, something like Indian muslin, stamped with gold arabesques. It threw up into capital relief the pale china vases with their tiny sunflower daisies, which formed the table decoration.

The dessert d'oyleys were of the same gold-stamped, foreign-looking stuff, which had a singularly pretty and elegant appearance.

* * *

Some one proposes quite a new idea. At the present time there are in every large town lots of people, who would like to know each other who cannot do so for want of introductions. In the country a new comer has an opportunity of making plenty of friends, but in the large towns there appears to be no system of etiquette for bringing people together who would like to know each other. There is no place more solitary in the whole world than a London suburb.

The new idea is that there should be in each district what is called a Parish Assistant, who will find out families who want to know people, and, after making proper inquiries, effect introductions.

It is a very common thing for a man to fall in love with a girl he does not know and has only seen. The attraction may be reciprocated. If the girl has any brothers, and the man has not the opportunity of knowing them as mutual friends, an introduction is almost impossible, and I have not the slightest doubt that many a happy marriage has been prevented by this unfortunate circumstance.

* * *

Owing to the early date at which this number is printed (nearly twelve days before you get the paper) I cannot say how many members of the Forget-Me-Not Club we shall have gained during the month. Up to the present we have not enrolled anything like a hundred names. Many are waiting for further particulars, no doubt. Additional information will be found in this issue.

* * *

"A Perplexed One" wants to know what she should do in the following case. She is governess in a family in London, but while she was at home for her last holidays an aunt took her to Scarborough, and she met there a man who paid her a great deal of attention.

Since she came back to London, she has had a letter from him, written to her home address, which he seems to have obtained from her aunt—and in this letter, which is of a sort any girl would like to have from the man she—well, she doesn't dislike—he says he has something which he particularly wants to say to her, and asks if he may call and see her.

Now comes in "A Perplexed One's" difficulty. She cannot get leave to go to her home, some hundreds of miles away, even to receive this call, which may be fraught with such important results, and yet she does not like to write and tell him the reason why, because she says his family are in a better social position than her own, and she is afraid, if he knows she is a governess, he will perhaps hesitate about asking that vital question at all.

So she wants to know what to do.

Now, my dear "Perplexed One," there can be only one course. If he is a man likely to be ashamed of you because you are bravely earning your own living, he is not a man to make you happy. Don't you see that? Besides, you would not, I am sure, want to act even the smallest deception towards him: it would be so wrong and unfair.

175

Write and tell him just how matters stand, and ask him to call and see you in London if he can. If that can't be, he will find another way of asking you that question: Love always finds out the way, you know. And you will know he is worth having for a husband.

* * *

SEVERAL of my correspondents ask what they can do for me in return for my confidential hints. Well, I never thought of a return, my dear girls; it's a pleasure to help you.

But if you really want to do something, you can mention FORGET-ME-NOT to your friends, and get them to take it, too.

* * *

WE are all wondering whether we are to have as bad a winter as last, or what will be the season that follows the remarkable spring, summer and autumn of this most unsatisfactory year. Most of the fashions point at least to the impression that we are to have it cold, and, indeed, those fashions are the wisest which, in this climate, provide for winter weather which is not pleasant.

* * *

DOCTORS are always telling us that macintoshes are unhealthy wear, because they retain the heat of the body and have no ventilation. A new patent has been brought out to change all this, and remove every objection. It is so simple and effective that the only wonder is nobody ever thought of it before. The middle of the back is lined with honeycomb cloth, which is so arranged as to let a free flow of air pass through it from the loose edges of the wings that cover the arms. This prevents the smothering feeling we are all so familiar with when we have to walk any distance in our waterproofs, especially on what we descriptively call a "muggy day."

YOUR EDITRESS.

17.6

Advice columns came in many forms, including didactic narratives. In the 1890s this tradition was put to new ends as editors began to recognise the new types of women who were potential readers and extended their advice into new areas such as room decor.

'The Home of a London Bachelor Girl', *Home Notes*, vol. 2, 1894, p. 126.

I DON'T wish to annoy a friend I have been calling on this afternoon by attracting attention to her, and therefore I will not mention her name, or even the district in which she lives. It is sufficient to tell you that when she is at home, she is in a dear little flat at the top of a high building, which is a favourite resort of many young artists and students, who make a nice colony, and who are remarkable for their pleasant sociability, and neighbourliness to one another.

It has been a hot day, and I reached the top of the long staircase tired, and rather breathless, so that my friend's pretty, cool, breezy little sitting-room seemed a perfect haven of rest of me.

"How pleasant and airy it is up here, even on this scorching day," I remarked after I had been there a little while.

"I am so glad you think so," my friend replied, "we like it, and think the extra light and air we get in our exalted position are worth climbing up for, and besides that it is so nice to have no one trampling about above our heads. We call our eyrie 'Air Throne,' do you think it a good name?"

"Capital, I think, and it is much prettier, I am sure, than the attic which Miss Keary's heroines dignified with that name. This room is perfectly sweet." I looked round lazily as I spoke, and appreciated everything, from the fragrant cup of tea, to the cool looking plants in the window, which were fluttering in the breeze that obtained free entrance through the outside reed blinds of Chinese manufacture, while all the glare and heat were excluded.

It was a very tastefully decorated room, and my friend and the cousin who lived with her were proud of it as being their own handiwork, so they showed me all their devices to make it pretty and homelike. The colours of this room were pale blues and yellows, and the leading idea of the decoration of it was butterflies.

The walls were a plain colour, and on one was a regular flight of butterflies of various colours, which were painted in water-colours, and on the dainty window curtains, and on some of the picture frames, were bright-coloured Japanese butterflies which looked as if they had just settled down there, tired of their flight this hot midsummer day.

In a room like this the butterflies need not be painted on the wall, but the effect can be gained by pinning up a flight of scrap butterflies, such as children buy for picture books. An open or half open fan or two over window or door has power to enhance the butterfly effect, and the same idea is carried out by having Japanese fans as photograph holders.

The fan is nailed up sideways and wide open, so that photographs can be stuck into the cane sticks. In the room I am describing I noticed some pretty rush-bottomed chairs, which had small triangular cushions hanging from the top bar; at each side of the top was a butterfly bow of ribbon.

My hostess told me that when Autumn came the cool matting on the floor would be supplemented by a warm, thick Oriental rug, and the light draperies, which have such an effect of Summer, would give place to others of warmer texture and colour, which would harmonize better with the aspect of nature at that season, and would impart an air of comfort to the room.

Before I descended from "Air Throne" I saw all the rooms of the little flat.

The girls' bedrooms were dainty and refined looking like their inmates, and I noticed the colouring of curtains and bedspreads was soft and cool-looking, and that there were no superfluous draperies or bric-à-brac to take up the air and make them unhealthy. Both rooms had floors painted a dark oak colour and varnished. This was in order that they might be washed with water, and to save the time and trouble of polishing with beeswax and turpentine.

There was a light rug or two in each room, which could be easily taken up and shaken every day, but the greater part of the floor was bare. I saw that both rooms were provided with a basket, lounging chair, and also one with a rather low seat and a high straight back, such as our grandmothers used to delight in, and which I think are far more restful than the greater number of easy chairs of to-day, in spite of their somewhat stiff and prim appearance.

The girls told me that it suited them to have a servant who came to them only in the morning and evening, and who lived at home; so, as she was not there then, I was invited into the kitchen. It was as breezy as the rest of the flat, and it was also shaded by an outside reed blind, which afforded shade to a window-box which was gay with nasturtiums and golden lemon thyme and parsley, so combining beauty and utility.

I give these brief notes because I think other denizens of cities might make use of the suggestion of changing the aspect of their surroundings, according to the seasons of the year.

17.7

Woman at Home (1893–1920) was a general illustrated magazine which became famous for its letters pages and advice columns, especially 'Over the Teacups' in which Annie S. Swan dealt with readers' letters. As was general by the 1890s in all kinds of magazine, this was only one of several advice columns under separate headings including: 'Health and Personal Appearance', 'Dress and Fashion', 'Love, Courtship and Marriage.'

'Over the Teacups', by Annie S. Swan, *Woman at Home*, vol. 5, 1896, pp. 709–10.

THE few paragraphs which appeared in recent number about business girls have brought me a large number of letters. Some of my correspondents appear to be indignant with me for having, in some way or other, decried their calling. To this I do not, however, plead guilty, as I did not commit myself in any way, except to say that the large salaries and enviable surroundings of some who wrote are the plums of this profession as all others; and I have no hesitation in repeating that the rank and file of the young ladies who serve in business houses find the work as hard and at times as unremunerative as in any other field of labour. The letters are so interesting that I think it would please my readers to have a few extracts made, though it will be impossible to quote from all.

* * *

GWYNETH assures me the picture drawn by "A Draper" is not isolated or exaggerated, and advocates more personal interest on the part of employers towards those under their care. She also makes a very good suggestion, that those who have happy homes, and are interested in the welfare of women workers, should extend some hospitality, especially on Sundays, to the girls who live in business houses and sometimes feel lonely on Sundays. This is an admirable suggestion. I am sorry "Gwyneth's" letter is too long for insertion.

* * *

The same applies to the letter of "L. M. S.," but she gives some practical details which may be useful to any of my girl readers who have had business life in contemplation. She says: "In good business houses the premiums vary from twenty to forty guineas, with two years' service, of course in the house; during that time it costs £20 to £25 per annum for dress and other expenses. Is it any wonder that these girls resent being classed, as I have seen them, scarcely one degree above factory girls? In every calling there are the foolish and vicious, but they need not be taken as types of the whole body. Most of the good houses study in every way the comfort of their employees, giving good living, separate beds, library, piano in each sitting-room, etc. I prefer country houses, as they are more home-like."

* * *

A retired business girl writes very sensibly and moderately, and though now happily married, finds life has still its worries and its cares. Space forbids any further quotation. I regret that I have inadvertently conveyed the impression that I regard the position of a shop-girl from rather a contemptuous point of view. God forbid that I, to whom all work is honourable and sacred, should so misjudge a large and honourable section of the working community. My desire in these columns is simply to refrain from giving any false impressions or drawing glowing pictures which experience will dissolve. For this reason I have quoted so largely from the letters of those who, knowing the life by experience, can write with authority, and here the matter may be left.

* * *

I send my sincere sympathy to AN ANXIOUS MOTHER. Her boy has arrived at that restless age when the desire is strong upon him to see life, and when the far lands across the sea beckon to him with persuasive smiles. I do trust she will be able to keep him with her, or at least in this country. I am no advocate for the emigration of boys to other countries. Our own colonies have swallowed up too many of our dearest and best. If all, or even a few, could come back to tell the tale, what bitter heartaches, what disappointment, what disillusionment would be revealed. Tell him that a moderate competency here is better than large means abroad, that there is more comfort, more peace, more true contentment to be found in one's own land among kinsfolk and friends than in an alien land. Perhaps I write with bitterness because of what has been and will be for ever to my heart a personal sorrow and regret. I think "An Anxious Mother" should talk frankly to the boy, and encourage him to state his views about the future, and what he expects to do or to achieve by emigration. I shall be glad to hear from her again.

* * *

LITTLE ROSEBUD would like the address of "Unreconciled," who wrote in a recent number. Being somewhat similarly afflicted, she thinks they might by correspondence cheer and help each other.

* * *

DAISY sends a word of cheer from Saffi, Morocco. She says: "I feel sure that you will like to know how much your magazine is appreciated by us far away in South Morocco. How anxiously we look for a steamer from the north to bring us letters and papers from the dear Home-land! As we have no harbour here, and are exposed to all the Atlantic gales, the steamers often pass in winter without communicating, and then we have to depend on couriers, who bring the mails from north to south and are often robbed. The Moors are a strange people, but in Saffi they are not at all fanatical. Two months ago we had fighting between the tribes, up to our very gates, and the town was for a time in a state of siege."

I do hope "Daisy" will send us a few more particulars of her life in that remote, inaccessible place. It is just possible that she may do a good work by making some discontented souls, whose eyes are presently holden, grateful for the mercies by which they are surrounded.

* * *

I am more than pleased to number LITTLE AFRICANDER among my friends and correspondents over-sea. She sends me a most delightful letter, with a brightly written and amusing account of family life in a doctor's house in Cape Colony. It does not differ so very much from life at home—that is, family characteristics are the same everywhere, and wherever a number of happy, healthy boys and girls are to be found under one roof, there will there be sunshine and shower, east winds and gentle breezes. I send my love to them all, but most particularly to the dear father, about whom his little daughter writes so lovingly. I shall be glad to hear from her again, for a glimpse into such a happy family circle is something worth repeating. . . .

18

Reviews

A whole range of reviewing appeared in women's magazines and this included reviews of books, exhibitions and theatres. Book reviewing was an integral part of the periodical press and this was also the case in publications aimed at women. The popular commercial titles included short reviews of a range of writing whereas certain types of magazine such as the drawing-room and feminist journals took reviewing more seriously and often produced lengthy and detailed reviews, often of recent works of fiction. Reviews of exhibitions, particularly of art followed a similar trend, whereas reviews for the theatre, popular in the fashion magazines, tended to be short with the emphasis primarily on information. Both theatre and art reviewing were particularly important in the ladies' papers.

18.1

The feminist journals took reviewing very seriously and *The Englishwoman's Journal* (1858–63) ran a substantial regular feature 'Notices of Books' that covered a range of reading material thought to be interesting to women interested in reform.

Extract from 'Notices of Books', *The Englishwoman's Journal*, vol. 1, 1858, pp. 196–97.

4.—*The Journal of Psychological Medicine and Mental Pathology.*
Edited by Forbes Winslow, M.D. John Churchill, New Burlington Street.

'CHARLOTTE BRONTÉ, a Psychological Study,' is the title of a paper in the April number of this Quarterly, which will not fail to attract many readers. The character of Miss Brontë was in itself so remarkable, the circumstances under which it was moulded so exceptional, the genius so vivid and impassioned, while the external life was so cold and constrained, that a finer or more generally interesting subject for psychological study it would not be easy to find. Owing, we conclude, to the difficulty of treating fully and freely a life and a being so recently passed from among us, a difficulty which should either have restrained the attempt altogether, or, in the interests of the science of mental phenomena, should have been wholly disregarded, the writer does little more than present in a condensed form the physical, mental, and spiritual peculiarities with which the public is already well acquainted through the medium of Mrs. Gaskell's interesting memoir. Here and there, it is true, the real gist of such an article as the title announces is incidentally touched upon, but with an evident embarrassment and timidity of expression which destroys its value as a "psychological study."

Ordinary readers and critics have not failed to discover for themselves that the painful and unnatural isolation of the Brontë family powerfully affected the development of their character, and that Jane Eyre is as faithful a transcript of Charlotte Brontë as any individual can give of him or herself. As an ordinary review this paper will be found interesting enough. As a psychological study, it is utterly valueless.

IF stays must be worn at all, by all means let us have scientific stay-makers like Madame Caplin, who has devoted herself to the study of the human figure and its artificial needs of requirement and support. We are not of those who think stays indispensable, providing always that from infancy upwards they have at no period been worn. Let nature have fair play, and the muscles will do their own work. It is the unnatural use of stays which renders the muscles flaccid and incapable of sustaining themselves. Still, while it remains the fashion to case the female "human form divine" in whalebone and steel, let all who wear the armour consult those who know what the peculiar figure requires, in preference to the fashion-mongers, who have but one pattern of stays for all shapes and sizes, and whose one ambition seems to be to conform nature to the senseless and arbitrary mode of the moment, manufacturing waists under the arms, or on the hips, as fashion requires. Madame Caplin's corsets are made on anatomical principles, and deserve the attention of all who value rational and sanitary modes of clothing. We commend her and her gay little volume to the notice of our stay-wearing readers.

18.2

The following review from *The Englishwoman's Domestic Magazine* (1852–79) demonstrates the commitment to reviewing very recent works of fiction by contemporary writers, expecially women.

'The Book of the Month', *The Englishwoman's Domestic Magazine*, vol. 1, new series, 1860, pp. 44–45.

The Mill on the Floss. By George Eliot, Author of "Adam Bede."

THE appearance of "Adam Bede," some twelve months since, was hailed by the readers of fiction as proclaiming the advent of a new, fresh, and powerful writer. The book excited an absorbing interest in the minds of the subscribers to the circulating-library, whose voracity for fiction is only paralleled by that of the Esquimaux for blubber and train-oil, and whose wants are met by caterers chief among whom is the magnate Mudie. Very natural was it, that a book which had so deeply affected the emotions of the novel-reader should also stir his curiosity. On concluding the final chapter, the delighted novel-reader turned once more to the commencement of the book, and fastened upon its title-page. After some reflection, a spirit of hardy scepticism came over this typical representative of his class—and, out of his gratitude, he began to doubt the sex of the author. Notwithstanding the very masculine christian and surname placed upon the title-page, it was considered that certain traits of style betokened the hand of a lady. "Jane Eyre" immediately recurred to the mind of the sceptic, and the transformation of Currer Bell into Charlotte Brontë was deemed a sufficiently good precedent for a similar change in this instance. Unfortunately, the feminine equivalent for George Eliot was not forthcoming at this stage. But, after some short epistolary skirmishing in the newspapers, it appeared that the author was really a lady—a Miss Evans; and, although George Eliot is again placed on the title-page of "The Mill on the Floss," all its readers—with the exception of a few illogical individuals who are said to consider the workmanship too good for a woman—will agree in assigning its creation to a feminine brain.

The novel opens with a dialogue between Mr. Tulliver and his wife, wherein the male member makes known to his better half his resolution about Tom, his son. Mr. Tulliver is the owner of Dorlcote Mill, standing on the "Floss"—a broad, navigable river, which "hurries on, between its green banks, to the sea." "I mean to put him to a downright good school at midsummer," says Mr. Tulliver. "The two years at th' academy 'ud ha' done well enough, if I'd meant to make a miller and farmer of him; for he's had a fine sight more schoolin' nor *I* ever got: all the schoolin' *my* father ever paid for was a bit o' birch at one end and th' alphabet at th' other. But I should like Tom to be a bit of a scholard, so as he might be up to the tricks o' them fellows as talk fine and write with a flourish. It 'ud be a help to me wi' these law-suits, and arbitrations, and things. I wouldn't make a down-right lawyer o' the lad—I should be sorry for him to be a raskill."

Thus speaks Mr. Tulliver, farmer and miller, apparently prosperous, but, in reality, sunk in embarrassment, through always being at law. Mr. Tulliver has a special hatred for lawyers— they are never spoken of but as "raskills"—the agents of Satan; and in giving his boy, Tom, a "scholard's education," it is with the view of making him a match for these wily gentry. We are presently introduced to Tom Tulliver and Maggie—the son and daughter of the miller. A considerable portion of the first volume is taken up in laying bare the minds of this boy and girl. Maggie is a wayward, impulsive, fretful, passionate, sensitive girl. Tom is a strong, practical, unromantic, domineering boy; and, in depicting their early characters, the authoress has made Tom, the boy, father to the man; and Maggie, the child, is but a foreshadowing of Maggie, the woman.

The father insists on putting his son to a better school than that which he is in at present, for the reasons above given. Mrs. Tulliver consents, after suggesting that she should "kill a couple o' fowl, and have th' aunts and uncles to dinner, next week, so that they may hear what sister Glegg and sister Pullet have got to say about it."

The portrait of Mrs. Tulliver is sketched, at this point, in a few powerful touches.

The three sisters of Mrs. Tulliver are drawn with remarkable force, but all their characters are so hard and disagreeable, that one feels the want of some relief. So uninviting are these three representatives of the awful "Dodson family," that one seeks to believe that, unlike all the rest of the book, they are unnatural creations. They are all vulgar, selfish, and narrow-minded. Mrs. Glegg, the eldest of the Dodson girls, is a bitter being, the wife of a "wool-stapler, retired from active business for the purpose of enjoying himself through the rest of his life." Mrs. Pullet is a tearful woman with a passion for tidiness and order. Mrs. Deane is a swarthy woman, of a sour disposition. One of these ladies has a daughter, Lucy Deane, a neat, pretty, amiable girl, and a most striking contrast to the daughter of Mr. Tulliver, Maggie, who is chiefly remarkable for her tall, graceful form, dark, heavy locks, and brown skin.

After some domestic deliberations, Mr. Tulliver sends Tom for his "first half" to the Rev. Mr. Stelling, a well-sized, broad-chested man, not yet thirty, with flaxen hair standing erect, and large, lightish-grey eyes, which were always very wide open. He had a sonorous bass voice, and an air of defiant self-confidence, inclining to brazenness. He had entered on his career with great vigour, and intended to make a considerable impression on his fellow-men. In short, Mr. Stelling meant to rise in his profession, and to rise by merit, clearly, since he had no interest beyond what might be promised by a problematical relationship to a great lawyer who had not yet become a Lord Chancellor. A clergyman who has such vigorous intentions naturally gets a little into debt at starting, it is not to be expected that he will live in the meagre style of a man who means to be a poor curate all his life. Under the direction of this worthy divine, Tom Tulliver's practical mind is plunged into all the awful miseries of Latin grammar and Euclid, these being the Rev. Mr. Stelling's text-books for making a sound scholar. He believes in no other sort of training for a boy. After some time, Tom finds a slight diversion in his toilsome studies in the advent of a new pupil, Philip Wakem, the son of Lawyer Wakem, old Mr. Tulliver's enemy. The boy Philip is a hump-back, but is endowed with a fine and sensitive nature. The lad has the perception of an artist, the soul of a poet. Tom's feelings on first seeing this poor youth are graphically detailed. He had a vague notion that the deformity of Wakem's son had some relation to the lawyer's rascality, of which he had so often heard his father talk with hot emphasis; and he felt, too, a half-admitted fear of him, as probably a spiteful fellow, who, not being able to fight you, had cunning ways of doing you a mischief by the sly.

So far there is very little complication of plot—indeed, the first volume is chiefly a collection of portraits, with a slight variation of incident, or, more properly speaking, it is a chain of events. But troubles for the house of Tulliver are at hand.

We should have liked to have quoted a series of bright, freshly-painted portraits from this novel. Our limited space forbids this. We must proceed, rather, to give our readers a slight notion of the plot. The miller has lost his great law-suit, and his ruin is impending. Lawyer Wakem has been the chief instrument in bringing the affair to a termination so disastrous to Mr. Tulliver. The violent struggle which ensues in the mind of the miller is described with a minuteness and a power truly marvellous. Mr. Tulliver must now become the agent of his hated neighbour, the "raskill" Wakem. He determines to serve him like an honest man, but, in the overwhelming force of his malice, he makes his son inscribe, at his dictation, a terrible curse in the family Bible. And so the Tullivers set out on their journey through the valley of humiliation. A long and weary journey it is, but the Tulliver family are stout of heart, and both Tom and his father are resolved to remove the disgrace of debt by years of manful energy. Time goes by. Maggie is now seventeen. Her form has developed into queenly proportions. Long intervals of silent, solitary self-communing have given her mind an unusual fervour and intensity. The deformed youth, Philip, has been abroad, and has now come home; and the childish gratitude of the maiden for his gentle sympathy with her has ripened into love for the son of her father's enemy and master. She has stolen interviews with her lover in the Red Deeps, an exhausted stone-quarry. Discovery awaits the lovers, however. Tom, who combines all the decision and inflexibility of the Dodson nature with the hard, practical character of his father, suspects his sister, and, on extracting a confession from her, forces her to spurn her lover, whom he cruelly insults. There is another pair of lovers in the shape of Lucy Deane and Mr. Stephen Guest, "whose diamond ring, attar of roses, and air of nonchalant leisure at twelve o'clock in the day, are the graceful and odoriferous result of the largest oil-mill and the most extensive wharf in St. Oggs."

Poor Maggie! Her whole heart belongs to Philip Wakem; but Stephen has been fascinated by her magnificent form and powerful intellect. The young man forsakes Lucy Deane for Maggie. Maggie's wild, impulsive nature betrays her into what will appear to most readers a cruel piece of treachery towards her cousin. Hardly has she realized the extent or nature of her feelings towards Stephen Guest, when this bold and disloyal lover rows away with her out to sea in a boat. He declares his passion; but honour and duty are not dead in Maggie's breast. She spurns the offer of his hand, and, with an angry resistance, demands to be taken back. She returns, but her absence has been remarked; the town of St. Oggs is scandalized, and unhappy Maggie is sacrificed on the altar of social propriety. The bitter reproaches of Tom cut like a whip; his words are awful in their intensity of scorn. The catastrophe approaches: the old mill is swept away by an inundation; Maggie and Tom seek to escape in a boat; the frail craft is borne along the dark flood; but, just as the sight of some tall, strong houses revives hope in their breasts, death, in a most horrible shape, starts up before them. The boat is driven against some immense fragments of wooden machinery, which are being driven along with the boiling current. Brother and sister are clasped in each other's arms as the boat is driven beneath the black water, and, when it reappears, keel upwards, both have gone down in an embrace never to be parted.

Although the "Mill on the Floss" may be set down as inferior to "Adam Bede," it displays no evidence of diminished powers in its author. In some quarters, surprise has been expressed that George Eliot—or Miss Evans—could have produced so grand a piece of literary workmanship within a year after the publication of her "Adam Bede." But it surely must have escaped these people, that such a book as that could never have been written without vast preparation.

A goodly pile of MS. must have been the forerunner of this first work. The order of publication is not necessarily the order of composition. Did not Charlotte Brontë's "Professor" appear as a posthumous work? And is it not known that this was the very novel which the lamented lady sent to almost every publisher in the United Kingdom without finding one willing to produce it to the public? And was not "Jane Eyre," the first novel published, in reality written subsequently to this last-issued work?

We believe the "Mill on the Floss" to be inferior to "Adam Bede," merely because it was written partly, if not totally, before "Adam Bede." To our mind, the comparatively crude sketches of the Dodson family were the first efforts of the author in that marvellous, minute, and daring style of word-painting which resulted in the more mellow and harmonious characters of Mr. and Mrs. Poyser, &c.

18.3

The drawing-room journals, like the feminist journals, were also committed to rather lengthy and serious reviewing. *The Rose, the Shamrock and the Thistle* (1862–65) devoted its review space to works largely written by women.

Extract from 'The Lady's Literary Circular', *The Rose, the Shamrock and the Thistle*, vol. 3, 1863, pp. 669–70.

LITTLE ADA AND HER CRINOLINE. BY MADAME DE CHATELAIN. (Dean & Son.)

THE authoress, a friend of the "little folks," has dressed *a la mode* one of her young friends in the odd costume that fashionable mothers put on their girls, and thus attired the nursery angel is, in Madame de Chatelain's story, carried through various adventures, each of which has the natural predicament of demonstrating the tasteless folly, and ever present danger incurred of making a pretty child wear a crinoline petticoat. Other little girls, whose mothers and fathers are wise, may have their game of romps, their rambles, their childhood's manor (*sic*) of careless enjoyment, but Ada the hapless carries about with her *fear* in its fifty shapes—fear of spoiling her stiff hops (*sic*), fear of the hydra-consequences which spring up round the crinoline encircled child. The volume is an appeal to mothers, and we may hope maternal love may be stronger than the wife's obstinacy—the latter holds against all the attacks of husbands and universal man; against all the fiery ordeals to which it has been exposed; nevertheless, we have a hope that the ice of fashion will lose its adamantine quality when touched by the glowing mother-love which would shield a child from every harm, and as a consequence leave the 'Little Adas' of our homes, their childhood's prerogatives of playing in peace and safety.

ESSAYS ON THE PURSUITS OF WOMEN. BY FRANCES POWER COBBE. (Faithfull.)

THE pen in a woman's hand is a sword with which she has to fight her way in establishing the standing-ground, the native-land of her right to labour. This is the little kingdom, which, as a freeborn woman, she claims, and surely it is but a social Belgium, the independence of which should be guaranteed by the Great Powers of civilized Europe. And, in truth, this is really the case; the claim has been preferred and allowed. The difficulty remaining is to fix the *boundaries* of woman's labour-fields, and this question continues an open and vexed one, which is only likely to be settled by public support rather than argumentative sanction. Now, there is a great deal of delicacy in that courted patron and giant-employer the public. This recent facts have abundantly proved—thus, nimble-fingered girls wanted work as telegraph clerks,—the public employed them.

Other girls wished to do the type work in our printing offices, and the public again smiled and encouraged them. So in a multitude of occupations (compared with former exclusiveness), woman has knocked at the door of workrooms and been allowed the privileges of man to labour and earn independence. Miss Cobbe's book attempts successfully to distinguish what should be, and may be, a woman's pursuits, and is, therefore, commended to philanthropic employers and social-thinkers, who, now that the gates are open, would throw them wide and free to admit work-women to perform every and any task they are competent to undertake.

In treating of female education one consideration, and that often the greatest, is usually passed over, the *expense* of any of the courses of study which men must pass through. Painting, music, and literature are alike free to both sexes, but science shuts her door on a woman's face. Boys at sixteen, advised by friends, choose an occupation, and usually they settle down to it *for life*. But what girl of the same age might do so? To name a profession that is not often named, but which, nevertheless, many women might follow. Who would make an *architectural* draughts-woman of his daughter? Paying a premium and supporting her for some five years during the appren-ticeship. Probably many fathers would do so if they felt sure the student would, *for life*, remain an architect. But there is always *the probability*, the great probability of marriage, which would render valueless the knowledge and practice acquired, at a cost which would have formed a dowry sufficient to be of real use to her husband, professionally or commercially. And this must ever be a woman's normal position. The avenues open are the byepaths; marriage is the highway of social woman's life, and, as a rule, only the waifs of orphanage, the strays of cruel circumstance, and the meteors of talent will have occasion to leave the broad pleasant road of domesticity, of wifehood and motherhood. As it is, the generous public earnestly desire to make the bye-paths of woman's life as numerous, as free from briars, as pleasant with wayside flowers as civilized manhood can make them.

18.4

The religious magazines approached the business of reviewing in the same way that they approached other areas, by aiming to be instructive and didactic. The following review from *The British Workwoman* (1863–96) takes the opportunity to comment on the lives of female street vendors, one of the topics covered by the subject of the review.

'London Labour and the London Poor', *The British Workwoman*, vol. 1, 1863, pp. 37–38.

ONE half of the world knows not how the other half lives, and better it were for both halves if they understood each other better. The trials, the perils, the temptations of the very poor are strange to a large number of those who "dwell in ceiled houses". Close at hand is want and misery—Lazarus at the very gate of Dives; but the purple and fine linen, the sumptuous fare every day, make Wealth too often forgetful of Want. Let us not be misunderstood. Good and charitable offices are rendered freely by the richest and noblest in the English Peerage. British nobility is not afraid of losing any of its lustre, by doing the work of the good Samaritan, the grand exemplar set before us all by Jesus Christ. But there is necessarily an estrangement between the well-to-do and the ill-to-do: the poor cluster together, and so do the rich; and anything that serves to bring them nearer to each other, to make them feel their common brotherhood, is of immense advantage.

In the comprehensive and circumstantial volumes of Mr. Henry Mayhew, entitled "London Labour and the London Poor", the circumstances and condition of the indigent classes in our great metropolis are fairly, fully, faithfully described. Those that will work, those that cannot work, and those that will not work,—the volumes form a cyclopedia of the condition and earnings of the poor and are one of the most valuable contributions to the benevolent agencies of this nineteenth century. A cheap re-issue of this work will be hailed with satisfaction, and we may confidently predict for the enterprising publishers* a large circulation. A new generation has sprung up since the work originally appeared—a generation deeply interested in the welfare of the London street folk—and to which the valuable information contained in its pages will be exceedingly welcome.

To the British Workwoman, no portion of "London Labour and the London Poor" can be more interesting than that of the female street-sellers, the women and girls who seek a livelihood by the sale of combs, wash-leathers, tapes, boot-laces, matches, and other minor articles. We cannot but look upon this class of street traders with extreme commiseration. They are exposed to very great hardships and very sore temptation. They are of all ages, and nearly all classes,—English, Irish, Scotch, Welsh and a few Jewesses. They are the wives of street-sellers, mechanics' and labourers' wives, who go out street-selling, while their husbands are at work, as a means of helping out the family income. They are the widows of former street-sellers, or they are single women, who appear to have no other honest means of obtaining a livelihood.

It is a sad pity that so many women in this great city of ours should be compelled, by the imperative demands of absolute starvation, to "try the streets". The battle for bread is hard at all times, but hard *and hazardous* when waged in the streets. Very few street-sellers—we allude to females exclusively in this remark—ever rise to any better position; they lose heart, they lose self-respect, they sink into apathy and endure bitter privations, without an effort to escape. It is a melancholy fact that is worthy of observation.

And here, in all kindliness, we may be permitted to say:—should this paper come into the hands of a street-seller, is there nothing you can find to do that would lift you out of this hard, hazardous life? It may be, that your husband is a street-seller, and that you work with him; that is better, but better still would it be if you could obtain some work in your own house, and there discharge your wifely duties and make that house, however humble, a home. And let us urge upon mothers the duty of preventing their girls engaging in street traffic. It seems an easy method of turning a child's labours to account, that of sending it out with pins, or tapes, or flowers; but consider the risk—remember your own responsibility, as mothers. Accept for yourselves, as for your children, any work, however, humble or laborious, but never for a moment think of "Street Labour".

In the section which Mr. Mayhew, in his work, devotes to women street-sellers, we find several very affecting and instructive narratives, which we are satisfied will be read with interest. The illustrations are excellent; most of them copied from photographs of well-known street-folk, As an example of these engravings, we print the "Street Comb-Seller" [not reproduced here].

* London Labour and the London Poor—Charles Griffin and Co.

18.5

The regular feature 'Literary Notices' from *The Ladies' Treasury* (1858–95) illustrates the shorter, more general kind of review popular in many types of women's magazine.

'Literary Notices', *The Ladies' Treasury*, vol. 13, new series, 1876, p. 740.

FORGING THEIR OWN CHAINS. By C. M. CORNWALL. (London: Ward, Lock, and Tyler.) —A well-written tale, describing many of the inevitable consequences arising from the combination of workmen against their employers, and familiarly known as "strikes."

The idle must live, and, if possible, in seeming respectability; but among them are men with brains, which, if rightly governed, would convert them into blessings to humanity. But as it is, their dominating influence is mischievously used to bring weaker minds to misery. In the form of presidents of certain associations they induce men to leave good wages and good masters, making their poor uneducated tools subscribe money, under pretence of paying others out of work, while the same funds go to keep these demagogues in luxury. There are love-scenes, in which the actors "forge their own chains," and which are well described. The book is worth reading, and the price (one shilling) is very trifling.

MIMI'S CHARITY. By S. DE K. (E. Marlborough and Co., 51, Old Bailey).—A story which children will appreciate, and which, if carefully read to them, cannot fail to impress the little folks that much happiness may result from treating human beings with kindness instead of hard words and harder usage. In this tale a child's charity, obtained by self-denial, was rewarded tenfold. The book will make an excellent present to a little girl.

FAIRY. By LIZZIE JOYCE TOMLINSON. (E. Marlborough and Co.)—The plot of the tale, about a little girl being cast on the shore from a wreck, saved, and adopted by a fisherman and his wife, to be finally claimed by her rich friends, is one which little children delight to hear about.

THE MOTHERS' FRIEND. (London: Messrs. Hodder and Stoughton, Paternoster Row.)—The eighth volume of this excellent serial increases in vitality with every issue. It is calculated to do great good among a large class of readers. One tale alone, "Asked of God," is certainly written with the best of aims, and there is scarcely a husband and wife but must be benefited by its perusal.

THE PICTORIAL WORLD for October (an illustrated weekly newspaper) is deserving all success (but that, we believe, it has). It is well edited and elaborately illustrated. We find the following in one of its columns:— "Hard water can be rendered very soft by, for instance, boiling a two-ounce phial bottle in a kettleful of water. The carbonate of lime and other impurities will be found adhering to the bottle." The *Builder* is credited with this presumed fact. Part XXXII. contains a beautiful clear and well-engraved full-page plate of "Hunting in the Rocky Mountains." We have seldom met with such a gem in the way of engraving.

THE VICTORIA MAGAZINE (edited by EMILY FAITHFULL) contains a good biography of Pope, "A Grandfather's Story," an article on Madame de Sevigné and her contemporaries, with Miscellanea, which make up a very good number for November. It is published at 85, Praed Street.

THE NATIONAL SCHOOLMASTER contains a good deal of information regarding education, and is a useful little work. It is published by Simpkin and Marshall at 1d.

OLD JONATHAN: the District Parish-Helper (1d.).—This serial is much improved during the year, and will prove an acceptable gift in many cottage and other homes.

A very charming volume, FINGER-RING LORE, has been issued by Messrs Chatto and Windus, of Piccadilly. We hope to call special attention to this work in the January number of the LADIES' TREASURY.

The GARDENERS' MAGAZINE, the GARDEN GUIDE, and SCIENCE GOSSIP have not been received.

18.6

Literary reviewing was not the only type of reviewing found in women's magazines. The following abridged extract from *The Englishwoman's Review* (1866–1910) illustrates the significance attached to calling the reader's notice to other developments in the world of art.

'Exhibition of the Society of Female Artists, 9 Conduit Street', *The Englishwoman's Review*, vol. 1, 1867, pp. 136–38.

THE standard of merit has risen steadily in the exhibitions of this Society, from the time of their first establishment, eleven years ago.

The pictures in the early exhibitions, with some exceptions, displayed a very humble order of genius, but persevering effort has, as usual, gained the victory over difficulties, and almost all the pictures in the present exhibition are creditable to the artists who produced them.

In former days, when pictures were usually painted to hang in churches, for the purpose of instructing, encouraging, or terrifying the congregation, artists were often under the necessity of painting ugly and painful subjects; but now, that pictures are merely required to adorn the walls of living rooms, it is essential that the subject should be pleasant. To persons whose avocations condemn them to spend many months in a town, it is a great source of pleasure to have before them the picture of a pretty rural scene, of a group of wild flowers, or the view of some beautiful spot which they visited in their summer wanderings. Such pictures remind them that there is still beauty left on the earth, which they may hope some day to enjoy again. Our lady artists seem to understand this secret, and have contributed but few pictures which are not the representation of scenes pleasant to behold.

In the following notes, no attempt is made to mention all the works that deserve commendation, but only to call attention to a few which particularly attracted our notice.

Miss Gastineau's "Lock Katrine" (No. 9), gives an excellent Midsummer effect of sunshine, water, and rich foliage.

"The Last of the Season" (28), a flower piece, by Charlotte James, is well painted.

We were not surprised to see that "The Old Well," a sketch by Miss Parkes, was ticketed, "Sold." Miss M. Raynor exhibits two interiors of churches (Nos. 91 and 136), which are remarkable for their breadth and vigour; as is also that of "Naworth Castle" (No. 147), by the Hon. Mrs. Lowther. "The Bay of Algiers," (No. 92), taken from Mrs. Bodichon's studio, by Lady Dunbar, is highly effective.

"Reconciliation" (No. 15), is a more ambitious effort. A naughty child, who has begged pardon, is being kissed, and forgiven, by its mother. The mother's face is concealed, but the child's expression, tearful and agitated, yet no longer miserable, is very good. The painter is Madame Noa.

"Divided" (No. 161), by Miss Macandrew, tells its story remarkably well. A lady is leaving a gentleman, having evidently refused his proposal of marriage, from a sense of duty or some other reason, which he regards as insufficient. He retains her by grasping her dress, while he is thinking of something further to say, which will overcome her resolution. The girl's face of sorrow, tenderness, and solicitude for him, is admirable. His expression is full of thought. It seems to us that the insignificant accessories of the scene are made too prominent. If a passer-by had chanced to behold the interview through an open door, he would certainly have had his attention arrested by the chief figures, and not by the pattern of the chintz chair covers or the carpet.

. . .

On the screens there are a few good miniatures, among which we noticed a Portrait of the Prince of Wales (No. 289), by Miss Landseer, sister of the celebrated Sir Edwin Landseer; also several good sketches. "The Study of a Negress" (No. 339), by Mrs. Lee Briddell, deserves attention, on account of the expression of resignation in the woman's face.

The Exhibition contains very few pictures of the "Bird's Nest and Group of Primroses" type, of which the public is so weary.

We believe the Exhibition will close very shortly after the publication of these pages, so any one who wishes to see it should hasten thither at once.

Theatre reviews were common in many types of women's magazines, but the short review illustrated here from *The London and Paris Ladies' Magazine* (1828–91) was a staple feature of the expensive fashion magazine and the ladies' papers.

'The Theatres', *The London and Paris Ladies' Magazine*, vol. 46, 1873, p. 8.

The Royal Italian Opera opens for the season on the first of this month. Mr. Gye has secured the co-operation of those talented artistes, Mdlle. A. Patti, P. Lucca, and Alboni: among the novelties announced are *Mosé in Egitto* and *I Promessi Spose*.

At Drury Lane, the revival of the *"Cataract of the Ganges"* has proved a great success. The characteristic music by Mr. Levey, and the scenery by Mr. William Beverly greatly contribute to the favorable reception this drama is receiving. The morning performances of *"Charles the First,"* which have taken place at the Lyceum during the month, have been very successful. Herr Bandmann and Mrs. Bandmann have appeared at the Princess's nightly during the month, in *"Hamlet"* and *"Macbeth,"* and have drawn large houses. The new burlesque *"Don Giovanni"* is meeting with great favour at the Gaiety, the principal characters are by Mr. Toole, Miss Farren, and Miss Loseby. The new scenery, dances, and dresses are very tasteful and elegant. The music by eminent composers, and arranged by Herr Meyer Lutz, is exceptionally attractive. The Queen's retain *"Old London,"* in which Miss Henrietta Hodson appears to great advantage.

19
Competitions

All commercial women's magazines used competitions and inducements to buy to boost sales and reader loyalty. The kinds of inducements and ideas for competitions grew in numbers and in imagination as the century progressed. The early pioneering incentives to purchase formulated by Samuel Beeton in *The Englishwoman's Domestic Magazine* and the late century competitions for increasingly expensive prizes set the agenda for the reader participation and product promotion of the modern women's magazine.

19.1

As a pioneer of the general illustrated magazine Samuel Beeton introduced many novel initiatives in *The Englishwoman's Domestic Magazine* (1852–79) and its sister paper *The Young Englishwoman* (1864–77). This early inducement to buy set the pace for the development of the idea of offering incentives to the reader beyond the magazine itself.

'Notice', *The Englishwoman's Domestic Magazine*, vol. 3, new series, 1862, p. 144.

THE SHILLING EDITION comprises, besides the components of this Magazine, an 8-page Supplement, containing illustrations of the CHEMISE RUSSE, New Stitches in Point Russe, Six Engravings of the Newest and most Fashionable Mode of Making Dresses, Hanging Sleeve, Muslin Fichu, Young Lady's Coiffure, Work-Basket Cover, Braiding Patterns, Parasol Cover in Venetian Embroidery, Knitted Square for Counterpanes, Braided Slipper, &c., with full directions for working and making the same. Also a Fashion Plate of large size, and a Photograph of the late Prince Consort.

19.2

As competitions grew in frequency and number the variety also proliferated, and with prizes ranging from money to gifts like bicycles and sewing machines they became an increasingly important feature of the later Victorian magazine. In the magazine for girls the emphasis was most often placed on testing educational and specifically literary attainments. This competition from the girls' monthly *Atalanta* (1887–98) was part of a regular feature 'Atalanta Scholarship and Reading Union' in which an annual scholarship prize was awarded along with a number of smaller rewards.

'Scholarship Competition Page', *Atalanta*, vol. 4, 1890, unnumbered page.

Compare and contrast the characters of Juliet (*Romeo and Juliet*) and Julia (*Two Gentlemen of Verona*). Essays must contain not more than 500 words, and must be sent in by January 25th. Competitors are requested to notice that their Papers are correctly stamped, as extra Postage has to be paid on many received each month.

Plays Selected for February.—Middle History. *King John. Richard II.*

SEARCH QUESTIONS IN ENGLISH LITERATURE.

I.

(*a*) Where, and by whom, were the following words written?

"Fain would I climb, but that I fear to fall."

(*b*) Give the answer, and say who completed the couplet.

II.

Mention any authors who lived at the following places:—1, Horton, Buckinghamshire; 2, Newstead Abbey; 3, Kilcolman Castle; 4, Canons-Ashby, Northamptonshire; 5, Stoke-Pogis; 6, Aldborough; 7, Donnington Castle; 8, Olney; 9, The Leasowes.

III.

What was the real name of Mr. "Silas Tomken Comberback?"

IV.

Who was the traveller who related the following as things he had really seen?—"In Æthiope are such men as have but one foot, and they go so fast that it is a great marvel, and that is a large foot, for the shadow thereof covereth the body from sun or rain, when they lie upon their backs." "In the Island of Macameran, the natives have the heads of dogs. In another island are white lions and double-headed geese. In a third are men with only one eye; in a fourth the natives are headless, and have their mouths and noses in their breasts, and their eyes in their shoulders. Another island is inhabited by giants twenty-eight feet high, who eat raw flesh; and beyond this is another, in which are giants fifty feet high."

V.

Quote a passage from Shakespeare which is supposed to refer to the book of travels mentioned in the preceding question.

VI.

Give author and work from which the following quotations are taken:—

(1) "Man is his own star; and the soul that can
   Render an honest and a perfect man,
   Commands all light, all influence, all fate;
   Nothing to him falls early or too late.
   Our acts our angels are, or good or ill,
   Our fatal shadows that walk by us still."

(2) "And a magic voice and verse
   Hath baptised thee with a curse;
   And a spirit of the air
   Hath begirt thee with a snare;
   In the wind there is a voice
   Shall forbid thee to rejoice;
   And to thee shall Night deny
   All the quiet of her sky;
   And the day shall have a sun
   Which shall make thee wish it done."

(3) "But little do men perceive what solitude is, and how far it extendeth; for a crowd is not company, and faces are but a gallery of pictures, and talk but a tinkling cymbal, where there is no love."

(4) "I've heard of hearts unkind, kind deeds
   With coldness still returning,
   Alas! the gratitude of men
   Has oftener left me mourning."

Answers to be sent in by January 15; they should be addressed to the Superintendent, R. U., Atalanta, 28, New Bridge Street, London, E.C., and must contain full Name and Address of sender.

This abridged piece from *Hearth and Home* (1891–1914) is part of a whole section including extracts from entries as well as a list of prizewinners for a number of art and literary competitions.

'The Literary Guild', *Hearth and Home*, vol. 1, 1891, pp. 76–77.

The HEARTH AND HOME Literary Guild does not consist simply of competitions and prizes, but includes criticism of and on every paper sent in, advice to young writers, practical help in the shape of occasional "model" papers, and the encouragement generally of literary talent. The subjects of competitions are as varied as possible, and range from "leaders" and essays to comic verse. Short stories are an especial feature in our competitions, and when suitable will be purchased by the Editor, even when they do not obtain the prize. *Prizes of ONE or TWO GUINEAS are offered every week for the best papers sent in which will also be printed.*

RULES.

1. Every competitor must send a statement with Coupon cut from the Wrapper of the current issue of this paper, declaring that he or she is not a professional writer, i.e., one who adds to or earns an income by writing regularly. Papers unaccompanied by the Coupon and Declaration will not be considered.

2. Every competitor must adopt a nom-de-plume, and at the same time forward a real name and address, which will be published in the case of prize winners.

3. MSS. can in no case be returned.

4. All competitions must be legible, written in ink, on one side of the paper only and addressed on the top corner of the envelope to

> *Critic,*
> *"Hearth and Home"*
> *6, Fetter Lane, London, E.C.*

5. The Editor's decision must in all cases be considered as final.

COMPETITION XIV.

A prize of ONE GUINEA is offered for the best original four-lined

VERSE SUITABLE FOR CHRISTMAS CARD.

All contributions must reach this office by to-day.

COMPETITION XV.

A Prize of ONE GUINEA is offered for the best short

CHRISTMAS STORY

of not more than 2,000 words.

All papers must reach this office by Dec. 24th.

COMPETITION XVI.

A Prize of ONE GUINEA is offered for the best written

INCIDENT IN SCHOOL LIFE

that is the actual experience of the writer.

Papers must contain not more than 1,000 words and reach this office by December 17th.

COMPETITION XII.
A TRUE GENTLEWOMAN.

I am pleased to be able to say that some really excellent papers, characterised by good sense, good taste, and good feeling were sent in for this competition, which seems to have been a very popular one. There is almost a complete unanimity of expression on the subject of "Emancipated Women," most of my contributors having pointed out with a good deal of sobriety and moderation that the path of the "true gentlewoman" lies between the positions taken by the schools headed by Mrs. Fawcett on the one side, and Mrs. Lynn Linton on the other. The prizewinner's paper is the best, because the writer has made some attempt, now and again very successful, to write with grace and elegance. It would, however, have been infinitely better if the opening remarks had been left out. Some extracts from the papers of other competitors are also given below, and are only a selection out of the really good and careful work sent in. The Prize of One Guinea has been awarded to "Daphne,"

Mrs. A. M. RAWSON,

Rosary Gardens, S.W.,

for the following

PRIZE ESSAY.

WE children of this prolific Nineteenth Century have much to be proud of. We have witnessed and shall, no doubt, witness many an interesting crisis in knowledge and in manners, many happy solutions of social and scientific problems. In such breathless times it is, nevertheless, hard to divide our attention equally between breadth and detail. Details in manners are specially apt to be slurred over, and it is to this non-recognition of the due importance of detail—in other words, of the *decline of grace*—I would now speak.

We pride ourselves, no doubt, on our cosmopolitanism, our indifference to class distinctions. We spend much of our wealth and energy in work amongst the lower classes in the belief that we are raising their moral and æsthetic standard, we consider ourselves as "gentle-folk" in contradistinction to them, yet I fear that more often than not we do not earn this title. To women especially it is given to mould the manners of those around them, to cherish and practice the "great and gracious ways," which are not veneer, but the outcome of a simple true nature. I cannot believe that these are consistently and universally cultivated when I see daily a want of chivalry and grace amongst women themselves. I shall add a special clause to my thanksgivings when I no longer hear of the social "boycotting," the foolish cliques, the absurd worship of "outsides," which mar the lives and dwarf the characters of many well-born, nay, highly-born women. I shall feel proud when I find a lady consistently treating a woman of inferior rank to herself, be she scullerymaid or milliner, with the same courtesy that she would use to a friend of her own standing.

There are several facts which, should they ever come to pass, I shall record with red letters in my diary—viz., when I see one of my own sex, who, on getting out of a railway train (underground or otherwise), will quietly close the door and turn the handle after her, lest her companions should be subjected to the rush of sulphurous vapour, followed by the guard's bang at the door, which sets all nerves a-thrilling. Also when a lady seated next the door of a railway carriage will have the courtesy to open the door for one who is getting out, instead of remaining passive while the latter trips over her feet and strews multitudinous parcels in the attempt to turn the handle.

Furthermore, when I am allowed to mount the step of an omnibus without being lifted down by a person, whose h's and appearance are alike irreproachable, in order that she may first ascend and secure a seat. (Do not smile incredulously, fair reader! I state a fact.)

I am proud of my sex, and would think myself honoured to die singing their praises, with just certain exceptions. I would that the army of women tattlers and scandalmongers were put to rout; not these only but the meanly ambitious souls, the matchmakers, the schemers, the "worldly-holy" and the "wholly worldly" who do not know what it is to cherish a gentle thought of their own sex. I should not be sorry to see these *disillusionées*, the nakedness of their ambitions, the emptiness of a life without beauty and without depth, without grace presented to them in all its sad reality.

A want of grace is often attributed to self-consciousness. Unconsciousness is the essence of a gracious manner. My earlier years were associated with a friend of my family, one of the most charming women I ever met. As children we called her "Old Miss Lavender," and the name exactly described her. Of the many happy recollections of her, two are as vivid as if they had but yesterday been painted on my memory's canvas—my first sight of her and my last. How well I remember that first meeting! She had stopped during a ramble in the fields to help an old man to steady a bundle of osiers on his back; she

193

ended by carrying half of it herself. leaving him at his cottage with a smile and a greeting that would have made an emperor proud. As she turned away her eye caught a bunch of pink-tipped daisies thrown in the dust by some idle hand; she stooped for the flowers and passed on. Those daisies graced her windowsill for full a week after their adventure. The last time I saw her in her rose-wreathed cottage the dear silvery head was leaning against the back of her favourite low chair, the eyes closed, the lips faintly smiling. An open Testament lay on her knee. In one hand was a bunch of myrtle, the other was pointing to the twenty-second verse of the seventh chapter of I Kings: "And upon the top of the pillars was lily-work. So was the work of the pillars finished." Sweet Old Miss Lavender had gone to her rest. The picture and the lesson have become my lasting heritage.

Lily-work? Ay, just as the lily-work was destined to adorn the pillars of Solomon's ancient temple, to soften the sternness of their straight lines, so woman with her inborn adaptability, her more delicate imagination, has it in her power to call forth such qualities in her brother man as will enrich his life and her own to the fostering of

> Merrie chere and courtesie,
> Ful manie a grace with dignitee;

and this not only in the lives of men, but women too, whose circumstances and education has left the graces of life uncultivated, unthought of.

Be she the poorest apple-woman or flower-girl that treads the streets, or be she a Portia in intellect, with the daring and brilliancy of a Diana of the Crossways, she may equally be what sweet "Old Miss Lavender" unconsciously was—"a true gentlewoman."

. . .

COMPETITION XI.
CRITICISMS ON PAPERS.

The following were crowded out last week:—

LAUREL.—Your lines are too sing-song. Listen to these two lines:—

> "Through courts by love's immortal ray
> To seek thy king whom thou hadst served
> alway."

Avoid also as far as possible throwing the emphasis on "had."

GREEN MANTLE.—For sixteen years old your sonnet is very creditable, and I am glad to see you take some eminent poet for a model. I suppose you had Mrs. Browning's sonnet, "What would we give to our Belovèd?" in your mind, did you not? You must try and keep the metre the same throughout.

> "Wax dim as changing centuries thunder by"

will not scan. I hope you will try again. Some of your lines are very graceful.

SERJAEM.—It is not wise for a poetaster to invite severe criticism by such a line as your sixth—

> "And anger with my inspiration blends."

Inspiration is rather a big word. Apart from their not scanning, the lines—

> "'Gainst those who sacrificed him to delay,"
> etc.,

are very jarring and unmusical.

TRUTH.—For a first attempt yours is not at all bad; but you do not know anything about "form" or metre, and it is impossible to criticise your production at present. It would be quite worth your while to get "Sonnets of this Century," and carefully study the introduction. You have a good deal of poetic "feeling" and have some command of words. After you have studied the introduction read Milton's "Thou should'st be living," etc., and "The world is too much with us," by the same poet.

AMOR.—Your lines are correct, but they are commonplace; and the lines—

> "Her bitter sorrow; while from East and West
> Asia and Europe mourn with each freed slave."

are not quite intelligible to me.

FIDELIS.—Please see first part of my answer to "Laurel," though your sonnet contains many better lines. You write with a great deal of facility, and if you will avoid the fault named above should do well.

G. H. B.—Your ear-sense wants cultivating; and your sonnet is altogether too confused. One is unprepared for

"The hero's cold and listless ear,"

immediately after hearing

"That his heart nigh bursts with scorn," etc.

If you will read the best sonnets, Shakespeare's, Milton's, Arnold's, etc., you will see there is a certain unity and sequence of thought which are essential to a successful poem of this kind.

Favo.—Your sonnet arrived after the given date.

COMPETITION XII.

American Girl. Your ideas are somewhat advanced, and the "true gentlewoman" would do well to avoid so liberal a use of slang; but there is some honesty and sincerity in your writing, which go a little way towards inclining your reader to look upon you with kindness. Another time please do not mix up questions on dress and literature. You will find an answer to your question for a good inexpensive dressmaker under the Dress column. No, I do not much admire Mr. Kipling's views of life, and women in particular. He is, however, still very young.

Issor.—Any coupon will do. We generally give a fortnight for each competition, but, of course, if you do not take Hearth and Home regularly, you do not see the subjects as soon as they are announced.

Stranger.—I have not handed your letter to the Editor, because I feel perfectly certain he would not publish it. You see Hearth and Home is read by persons of all ages and both sexes, and it would not, therefore, be advisable to print these details. You have, however, expressed yourself with great moderation and restraint, and I strongly advise you to write to the editor of the *Lancet*. The doctor acted disgracefully. I cannot advise you to be guided in your choice of a doctor by anything that appears in a lay-paper, but if you will send me a stamped directed envelope I will send you the name of—so far as my experience goes —the very best consulting specialist for nervous, etc., complaints. As regards your MS., I am sorry not to be able to give you any criticism, but you must *write on the subject set*.

Madge.—Please see latter part of reply to "Stranger." Anyone is at liberty to enter for the competitions.

Victoria Catling.—Your essay is a great improvement on your other productions, but you still need great care in your composition and choice of words.

⁂ *A large number of criticisms are unavoidably held over until next week.*

19.4

Although competitions were used primarily to boost sales, encourage reader loyalty and gain revenue from advertising, the kinds of competitions a magazine ran indicated much about its general ethos. This prize competition from *The Woman's Signal* (1894–99) illustrates the way in which the feminist press in the later century utilised this commercial aspect of journalism to complement its ideological aims. Some magazines like *The Englishwoman's Domestic Magazine* (1852–79) banned male entrants, but this was not the case for many others including this one.

'Why I am an Abstainer. Our Prize Competition', *The Woman's Signal*, vol. 8, 1894, p. 105.

In response to our offer of a guinea's worth of books for a post card on which was written the best reason "Why I am an abstainer," we have received a large number of replies. These were placed in the hands of a lady well known in the temperance world, who had kindly consented to award the prize. After a careful perusal of all the cards she has awarded the prize to—

MR. JOHN WILSON,
Duke street, Eldon Lane,
Nr. Bishop Auckland, Durham.

Mr. Wilson is a miner, and we shall have much pleasure in sending him any books he may choose to the value of one guinea. We now publish the prize card, and one or two others as well.

THE PRIZE CARD.

I am a total abstainer because, 1st: As a miner and a coal hewer I can do more work without drink than with it. 2nd: That I cannot so far forget myself as to let the devil have so firm a hold on my soul by so degrading a habit as being a drunkard. 3rd: That I cannot be a Christian and fear God by wrecking His noble work by ruining my system with drink. And 4th: That I cannot so far forget the promise I made before God at the altar as to starve my wife and children by drinking my wages at those hells of iniquity that are spread throughout our land.

For my own sake. For the sake of others. For the sake of future generations.
M. ALABASTER.

The "reasons why" I am a total abstainer may be briefly summed up as follows:—For the sake of health, wealth, beauty, example, principle.
EDITH A. ATKINSON.

My reasons for being a teetotaler are as follows:—1st: My duty to myself. 2nd: My duty to my neighbour. 3rd: My duty to my country.
MINNIE ELVEN.

"To make some nook of God's creation a little fruitfuller, better, more worthy of God; to make some human hearts a little wiser, manfuller, happier, more blessed, less cursed" (Carlyle)—this is my aim in becoming a total abstainer.
AMY H. TILLY.

Because duty to God and man alike demand it. Duty to God says, "I ought" to abstain. Duty to man says, "I must" abstain. Since the doctor says, "I may" abstain, my resolve has been "I will" abstain.
C. G. MYLREA.

Because all that is good and true in my nature cries out in protest at the poverty, demoralisation of intellect, death of home affection, and enervating social intercourse, which meet me at every turn as the effect of drink.
A. INGE.

Because when I was about six years old I was taught by my aunt what intoxicating liquors were made of, and what they led to. I am now fourteen years old, and I mean to carry through from beginning to end, so that I may do somebody else good.

W. HOGAN.

Because in the flood of light now cast upon the subject by physical, medical, moral, and social science I cannot, without disregarding conscience, be any other; and because in being a total abstainer, I am allying myself with the best of men and the noblest of women, in their efforts to be co-workers together with Him who came to save a lost world.

JESSY H. GEDDES.

I am a total abstainer because I feel it to be my duty as a Christian, my duty to myself as a woman, and to future generations who may be affected by my abstinence. I also feel that unless I am on the right side of the question, I cannot have the privilege of influencing the children I teach, and others I come in contact with, by my example and persuasions, to loathe the drink and its associations as I do myself.
M. OLIVE PARKER.

I am a "total abstainer" because careful, candid investigation increasingly shows that the regular and frequent use of alcohol, whether as beer, wine, or spirits, as an article of diet or refreshment, is *unnecessary* and positively *injurious* to health; and that, in varying order, rate, and degree, *lessens* peace, power, purse, prosperity, personal and domestic happiness, opportunities of influencing others for their highest good, and promoting the glory of God. Preaching without practice is useless, and the constant, silent, influence of self denial for the good of others is simply *immeasurable*.
ROBT. N. INGLE, M.A., M.D.

196

OUR PRIZE COMPETITION.

WE offer a prize of a guinea's worth of books (to be chosen by the winner) for the best post-card paragraph on

"WHY WOMEN SHOULD HAVE THE VOTE."

I. The competition is open to all our readers.

II. All paragraphs must be written on post-cards, and sent on or before March 15th to the Editor of THE WOMAN'S SIGNAL, Memorial Hall, Farringdon Street, London, E.C.

III. We reserve the right to print any of the paragraphs sent in, whether they win a prize or not.

19.5

Home Chat (1895–1958), like other cheap domestic magazines, ran regular competitions for its readers. The following extract illustrates both the way such competitions worked and also gives a good idea of what was considered appropriate reading for girls.

'The Best Hundred Books for a Girl to Read', *Home Chat*, vol. 2, 1896, p. 431.

WHEN, some weeks ago, we offered an award of £5 for the best list of 100 books suitable for girls' reading, we scarcely expected that the competition would prove so popular as it has done. Lists have been sent in by well-known clergymen in all parts of the kingdom, and the task of deciding the competition has been a long one. Each book mentioned by a competitor received one mark; and the hundred best books were considered to be those which received the greatest number of marks.

Of these hundred books, the Reverend J. Lawson, Forest House, Ovenden, Halifax, included seventy-eight in his list. No other competitor mentioned more than seventy-five; the prize of £5 has, therefore, been awarded to the Reverend J. Lawson.

The following is a list of the hundred best books for girls to read, as decided by the votes of our competitors:—

Bible.
Pilgrim's Progress.
Thomas à Kempis.
Farrar's Life of Christ.
Shakespeare's Poems.
Longfellow's Poems.
Tennyson's Poems.
Wordsworth's Poems.
The Golden Treasury.
Robert Browning's Poems.
Elizabeth Barrett Browning's Poems.
Proctor's Legends and Lyrics.
Green's History of the English People.
Macaulay's Essays.
Ruskin's Sesame and Lilies.
Ruskin's Crown of White Olive. (*sic*)
Ruskin's Ethics of the Dust.
The Opening of a Chestnut Burr (E. P. Roe).
Carlyle's Heroes and Hero Worship.
Breakfast Table Series (O. W. Holmes).
Huxley's Physiography.
Lady Brassey's Voyage of the Sunbeam.

Robinson Crusoe.
Arabian Nights.
Grimm's Fairy Tales.
A Flat Iron for a Farthing (Mrs. Ewing).
Little Lord Fauntleroy.
Rudder Grange.
Life of Sister Dora.
Memorials of F. R. Havergal.
Vicar of Wakefield.
Uncle Tom's Cabin.
Tom Brown's Schooldays.
Pride and Prejudice.
The Scarlet Letter.
Kenilworth.
The Bride of Lammermoor.
The Abbot.
Adam Bede.
The Mill on the Floss.
Jane Eyre.
Shirley.
Mary Barton.
Westward Ho.

Two Years Ago.

Hypatia.

The Cloister and the Hearth.

Last Days of Pompeii.

David Copperfield. Old Curiosity Shop. Oliver
   Twist. Nicholas Nickleby. Christmas Tales.

Vanity Fair.

Princess of Thule.

A Daughter of Heth.

Lorna Doone.

Far from the Madding Crowd.

Robert Falconer.

All Sorts and Conditions of Men.

Treasure Island (R. L. Stevenson).

Kidnapped (R. L. Stevenson).

A Window in the Thrums (J. M. Barrie).

The Little Minister (J. M. Barrie).

A Lilac Sunbonnet (S. R. Crockett).

The Stickit Minister (S. R. Crockett).

Beside the Bonnie Briar-Bush (Ian McLaren).

For Auld Lang Syne (Ian McLaren).

Sherlock Holmes.

A Gentleman of France (Stanley Weyman).

Donovan.

We Two.

John Halifax; Gentleman.

The Channings.

Pillars of the House.

The Heir of Redcliffe.

The Wide, Wide World.

Queechy.

Little Women.

Good Wives.

Chronicles of Schonberg Cotta Family.

Alice in Wonderland.

Alice through the Looking-glass.

The Daisy Chain.

Jessica's First Prayer.

Strickland's Lives of the Queens.

Self Help (Smiles).

Scott's Poems.

Christian Year (Keble).

Farrar's Life of St. Paul.

Mrs. Heman's Poems.

Milton's Poems.

McCarthy's History of our own Tunes.

Drummond's Natural Law in the Spiritual
   World.

Spenser's Faerie Queen.

Drummond's Ascent of Man.

Mr. Gatty's Parable from Nature.

Little Pilgrims' Progress.

Roland Yorke.

The Water Babies.

RESUMÉ COMPETITION

I offer a prize of one guinea for the best resumé or synopsis sent in to me, before June 14th, of the plot of any well-known work of fiction.

The resumé should not exceed 800 words in length, and should be addressed to "Resumé," HOME CHAT, 24, Tudor Street, London, E.C.

19.6

In some literary competitions the prize was publication of the winning essay, poem or short story. This prize composition from the fashion weekly *Ladies' Fashions* (1897) is one such example.

'Our Prize Story. So Sorry for Her!', by E. S. Curry, *Ladies' Fashions*, vol. 1, 1897, p. 59.

"BUT surely it is very funny and impertinent," angrily.

"The road is open to all, my dear."

"If it were a man, now, hanging on to us like this!"

"A man wouldn't 'hang on,' as you call it."

"Then why should she?"

A couple of bicyclists—a man and his wife—had just ridden through Dorking towards London. Nearly all the way from Horsham they had been accompanied by a third bicycle, ridden by a girl in brown, now a few yards in front, now a few behind. Though her machine was a fine one, she was an unskilful rider. Sitting awkwardly, crouched over her handle-bar, she had only, by great effort, kept up the moderate pace of the other two, making up by frantic rushes downhill for her loss of ground uphill. She kept to no rules of the road—passed on either side, jumped off just in front of them, or wobbled across their track, as the whim seized her. A rather thick white veil with a pattern on it partially concealed her features. Her figure, though tall and finely formed, was youthful and immature, and her hair was a sunny brown.

"I shall get desperate soon," Mrs. King said, as, at the top of Mickleham Hill, this perplexing figure pedalled by energetically on the wrong side of the speaker, nearly running into her. "Can't she see 'Dangerous to Cyclists,' I wonder?"

"I think she is afraid of being left behind," her husband answered. He had owned to a rather pitying interest in the unknown. "For some reason or other she wants a companion."

"I wish she would choose somebody else, then. She has quite spoilt our ride."

"Again I say the road is open to all, my dear. Isn't that Amy coming?"

They had arranged to meet at Leatherhead and ride back to London with Mrs. King's sister, the Amy now in view. As she recognised them, she turned on the hill and ranged herself alongside her sister.

"Did you see that girl in brown?" she asked, breathlessly.

"See her! I should think so!" Mrs. King replied. "We have seen her ever since we left Horsham."

"Couldn't she get away?" eagerly.

"Get away? She has never shown the least desire to get away. I wish she would."

"But I don't," said Amy. "Didn't you see? Oh, you blind people! She was on my bicycle!"

"Your bicycle! Your new Beeston Humber—your new one?"

"Yes. She stole it yesterday afternoon—during that minute I ran indoors with you. Don't you remember, that old thing of Jane's was outside, and another—this horrid thing I'm on—we thought it was calling next door. After you had gone, I found that my bicycle had disappeared, and this one been left."

"Amy! And that girl took it?"

"Yes. I happened to see her go into the house—I was looking out for you. I thought I was late, or I should never have left mine for a single minute. And now I have got her!" triumphantly, gazing after the struggling figure ahead, now slowing up on the ascent of the hill into Leatherhead.

"You must be mistaken," Mr. King said, refusing to see a certain "I told you so" kind of look on his wife's face.

"I am not. That is my bicycle—and what is more, I'm going to have it."

"I should think so! But how?" asked Mrs. King.

"How? I don't care how! I shall run her down, and take it."

A twinkle came into Mr. King's eyes. "I think I'll ride on, and order tea," he said. "I suppose you want tea at the old place?"

"Yes, and muffins," said his wife.

"How like a man!" said Amy, malevolently. "Fleeing from a row, instead of helping me to recover my own paid-for property!"

But he was gone—darting ahead with an energy which soon brought him alongside the figure in brown, on whose movements Amy's eyes were steadfastly fixed.

"I do believe John is speaking to her," she said suddenly. "I'll never forgive him, if he helps her to get away. This thing has no go in it; I couldn't catch mine with it. You must back me up, Kate, whatever I do. Do you hear?"

"Yes. Only don't make a row in the street, Amy. Wait till after tea."

"I shall have it wherever I can get it—my bicycle, I mean. Ah, she's off!"—with satisfaction —"I thought she'd find that gearing too much for her up hill. How *can* he?"

Restrained by her sister from rushing ahead, Amy dismounted at the little teashop at Leatherhead, still lacking her paid-for property. It stood in its shining newness—a most attractive and desirable sight in its owner's eyes—by the curb in front of the shop, and close to it stood Mr. King's.

"Really," said Mrs. King, exasperatedly, as she glanced in at the shop window, "the woman haunts us."

"Glad she does," said Amy, fixing the machine she was riding nose to nose with the machine she owned. "Now I resume possession. You can go in to tea; I stick to this!" laying hold of the handle of her own machine.

Meanwhile, inside the shop a rapid and somewhat agitated colloquy was proceeding.

"Say nothing when they come in. Mount your own and go." Mr. King was a man who objected to feminine explanations.

"But it must seem so strange!"

"I'll explain. The only strange part was your recognising my wife to-day."

"I was so thankful. I thought if I kept with you the police could not take me. You see, I did not discover yesterday what I had done for some time. You don't particularly notice a hired machine. And I had to get home, so I thought the best thing was to do what I have done, and bring it back to-day. It was a horrid mistake. I was so frightened. No one knows what I have suffered."

Mrs. King entered the shop, glancing haughtily at the lady in brown, whose tea-cup her husband had just taken from her. Mr. King's eyes laughed as he placed a chair for his wife before the tea-tray.

"Where's Amy?" he asked.

"Outside," shortly.

"Doesn't she want any tea?"

"She has found her bicycle, and is afraid of having it stolen again if she leaves it."

"Not again. Oh, never again!" came in an agitated murmur from the veiled lady.

Mr. King held the door open, and said something to her in a low tone as she passed through, of which his astonished wife only heard "Now's your time."

The girl bowed, and, walking out of the shop, mounted the machine Amy had relinquished. A portentous wobble, threatening an upset, signalised her departure as she and her machine disappeared down the street.

"Well, I never!" said the amazed Amy, breathlessly. "She's a cool hand. How did you manage her, John? Does she know? Was she afraid? Oh, yes, I'll have some tea now. I suppose she won't come back?" anxiously.

"Now, my dear," Mr. King said to his wife, as he entered with Amy, "I hope you'll concede that a man manages difficult situations with less fuss than a woman? That poor thing——"

"Poor thing, indeed!" sniffed Mrs. King.

"Was in an agony of fear. She took Amy's bicycle quite by mistake yesterday——"

"Fudge!" said Mrs. King.

"And did not find out till she was half way home, that it was not the one she had hired."

"Oh!" Amy said in incredulous scorn. 'Why my bicycle——"

"Oh, let him go on, Amy," said Mrs. King, "if he can be taken in by such rubbish."

"She was bringing it back to-day," went on Mr. King, with the rude persistence of a man, "to try and find its owner, when she recognised you, having noticed you yesterday."

"And she couldn't get away, I expect," put in Amy.

"And she was so relieved to think she had a clue, and was trying to make up her mind to explain to me—to us, when Amy——"

"Oh, John," exclaimed his wife, "have you turned foolish? Fancy your being deluded by such a story. Believe it if you like, of course. It is just like the misplaced sentiment of men who think they manage things better than women. Which of us," severely, "you or I, is to pay for her tea?"

A cheque for One Guinea has been forwarded to—

MRS. CURRY, Rectory, Merrick Square, Southwark, S.E.

20
Illustrated biography

The biography, usually illustrated with an engraving of the subject, had been a feature of the drawing-room journal before the Victorian period and the genre was carried forward into a range of magazines. In the mid-Victorian period it was deployed in the religious, general illustrated and ladies' papers where it was an occasional rather than a regular feature. However, the illustrated biography came into its own at the end of the century, alongside the much newer genre of the interview. Female figures were most frequently the subjects and it was heroines of the past, writers, artists and royalty who were the most popular and frequently featured. In the general illustrated and cheap domestic weeklies of the 1890s biographies of different royal ladies from across Europe featured beside the short prose, which in many women's papers routinely included royal news. The illustrated biography tended towards hagiography rather than critical examination of the subject and was usually intended to provide a positive role model for whatever kind of femininity the magazine represented.

20.1

General illustrated magazines did carry illustrated biographies of notable women, including writers, from time to time, though this was not one of their regular features. This is an abridged copy.

'Mrs. Jameson', *The Englishwoman's Domestic Magazine*, vol. 2, new series, 1861, pp. 36–37. See also FIGURE 41.

THIS celebrated authoress, whose sudden and recent death we have all to deplore, was of Irish extraction, being the eldest daughter of Mr. Murphy, painter in ordinary to the Princess Charlotte, an artist well known during the earlier years of the present century. His eldest daughter, Anna, was very naturally taught by him the principles of his own art, but she had instincts for all—a taste for music, a feeling for poetry (some short pieces of hers are still preserved), and a delicate appreciation of the drama. As a young woman, she occupied the post of governess in two or three families of distinction, and to the last used to speak occasionally of the young girls who had been her pupils, particularly of one who had died early.

At thirty years of age, however, she had entered on her literary career, by the publication of notes on foreign travel, under the title of the "Diary of an Ennuyée." It appeared anonymously, and had only a partial success, never reaching a second edition. 'About the same time she married Mr. Robert Jameson, late Vice-Chancellor of Canada, a man of some talent and artistic taste; but the marriage was notoriously an unhappy one, and a separation eventually took place. Mrs. Jameson only survived her husband six years.

The "Diary of an Ennuyée" was followed by "Visits and Sketches at Home and Abroad," which consisted, in a measure, of a reprint of the "Diary of an Ennuyée," and of reprints of some smaller pieces. Three years later her "Loves of the Poets" appeared; after that, "Female Biography," "Romance of Biography," "Beauties of the Court of Charles II.," "Female Sovereigns," "Characteristics of Women" (chiefly Studies from Shakspeare), one of her most popular and deservedly popular works; and in 1838, "Winter Studies and Summer Rambles in Canada," the latter work containing recollections of a visit undertaken to that country in a hopeless attempt to arrange her family affairs. In this book there is the account of her solitary canoe-voyage, and her residence among a tribe of Indians.

To this list of Mrs. Jameson's literary works may be added her "Reminiscences of Munich," and a translation of the "Dramas of the Princess Amelia of Saxony."

Mrs. Jameson's literary life may, to use the words of a contemporary journal, be divided into three epochs. The first includes various books of foreign travel, containing social and artistic criticism—in short, all the works that we have already named belong to this period; to the second epoch belong her elaborate works on Art proper, beginning, in 1842, with a "Handbook to the Public Galleries of Art in and near London;" and the third is represented by her two celebrated lectures on the "Communion of Labour" and "Sisters of Charity," and her "Letter to Lord John Russell."

Mrs. Jameson only busied herself with "Art" as it was understood in the last generation, when it meant almost exclusively painting and sculpture. To appreciate her labours aright, it is essential to remember the state of literature and art before she commenced adding to it. The Germans had, indeed, begun their laborious reconstruction of the history of art; but in France there was not much, and in England still less; for there were only Richardson's old world talk and Walpole's gossip, Reynolds's *discourses*, and a few fossil lectures of the Academicians; Ruskin, Lord Lindsay, Fergusson, and others, were all subsequent to Mrs. Jameson's first appearance in the field.

Her contributions to the literature of art, or, rather, of painting—the direction in which she created for herself her soundest and most enduring reputation—stretch over nearly twenty years. After the "Handbook to the Public Galleries" (1842), came her popular memoirs of "Early Italian Painters," first published by Charles Knight in the "Penny Magazine," then as two one-shilling volumes, and finally they were reprinted, in a revised and more expensive form, by Murray, in 1858. As a condensation of Vasari, and a *resume* of all that need be said about the early painters and their works, these volumes are invaluable.

Other books of a similar scope are the "Companion to the Private Galleries in London," "Memoirs and Essays Illustrative of Art and Literature," collected from various periodicals. Then came the large and copiously-illustrated volumes of sacred and legendary art, "Legends of the Monastic Orders," "Legends of the Madonna;" and death found her busy in the completion of a "History of the Life of Our Lord, and of His Precursor, St. John the Baptist; with the Personages and Typical Subjects of the Old Testament, as Represented in Christian Art." For two long years had Mrs. Jameson been engaged upon this work; she had taken many and exhausting journeys, made diligent

FIGURE 41 'Mrs. Jameson', portrait, p. 36

examination of far-scattered examples of art, and, in completion of this labour, had revisited Italy, and passed several months in Rome and other Continental cities. Mrs. Jameson was putting the last finish to the work (which we are happy to hear is nearly ready for the press) when she was, after a very brief illness, bidden to cease for ever.

Of her "Communion of Labour" and "Sisters of Charity" we cannot speak too highly. Prisons, reformatories, schools, hospitals, workhouses, all engaged her attention; and she most eloquently pleads that women may take their share in every good work with men. When the "Letter to Lord John Russell" was written and published, she said—

"Now I have said all I can say upon these subjects, and I must return to art." But at the meeting of the Association for the Promotion of Social Science, at Bradford, in October last, she attended, and sat, during the whole of one day, in section B., where papers on the employment of women were being read, and occasionally joined in the discussions which ensued, while her brief observations and suggestions were received with marked respect.

In the course of her indefatigable literary career, she drew around her a large circle of steady friends, and

> "many foreign households will grieve for the English friend who knew how to sympathize with every nation's best; how many learned and literary circles in Rome, in Florence, in Vienna, in Dresden, in Paris, will regret the bright mind, the accomplished talker, the affectionate heart, which recognized merit, and cheered the student, and made the studio and the salon gay and pleasant with her cordial smile." . . .

20.2

The ladies' papers took up the illustrated biography and used it in a number of ways. In the first example, from *The Lady's Own Paper* (1866–72), the engraving is the hook for the article and its subject is a remarkable woman.

'Dr. Mary Walker', *The Lady's Own Paper*, vol. 1, 1866, p. 1. See also FIGURE 42.

THE subject of this week's engraving is so well-known, through our own articles and those of the daily press, that it is unnecessary for us to do more on the present occasion than draw prominent attention to two or three points in her eventful life.

She may be considered in two aspects, not only as a lady who by marvellous perseverance in the face of almost insuperable difficulties has won her way into public notice and position; but also as the representative of a class of ladies who of late years have earnestly striven to redress the grievances under which their sex has too long laboured.

We will devote our remarks more especially to Dr. Mary Walker in the former relations; in the latter capacity she is tolerably well known.

In reference to her early training for the Medical profession, and the motives that prompted her to enter it, we cannot do better than let her speak for herself. She was one of those, she stated in her recent lecture at St. James's Hall, who thought it better and easier to live out their own individual lives, and to use the powers specially bestowed upon them, than to live according to other people's notions—to live, in fact, the lives of other persons. More than 15 years ago she resolved thus to do her whole duty to humanity, as she comprehended it, leaving the results to care for themselves. Her own approval of her own conduct was worth more to her than the applause of all the world would be without such self-approval. At 17 years of age she entered the seminary, where large classes of both sexes were held, and among her greatest troubles were the reproaches levelled at the supposed immodesty of desiring to be present at operations, and the perpetual worry attendant on long dresses. This dress question has been a sore trial to her. At the lyceum, when she attended the classes with two other ladies, many of the male students threatened to secede, but did not do so. The other ladies discussed the subject of dress freely with her, but did not like to make themselves remarkable, declaring that it was no use to go against the fashion.

She held out, however, and succeeded in overcoming a great deal of the obloquy first cast upon her. Her opinions on this point are very decisive. She holds it as a fact, admitting of no denial, and one perfectly well known to doctors, that long dresses are killing women; and she attributes the failure of the Bloomer movement, some years ago, to the circumstance that the ladies who favoured it then were for the most part incapable of appreciating and explaining the physiological, hygienic, and moral bearings of the question.

FIGURE 42 'Dr. Mary Walker', portrait

Doubtless there are very many of our readers who may dissent from these opinions; yet they will not fail to admire the courageous manner in which Miss Walker set herself, in the face of all but overwhelming opposition, to redress what she conscientiously considered a great social anomaly.

Dr. Mary Walker's professional career has been as chequered as her student life. She practised medicine in New York for five years before the war broke out, then volunteered for the Federal army medical service, and served through a campaign of four years, during the first three years being with the Army of the Potomac. In the course of her military career, she was taken prisoner of war, and, after a captivity of four months, was regularly exchanged, the "happy rebel whose freedom was thus purchased being a full-grown and moustached surgeon, six feet high."

In Dr. R. T. Trall's "Herald of Health," published in New York, are some interesting particulars bearing upon her army practice, from which we learn that, in 1862, the United States Congress passed an act giving to the soldiers of the United States Army a medal of honour for special meritorious services, and the President of the United States decided who were to receive such honours. Amongst the number selected for the distinction of a "testimonial and medal of honour" was Miss Walker, who had achieved a distinction in the annals, not only of military surgery, but of military service, never before accorded to one of her sex. The *Washington Republican* says:—

"President Johnson, carrying out the purpose of his predecessor, President Lincoln, and acting upon the recommendations of such high military authority as Major-Generals Sherman, General Thomas, and McCook, has been pleased to issue his order in favour of Doctor Mary E. Walker. The order is handsomely inscribed upon parchment, and is the only compensation under the law that the President is empowered to bestow upon the Doctor, because she happens to be a lady. Much of the service rendered by her to the Government could not have been accomplished by a man. She risked her life many times, and nearly sacrificed her health, in her efforts of patriotism, as time will hereafter tell. Until Congress can do Dr. Walker some degree of pecuniary justice, she must be content with the noble parchment testimonial of the President, so justly bestowed, and all that he has the power legally to give."

This document was signed by Andrew Johnson, and bears date November 11th, 1865.

In concluding this slight sketch, we may mention another interesting fact. Dr. Mary Walker stated in her lecture, that she had been anxious to volunteer for service in the Crimean hospitals, but the war closed too speedily. She therefore devoted herself to private practice among women and children, only attending husbands at the special request of their own wives. The practice which she acquired might be attributed to various causes. Some employed her because she lived near them; some because she made her toilette quicker than the gentleman; some because they liked her personally; and some because they believed it to be the true position of a woman to be a physician to her own sex.

Dr. Walker intends writing a history of her doings and sufferings as soon as she regains her full health and strength. Throughout her whole war-life of four years she has persisted in wearing the "short dress," and by the indomitable energy of her will, and inexhaustible resources of her "strategy," she has not only won the admiration of the military authorities of the country, but compelled, as it were, a recognition of woman's right to dress as she pleases, and to fill any station, public or private, which capacity and inclination fit her for.

20.3

Even the religious magazines carried illustrated biographies of female role models. In this article the interest in royalty which was generally a feature of other kinds of magazine was linked to the characteristically serious account of an exemplary life.

'Out and at Home. Twice Royal, or a Royal British Workwoman', by Grace, *The British Workwoman*, vol. 12, 1879, pp. 36–37.

A YOUNG GIRL of eighteen, little more than seventeen years ago, suddenly became famous. One of a noble line, one of the members of a royal family, not much more had been known of her than her name, outside her own circle, until the winter of 1861. Suddenly she stood forth before the whole world, in the halo of her own sweet, noble individuality. In the tender humility of her disposition, she had willingly accepted comparative obscurity; but the time came for her to take upon herself a duty, which, from its very nature, was a public one, and she so fulfilled it that, her light shining before men, they saw her good works, and glorified her Father which is in heaven.

Some people have a crude notion that a workman or a workwoman necessarily means a poor person, and one who works with his or her hands. No such narrow signification belongs to the words at all. The royal maiden of whom we are now writing was as truly a workwoman, in the right sense of the term, when she kept back her tears to sing hymns to her dying father, as any sempstress, or toilsome charwoman on the earth. But our beloved young Princess Alice, for of course you know to whom we refer, was also a worker in the commonest meaning of the term. It has been said that in that Book, upon whose precepts she strove to form her life, "Whatsoever thy hand findeth to do, do it with thy might." And so it came to pass that her father on his bed of sore sickness liked best to have his pillows arranged by her, liked best to take his medicines from her hands, because she did her work so well. No fuss, no officiousness, no ostentation; no laxity or forgetfulness, either from weariness or grief. She had worked earnestly and heartily as a child in the schoolroom. Reports say that she showed superior excellence even in the schoolroom cooking kitchen that her wise Queen-mother instituted, both at Osborne and Windsor, for her children's good. We once heard it said that the Princess Alice's potatoes were the models of perfection!

She had been faithful in little, now much was given to her, even the sweet sad work of sooth-ing inexpressibly the dying bed of her father, and comforting her widowed mother. And her tasks were performed with such a pure simplicity of self-forgetting grandeur, that a low murmur began, and gradually rose and spread throughout the world, of the deepest admiration for the British workwoman, of whom Britain had such good right to be proud, the young Princess Alice.

It may well be that her acts during those sorrowful December days of 1861 have taught many a useful lesson to her humbler sisters plodding on through this work-a-day world, and also to those in a sphere more on a level with her own. Some people think that two of the special privileges of wealth and high birth are idleness and incapacity for usefulness. Had Princess Alice been endued with such mean ideas of her blessings, where, think you, would have been the clear power of right thought at the right moment, the brave sternness of self-control, the ready useful hand, all of which were found of such priceless helpfulness at the sick beds of those who were near and dear, not only to her, but to the whole nation of her countrymen. The fact is, our beloved and mourned Princess shared with her royal parents a very keen appreciation of the capabilities afforded her by high station for devoting herself to work, real, earnest work, with no pretence or outside show about it, for the sake of others.

At the time of Prince Albert's death, his favourite young daughter had already been betrothed some little time to Prince Louis of Hesse, and in obedience to his own express wish, uttered on his dying bed, the wedding was not long postponed from the date originally decided upon. Between six and seven months Princess Alice remained beside her mother, her chief consoler, almost the only comfort our bereaved Queen could accept in those early days of bitter trial; and then, on the 1st of July, 1862, there was a quiet marriage at Osborne, made sombre by the few guests in mourning garb, and our English Princess became the wife of the heir to a German dukedom, and had a home thenceforth in a foreign land.

Her new found happiness, and her new dignity, were received by Princess Alice as fresh talents committed to her charge to be employed for her Master's service. All her sympathies were aroused on behalf of those less favoured than herself, and the proof of power and intelli-gent comprehension which she had given at Windsor Castle, removed from her all suspicion of idle curiosity, or unproductive philanthropy, when the young maiden took advantage of her increased measure of independence to visit hospitals and the homes of the sick poor, that she might the better learn how to alleviate suffering, and in what directions her aid would be most useful.

Many a time, when Princess Alice crossed the English Channel to make a few weeks' stay in her native land, some poor creature, bowed down under the combined evils of poverty and ill-ness, has received a visit from an unknown lady of sweet face and gentle manners, who thought no scorn to smooth the patchwork counterpane, or hold the cracked cup to the poor fevered lips. England is proud of a good many things that it is not worth being proud about, perhaps, if we come to consider the matter; but we may all be proud of our working Princess, of our Princess who followed in her Lord's footsteps, and "went about doing good;" of our Princess whose uncon-scious motto was, "Little children, love one another."

When the Franco-Prussian war broke out in the summer of 1870 our two English princesses —the Princess Royal, married to the heir of the German Empire, and her sister Alice—were among the first to think for those who would suffer during its progress, and to work for their relief. Many a poor wounded soldier, we have been told by an eye-witness, had reason to bless the kind, skilful hands and pitying looks of his royal nurses, who gave not only their money, their thoughts, and their prayers, but also their personal labour and supervision.

The following year, December 1871, home ties again appealed to the closest sympathies of the English Princess of Hesse-Darmstadt. The Prince of Wales fell ill of the same insidious dis-ease that had so early robbed him of his father, and the experienced sick-nurse, his sister Alice, was summoned to his bedside, and welcomed with warm, trusting thankfulness by the anxious, half heart-broken mother, and young wife. On this occasion her untiring efforts were blessed not only with soothing power, but with glad success. There can scarcely be a reader of this Magazine, or indeed a reader in the British Isles at all, who does not remember the terrified suspense that hung heavily over these dominions during the early weeks of that December of seven years ago, and few can have forgotten the thrill of thankfulness with which the news was received that the Prince's sister Alice had reached his bedside. He was sure to receive good nursing; his mother and wife were sure to have the tenderest and truest sympathy, and the precious words in season of Christian support and consolation.

No greater honour can be bestowed upon a woman than to be deservedly welcomed in a sick room. This honour was abundantly earned and won by our dear Princess, and strangely enough she fell on the battle-field she chose. She fought, as long as her Father ordained that she should fight, against sorrow and sin, and pain, and weariness, and then she fell, as a warrior would wish to fall, in the forefront of the battle. She "rests from her labours, and her works do follow her."

[. . .]

20.4

The Ladies' Pictorial (1880) appeared in a cheap broadsheet format. It was illustrated and in three columns. This is a more typical example than the one above of the kind of subject usually featured in these biographies.

'Miss Ellen Terry', by A. H. Doubleyew, *The Ladies' Pictorial*, vol. 1, 1880, pp. 1–2.

WHEN Shakespeare's *Winter's Tale* was played at the Princess's Theatre, in April, 1856, as one of Charles Kean's series of grand spectacular revivals, the precocious talent of Miss Ellen Terry, then eight years old, who made her first appearance therein, awakened no little wonder. She personated Mamillius, and spoke her lines with so much feeling and expression as to create considerable interest in the future career of a child displaying such precocious talent. Graceful, pretty, quick to perceive and anxious to excel, she soon became a favourite both before and behind the curtain.

In the following October, when the *Midsummer Night's Dream* was produced, she personated Puck, playing his mischievous pranks with such elfish glee and with such a thorough and forcible conception of the poet's fantastic creation as produced both wonder and delight.

She appeared in several of the succeeding Shakespearian revivals, until in *King John* (October 18th, 1858) her fame as child-actress culminated in the part of Prince Arthur, a piece of acting in which refined taste, a sweet clear voice, and excellent elocution, aided by earnestness and a just conception of the character, produced a very marked effect. The part had been previously played under Charles Kean's management, and, on the same boards, by her sister Kate. This was one of the last of the famous revivals to which old playgoers still look back with so much pleasure, and with the close of that season – the last revival being Shakespeare's *Henry the Fifth* – Mr. Kean retired from the management of a theatre to which he had given the greatest dignity and importance – one now undergoing the process of destruction previous to re-building not, we trust, for the production of vulgar spectacle and modern sensational melodrama.

In March, 1863, Miss Ellen Terry re-appeared at the Haymarket Theatre as Gertrude in *The Little Treasure*, an adaptation from the French of *La Joie de la Maison*. In this part her grasp of the frank simplicity and fearless innocence depicted by the author was most complete. Generous, impulsive, full of feeling, and awfully unconventional, her impersonation of Gertrude laid the foundation of her after reputation. In the following year, and in a part somewhat akin to the above – that of Philippa in Charles Reade's *Wandering Heir* – but with touches of pathos, deep feeling, and artistic subtleties of expression, to which she did full justice, Miss Terry fairly established her claim to a reputation which from that time forward succeeding years have elevated and extended. In the same year she played Susan Merton in the same dramatist's *It's Never Too Late to Mend.*

When, towards the end of April, 1875, the Bancroft management essayed its flight into the regions of tragedy with far more ambition than judgment, producing some admirable and most artistic pictures of old Venetian costumes, scenery, and customs, with a genteel-comedy-version of Shakespeare's *Merchant of Venice*, Miss Terry played Portia. Despite the frigid, lifeless personations by which she was surrounded, and the depressing influences exercised by critical and popular disapprobation of the curious attempt, her triumph was a great one; and all that has been said of her in the same part at the Lyceum Theatre since would have been equally true if said then. The critics did indeed award her the highest praise, and if it had been possible to have saved the revival by the efforts of any one player standing out in such palpable and strong relief from the rest of the cast, Miss Terry would have spared the little theatre in the Tottenham Court-road a very costly failure. The evidence of careful, earnest study was apparent in her conception of the character; the bending of her entire mind and energies to its forcible realisation was not less palpable. It was a picture finished in all its details; even the most minute touches of look and movement were the result of careful study, and the general effect was that perfection of art which is seen in the complete concealment of art, a conquest which only the true artist can possibly achieve. The critic of the *Daily News* said of this performance, 'This is, indeed, the Portia that Shakespeare drew. The bold innocence, the lively wit and quick intelligence, the grace and elegance of manner, and all the youth and freshness of this exquisite creation can rarely have been depicted in such harmonious combination.'

When *The Merchant of Venice* was withdrawn in May, 1875, Mr. Bancroft revived, and Miss Terry appeared in, Sir Bulwer Lytton's famous stock piece *Money*, a play which critics would now fain sneer down as out-of-date in its characters and old-fashioned in its sentiment; although it invariably commands the entire sympathies of all kinds of audiences, and, in one place or another, is seldom absent from 'the boards.' Although a somewhat shallow, weak-kneed drama from an artistic view-point, *Money* shows in triumphant contrast with the empty, spasmodic dialogue, bare, bald incidents, and undeveloped characters which too often represent our less successful dramatist of to-day – plays in which no actresses sway the emotional thoughts and sentiments of an audience as Miss Ellen Terry swayed them on this occasion in the part of Clara Douglas. In this, as in her preceding creations, she displayed the refinement and [. . .] of a most accomplished artist. Every indication of thought, feeling, and sentiment which by tone, look, or gesture could lend force and emphasis to the author's words appeared. She conveyed the heroine's changeful feelings, womanly pride, self-devotion and tenderness, anguish and despair, the patience of a martyr, and the passionate outburst of joy which crowns and ends her sufferings, with intense power, but without the slightest touch of stage exaggeration. 'Nothing,' said the *Athenæum* of June 5, 1875, 'will distinguish this revival so favourably as the exquisitely graceful, tender, and charming performance of Clara Douglas by Miss Ellen Terry. Not only are voice and gesture alike winning and sympathetic, but in a hundred little details which would escape the notice of any but an actress of the highest capacity does Miss Terry prove her power. The expression of her face during the reading of the will which gives fortune to Evelyn is supremely beautiful.'

In August, 1875, *The Lady of Lyons* was revived for one night only at the Princess's Theatre, and Miss Terry played Pauline. She again displayed that harmony of conception and execution, conscientiously elaborated in detail, which had won her such high praise. But, as was pointed out, she hardly realised in its full strength the pride which makes Pauline's struggle with her love so full of agony and bitterness.

In the November of the above year she played at the Prince of Wales's Theatre as Mabel Vane in *Masks and Faces*, and in 1876 as Blanche in *Ours*, attracting in each the favourable attention of the press. In the same year she appeared at the Royal Court Theatre, where she afterwards achieved another remarkable triumph as Olivia in *The Vicar of Wakefield*.

In December, 1878, Miss Terry joined the company of Mr. Henry Irving at the Lyceum Theatre, which re-opened under that gentleman's management with a revival of *Hamlet*, in which she played Ophelia, achieving therein, perhaps, the greatest triumph of her histrionic career. The gentle calm which hides so strong and deep a current of feeling was never more completely realised, and in the mad scene her vague, wandering glances, half-formed, bewildering ideas, and disconnected utterances conveyed a picture of madness at once touching and terrible in its wonderful truthfulness and intensity.

In the following year she again played Pauline, and, in the revival of *Eugene Aram*, Ruth Meadows. Her recent reappearance as Portia is an event of yesterday, of which the general verdict is yet fresh in every reader's memory.

Miss Terry may take rank with the proudest as an actress of genuine talent and power. She is natural without falling into that common-place tameness which has of late been so often dignified with that title, displaying a naturalness which has its origin in the perfection, not the entire absence, of art. She can declaim passionately without descending to rant, and express love and tenderness with that graceful simplicity and directness of speech and gesture which so greatly surpasses the more conventional and artificial methods in ordinary use. She has a graceful figure and a very expressive face, with a smile of singular sweetness; her voice is clear and pleasant to hear, and she manages it with singular ability.

20.5

This genre was important in the magazines for girls at the end of the century. This extract is by Sarah Tooley, who frequently wrote interviews for the women's press, and gives an illustrated account of the lives of several women authors with facsmiles of their handwriting. It includes material on L. T. Meade, who was among the most prolific writers for the women's and girls' press.

'Some Famous Authors as Girls', by Mrs. Tooley, *Girls' Realm*, vol. 1, 1899, pp. 447–48.

NEARLY all the women who are prominent to-day in literature began to write original compositions of some kind or another as soon as they could hold a pen; for the writing faculty, like that of music or of art, is not an acquirement, but an inborn talent which early seeks expression, and the future very much depends upon the sympathy and guidance which are given to these early efforts. I am sure you will be interested to read of the earliest compositions of some of the authors whose stories you have learned to love, and also to hear about their girlhood.

There is no greater favourite as a writer for girls than Mrs. L. T. Meade, as the recent competition in this magazine has fully proved. Mrs. Meade has a very warm place in her heart for girls, and is always anxious to use her pen not only to entertain them, but to give sympathy and encouragement to those who are entering upon life with a determination to win success in the various fields of occupation open to the modern girl. Mrs. Meade has produced over one hundred works of fiction, and is still a lady in her prime. She was born at Bandon, co. Cork, and was the daughter of a clergyman. At a very early age she began to scribble, but her father did not like her literary proclivities, and all writing-paper was taken from her. This, however, did not put an end to her compositions, for she now wrote her stories on the margins of the newspapers.

. . .

While yet a girl in her teens, Mrs. Meade left her Irish home and settled with some friends in London, and began to study the lives of the poor. The result was her first novel, "Great St. Benedict." This was followed by that charming and pathetic story of child-life amongst the London poor, "Scamp and I." With this the girl author secured fame and a recognised position in literature. Few novelists have indeed made their name at such an early age as Mrs. Meade . . .

21

The personal interview

The interview as a journalistic genre was associated with the rise of the 'New Journalism' of the 1880s and 1890s and particularly with W. T. Stead, the editor of the *Pall Mall Gazette*, who was credited with importing it into Britain from America. However, as these examples show, this form of journalism was being developed immediately before the 1880s as an alternative to the short biography. As with other elements of the 'New Journalism', it brought a more personal touch to the representation both of the person interviewed and the interviewer. Interviews, usually illustrated, became a staple of many kinds of women's magazine in the 1890s. Almost always the interviews would be conducted in the home of the subject which meant the editor could include illustrations and discussions of home furnishing, an important feature particularly in the ladies' papers and general illustrated magazines at this time. Those interviewed ranged from aristocratic ladies to 'New Women' but frequently they were themselves authors or journalists. Sometimes, as with Sarah Tooley in *Woman at Home* or Helen Black in *The Lady's Pictorial*, a woman journalist undertook interviews with celebrities 'at home' as a regular feature. Like the increasing use of the by-line instead of the anonymous journalism of the mid-century, this made writing, including journalism, more visible as a career for women.

21.1

The feminist journals used the device of the interview to bring to the reader's attention the work of women furthering their cause, and perhaps to humanise their politics. Much more cheaply produced than their commercial rivals, these journals could not afford the kinds of illustration which usually accompanied the interview in other publications.

'Interview. Mrs. Florence Fenwick Miller', *Women's Penny Paper*, vol. 1, no. 18, 1889, p. 1. See also FIGURE 43.

AMONG the eminent women of the day Mrs. Florence Fenwick Miller takes a prominent place. It was as a leading lady journalist that I had requested the honour of an interview with her, for, during the few years that she has made newspaper-writing a profession, she has achieved a high reputation and solid success. But it is by no means on this alone that her name and fame rest. She is a lecturer and public speaker of wide-spread popularity; her name invariably attracts a large audience, and in an electioneering campaign she is a tower of strength. In yet a third capacity Mrs. Fenwick Miller has gained distinction of no ordinary kind. She is the author of seven books, all of them—with the exception of the *Life of Harriet Martineau* (in the Eminent Women series)—of a scientific character. Had she been none of these things Mrs. Fenwick Miller would in all probability have taken a high place among women medical practitioners. She has a very scientific habit of mind, and her favourite studies are anatomy, physiology, biology, and medical science generally. At the age of seventeen she was visiting Edinburgh, and not only went heart and soul into the controversy over the admission of women to the medical classes of Edinburgh

University, but sat for the Preliminary Examination, and passed in English with "distinction" marks, in French and in Logic. Returning to London she entered at the Ladies' Medical College, passed brilliantly in the Examination for Honours, and took up practical work at the British Lying-in-Hospital. She had an extensive practice for about three years among women and children, but abandoned medicine as a profession on her election to the School Board in 1876. It need thus scarcely be said that Mrs. Fenwick Miller is first of all a thinker—a vigorous and original thinker—and her writing like her speaking is marked by a force and freshness which never fail.

"How do you get through such an amount of work?" I asked, for I knew that a very carefully written signed article in *The Illustrated London News*, and three leaders a week for provincial papers formed but a section of Mrs. F. Miller's journalistic work.

"That is what everyone says," was the reply, "my practice in speaking has probably given me facility in writing." Whatever the cause, there is no manner of doubt that Mrs. Miller writes with remarkable rapidity—a *sine qua non* in journalism.

"What do you think of journalism as a profession for women?"

"At present I think it is a good one; I know several women of moderate capacity who earn three or four pounds a week, who would otherwise have been struggling along in the overcrowded ranks of teachers. That women would display observation and versatility was to be expected, but they have shown a staying power and a push that were not anticipated. To be a journalist you must possess the capacity of meeting your engagements, and also of seizing every opportunity. Women are showing that they are equal to both."

"Do you consider journalism a healthy pursuit, or are late hours an objection to it?"

"I do not think much of the late hours, they are nothing more than those which amusements demand of other women. Where some women make a mistake is that they try to be literary women and society women as well, and then they break down. They should be content with one or the other."

To Mrs. Fenwick Miller writing for the Press is not merely a business but a serious responsibility. "To address," she said, "as I have done, three thousand persons in the Birmingham Town Hall is a very important task—it almost takes one's breath away to feel that for a whole hour one has to influence and interest that vast concourse—but through the Press one speaks to many thousands more than the voice could reach." "In all my work," she continued, "I have very deeply at heart the influence I can bring to bear on the woman question."

Like many independent thinkers she is not wholly in sympathy with any of the political parties.

As a child Mrs. Fenwick Miller's favourite book was the Bible. Books two rows deep almost cover the walls of her study. There is a long row of scientific volumes which must have been well read before such works as "An Atlas of Anatomy" (1879), a third edition of which appeared last year, or "The House of Life," could have been produced. Of the first of these *The Athenæum* said, "it is excellent, and will, we believe, play no mean part in the diffusion of true, pure scientific knowledge." She has also a singularly good collection of works by women, including the now rare "Vindication of the Rights of Women" by Mary Wollstonecraft. One corner of her sanctum is quite a portrait gallery of famous women. I noticed with special interest the little known but truly memorable Maria Schurman, the mistress of eleven languages, but who at the age of twenty-five buried herself as a Quietist.

Mrs. Miller's last book, published in 1884, was *The Life of Harriet Martineau*, and she has in her possession two excellent portraits and other interesting relics of the famous writer, such as a lock of hair when silvery white, and several specimens of her handwriting. This is the list of her own books:—"Simple Lessons in Health" (published in 1877); "The House of Life: Human Physiology in its application to Health" (1878): "An Atlas of Anatomy" (1879); "Physiology in Schools" (1881); "Readings in Social Economy," and "Natural History for the Standards" (1883); "Life of Harriet Martineau" (1884).

Mrs. Fenwick Miller is a lecturer of some reputation, but as a speaker her power shows itself not so much in lecturing as in debate. From my place in the gallery of the London School Board, I have seen men grow visibly paler as she dissected—or rather vivisected—their halting arguments with her pitiless logic; she would leave nothing but shreds behind. She sat for nine years on the Board.

In April 1877, the following announcement appeared in *The Times*: "On April 28th, at the office of the Registrar of the City of London, Frederick A. Ford, to Florence Fenwick Miller. By mutual desire the bride will retain her maiden name, and will be addressed as Mrs. Fenwick Miller." Very high legal opinion was taken on this matter by the Chairman of the London School Board before

FIGURE 43 'Mrs. Florence Fenwick Miller', portrait

he would call out her name on the division lists as "Mrs. Fenwick Miller," and a fruitless attempt was made to upset the first election to the School Board which she fought in that name after she became the wife of Mr. Ford. The only other precedent for not taking the husband's name exists in the peerage; many widows of baronets, on re-marrying with commoners, retain the dead husband's name for the sake of continuing the title. There are numbers of cases in which professional women retain their maiden name, but it is only as an alias; they sign their husband's in legal documents and are known by it in private life. Mrs. Fenwick Miller is convinced that in the course of a generation or two the action, of which Lucy Stone in America and she in England have been the pioneers, will become general. As she justly says: "The name expresses the individuality; and to resign that name which stands on the covers of my books, and in the reports of my speeches in the columns of many newspapers, would be to sink my whole past life and work in oblivion."

Mrs. Fenwick Miller is one of the few ladies who have joined the Society of Journalists.

21.2

Interviews with women authors appeared in magazines for girls as well as women. L. T. Meade was one of the most prolific magazine writers of the end of the period and editor of *Atalanta* (1887–98). See 20.5 above.

'How I write my Books. An interview with L. T. Meade', *The Young Woman*, vol. 6, 1892, pp. 122–23.

MRS. L. T. MEADE has probably written a greater number of stories than any other living author. A healthy tone pervades all her works, and her pictures of English home life in particular are among the best of their kind. Calling on the novelist (writes our Special Commissioner) at her City office, I found her at her desk hard at work. Her personality is like her writings—bright, fresh, vivacious; and to say that she is of a well-favoured countenance is to understate the fact. She retains much of her girlish appearance, though a rather worn look about the eyes suggests midnight oil and an ever-active brain. Knowing how Mrs. Meade values her time, I plunged at once into the subject of my visit by remarking that nowadays people take a very friendly interest in those who delight and instruct them by their writings, they like to know how their favourite books are written; and asked whether she was willing to satisfy this natural curiosity.

"I shall be happy to tell you anything you want to know," she replied in a soft, musical voice. "As to how my books are written, well, I simply get a thought and work it out. I have no particular method of writing. My stories grow a good deal as I write them. I don't think the plot out very carefully in advance. My children's stories, for instance, before they are written, are, as a rule, first told to my own children to amuse them—at least, I have tried that plan since the children have become old enough to be interested in them, and I have found it very successful; as a rule, what one child likes, another child will like. I write my stories a good deal because the publisher wants the book; I simply write it to order, and, of course, if he asks for a girl's story he gets it, and if he asks for a novel or children's story he gets that. I may say that I am a very quick writer; I produce four or five books in a season. I have written in less than three months a rather important three-volume novel."

"Do you ever take your characters from real life?"

"Yes, but not intentionally. I don't deliberately say I will put such a character here or there; I take traits rather than a whole character. I find that deliberately setting my mind to delineate a certain character produces considerable stiffness, and the character is not so fresh. Authors are a good deal governed by their characters in writing fiction. If your book is to be successful, your characters guide you rather than you guide your characters; they are so very living and very real that you have not complete control over them."

"Your experience, then, is similar to that of Charles Dickens and some living writers, who have stated that their characters become their masters, and, as it were, take their destiny into their own hands?"

"Exactly. I find it a good plan, when a novel is in process, after a certain stage, to cut out every character that is not intensely alive. I am now speaking, of course, of my larger stories; in a short story there is not room for development of character."

"May I ask how many stories you have written?"

"I am afraid to tell you—between fifty and sixty volumes, besides a great many short stories. I have been writing now constantly for fifteen years. An enormous quantity to have produced?— so it is; I don't know any other author who has done so much work as I have done in the time. I will give you an example. I have recently brought out four volumes (none cheaper than 3s. 6d., which gives you some idea of the size) and a three-volume novel, not to mention a complete Christmas number of the *Sunday Magazine*, of nearly sixty thousand words. They have certainly all been written under two years. I write on an average every day in the year a little over two thousand words; on some occasions I write a great deal more."

"Do you write everything with your own hand?"

"I write nothing with my own hand—I almost forget how to write. I employ a shorthand-writer, and I revise the type-written transcript."

"Do you write at regular hours or at uncertain intervals; in other words, do you wait for an inspiration, or do you sit down and write whether you feel inclined for it or not?"

"I never wait for an inspiration." Mrs. Meade added, with a laugh, "I might never write at all if I did. I write every day at a certain hour, and it would be impossible for me to write in the way you suggest. I have a great many books promised against a certain time. I always write against time."

"And you find that your work does not suffer from that somewhat mechanical method?"

"I don't think it does. I believe that to write against time puts your work into a frame, and is improved by it. To have to write a certain length, and for a certain publisher, who requires a certain kind of work, is splendid practice; it makes your brain very supple, so that you can turn to anything. It is a matter of habit with me now, and I rather like it."

"Are you never at a loss for ideas when working under such pressure? Don't you ever feel impoverished?"

"Sometimes, perhaps; but not as a rule. I often sit down, my secretary has a blank sheet of paper, I say 'Chapter I.,' and that is all I know when I begin. I suppose my ideas do flow very rapidly, for some writers who are very much beyond me in power can't write quickly. They have to think out their subjects a great deal. I could not write if I gave much labour to my work."

"But surely you must sometimes stop and think when you are dictating?"

"No; as a rule, I dictate straight ahead continuously, and never pause for an instant. I see the whole scene, and I talk on as I see it."

I could not help feeling that, if Mrs. Meade dictates as rapidly as she was speaking to me, her stenographer must be exceptionally expert. Her readiness and fluency were such, that of all the people I have interviewed, not one covered so much ground in so short a time. To this hard-working novelist our conversation was but a momentary interruption.

"Then you create as you speak?"

"Yes. Of course all writers must feel they do better work on day than another, but there is no day I don't write except Sunday. *Atalanta* takes up a great deal of time; more than half my days are occupied with it. I have a very large life outside my books."

A portrait of a sturdy, happy-looking youngster in cricketing costume, which his mother showed me, was an illustration in point. Mrs. Meade told me that he was the original of *Daddy's Boy*— one of the most fascinating of her numerous children's tales.

. . .

"Do you do most of your work at home, or here in the City?"

"I write in the morning at my own house at Dulwich. I do most of my original work at home, and my editorial work here, though I have done a great deal of original work here also. I don't go by any fixed rule. The only fixed rule in my life is that I never can get a holiday."

"I hope that is not to be taken literally?"

"Well, we are going away to-morrow for three or four days. Such an event is so rare that I can hardly believe it is coming to pass. I never get more than about a fortnight's holiday in the year. That is mostly because of my magazine work, which, of course, never ends."

21.3

The penny weekly, *Woman* (1890–1912), was typical of the new journals of the 1890s in that it sought to engage readers through a chatty and informal style. The interview was an important part of this. The novelist, Sarah Grand, whose book *The Heavenly Twins* made her perhaps the most famous 'New Woman' of 1894, was here interviewed by an anonymous male journalist calling himself 'Jim's Wife's Husband'. It was typical of this kind of journalism that it emphasised the immediacy and intimacy of the interview as against the more studied and reflective biography.

'A Chat with Mme. Sarah Grand', by Jim's Wife's Husband, *Woman*, 21st May, 1894, *Literary Supplement*, pp. i–ii.

CONSIDERING that I am a man, and but an average one, I felt flattered when Mme. Sarah Grand asked me to look in and have tea and a chat with her. I must confess, however, that when I arrived at the door of the house which contains her little Kensington flat, and saw written in bold type in the entrance hall the name of her whose doctrines have been discussed in hushed whispers, the sense of self-congratulation for a moment gave way to a feeling of timidity.

But it was too late to turn back. I pulled myself together, ascended and knocked, and a moment after was awaiting my hostess in a pretty blue and white drawing-room. Her greeting re-assured me and Mme. Grand, whom I had until then seen only in evening dress—which in a woman is often deceptive, although it sometimes conceals but little—bore none of the outward signs of feminine aggressiveness.

However, I thought it wiser to stick to common everyday subjects, as I have always been nervous in the presence of a woman with a mission. So I began with the weather, and then was about to commence with the first link of the conventional conversational formula of the moment by asking my hostess whether she had read *The Heavenly Twins* when I realised just in time that this question—the great stand-by of stranded conversationalists of to-day—would, under the peculiar circumstances, be a little out of place. Having missed the first link, I failed to get the second. *Dodo* ought to have come to my rescue; but I could not for the life of me, recall the name of Mr Benson's "boom book". And to make matters worse, there had been no bomb outrage for several days, and I had not seen the new play of the previous week. But I happily recalled a paragraph I had just read in that evening's *Globe* which referred to Mme. Grand, with no particular object beyond that of ventilating two terrible puns upon her book and her name, which the writer had presumably been treasuring up in one of the pigeon-holes of his mental store cupboard. I referred to it with many apologies for the profession of journalism, and we wondered why such things were written, and whether or not the County Council could interfere; and thus we got on to the subject of the Press in general, and of her critics in particular.

"Nothing annoys me more," said Mme Grand, "than the mistake made by so many in supposing that I took Colonel Colquhoun as a typical man. Only last night at a dinner party Mr.—" (naming a well-known literary character) "told me how mistaken I was in supposing that my principal male character was a fair type of the sex. Of course I only meant him to be typical of a particular type—not of the whole sex."

"And you do not think us very bad?" I asked, feeling more at ease.

"Oh! Dear no. I am far from being a man-hater, I like and respect many men. Moreover, there is not, and never can be, any quarrel between the sexes. Women will always be women, and men always men, and marriage, in my opinion, must always be the ideal state."

"But do you not sympathise with the bachelor girl?"

"Yes, certainly. I do not think any worse of a woman because she won't run the risk of matrimony. The glorified spinster distinctly interests me."

"And your ideal married life?"

"That there should be absolute equality between the two, but not on the same lines; each in her or his own sphere, and that if there is to be a head it should be the husband. Personally, I should most admire a husband to whom I could show deference, whom I could consult on every subject. It would be such a pleasant, lazy, irresponsible existence, but it would not be quite ideal from a wider point of view."

"And you think a woman should be domesticated?" I asked, prepared for another surprise.

"Absolutely. That is her line. I myself, busy as I am, know all the details of my *ménage*. I love domesticity, and sometimes long to throw down my pen and take up a piece of plain needlework."

(Mrs. Grand's tea, at any rate, was excellent, and I wondered whether a housewife's character could be judged by tea as by handwriting.)

"Then you do not believe in emancipation?" I asked, more surprised and certainly more at my ease than ever.

"Not in the hackneyed use of the expression; not in the emancipation of women from womanliness and the natural ties of wedlock, but certainly in emancipation from shallowness and ignorance."

"And a woman's dress?"

"Should be suitable to the sex and the occasion. I cannot bear to see a woman lounging on a London drawing-room sofa in what is little less than a Highland shooting costume, any more than I should admire a woman riding in the Row in a teagown. Affected masculinity in dress seems to me foolish, because inappropriate and uncomfortable."

"I presume you have made many enemies in consequence of your book?"

"Many more friends than enemies. For instance, I am quite surprised myself at the number of clergymen who have written expressing their appreciation of *The Twins*. The way in which the book was received by the Press affords an interesting study. Papers representing the very young school of affected culture, or those which I believe unconsciously reflect the private characters of journalistic Don Juans, attacked me furiously in the most bitter manner, but gave me good advertisement thereby. Other papers showed extreme caution, combined with faint praise. The *Daily Telegraph* was, I think, the first important paper that 'discovered' my book and foresaw its success."

"I suppose you have a very extensive correspondence?"

"Yes, very. In fact there is no end to it. Fortunately one of my stepsons is at home now, and acts as my secretary, and his post is no sinecure. I get letters from 'sincere admirers' who want to borrow sums varying from £5 to £50, on the ground that they have failed while I have succeeded. I receive poems, too, from ladies who are sure they are born to win fame by their poetry, 'if only they can get a start,' and ask my opinion of worse than commonplace verses; and one lady threatened to commit suicide if I did not get her poetry published very soon."

"Is it published?"

"I am afraid not, but I think she is still hopeful. It is very sad, this curious phase of life that one sees in the letters that I suppose are received by everyone who has made more or less of a name." And so on to subjects that savoured less of "shop," until when I rose to leave, I realised that there was nothing unwomanly—quite the reverse—about the author of *The Heavenly Twins*.

Bibliography of titles

This listing is more definitive than anything which currently exists. As more scholars and bibliographers begin to work in this area accuracy and detail will improve. We provide the dates of run for all titles, with the exception of a small number of queries, and we also provide start prices, frequencies and first editors where this information is known. Information on title changes, mergers and publications with the same contents but different titles is also provided wherever possible. In the frequent instances where titles change name or merge with another more than once we have not listed each as a separate alphabetical entry, except where an influential title is at the end of a number of changes. The place of publication is London unless otherwise stated.

Key to abbreviations
- *w*   weekly
- *f*   fortnightly
- *m*   monthly
- *q*   quarterly
- *d*   penny
- *s*   shilling

Advice to Young Wives (1859–60)

Aglaia (1894)

The Alexandra Magazine (1864–65) *m*, 6*d*, Bessie Parkes

Atalanta (1887–98) *m*, 6*d*, L. T. Meade

Baby (1887–1915) *m*, 4*d*, Ada Ballin

Babyhood (1884–1892) *m*, 5*d*, London and New York
   becomes *The Mother's Nursery*

The Barmaid (1891–92) *w*, 1*d*

Le Beau Monde (1831–43) *m*
   becomes *Le Nouveau Beau Monde*

Beau Monde (1862–73) *m*
   becomes *The Draper's and Milliner's Gazette of Fashion* (1873–77) *m*, 1*s*
   becomes *Beau Monde* (1878–1905) *m*, 1*s*

Le Beau Monde (1879) *m*, 1*s*

Beauty (1889)

Beauty and Fashion (1889)

Beauty and Fashion (1890–92)

Biblewomen and Nurses (1889–1915) *m*, 2*d*

Blackwood's Lady's Magazine (1836–60) *m*, 1*s*

The Bouquet Culled From Marylebone Gardens (1851–55) *m*, 1*s*

The British Mother's Magazine (1845–55) *m*, 3*d*, Mrs Bakewell
   becomes *The British Mother's Journal* (1856–63) *m*, 3*d*
   becomes *The British Mother's Family Magazine* (1864) *m*

British Women's Temperance Journal (1883–1892) *m*
  becomes *Wings*

The British Workwoman (1863–96) *m*, 1d

Butterick Fashion Guide (1898–1906) 1d

Butterick's Quarterly Report of Metropolitan Fashions (1881–96) *q*

Cartwright's Lady's Companion (1892–1915)

Cartwright's Monthly Review (1898–1905) *m*

The Christian Lady's Friend (1832–33)

The Christian Lady's Library (1850) *q*, 1s

The Christian Lady's Magazine (1834–49) *m*, Charlotte E. Tonna

The Christian Mother's Magazine (1844–45) Mrs Milner
  becomes *The Englishwoman's Magazine and Christian Mother's Miscellany* (1846–54)
  becomes *The Christian Lady's Magazine* (1855–57) Mrs Milner

The Churchwoman (1895–1903) *w*, 1d

The Court Herald and Ladies' Monthly Magazine (1873) *m*

The Court Magazine and Belle Assemblee (1832–38) *m*
  becomes *The Court Magazine and Monthly Critic* (1836–38) *m*
  merges with *The Lady's Magazine and Museum* (1832–48) *m*, 6d
  and becomes *The Court Magazine and Monthly Critic* (1838–47) *m*

The Court Suburb Magazine (1868–70) *m*

The Daughter (1897) *w*, 1d

The Daybreak (1886–1918)

Dorothy (1890–99) *m*, 1d

Dress and Fashion (1870–71) *m*, 6d
  merges with *The Young Ladies' of Great Britain* (1869–71) *w*, 1d, E. Brent
  becomes *Young Ladies of Great Britain: Dress and Fashion* (1871–72)
  becomes *The Month's Dress and Fashions* (1872–74) *m*

The Dressmaker and Milliner (1895–96) *q*, 1s 6d

Dressmaking at Home (1895)
  becomes *Isobel's Dressmaking at Home* (1895–1905) *m*, $1\frac{1}{2}d$
  absorbs *Isobel's Fashions for Children* (1895–99)

The Edinburgh Ladies' Magazine (1843) 1s, Edinburgh

The English Girl's Journal and Ladies' Magazine (1863–64) *w*, 1d, Edward Harrison

The Englishwoman (1834–35) 2d
  see *The Ladies' Penny Gazette*

The Englishwoman (1895–99) *m*, 6d, Ella Hepworth Dixon

The Englishwoman's Domestic Magazine (1852–79) *m*, 2d, 6d, Samuel Beeton
  absorbed by *The Milliner and Dressmaker and Warehouseman's Gazette*

The Englishwoman's Journal (1858–64) *m*, 1s, Bessie Parkes and Matilda Hays

The Englishwoman's Review and Drawing Room Journal (1857) *w*, 5d, E. Duckworth
  becomes *The Englishwoman's Review and Home Newspaper* (1857–59) *w*, 3d, Sarah Sutton
  becomes *The Englishwoman's Review of Literature, Science, and Art* (1859)

The Englishwoman's Review of Social and Industrial Questions (1866–1910) *q*, 1s, Jessie Boucherett

Every Girl's Magazine (1878–88)

Fashion (1898–1904)

Fashion Illustrated (1898–99)

Fashions and Fancies (1898–99)

Fashions Illustrated (1896–98)

Fashions and Patterns (1898–1902)

The Female's Advocate (1838–45)

The Female's Friend (1846) *m*, 3d

The Female Missionary Intelligencer (1858–99)

The Female Servant's Union News (1892) *m*, Mrs M. J. Sales

Fiction and Fashion (1890–91)

Le Follet (1846–1900) *m*, 1s 6d, London and Paris

Forget-Me-Not (1891–1918) *w*, 1d

Friendly Leaves (1876–1917) *m*, 1d, Mrs Jerome Mercier

Friendly Work (1883–1917) *m*

The Gatherer (1882–83) Mrs Rawlinson Ford

The Gem and Ladies' Album (1838) *w*, 2d

The Gentlewoman (1890–1926) *w*, 6d

The Girl of the Period Miscellany (1869) *m*, 6d, Augustus Mayhew

Girls (1893)

Girl's Best Friend (1898–99) *w*, $\frac{1}{2}$d
    becomes *The Girls' Friend* (1899–1931)

Girls' Favourite (1898)
    see *Sweethearts*

Girls' Friendly Society Advertiser (1880–82)
    becomes *The Girls' Friendly Society Associates Journal and Advertiser* (1883–1919)

Girl's Home (1900–18)

The Girls' Mistress (1893–95) *w*, 1d

The Girls' Own Messenger (1895) Ymal Oswin

Girls' Own Paper (1880–1927) *w*, 1d, Charles Peters

Girls' Realm (1898–1915) *m*, 6d

Girls' School Magazine (1892–93) *m*, 1d

The Glass of Fashion up to Date (1896–1902) 3d
    see *The Ladies' Monthly Review*

Go Forward (1891–1908) *m*

The Golden Penny (1895–1903) *w*, 1d

Golden Stories (1898–1913)

The Governess (1854–56) *m*, 6d

The Governess (1882–84) *m*, 6d, Joseph Hughes

The Grain of Mustard Seed (1881–98) *m*, 1d
    becomes *Women in the Mission Field*

Harrison's Complete Dressmaker (1898–1902) *m*, 3d

Hearth and Home (1891–1914) *w*, 3d

The Helpmeet (1891–1900) *q*, 1d

Home Chat (1895–1958) *w*, 1d

Home Circle (1894–97) *w*, 1d

The Home Friend (1880–1925)
    see *The Homely Friend for Young Women and Girls*

Home Life (1893–98)

Home Notes (1894–1957) *m*, 1*d*

Home and Society (1893)

Home Sweet Home (1893–1901) *w*, 1*d*

The Homely Friend for Young Women and Girls (1877–79) *m*, 1*d*
   becomes *The Home Friend*

The Household Dressmaker (1877) *m*, 2*d*

Household Hints and Mother's Handbook (1899–1901) *w*, 1*d*

The Housekeeper (1875–6)

The Housewife (1886–1900)

India's Women (1881–1957)

Iris (1892) 4*d*

Isobel's Home Cookery (1896–1904)

Jose Lille's Juvenile Dressmaker (1895–1918)

Jose Lille's Practical Fashions (1898–1920) $1\frac{1}{2}d$

The Journal (1893) Mrs Ward Poole

Journal of the University Association of Women Teachers (1892–95) *m*, 3*d*

Journal of the Workhouse Visiting Society (1865) *f*, 6*d*, Miss Louisa Twining

The Ladies (1872–73) *w*, 6*d*

Ladies' Bits (1892)

The Ladies' Book of Fashion (1858–59)

The Ladies' Cabinet of Fashion, Music and Romance (1832–70) *m*, 1*s*, M. and B. De Courcy
   see *The Ladies' Companion* and *The New Monthly Belle Assemblee*

The Ladies' Companion (1849–70) *m*, 3*d*, Mrs Loudon
   same as *The Ladies Cabinet from 1852*

The Ladies' Companion (1850)

The Ladies' Companion (1871) *m*, 1*s*

The Ladies' Daily News (1901)

The Ladies' Directory or Red Book of Shanghai (1876)

The Ladies' Edinburgh Magazine (1875–80) *m*, 6*d*, Edinburgh

Ladies' Fashions (1897) *w*, 1*d*

The Ladies' Fashionable Repository (1809–1905)

Ladies' Field (1896–1928) *w*, 6*d*

The Ladies' Free Lance (1880) 1*d*, Southport

Ladies' Friend (1887) *w*, 1*d*, Glasgow

Ladies' Gazette (1895–99) *w*, 1*d*

The Ladies' Gazette of Fashion (1834–94) *m*, 1*s*

Ladies' Home (1898–99)

The Ladies' Journal (1847) *w*, 1*d*

The Ladies' Journal of Decoration (1886) *m*, 2*d*

The Ladies' Keepsake (1843)

Ladies' Kennel Journal (1895–1901) *m*, 1*s*

The Ladies' League Gazette (1900–1903)

Ladies Magazine of Gardening (1842) *m*, 1*s* 6*d*, Mrs Loudon

The Ladies' Monthly Magazine (1852–79) *m*, 1s
   see *The World of Fashion*

The Ladies' Monthly Review (188?–96) *m*
   becomes *The Glass of Fashion up to Date*

The Ladies' Quarterly Review (1880) *q*, 1d

Ladies of all Nations (1869) *w*, $\frac{1}{2}$d

The Ladies' Novelette (1880) *w*, 1d, John Holloway

The Ladies' Occasional Paper (1885) *q*

The Ladies' Own Journal and Miscellany (1844–74) *w*, $\frac{1}{2}$d, Edinburgh

The Ladies' Own Magazine and Mirror of the Months (1843)

The Ladies' Penny Gazette (1832–33) *w*, 1d
   becomes *The Englishwoman*

The Ladies' Pictorial (1880) 3d

Ladies' Pocket Magazine (1824–39) *m*, 6d

Ladies' Polite Remembrancer (1843–45)

The Ladies' Portfolio (1853) *m*, 2s, Mrs Warren

The Ladies' Quarterly Review (1880) *q*, 9d

The Ladies' Reciter (1891) A.H.M.

Ladies' Review (1892–1908) *m*, 1d

The Ladies' Sunday Reader (1879) *w*, 1d, Edwin. J. Brett

Ladies' Tailor (1884–1936) *m*, 9d

The Ladies' Treasury (1858–95) *m*, 7d, Mrs Warren

The Ladies' Weekly Fashions (1832) *w*, 1d

Ladies' Work Penny Series (1894) *m*, 1d

Ladies' World (1880) *w*, 1d

The Lady (1885–) *w*, 3d

Lady Cyclist (1895–97) *m*, 3d, Charles Sisley
   merges with *The Wheelwoman*

Ladyland (1893) *w*, 1d

Ladyland (1898–99) *m*, Smedley North

The Lady's Album of Fancy Work (1880)

The Lady's Companion (1900) *w*, 1d

The Lady's Companion for Daughters (1892)

Lady's Gazette (1901–04) *w*

Lady's Home Journal (1895) *m*, 1d

Lady's Idler (1894) *m*, 6d, Robert Barr, Coventry

The Lady's Journal of Decoration and Magazine of Fine Art (1888) *m*, 3d

Lady's Magazine (1894) *m*, 1s

Lady's Magazine (1901–04)

The Lady's Newspaper and Pictorial Times (1847–63) *w*, 6d
   merges with *The Queen*

Lady's Own Magazine (1898) *w*, 2d, Ferguson Weir

The Lady's Own Novelette (1889) *w*, 1d

The Lady's Own Novelist (1880)

The Lady's Own Paper (1866–72) *w*, 2d

The Lady's Pictorial (1881–1921) *w*, 6d, Helen Black

The Lady's Realm (1896–1915) *m*, 6d

The Lady's Review (1860) *w*, 3d

The Lady's World (1886–87) *m*
    becomes *Woman's World*

The Lady's World (1893)

The Lady's World (1894) *m*, 6d

The Lady's World (1898–1926) *m*

Latest Paris Fashions (1898–1902) 1s 6d

Leach's Children's Dressmaker (1894) *m*, 1d

Leach's Fancy Work Basket (188?–1915)

Leach's Practical Family Dressmaker (1894) *m*, 2d

The Little Dressmaker (1872–77) *m*, 6d, Mme Marie Schild
    becomes *Mother's Help and the Little Dressmaker*

Little Women and Good Housewives and Home Industries (1887–89) *m*, 6d, Leeds
    becomes *Good Housewives* (1890)
    becomes *Little Women and Good Housewives* (1890)
    becomes *Good Housewives* (1890–91)
    becomes *Housewifery* (1892–95)

The London and Paris Ladies' Magazine (1828–91) *m*, 1s, Mrs Edward Thomas
    see *The World of Fashion*

The London and Paris Magazine (1894)

The Magdalen's Friend (1860–64) *m*, 3d, Rev. W. Tuckniss

Madame (1895–1913) *w*

Madame Aubert's Governess List (1883)
    becomes *The Girton Governess School Agency* (1884–86)
    becomes *Madame Aubert's Governess List* (1886–1914)

Madame Bayard's Bouquet of Summer (and Winter) Fashions (1879–84) *m*

Milliner and Dressmaker and Warehouseman's Gazette (1870–81) *m*
    becomes *The Milliner, Dressmaker and Draper* (1881) *w*, 1s
    see *The Englishwoman's Domestic Magazine* and *Le Moniteur de la Mode*

La Mode Illustree (1896–99)

La Mode Practique (1892–94)

La Mode Unique (1879) *f*, 1s

Les Modes Parisiennes (1871–2)

Les Modes de la Saison (1886) *m*

Les Modes Francaises (1873–87)

Le Moniteur de la Mode (1882–96)
    merges with *Milliner and Dressmaker*

The Month's Fashions (1868) *m*, 1s 6d

The Monthly Packet (1851–98) *m*, 6d, Charlotte Yonge

The Mother (1871) 1d

Mother (1893) *w*, 1d

Mothers in Council (1891–?) Charlotte Yonge

Mother's Companion (1887–96) *m*

The Mother's Friend (1848–95) m, 1d, A. J. Morgan

Mother's Help and the Little Dressmaker (1878–1905) m, 6d, Mme Marie Schild
  see The Little Dressmaker

The Mother's Magazine (1834–62) (reprinted from the American) m, Mrs Whittelsey

The Mother's Nursery (1892)
  see Babyhood

The Mother's Treasury (1864–89) m, 1d

Mother's Union Church Journal (1888–1925) Winchester

Mothers and Daughters (1892–98) w, 1d, Mrs Reaney

Mrs Ellis' Morning Call (1850–52) m, Mrs Sarah Ellis

Mrs Leach's Practical Family Dressmaker (1881–1921)
  see The Practical Dressmaker

My Lady's Novelette (1890) w

My Magazine (1899)

My Paper (1895)

Myra's Journal of Dress and Fashion (1875–1912) m, 3d

Myra's Mid-Monthly Journal and Children's Dresses (1877–82) m

The Needle (1852–55) m, 6d, Mme Eleanor Riego de la Blanchardiere

The New Monthly Belle Assemblee (1834–70) m, Mrs Cornwall Baron-Wilson
  same as The Ladies' Cabinet after 1852

Le Nouveau Beau Monde (1844–46)
  merges with The London and Paris Ladies' Magazine
  see Beau Monde
  was Le Beau Monde

Nursing Notes (1887–1939)

Nurse's Diary and Quarterly Review (1896–97) q

Nurse's Journal (1891–1918)

Nursing Mirror (1886–?)

The Nursing Record (1888–89)
  becomes The International Nursing Record (1889–90)
  becomes The Nursing Record and Hospital World (1890–1902)

Our Home (1898–1927)

Our Magazine (1875–1923) Miss Aitken

Our Own Gazette (1884–1928) $\frac{1}{2}$d

Our Paper (1883–1903) q

Our Journal (1871)

Our Sisters in Other Lands (1879–1937) q, 1d

Paris Fashions (1901–14) w, 3d

The Pelican (1874–75) q, R. King

Pioneer of Fashion (1892–94) q, 6d

The Practical Family Dressmaker (1878–81)
  becomes Mrs. Leach's Practical Family Dressmaker

The Princess (1873) w, 3d

The Princess (1880) 1s

The Princess (1890–98)

The Protestant Girl (1895–1900) *m*, 1d

The Protestant Woman (1894–95) *m*, 1d

The Queen (1861–1967) *w*, 6d
    merges with *The Lady's Newspaper*

Queen's Own (1841–77) *w*, 3d

The Rational Dress Society's Gazette (1888–89) *q*, 3d

The Rose, the Shamrock and the Thistle (1862–65) *m*, 1s, Mary Anne Thomson, Edinburgh

Ross's Monthly Toilet Magazine (1861–76) *m*, 1s6d, Alexander Ross

Schild's Home Journal (1897–1906)

Schild's Illustrated Magazine of Fashion (1882–1905)

Schild's Parisian Dress Patterns (1894–1902)

Schoolgirls (1894–95) *w*, 1d, Olivia Landale

School and Home for Mother's Meetings (1889)

School Mistress (1881–1935) *w*

The Sempstress (1855) *m*, 1d

The Servant's Magazine (1838–69) *m*, 1d

Shafts (1892–99) *m*, 3d, Margaret Sibthorpe

Sisters (1895–98) *m*, 1d, Mrs Hooper

Social Review (1872) *w*, 2d, Amelia Lewis
    see *Woman* [1]

Sweethearts (1898) *w*, ½d
    becomes *Girls' Favourite*

A Threefold Cord (1891–96) *q*, Emily James

Townsend's Monthly Selection of Parisian Costumes (1823–88) *m*, 1s
    see *The World of Fashion*

The Victoria Magazine (1863–80) *m*, 1s, Emily Faithfull

The Vineyard (1867) *m*, 8d

Waverley Journal (1856–57) *f*, 5d, Eleanor Duckworth, Glasgow

Wedding Bells (1870) *w*, 1d, Edwin Brett

Weldon's Bazaar of Children's Fashions (1881–?) *m*, 1d

Weldon's Home Dressmaker (1895–?)

Weldon's Home Milliner (1895–1928)

Weldon's Illustrated Dressmaker (1880–1935)

Weldon's Knitted and Crochet Comforts (1900)

Weldon's Ladies' Journal (1879–1954) *w*

Weldon's Practical Milliner (1889)

Weldon's Practical Needlework Series (1881–?)

The What Not (1859–64) *m*, 3d

The Wheelwoman (1896–1928)
    see *Lady Cyclist*

White Ribbon (1896–1925) *m*

Wings (1893–1925) *m*
    see *British Women's Temperance Journal*

Woman (1872) *w*, 3d, Amelia Lewis
    becomes *Social Review*

Woman (1887)

Woman (1890–1912) *w, 1d*

Woman at Home (1893–1920) *m, 6d,* Robertson Nicoll

Womanhood (1898–1907) *m, 6d,* Ada Ballin

Woman's Agricultural Times (1899–1904)

Woman's Gazette, or News About Work (1875–79) *m, 2d,* Louisa Hubbard
   becomes *Work and Leisure* (1880–93)

Woman's Guild: Life and Work (1890–1928)

Woman's Life (1895–1934) *w, 1d*

Woman's Opinion (1874) *w, 1d,* Amelia Lewis

Woman's Signal (1894–99)
   see *Women's Penny Paper*

Woman's Tribune (1888)

Woman's Weekly (1898–1900) *w*

Woman's Work (1895) *q, 1d*

Woman's Work in the Great Harvest Field (1872–94) *m, 4d*

Woman's Work on the Mission Field (1859–?)

Woman's World (1868) *m, 6d,* Charles Jones
   becomes *The Kettledrum* (1869) *m, 1s*
   becomes *Now A Days* (1869) *m*

Woman's World (1887–90) *m, 1s,* Oscar Wilde
   see *The Lady's World*

Women at Home (1893–1917)

Women in the Mission Field (1899–1903)
   see *The Grain of Mustard Seed*

Women and Work (1874–76) *w, 1d,* Emily Faithfull

Women Workers (1891–1924) *q,* Birmingham

Women's Education Union Journal (1873–82) *m, 6d,* Emily Shireff and George Bartley

Women's Employment (1900)

The Women's Gazette and Weekly News (1888–91) *w, 2d,* Miss Orme, Manchester and London

The Women's Industrial News (1895–1919) *q*

Women's National Liberal Association (1895–) *q*

Women's Penny Paper (1888–90) *w, 1d,* Helena B. Temple
   becomes *Women's Herald* (1891–93) *w, 1d,* Helena B. Temple
   merges with *The Journal* (1893)
   becomes *The Woman's Signal* (1894–99) *w, 1d,* Mrs Henry Somerset, Annie Holdsworth

Women's Protestant Union (1893) East Grinstead

Women's Suffrage Journal (1870–90) *m, 1d,* Lydia Becker, Manchester

Women's Suffrage News (1894) *m, ½d,* A. B. Louis

The Women's Union Journal (1876–90) *m, 1d,* Mrs Emma Paterson
   becomes *Women's Trade Union Review* (1891–1918) *q,* Gertrude Tuckwell

Women's Work in Heathen Lands (1890) *q, 1d,* Paisley

Work and Leisure (1880–93) *m, 3d,* Louisa Hubbard
   see *Woman's Gazette*

Worker's Paper of Young Women's Help Society (1892–94) *q*

The World of Dress (1898–1908)

The World of Fashion (1824–51) *m*, 2*s*, Mr Bell
  becomes *Ladies' Monthly Magazine* (1852–79) – still known as *The World of Fashion*
  same as *Townsend's Monthly Selection of Parisian Costumes* and *The London and Paris Ladies'*
  Magazine of Fashion
  becomes *Le Monde Elegant* (1880–91)

The Young Englishwoman (1864–77) *w*, 6*d*
  becomes *Sylvia's Home Journal* (1877–91) *m*, 6*d*
  becomes *Sylvia's Journal* (1892–94)

Young Gentlewoman (1892–1921) *m*, 6*d*, J. S. Wood

The Young Ladies' Herald (1879) *w*, 1*d*

The Young Ladies' Journal (1864–1920) *w*, 6*d* and *m*, 9*d*, Edward Harrison

The Young Ladies' Magazine of Theology (1837–38)

The Young Ladies' Reader (1881) *w*, 1*d*

The Young Widow (1838)

The Young Woman (1892–1915) *m*, 3*d*, Frederick A. Atkins

Zenana Missionary Herald (1893–95) *m*

Selected further reading

This is an introductory booklist and suggests a range of general reading on the Victorian press and on women's magazines. However, there is a growing wealth of scholarship on Victorian periodicals, particularly in *Victorian Periodicals Review* the journal of the Research Society for Victorian Periodicals, to which we direct our readers.

Adburgham, Alison, 1972. *Women in Print: Writing Women and Women's Magazines*, Allen & Unwin: London

Altick, Richard, D., 1957. *The English Common Reader: A Social History of the Mass Reading Public 1800–1900*, University of Chicago Press: Chicago

Ashdown, Dulcie, 1971. *Over the Teacups*, Cornmarket Press: London

Ballaster, Ros, Beetham, Margaret, Frazer, Elizabeth and Hebron, Sandra, 1991. *Women's Worlds. Ideology, Femininity and the Woman's Magazine*, Macmillan: London

Beetham, Margaret, 1996. *A Magazine of Her Own? Domesticity and Desire in the Woman's Magazine 1800–1914*, Routledge: London

Brake, Laurel, Jones, Aled, and Madden, Lionel (eds), 1990. *Investigating Victorian Journalism*, Macmillan: London

Brake, Laurel, 1994. *Subjugated Knowledges. Journalism, Gender and Literature in the Nineteenth Century*, Macmillan: London

Braithwaite, Brian and Barrell, Joan, 1988. *The Business of Women's Magazines*, (2nd edn), London Associated Business Press: London

Brown, Lucy, 1985. *Victorian News and Newspapers*, Oxford University Press: Oxford

Dancyger, Irene, 1978. *A World of Women: An Illustrated History of Women's Magazines*, Gill and Macmillan: Dublin

Donn Vann, J. and Vanarsdel, Rosemary, 1996. *Periodicals of Queen Victoria's Empire*, University of Toronto Press: Toronto

Drotner, Kirsten, 1988. *English Children and Their Magazines 1875–1914*, Yale University Press: New Haven and London

Doughan, David and Sanchez, Denise, 1987. *Feminist Periodicals, 1855–1984: An Annotated Critical Bibliography of British, Irish, Commonwealth and International Titles*, Harvester Press: Brighton

Ellegard, Alvar, 1957. *The Readership of the Periodical Press in Mid-Victorian Britain*, Goteburg University Press: Goteburg

Ferguson, Marjorie, 1983. *Forever Feminine. Women's Magazines and the Cult of Femininity*, Heinemann: London

Forrester, Wendy, 1980. *Great Grandma's Weekly. A Celebration of the Girls' Own Paper 1880–1901*, Lutterworth Press: London

Freeman, Sarah, 1977. *Isabella and Sam. The Story of Mrs Beeton*, Victor Gollancz: London

Graham, Walter, 1966. *English Literary Periodicals*, Octagon Books: New York

Harris, Michael and Lee, Alan (eds), 1986. *The Press in English Society from the Seventeenth to Nineteenth Centuries*, Associated University Press: London

Hindley, Geoffrey and Hindley, Diana, 1972. *Advertising in Victorian England, 1837–1901*, Wayland Publishers: London

James, Louis (ed.), 1976. *Print and the People 1819–1851*, Allen Lane: London

Kramarae, Cheris and Russo, Ann (eds), 1991. *The Radical Women's Press of the 1850s*, Routledge: London

Lee, Alan, J., 1976. *The Origins of the Popular Press, 1855–1914*, Croom Helm: London

Madden, Lionel and Dixon, Diana, 1976. *The Nineteenth Century Periodical Press in Britain*, Garland Publishing Inc: New York

McCracken, Eileen, 1993. *Decoding Women's Magazines*, Macmillan: London

Mitchell, Sally, 1995. *The New Girl: Girls' Culture in England, 1880–1915*, Columbia University Press: New York

Palmegiano, Eugenia, M., 1976. 'Women and British Periodicals, 1832–1867. A Bibliography', *Victorian Periodicals Newsletter*, 9, pp. 3–36

Reed, David, 1997. *The Popular Magazine in Britain and the USA*, The British Library: London

Scanlon, Jennifer, 1995. *Inarticulate Longings. The Ladies' Home Journal, Gender, and the Promises of Consumer Culture*, Routledge: London and New York

Shattock, Joanne and Wolff, Michael (eds), 1982. *The Victorian Periodical Press: Samplings and Soundings*, Leicester University Press: Leicester

Shevelow, Kathryn, 1989. *Women and Print Culture. The Construction of Femininity in the Early Periodical*, Routledge: London

Tye, Reginald, 1974. *Periodicals of the Eighteen Nineties: A Checklist of Literary Periodicals Published in the British Isles at Longer than Fortnightly Intervals*, Oxford Bibliographical Society: Oxford

Varty, Anne, 2000. *Eve's Century. A Sourcebook of Writings on Women and Journalism 1895–1918*, Routledge: London

White, Cynthia, 1970. *Women's Magazines, 1693–1968*, Michael Joseph: London

Wiener, Joel (ed.), 1985. *Innovators and Preachers. The Role of the Editor in Victorian England*, Greenwood Press: Westport and London

Wiener, Joel (ed.), 1988. *Papers for the Millions: The New Journalism in Britain, 1850s to 1914*, Greenwood Press: New York

Winship, Janice, 1987. *Inside Women's Magazines*, Pandora Press: London

Woolf, M., North, J. and Deering, D. (eds), 1976. *The Waterloo Directory of Victorian Periodicals 1824–1900*, Waterloo: Ontario